THE INQUIRING READER

IDELLE SULLENS
EDITH KARAS
RAYMOND FABRIZIO

All of Monterey Peninsula College

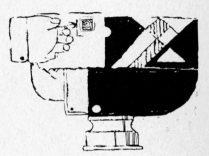

D. C. HEATH AND COMPANY · BOSTON

THE

INQUIRING

READER

Printed April 1967

PREFACE

Collections of readings for college English students appear in more abundance every year, and the instructor who opens this one with, "Ho hum, another anthology," will echo his colleagues everywhere. Among our most compelling reasons for writing it was the desire to read some new material with our students, and we hope that it will be stimulating to other seasoned instructors and to their unseasoned students as well. The majority of selections in this anthology are interesting contemporary materials, many of them reprinted here for the first time. But there are also certain old stories, essays, and poems so dear to us that we could not leave them out. They are classic statements of their kind, the pieces that some of us feel we must continue to present to every class, partly because nothing better has been written to take their place.

So we have made room for both the old and the new. The criteria of choice in every instance was the intrinsic value and potential interest to the students in our classes today. We hope that we have provided a wide range of readings without sacrificing the literary point of view.

We have found that interest and enthusiasm vary greatly among our students, even in the most rigidly "selected" classes. Many of our students, of course, have had excellent preparation for literary study while in high school. Others—alas—have become alienated from literature by a diet of pablum. We would like to introduce every student to the literary values appropriate to the adult world in which he finds himself. We want to make it possible for him to examine his own beliefs while he questions those of others.

One of our major goals was to avoid dictating the way an instructor should use this book. We have arranged the pieces rather arbitrarily by genre, with the expectation that every instructor will assign them in a way that seems best to himself. There is, of course, a thread of continuity in the arrangement; it will be discerned easily by the sequence of subjects, but it is not inviolate. For the sake of keeping students awake to the breadth of modern literature, instructors may sample any section, group, or individual selection at any time they wish.

As anthologists, our collective taste speaks for scholars of widely varying persuasions. If all the selections represented the irrevocable choice of any one of us, we would be addressing the book only to instructors of precisely the same taste as our own.

Our greatest debt is to those hundreds of inquiring students who have struggled with us through other anthologies. They have tried to teach us what they like and have sympathized with us in our often misguided attempts to understand their world of ideas, the important concepts about life and literature which we so easily forget when we become older than they. We owe more personal debts to our colleagues at Monterey Peninsula College who have encouraged us to attempt a new arrangement of reading materials for the freshman English course. If the selections in this book seem to provide the student with more questions than answers, we will count our anthology a success.

I.S. E.K. R.F.

CONTENTS

INTRODUCTION TO THE INQUIRING READER

ESSAYS

PERSONAL ESSAYS

CONTROVERSY

REPORTAGE

STORIES

POEMS

FOLLY AND TURMOIL

LOVE AND CELEBRATION

INTRODUCTION
TO THE INQUIRING READER

That stack of new textbooks you bought today, or yesterday, or the day before rushing and classes began, contains the reason for this one: when you start to read what your instructors have prescribed for you, you are opening the door to scholarship.

And how are you going to read all of it? That is a rhetorical question, and you may never find a precise answer. This book will help you to discover some of the ways to read your college texts, but its main purpose is simply to make reading in general easier, more efficient, and more enjoyable. For unless you can become concerned about the ideas you are discovering, conscious of the beauties of language and the delight of literary experience, you will find college study to be drudgery all the way.

Many students tell us that they don't read much. Secondary schools provide an astonishing range of information and develop some amazing skills by other methods. For example, many laboratory courses require little reading; instead, you are provided a laboratory workbook with a specific set of directions, accompanied by diagrams, pictures, and formulas, which make reading a prose version of the laboratory problem rather superfluous. History, grammar, and related subjects are often taught with visual aids—tapes, records, films, and slides—making learning easy.

Then in leisure hours, the television provides a vast amount of information and an even greater amount of entertainment. All those hours seem well-spent when you think you have been comfortably entertained and painlessly educated. The day of television teaching is also at hand. The range of instruction is becoming much wider and the variety of knowledge offered seems to be greater in the classroom as well as on the educational television programs available at almost any hour of the day or night.

The art of reading rapidly and efficiently is not very easy to master under these circumstances. The first shock a new college student receives is the paralyzing fact *that practically everything he will be expected to learn in college comes out of a book.* And the books he will be expected to read deal almost exclusively with adult ideas, in sophisticated—even academic—language; furthermore, he is expected to have done a lot more reading in high school so that he will have the skills to read discriminatingly and with almost perfect comprehension of everything on the printed page.

Some students have gone to schools in which these reading skills are regularly and systematically taught. But the great majority have not, and the loss of practice in reading—those hours lost as we have developed skill in learning by other methods— will be crippling to a college student who cannot quickly develop a technique for reading rapidly and accurately.

Quite aside from the matter of basic efficiency in reading, but equally as important, is the discovery of adult ideas, your introduction to a whole new range of *the intellectual realities of the college scene.* The campuses of America today are seething with vital questions: the students who only yesterday were content to accept the ideas of the secure and explainable world around them, the ideas of progress and perfectibility, are now exploring their old prejudices and preconceptions in a very militant fashion.

They are discovering that they can think for themselves and that the very essence of education is thinking and talking about and acting upon the new ideas crowding the campus scene from Student Union to Theater to Passion Pit. The generation of students whose major concerns were telephone-booth-stuffing, bed-pushing, and panty-swiping has gone to a comfortable little box in suburbia, content to commute and mow the lawn on weekends. Students today are literally attacking the old ideas, clamoring for more knowledge of recent and ancient history, exploring the old verities and renouncing the dogmas of their elders as fast as possible.

The ideas that made the world came from books. The heritage of the ages is wisdom; it is to be found only in prose, poetry, essay, and drama, those things in print that today's student scarcely knew existed until he came to college and discovered that his education would no longer be delivered in moving pictures, painlessly and without effort. Your instructor, with the help of this book, can get you into the active framework of the college thinking explosion very quickly.

Part of our purpose in collecting this wider range of readings has been to provide some enjoyment, too. Essays give us information and stimulating ideas, but stories and poems provide another dimension of literary experience. A poem is rather intimate; we can share a feeling with a poet, and with only a few other people. Similarly, stories give us insight into character and provide a new dimension to help us understand the people in our world. The author who shaped the story gives us a view of his world, colored with his vision, his fantasy, and his own response to it. Perhaps you will not always like what the author does, but seeing how he does it and understanding his meaning and interpretation of his world can be tremendously exciting, nevertheless. Enjoyment of literature is one of the rarest rewards of an education. As you read, you will suddenly find yourself in an expanding world. Those racks of paperbacks, those collections of hitherto uninteresting oddments you used to stumble past in the library and the bookstore will become endlessly fascinating—even irresistible.

The editors welcome you to the world of ideas contained in this book. It was written with you in mind, from the choice of pieces to the last detail of their arrangement. We hope you will enjoy it and mark it up, turn down the pages, and kick it around until it is an old friend.

ESSAYS

Students today live in several different cultures simultaneously. In schoolrooms there is an orderly, idealized, and usually conventional—sometimes artificial—world, more or less closely controlled by the values of the community around that world. At home, a vast number of students live in a different world conditioned by differences in language, religion, or custom. Among friends, another set of values applies, though it is similar to the others and shares many aspects.

A student may be able to reconcile his different worlds only through independence and sometimes, unfortunately, through rebellion, for the values of these worlds are often in conflict. The demands of school, the traditions of the family—or the lack of them—and the social pressures of friends force young people to accept or question, to conform or rebel, at least until being away from families and schools eases some of the most urgent pressures.

The journey from school to college may be far more catastrophic than students or parents realize. The conventions of home and school must be compared with the wide, challenging world of ideas which a student encounters in college. The high school friends left behind may fade into some limbo of old acquaintances, to be replaced by new friends who come from other worlds with other, more fascinating plans and dreams.

The essays in this book are intended to help students in the sudden and exciting discovery of a new world of ideas in college. In this path of discovery, an awareness of some of the exemplary English prose of our time, along with a forthright introduction to some pressing problems of the general culture, will be useful for the sophisticated tasks of thinking and writing which college study will demand in the next few weeks or months. A student cannot meet the demands of the academic world without a conviction that he is a part of it, a contributor to it, and an active member of his own generation.

For the student just beginning in college to contribute to this world of ideas, the following general statement provides a helpful overall view of what he may expect from a liberal education: *

"The purpose of education must remain what it has always been: to develop a free, reasoning person who can make up his own mind, who can understand his culture, and who can live compassionately with his fellow man.

"Great literature raises the problems and questions that have perplexed man through all history: for example, the relationship between power and moral responsibility, or the problem of undeserved human suffering. It presents the solutions and answers of the greatest minds the world has known. . . . In this imaginative search into the values and ideas of our culture lie both our humanity and our salvation. Those who do not remember the past, Santayana reminds us, are condemned to relive its mistakes."

The essays in this book are presented in three groups: personal essays, controversy, and reportage (the Table of Contents shows these groups).

Among the *personal essays* are a group of reminiscences and several short *satires;* these are identified in the headline notes). The satirical essays show an important form of expression that frequently appears in speech and cartoons as well as in writing. A fundamental element in satire is irony, the reversal of meaning. With ironic statement, readers are exposed to a writer or character who makes a pose of stating an attitude opposite from the one he intends. (In casual conversation, a somewhat bitterly sarcastic irony appears in the expression "Big Deal!") The result is usually ridicule of whatever is being discussed, and for readers, a new view of some social situation that the satirist wishes to expose.

The *controversial essays* concern aspects of the modern world which invite argument or lead to critical analysis of our culture. Among the pieces included under *reportage* are news accounts and several editorial pieces concerning problems still unsolved. The question, sometimes, is more valuable than the answer; the solution to the problems of our culture can be seen only in the perspective of time, but we must still live with the question.

President John F. Kennedy's Inaugural Address marks the beginning of an era in our culture which has not yet ended. It is a statement on the highest level of idealism from a man whose vocation for leadership was not extinguished by his untimely death. As he said, "The torch has been passed to a new generation of Americans—born in this century . . ." and it is still alight. "But let us begin."

* Reprinted by permission of the National Council of Teachers of English from the pamphlet, "The Students' Right to Read." Copyright 1962 by the National Council of Teachers of English.

JOHN F. KENNEDY

INAUGURAL ADDRESS

"...If a free society cannot help the many who are poor, it cannot save the few who are rich...."

MY FELLOW citizens: we observe today not a victory of party but a celebration of freedom—symbolizing an end as well as a beginning—signifying renewal as well as change. For I have sworn before you and Almighty God the same solemn oath our forebears prescribed nearly a century and three quarters ago.

The world is very different now. For man holds in his mortal hands the power to abolish all forms of human poverty and all forms of human life. And yet the same revolutionary beliefs for which our forbears fought are still at issue around the globe—the belief that the rights of man come not from the generosity of the state but from the hand of God.

We dare not forget today that we are the heirs of that first revolution. Let the word go forth from this time and place, to friend and foe alike, that the torch has been passed to a new generation of Americans—born in this century, tempered by war, disciplined by a hard and bitter peace, proud of our ancient heritage—and unwilling to witness or permit the slow undoing of those human rights to which this nation has always been committed, and to which we are committed today at home and around the world.

Let every nation know, whether it wishes us well or ill, that we shall pay any price, bear any burden, meet any hardship, support any friend, oppose any foe to assure the survival and the success of liberty.

This much we pledge—and more.

To those old allies whose cultural and spiritual origins we share, we pledge the loyalty of faithful friends. United, there is little we cannot do in a host of cooperative ventures. Divided, there is little we can do—for we dare not meet a powerful challenge at odds and split asunder.

To those new states whom we welcome to the ranks of the free, we pledge our word that one form of colonial control shall not have passed away merely to be replaced by a far more iron tyranny. We shall not always expect to find them supporting our view. But we shall always hope to find them strongly

"Inaugural Address, January 20, 1961," from *To Turn the Tide* by John F. Kennedy (Harper and Row, 1962). Reprinted by permission of Harper and Row, Publishers.

supporting their own freedom—and to remember that, in the past, those who foolishly sought power by riding the back of the tiger ended up inside.

To those peoples in the huts and villages of half the globe struggling to break the bonds of mass misery, we pledge our best efforts to help them help themselves, for whatever period is required—not because the Communists may be doing it, not because we seek their votes, but because it is right. If a free society cannot help the many who are poor, it cannot save the few who are rich.

To our sister republics south of our border, we offer a special pledge—to convert our good words into good deeds—in a new alliance for progress—to assist free men and free governments in casting off the chains of poverty. But this peaceful revolution of hope cannot become the prey of hostile powers. Let all our neighbors know that we shall join with them to oppose aggression or subversion anywhere in the Americas. And let every other power know that this hemisphere intends to remain the master of its own house.

To that world assembly of sovereign states, the United Nations, our last best hope in an age where the instruments of war have far outpaced the instruments of peace, we renew our pledge of support—to prevent it from becoming merely a forum for invective—to strengthen its shield of the new and the weak—and to enlarge the area in which its writ may run.

Finally, to those nations who would make themselves our adversary, we offer not a pledge but a request: that both sides begin anew the quest for peace, before the dark powers of destruction unleashed by science engulf all humanity in planned or accidental self-destruction.

We dare not tempt them with weakness. For only when our arms are sufficient beyond doubt can we be certain beyond doubt that they will never be employed.

But neither can two great and powerful groups of nations take comfort from our present course—both sides overburdened by the cost of modern weapons, both rightly alarmed by the steady spread of the deadly atom, yet both racing to alter that uncertain balance of terror that stays the hand of mankind's final war.

So let us begin anew—remembering on both sides that civility is not a sign of weakness, and sincerity is always subject to proof. Let us never negotiate out of fear. But let us never fear to negotiate.

Let both sides explore what problems unite us instead of belaboring those problems which divide us.

Let both sides, for the first time, formulate serious and precise proposals for the inspection and control of arms—and bring the absolute power to destroy other nations under the absolute control of all nations.

Let both sides seek to invoke the wonders of science instead of its terrors. Together let us explore the stars, conquer the deserts, eradicate disease, tap the ocean depths and encourage the arts and commerce.

Let both sides unite to heed in all corners of the earth the command of Isaiah—to "undo the heavy burdens . . . (and) let the oppressed go free."

And if a beachhead of cooperation may push back the jungles of suspicion, let both sides join in creating a new endeavor—not a new balance of power, but a new world of law, where the strong are just and the weak secure and the peace preserved.

All this will not be finished in the first hundred days. Nor will it be finished in the first thousand days, nor in the life of this Administration, nor even perhaps in our lifetime on this planet. But let us begin.

In your hands, my fellow citizens, more than mine, will rest the final success or failure of our course. Since this country was founded, each generation of Americans has been summoned to give testimony to its national loyalty. The graves of young Americans who answered the call to service surround the globe.

Now the trumpet summons us again—not as a call to bear arms, though arms we need—not as a call to battle, though embattled we are—but a call to bear the burden of a long twilight struggle, year in and year out, "rejoicing in hope, patient in tribulation"—a struggle against the common enemies of man: tyranny, poverty, disease and war itself.

Can we forge against these enemies a grand and global alliance, north and south, east and west, that can assure a more fruitful life for all mankind? Will you join in that historic effort?

In the long history of the world, only a few generations have been granted the role of defending freedom in its hour of maximum danger. I do not shrink from this responsibility—I welcome it. I do not believe that any of us would exchange places with any other people or any other generation. The energy, the faith, the devotion which we bring to this endeavor will light our country and all who serve it—and the glow from that fire can truly light the world.

And so, my fellow Americans: ask not what your country can do for you —ask what you can do for your country.

My fellow citizens of the world ask not what America will do for you, but what together we can do for the freedom of man.

Finally, whether you are citizens of America or citizens of the world, ask of us here the same high standards of strength and sacrifice which we ask of you. With a good conscience our only sure reward, with history the final judge of our deeds, let us go forth to lead the land we love, asking His blessing and His help, but knowing that here on earth God's work must truly be our own.

ANNE SINCLAIR MEHDEVI

A PERSIAN COURTSHIP

"... Sari was a faithful acolyte at Shem-
shad's Beauty Emporium ... and when she
came home ... she looked as if she were on
the brink of adventure...."

IN MY husband's family, as in so many Teheran families, everyone depended on everyone else. Thus, while we waited for our own villa to be made ready, we quite naturally lived with his sister Mitrah. It was there that I formed my friendship with Sari, Mitrah's twenty-year-old daughter. Sari was my mentor and guide during my early days in Teheran.

She had studied four years in England, where she had picked up a devotion to the latest thing—whatever it might be. England, however, had given Sari no more than the longing for up-to-date-ness. America was her arbiter of fashion. She gleaned her slang from American phonograph records and styled her clothes according to American picture magazines.

In spite of her efforts to lacquer herself with a Western veneer, Sari looked to me like one of those houris pictured in seventeenth-century Persian miniatures. Her face was a perfect oval dominated by her enormous, sleepy eyes—their lids slightly tilted at the outer corners. Her nose was long, narrow, and delicately pointed, while her short upper lip gave her face an expression of doll-like wonderment, a quality emphasized by the fashions she followed. She outlined her eyes with black grease pencil and carmined her lips with an opalescent paste. The harsh paint against her petal-like skin created an illusion of innocence and guile, of purity mated with artificiality.

Though she was twenty and a beauty, Sari had never been to a dance or even to the movies with a young man. She had never been kissed, had never received flowers or love letters, had never worn an evening dress. She hadn't even danced with anyone who wasn't a relative, and in a relative's home.

This was nobody's fault. It was just that teen-age girls had not been provided for in Persia's breathless changeover from a feudal to a nuclear-age society. Until a generation ago, a girl's marriage was arranged by her parents when she was still playing with dolls. (Sari herself had been affianced to a cousin when she was nine years old, but he went abroad to study and perfidiously married a foreigner before Sari grew up.) At fourteen or fifteen a girl was given in marriage to a previously hand-picked man. It was a contract for life, and that was the end of it.

But until the day of her marriage a Persian girl was treated as a child at home. She stood up when her elders entered a room, she never spoke unless spoken to; she was not invited to partake of the adult problems of the family. When she was not sitting in obedient attendance on her elders, she was expected to romp with the younger children. She had, in reality, no adolescence. That treacherous period was simply by-passed. From dolls and giggles she went directly to motherhood and responsibility.

Today Persian girls of the educated classes do not marry any younger than Western girls do. And though parental pressure is subtle and strong, the girl is allowed a certain say—a veto, if nothing else—in the choice of a husband. But it is an illusory privilege, for she has few means of meeting eligible young men. In all of Teheran there is no teen-age club where well-bred girls can meet other youngsters of their own age, nor do the schools provide such outlets. There are no hangouts where girls can meet boys, no soft-drink dancing halls, no milk bars, no drugstores.

As a kind of universal substitute, the girls have taken over Teheran's beauty parlors. But it is a poor and harem-like substitute. All girls who can afford it go twice or three times a week to meet their friends and exchange gossip while getting their hair and nails done. The problem of mass attendance at beauty shops has become so acute that recently the city government of Teheran passed a law that no beauty shop would be licensed unless it was at least three hundred yards from any other beauty shop.

Sari was a faithful acolyte at Shemshad's Beauty Emporium. At least twice a week, she was chauffeured there. The car waited outside until, two hours later, Sari emerged, smelling of lilac and banana oil, her nails enameled with silver, her hair piled high. She always wore her best clothes to Shemshad's, and when she came home, eyes bright and newly mascaraed, hair shining, dress immaculate, she looked as if she were on the brink of adventure. Then she would wander around the house, fretful and aimless.

"You look fit for a king's ball," I would say. "Why don't you go somewhere?"

"Where?" she would ask eagerly.

"Well, I don't know. But, surely, you can visit someone. It's a shame to waste your pretty getup on me."

"Oh," and she would shrug. Soon she would settle in a chair, pretending to read last month's movie magazine.

It used to hurt me to watch Sari's enthusiasm dim and wane as each day wore on. Yet there was nothing for her to do—not even a task around the house. Servants attended to everything with jealous pride. Sari did not know how to cook an egg and had no way of learning, for the cook would have quit in a huff had Sari invaded his kitchen.

My arrival at Mitrah's was a godsend to Sari, for I was a breath of new-ness in the old routine. One day, when the others of the family had dispersed after breakfast to go visiting, Sari and I lingered at the table.

"There's going to be a wedding," she said. "Maybe you'd like to go."

"I'd like it very much. When is it?"

"Tonight. Here, at our house. Our chauffeur is marrying our cook's daughter and Mother is giving them a wedding." Sari paused and looked down her nose. "It's the girl who helps Tai Aga with the laundry, you've seen her."

"Anyway, it will be nice."

"Yes, quite. But . . ." and she looked rather affronted at my interest. "You know, she's terribly old-fashioned, like all servants. She didn't even choose her husband. In fact, her father sold her to the chauffeur."

"Oh, nonsense, I know all about that custom. It's not 'selling' her. The money is a kind of dowry for her—and the bridegroom's family has to pay it."

Sari looked downright offended. "I wouldn't care to be married off like that. I'm going to fall in love."

I remained silent.

As if she were angry, Sari burst out: "How do people expect our country to get modern if all this old-fashioned business is still carried on? The wedding will be a terrible bore. The girl is really homely anyway."

"Why, Sari," I said. "You're jealous."

The chauffeur's name was Later-On. It was a name that teased my fancy and made me smile every time I heard it, though it didn't suit him at all, for he was a prompt and reliable fellow. Persia abounded in wonderful last names. There were Mr. Give-Me-Water, Mr. Snowy, Mr. Good-Handwriting. This surprising variety began forty years ago when the government decreed that everyone must have a name. Identity cards were to be issued and every-one, it was felt, should possess not only the name he was always called, but a last name as well. Before that, most people had lived and died with only a first name.

The pleasant thing about the name-giving decree was that each man was allowed to choose whatever name he fancied. As a result, there are quite a number of Mr. Kings and Mr. Emperors and Mr. Bigs. I ran into one Mr. King-*and*-Emperor. Those without imagination called themselves after the town in which they were born.

Guests for the wedding began to arrive about five-thirty. They were, for the most part, members of our family who had come to honor Later-On. The bridegroom himself was at the door to nod his greetings—a handsome, lean boy of twenty, with dark, snapping eyes, looking excessively uncom-fortable in his new brown suit and pointed polished shoes.

There were many faces I did not recognize, for the crowd soon grew very large. Both Mitrah's living rooms were thrown open, as well as the entrance hall, where her servants sat on a bench, ogling the perfumed and bejeweled crowd. Children of all ages ran about the rooms, snatching sweets from the overloaded tables.

Little by little I was able to place most of the guests—except for two women. They were the liveliest people at the party. One wore a pale green dress of tulle, very short and flouncy, and her neck and shoulders were bare. The other looked like a gypsy; she was looped with bangles that tinkled when she moved, and her hair fell in damp curls over her bony shoulders. These two women were attended by a fat man in a baggy suit and plaid bedroom slippers. All three seemed very much at home. They buzzed about everywhere.

Stimulated by the three gypsylike guests, and fortified by nips from the Arak bottles lavishly placed about the rooms, the crowd of some hundred persons soon grew flushed and noisy. A kind of wayward and earthy gaiety took over. Then the three odd guests produced a stringed musical instrument that resembled a long-necked ukulele, and began to dance and sing.

They were hired entertainers, the wedding musicians. The rest of us fell back into a circle and the performance was on.

The woman in green tulle did a belly dance, singing as she twisted her body and winking broadly at several graybeards in the audience. Then she circled among the guests and tried to entice some of the men to dance with her. When they refused she asked for money, wiggling and shaking her body in front of her victim, until he was forced out of sheer embarrassment to hand her a bill, which she popped down the front of her dress. Meanwhile, the fat man in the baggy suit was singing—his jokes were about weddings and brides and were not very proper. The audience whooped with laughter; the entertainers roared out their bawdy songs.

As suddenly as the entertainers began, they stopped. A hush fell over the room. The bride was coming, led in by her father, a little wrinkled man. She was veiled from head to foot in white netting, through which her sweet face could be seen as if swimming in a mist. Her dark hair was fastened with a circlet of jasmine blossoms.

A sheet was then spread in the center of the floor and the bride knelt upon it. The crowd, now silent, watched the girl curiously. The white sheet seemed so large, and she—so trembling and so alone in its center. With head bowed, she knelt motionless, her hands clasped together in her lap. She appeared as fragile as a China figurine. The crowd, as if reprimanded for their feverish and unchaste gaiety, spoke now in whispers. The entertainers drifted out of the room, like minions of evil routed by the purity of the little maiden.

In the hall a bustle announced the arrival of the *mollah*, or priest, a great hearty man in brown homespun cassock with a towering beehive of a turban on his head. He was given tea and cookies, of which he took a token sip and bite. Then he sat on a couch in front of the girl. A little table was placed before him on which he opened a great ledgerlike book. All the time the girl did not look up. Now a mirror was placed in front of her, a copy of the Koran beside her, and beside it a large cone of the rock sugar that I recognized as "sweetening life."

The *mollah* asked her three questions, to which she murmured assent.

Then she looked into the mirror as Later-On stepped up behind her, so that she could see his reflection in the glass. That was all. The ceremony was over. Later-On led his bride to the side of the room and everyone lined up, to congratulate them and toast them.

After the entertainers had begun their performance, I had lost sight of Sari in the crowd. Now I noticed her standing with her friends, Shayla and Layla, in a corner. The three girls, dressed in the latest Paris fashion—one of them in black velvet tights and chain-gold high-heeled boots—were watching the bride intently and sadly. Upon each of the three faces was written a passionate envy of the old, old ways which they had chosen to deny and deride and which could, now, never be theirs.

Next morning Sari asked me how I had met my husband.

"A friend gave me Mohamed's address when he heard I was going to New York, and when I got there I called Mohamed up. I liked him and he liked me, and after a while we decided to get married."

"How do you mean? Didn't he ask you?"

"Well, no. He didn't believe in marriage. So I asked him."

Sari clapped her hands. "You asked him! That's the way I want to get married. I shall never marry a Persian. I'm going to fall in love with a foreigner and I'm going to tell him so and ask him to marry me. And I'm not going to tell my mother or my father or anyone."

On other mornings we talked of polygamy—in Iran, an accepted state of affairs. Sari, like all women of her class, was against polygamy as far as *she* was concerned. These women have outlawed the practice in Iran simply by boycotting it, by refusing to marry anyone who already has a wife. But they cannot prevent their husbands from marrying some lower-class woman as a second wife after they have grown gray, and they have no recourse, for divorce is forbidden to women except in very rare cases.

Strangely enough, Sari upheld the custom in theory and pointed out its advantages. "What about that student who came back from Switzerland with a Swiss wife after his family had already arranged a marriage contract for him with a girl from Yazd? If it hadn't been for polygamy, he wouldn't have been able to marry the Yazd girl too and thus save the family's face."

"I thought you told me that modern Persian girls wouldn't marry a man who already had a wife."

"Oh," said Sari brightly, "foreign women don't count." I lifted my eyebrows. "Besides," she said, "it's unfair for foreign girls to marry Persian boys."

"Oh?"

"What are we Persian girls supposed to do? All the best boys go abroad to study and we have to sit here, waiting like ninnies. Then they come back with an American or English wife and we are supposed to shout 'hooray' and be glad to be old maids."

Didn't you notice?" Sari said to me a few mornings later. "Mother and I aren't speaking."

I had noticed, but had decided not to venture any comment. "Not speaking" was a favorite method of reprimand in Iran. My husband and I were the indirect cause of Sari's fall from favor. A few days before, I had persuaded Mohamed to escort Sari, Shayla, Layla, and me to a charity ball and raffle given by the American Women's Club of Teheran. I had proposed the evening, secretly hoping Sari and her friends might meet and dance with a few eligible young men.

The evening had been a frost. None of the girls won a door prize, though Sari had been convinced she would win the trip to Beirut. When she didn't, she fell into a pout. The place was crowded and unbearably hot, and the worst of it was that no young men asked my three charges to dance, except the boys they already knew—cousins and friends of the family.

We went home early and in profound silence.

Two days afterwards there was a mysterious phone call to the house. Golam Ali, a servant, answered and announced that an Aga wished to speak to Sari's father. When he went to the telephone, we all listened unashamedly. Sari's father said, "Yes," in a vague and guarded voice. Then, rather unwillingly: "If it is your pleasure." And, then, after a longer pause: "Very well, Thursday at five o'clock, if it pleases you." He hung up, explained nothing, and went off to his office.

This phone call was followed by two more that same afternoon. Sari's mother, Mitrah, took the calls. Afterwards she left the house, dressed in her best. Something was stirring. The whole household sensed it, and the servants smiled to themselves.

They knew about it before Sari was told, for Golam Ali had informed himself about the mysterious phone calls by means of his own. An unknown couple, Aga and Khanoum Jambani, had asked for a meeting with Sari's parents. Their son had seen Sari at the American Women's Club Ball and the parents were proposing marriage.

Late that evening, when the rest of the family had left Sari and me at home, Sari began to coax Golam Ali for information.

"The father is desperate, out of his senses," he said as Sari translated for me. "His son refuses to eat, can't sleep nights. He is reading poetry all day and says he can't live another hour. His parents are angry. They had a girl picked out for him, but he says he will kill himself . . ."

Sari's eyes popped open. "How?" she wanted to know.

"Opium. He says he will eat opium. He must have Sari Khanoum or he will die of grief." Pleased with himself, Golam Ali smiled a little and left the room.

Sari leaned back in her chair, her face a mirror of conflicting emotions—surprise, delight, hesitation. At last her features settled into a pout. "Imagine!" she burst out. "It's just like tribal days. Sending his parents to my parents! Well, I told my mother long ago that such proposals are out of the question. I'm not a piece of goods to be negotiated about." She tossed her head and lighted a cigarette.

"Which young man was he?" I asked, trying to recall faces from the evening of the dance.

"But that's it!" she exploded. "I haven't the faintest idea. I didn't dance with anyone I didn't know—only with my wretched cousins that I always have to dance with. This boy must be a sop, not even having the courage to ask me to dance—or at least to flirt a little. He's probably some middle-aged guy with a paunch."

"But Sari," I said, "I think it's exciting."

Her eyes opened wide. "You do? But I thought you were up-to-date."

"Well," I said, "if someone had seen me at a dance only for a moment and had been so affected that he was ready to propose marriage the next day, I would certainly have a look at him. Love at first sight isn't old-fashioned."

"You would see him?"

"Yes. Maybe he's handsome and rich. Maybe he's wonderful."

She looked thoughtful. "That's what Mother will want me to do, no doubt. Just meet him. His parents want to bring him over on Thursday at five o'clock, Golam Ali said. Then after we two get a look at each other close-up, and if I agree and if my parents like his looks and his character, then they'll enter into the serious negotiations—they're always financial, you know, never anything about love."

"I would be dying of curiosity to meet him," I said.

"Well, I won't. That's final." And she must have repeated this to her mother, for that was the morning they weren't speaking.

Two days later Sari was in the garden when the daily newsboy, after delivering the papers at the front door, ran over to her, threw a note at her feet, and hurried away. The note was unsigned and contained a single poem; rendered into English, it went something like this:

The night wind kissed the scented curl
On the white brow
Of a capricious girl;
And, in passing,
Gave me half the stolen kiss.

Oh, that my heart would bleed and break
For such a little thing as this.

On the third morning after the first mysterious phone call, Sari's mother was speaking to her again at breakfast, and with a smiling face. As Mitrah rose to go, she said to Sari, "At five o'clock, then." It was Thursday.

Sari looked at me sheepishly when we were alone. She shrugged. "You think I'm weak-minded."

"Not at all."

"It's really for Mother's sake. She's miserable when we're not speaking, so we had to start speaking again—that's the only reason I agreed."

"Of course. When will you meet him—this afternoon?"

"Yes. At five. He and his parents are coming."

Sari passed the day digging through her closets. She was not a tidy girl, and to her horror, everything she possessed seemed unsuitable. There was a spot on one dress; she had grown too plump for another; a button was off a third, and it needed to be washed, anyway. Around four o'clock she had a fit of tears.

She began to make up her face at four-thirty. I watched with fascination as she proceeded with great deliberation to obliterate the peach-like flush from her cheeks with a heavy theatrical paste. She piled her hair high and stuck bunches of false hair into it until her head was the size of a melon. She donned a black velvet blouse and tight gold-threaded trousers and gold slippers.

Every once in a while she would make a comment. "He's a graduate of some American university. That's a good sign." Or, "What if his parents don't like me?" Then she would bite her lip. "I should care," she would say loudly. "I don't care a bit. It's all so horribly old-fashioned."

We were still upstairs when we heard a car drive up and stop in front of the garden gate. We heard the car door snap open and then click shut.

Sari jumped up and wrung her hands. "What shall I do?" she cried. "What if he doesn't like me now that he sees me close?"

She grasped my hands in hers. "Please hide at the top of the stairs. Please do. You can crouch at the landing and no one will see you. Take a look at him. Oh, I can't bear it."

While Sari paced in her room, I went to the top of the stairs and looked below. The doorbell rang and Golam Ali opened the door. A heavy-set man with a double-breasted overcoat and a homburg hat walked in with slow dignity. Behind him came the mother, a rotund little woman in a very short, tight black dress and a fur stole. She was flashing with jewels and her fat little legs teetered uncertainly on high heels. The mother's face was grim and forbidding. I wondered how she would take to Sari's golden tights. Not very favorably, I decided.

Behind them came Sari's suitor, also in an overcoat and homburg. "Oh, he's short!" I said to myself automatically. He was, indeed, but his face looked gentle and his eyes were soft. He was twisting his gloves in his hand and his forehead was slick with sweat. "He doesn't like this, either," I thought, and I liked him for that.

The three visitors passed majestically through the hall and disappeared within the larger and more ornate salon, while Golam Ali went to call Sari's parents from the left wing of the house.

"Psst," I heard behind me. There was Sari on the landing, furiously puffing a cigarette. "I've decided to smoke as I go down to meet them," she announced. "Really, they might as well know what I'm like from the beginning."

She waited for my comment, standing with her gold-clad legs apart, hands on her hips. "Well?"

"You can't judge a man by his appearance," I said hesitantly.

"Oh!" she cried. "Then he's ugly, ugly as sin."

"No, he's not. It's just that he's not strikingly handsome," I said. "But don't forget, he's as nervous as you are. That makes a man look his worst."

"Oh," she said again, stamping out her cigarette on the tiles. "I won't go down. I absolutely refuse." She spun on her heel and ran to her room, where she threw herself on the bed.

When Golam Ali came to call her, after half an hour, she refused to go downstairs. But when her mother came up ten minutes later, she followed with a stony, set face. I watched her with mixed feelings as she trudged reluctantly down the stairs and through the entrance corridor—her melon head held high upon her fragile neck, her absurd costume twinkling in the afternoon light.

I waited upstairs, apprehensive and doubtful, expecting Sari to come scrambling back, bathed in tears. When she didn't after an hour, I tiptoed onto the landing and leaned over the balustrade. I heard sounds of laughter from the living room. I recognized Sari's melodious voice and pert answers, and went back to my room.

I didn't see Sari again until late the next afternoon. She seemed silent and pensive. "Did you like him?" I asked.

She shrugged. "He's short and chubby."

"What did your parents think of him?"

"Oh, they say it's up to me. Mother wants me to get married. I'm already twenty. She had two children by the time she was twenty. His family is quite rich, though not politically important . . ." She glanced up at me obliquely. "That poem of his was nice, wasn't it?"

There was a pause. Then Sari brightened. "I'm getting a car, a white two-seater."

"Oh?"

"It's kind of an engagement present—that is, *if* I get engaged. I suspect it's a bribe. You know, once a boy and girl are engaged, they can go out together—as long as a third person is along. I'll take Layla, because it will make her jealous. We could go out together in the car—that is, if I accept him."

I smiled. "Well. Are you or aren't you going to get engaged?"

She made a bored face. "Maybe. I haven't decided. I wish he weren't so short. And he can't dance."

There was another pause.

Then: "Of course, I'm short too, so his shortness shouldn't matter too much."

I still said nothing.

She chuckled proudly. "His parents are going to pay one hundred thousand for me. That's a lot of money."

Sari *did* get engaged. I could no longer follow the mercurial course of the courtship, for my husband and I moved to our villa shortly after the suitor's first call. But Sari lived next door. I often saw her of a morning, heading off to Teheran in her white sports roadster with Layla or Shayla beside her, their scarves flying, their eyes laughing.

One day Sari and I met on the sidewalk. She was loaded with packages, her face incandescent; she bustled about her car, locking the doors and checking that the ignition was off.

"Hello, Sari," I said.

There was a slight formality in her greeting. She was a woman of some importance now, and perhaps regretted the confidences of earlier weeks. She asked: "How is your new house, I hope you are contented with it?"

I smiled and mumbled an agreeable response.

"Are you now engaged?" I asked, though I was being a hypocrite, for the family grapevine had informed me long ago.

"Yes."

"Yes." She hesitated. She looked to see if anyone was watching. All at once she threw her packages helter-skelter on the ground. "Oh, you'll never guess," she burst out, hugging me. "He can play the guitar—like poetry. And he's so fond of me. And I'm teaching him to dance."

She stood back, slightly embarrassed at her show of emotion. "And, oh, my dear aunt," she added in a whisper, "I've been kissed at last."

JOHN FISCHER

A SMALL BURIED TREASURE

"'...We stopped our nighttime ventures, and for days we sat around the café and talked about this problem. In the end we worked out a very clever scheme....'"

ALEKO became a grave robber mostly out of boredom, though hunger had something to do with it.

He is not a talkative man, so I learned about his profession only obliquely and over a considerable period of time. (His former profession, that is. Now he is a businessman of monumental respectability, the owner of a cherished secondhand Cadillac in which he will drive you anywhere in Europe for quite a reasonable fee.) The first hint came in Salonika, after we had been traveling for days over the rutted, dusty roads of northern Greece.

We had stopped at a sidewalk cafe for a cup of coffee. On the way back to the car we passed one of those little open-front shops which seem to be the commonest form of enterprise in Macedonia. Its counter was piled with canvas shoes, old clothes, battered lamps, and similar castoffs. At one end was a tray of jewelry. I wouldn't have given it a second glance if Aleko hadn't stopped and begun to poke around among the earrings and bangles. Most of them looked as if they had come originally from the Greek equivalent of a dime store, and the one he pointed out to me—a copper-colored bracelet was even more tarnished than the rest.

"You might buy that," he said. "It won't cost much."

There was nothing I needed less, but I had learned to follow Aleko's suggestions, however odd. He conducted the mandatory haggling and bought it in the end for a few drachmas.

When we were on the road again I asked him why.

"It's old," he said. "Probably about eighth century B.C. I think it came, maybe, from the grave of a little girl. Because it wasn't gold, the grave robbers sold it cheap. They are ignorant fellows mostly." He was silent for a couple of miles, and then added: "I know a little about such things."

(At the time all this sounded unlikely, but weeks later I found out that Aleko was right. Museum people told me that the bracelet was bronze, not copper; its incised decorations were Early Geometric; a few similar pieces are in the Binaki collection in Athens.)

Two days later Aleko asked, diffidently, if I would mind our making a short detour. We were driving east, toward the Turkish border, along the narrow strip of coastal plain at the top of the Aegean Sea. The road originally had been built by the Roman emperors to link their two great seats of power, Constantinople and Rome, but it had deteriorated considerably since their time. A few miles to the north rose the long crest of mountains that mark the Bulgarian border. In their foothills, Aleko said, was the village of Moustheni. No, I wouldn't find it on the map—just a dozen or so stone huts.

"When I left there twenty years ago," he said, "I wore handcuffs. I never expected to go back—but now that we are so close, I would like to drop by and see if they remember me. It would be good for them to see me traveling in my own car and with an American friend."

As we turned onto the rocky track that led toward the foothills, he told me about his boyhood in Moustheni. His family, like most of the others, were tobacco farmers. Except for the few weeks each year when he helped plant, hoe, and harvest their three-acre patch, he had no work. Nor was there much else to do—no school, no movies, not even any girls; for in this part of the country, so long under Turkish rule, the women are still secluded. (Many of the older ones never appear in public without their heavy, tentlike veils; the younger ones, never without a chaperon.) So Aleko spent much time with a few other idle youngsters at a table in front of the town's only café, playing cards, nursing a thimbleful of coffee through the long hot afternoons, grumbling about their poverty and boredom.

He doesn't remember who first thought of the tumuli. These are mounds, about ten feet high, which rise like pimples all over the Macedonian plain; along some stretches of road you pass one about every quarter of a mile.

Each of them covers a tomb, usually a rough stone enclosure which contains (or once did) the bones of some Bronze Age chief, and sometimes those of his family, servants, and horses. (Common people were, presumably, buried with less pretension.) A stranger finds it hard to believe that there could have been so many of them; but, as Aleko pointed out, people as bellicose as the Achaeans and Dorians could manage over a few thousand years of tribal warfare to run through quite a few chiefs.

The young men of Moustheni had heard that archaeologists from Athens recently had been digging in such a mound near the ancient ruins of Amphipolis, not far away. Nobody knew for sure what, if anything, they had found; but there were rumors of much treasure—jeweled sword hilts, necklaces, armlets, statues of solid gold. Why shouldn't the boys do a little digging on their own?

Such enterprises are of course illegal in Greece, and the penalties are severe. But policemen are scarce in the country districts; besides, the Moustheni explorers planned to work at night. As an extra precaution they organized themselves into two shifts of four men each—one to stand sentry while the others dug.

"For the next year," Aleko said, "I labored harder than I ever have in my life. We would tackle a grave just like the archaeologists do—cutting a trench about two feet wide straight through the middle of the mound. If we hit anything promising, we would then open branch trenches to the left or right. And always we would try to finish the job and fill in the trenches before daybreak. We even replaced the sod and bushes as best we could, to avoid attracting attention to our business.

"We must have opened a hundred tumuli without finding a thing except bones and bits of useless pottery. Other grave robbers, you see, had got there first, maybe hundreds of years ago. So all we got for our trouble was calloused palms and aching backs, and naturally we began to get discouraged. Then one night we found it.

"This mound looked exactly like all the others, but somehow the earlier diggers had missed it. Alongside the bones of the old warrior we found all the equipment his people had given him for his last journey—three pots that must have held food and wine, a bronze spearhead, a wreath of gold leaves, and a little statue of Hercules. It was only about six inches high, but it was gold—probably from the ancient mines near the headwaters of the Strymon River—and to us the workmanship seemed very fine. None of us had ever seen anything like it.

"But what could we do with it? If we tried to sell such a rarity anywhere in Greece, the authorities would begin to ask questions at once. And how could we find out what it was worth? After so much labor, you understand, we didn't propose to let ourselves be cheated.

"We stopped our nighttime ventures, and for days we sat around the café and talked about this problem. In the end we worked out a very clever scheme. . . ."

At this point Aleko's account was interrupted by our arrival at Moustheni.

It looked even grimmer than he had led me to expect—a single cobbled street twisting up the hillside between two rows of gray hovels. But there was nothing grim about the people. As we came abreast of the first house, Aleko began to honk his horn, and the whole village—including a remarkable number of dogs and babies—poured out to follow. The appearance of any automobile here was cause for excitement enough, but when they recognized the man at the wheel the uproar really cut loose. If St. Demetrios himself had ridden into town on his spectral white stallion, he couldn't have produced more astonishment, or noise.

Aleko inched the car along to the café, where he had plotted with his friends so many years ago, and stopped to receive homage. At this place the street widens a little, to form a sort of village square. Though it was crowded to the walls, somebody managed to drag a couple of tables out to the center, and after Aleko had introduced me to what I took to be the village elders, we sat down with them for a ceremonial round of *ouzo* and thick, bitter coffee. Aleko insisted on paying for everything. While I couldn't understand a word of the conversation, it was clear that he was enacting—with great dignity—the Prodigal's Return.

His sense of timing was flawless. In precisely twenty minutes he rose, shook hands again with everybody, and led the procession back to his car—the very image of the man of affairs who has to be off to the pressing business of the outside world. A swarm of children and dogs, in full cry, raced beside us until we passed the last house.

All the way back to the main road Aleko grinned in silent satisfaction. I had a hard time getting him to pick up the thread of his story.

"One of the men you met back there—the one who passed around the tobacco and cigarette papers—is Philip Galas," he said. "He is a farmer now, but in the old days he was one of our diggers. He had relatives in Kavala, and there he had met a jeweler and pawnbroker—a rich man but trustworthy. To get our scheme under way, Philip took the statue to him and persuaded him to make an exact copy. Naturally we had to promise him a share—a full one-ninth—of the wealth we expected to have before long.

"The jeweler then carried his copy to the local museum and tried to sell it, saying that it had been pawned in his shop over a year ago and that the owner had never reclaimed it. The curator, of course, refused. He explained that it was only a modern reproduction, though a good one, and therefore worth little more than the metal it contained. Our friend pretended great disappointment. But if it *had* been genuine, he asked, what price would it have brought? At least a million drachmas, the museum man told him. Perhaps more, for such works of art from the archaic period were very rare indeed.

"Once we had that information, we knew just what to do next. From our fathers and the jeweler we borrowed enough money to send one member of our band—you will forgive me if I don't mention his name—to Paris. He carried the little Hercules, the real one, baked inside a loaf of bread. It was a safe hiding place, since nearly all peasants carry a parcel of bread and sausage when they go traveling, and the customs guards never pay it any attention.

"In Paris our messenger had no great trouble in finding a dealer willing to pay a fair price and ask no questions."

Aleko lapsed into one of his long silences; I thought the story was finished. When he began talking again, it was about Greek history.

"The habit of betrayal has always been our great weakness," he said. "Remember Alcibiades? Remember Ephialtes, who sold the pass at Thermopylae? Such men are more typical than you might think. Every city in Greece has its legend of at least one betrayer. So has Moustheni.

"Our agent didn't come home. Instead he went to Athens with our money in his pocket, and wrote an unsigned letter to the national police, telling them all about our little venture in midnight archaeology. So a truckload of policemen pulled into the village one morning, and arrested all seven of us. They took us to the Kavala court, where the judge sentenced us to a big fine and many years in jail. If the war hadn't broken out that fall, I might have been in prison yet."

What happened, he explained, was that the royal government had opened the jail doors for every man who wanted to fight the invaders. Aleko and his friends set off for the mountains, with no equipment except a rifle and a belt of cartridges apiece, and fought for five years against Italians, Germans, and Bulgarians. When the war was over, nobody felt inclined to remember the old charges.

"But the archaeologists didn't forget our statue," he added. "With the help of the French police they eventually got their hands on the little Hercules. You can see it any day you like in the Kavala museum—the finest piece in its collection. We never got a penny for it, of course."

Did he know, I asked, what had become of the man who turned them in?

"Yes," Aleko said, "he came back to Macedonia after the war. Perhaps he too thought that old scores would be forgotten. He was mistaken."

For a long while we had met no one along the road. Now we saw ahead of us two old women on minute donkeys, riding side-saddle in the fashion of the country. Aleko pulled up beside them to ask about the turnoff for Keramoti, the fishing village where he was to leave me and where I hoped to find some sort of boat to take me on the next leg of my journey. When we were on our way again, he said:

"There is one thing about these old graves. When everybody knows that one of them has been opened—as, for example, the one where we found the treasure—it is no longer of interest. Nobody else is likely to look inside it again, maybe not for centuries. It makes an ideal place to hide a body."

JOHN FISCHER

LEGEND ALOFT

". . . the DC-3 . . . is designed in . . . the American Vernacular, the great tradition ranging from the Mississippi steamboat to the San Francisco Bay Bridge, the Johnson Wax Company . . . and the Hoover Dam. . . ."

NEXT to the covered wagon and the Model T Ford, the DC-3 probably is embedded deeper in American history and legend than any machine we have ever made. It is the plane in which most of us made our first flight. It also is a work of art—clean, functional, and (like a good piece of sculpture) superbly balanced from any angle of vision. It is designed in what John Kouwenhoven has christened the American Vernacular, the great tradition ranging from the Mississippi steamboat to the San Francisco Bay Bridge, the Johnson Wax Company Building, the New Jersey Turnpike, and the Hoover Dam. (Every culture, of course, develops its own distinctive idiom and media. The materials of our major artists are steel, aluminum, glass, and concrete, rather than canvas, paint, and marble; and they are intended for the delight and use of millions, rather than for the private pleasures of an elite. Because European intellectuals find this hard to understand—because they can hardly conceive of any culture so different from their own—many of them still cling to the illusion that America simply doesn't have any.)

Then, too, the DC-3 has become legendary because it figures in the sharpest memories of so many Americans. Hundreds of thousands of us have had some experience with the plane which we are never likely to forget—a magic-carpet arrival in a strange land, a journey to a sick child, a glimpse of Manhattan's towers at night, an air drop into battle, or an encounter with fear.

For example, on a hot August morning in 1944, three strangers climbed aboard a DC-3 cargo plane at Dum-dum airfield. (This ancient military post, near Calcutta, is memorable only because the dum-dum bullet—which mushrooms on impact—was invented there about a hundred years ago; and because the outlawry of this unpleasant weapon is almost the only international Rule of War which is still universally respected.) None of the three had any proper military authorization to get on that plane; they were merely hitchhikers, thumbing a ride to Delhi.

Like most cargo planes at that time and place, this one was overloaded. It took off heavily, under a five-hundred-foot ceiling, and slid up into the monsoon cloudbank—some 16,000 feet thick—which covered most of India and Burma. You couldn't see the wingtips; everybody felt claustrophobic and uneasy.

Forty minutes out of Dum-dum the starboard engine quit. The pilot revved up the remaining engine, and swung into a slow turn, back toward the field. Then the second engine began to splutter.

At this moment the navigator opened the door from the pilot's compartment, and grinned at his three passengers.

"Looks like we may have to get out," he said. "We got a couple of extra parachutes—you guys divide up."

He tossed the two khaki packs on the floor, between the rows of bucket seats, and closed the door.

For perhaps thirty seconds, the three strangers stared at each other, each one grappling in silent panic with the same moral problem: Do I let the others have the chutes—or do I fight like a tiger to get one for myself?

Before anybody could make up his mind, the port engine stopped spluttering and a few seconds later the starboard motor roared back to life. The passengers fumbled for cigarettes with sweaty fingers and talked about something else. The two parachutes were still lying untouched on the floor when the plane rolled down the landing strip.

At least one of the passengers still bothers about the incident now and then. He wonders: (a) What should he have done, if the engines hadn't caught on?—Toss a coin? Try to guess whose life was most important to the war effort?—and (b) What would he actually have done? These unanswered questions—and the awareness that one of them now cannot ever be answered for sure—leave an annoying kind of gap, a hole in his psychic sock. He remembers it uncomfortably every time he sees a DC-3 parked at an airport.

LEE STROUT WHITE

FAREWELL, MY LOVELY!

". . . there was always . . . a certain dull rapport between engine and wheels, and even when the car was in a state known as neutral, it trembled with a deep imperative and tended to inch forward. . . ."

I SEE by the new Sears Roebuck catalogue that it is still possible to buy an axle for a 1909 Model T Ford, but I am not deceived. The great days have faded, the end is in sight. Only one page in the current catalogue is devoted to parts and accessories for the Model T; yet everyone remembers springtimes when the Ford gadget section was larger than men's clothing, almost as large as household furnishings. The last Model T was built in 1927, and the car is fading from what scholars call the American scene—which is an understatement, because to a few million people who grew up with it, the old Ford practically *was* the American scene.

It was the miracle God had wrought. And it was patently the sort of thing that could only happen once. Mechanically uncanny, it was like nothing that had ever come to the world before. Flourishing industries rose and fell with it. As a vehicle, it was hardworking, commonplace, heroic; and it often seemed to transmit those qualities to the persons who rode in it. My own generation identifies it with Youth, with its gaudy, irretrievable excitements; before it fades into the mist, I would like to pay it the tribute of the sigh that is not a sob, and set down random entries in a shape somewhat less cumbersome than a Sears Roebuck catalogue.

The Model T was distinguished from all other makes of cars by the fact that its transmission was of a type known as planetary—which was half metaphysics, half sheer fiction. Engineers accepted the word "planetary" in its epicyclic sense, but I was always conscious that it also meant "wandering," "erratic." Because of the peculiar nature of this planetary element, there was always, in Model T, a certain dull rapport between engine and wheels, and even when the car was in a state known as neutral, it trembled with a deep imperative and tended to inch forward. There was never a moment when the bands were not faintly egging the machine on. In this respect it was like a horse, rolling the bit on its tongue, and country people brought to it the same technique they used with draft animals.

Its most remarkable quality was its rate of acceleration. In its palmy days the Model T could take off faster than anything on the road. The reason was simple. To get under way, you simply hooked the third finger of the right hand around a lever on the steering column, pulled down hard, and shoved your left foot forcibly against the low-speed pedal. These were simple, positive motions; the car responded by lunging forward with a roar. After a few seconds of this turmoil, you took your toe off the pedal, eased up a mite on the throttle, and the car, possessed of only two forward speeds, catapulted directly into high with a series of ugly jerks and was off on its glorious errand. The abruptness of this departure was never equalled in other cars of the period. The human leg was (and still is) incapable of letting in a clutch with anything like the forthright abandon that used to send Model T on its way. Letting in a clutch is a negative, hesitant motion, depending on delicate nervous control; pushing down the Ford pedal was a simple, country motion —an expansive act, which came as natural as kicking an old door to make it budge.

The driver of the old Model T was a man enthroned. The car, with top up, stood seven feet high. The driver sat on top of the gas tank, brooding it with his own body. When he wanted gasoline, he alighted, along with everything else in the front seat; the seat was pulled off, the metal cap unscrewed, and a wooden stick thrust down to sound the liquid in the well. There were always a couple of these sounding sticks kicking around in the ratty sub-cushion regions of a flivver. Refuelling was more of a social function then, because the driver had to unbend, whether he wanted to or not. Directly in front of the driver was the windshield—high, uncompromisingly erect. Nobody talked about air resistance, and the four cylinders pushed the car through the atmosphere with a simple disregard of physical law.

There was this about a Model T: the purchaser never regarded his purchase as a complete, finished product. When you bought a Ford, you figured you had a start—a vibrant, spirited framework to which could be screwed an almost limitless assortment of decorative and functional hardware. Driving away from the agency, hugging the new wheel between your knees, you were already full of creative worry. A Ford was born naked as a baby, and a flourishing industry grew up out of correcting its rare deficiencies and combatting its fascinating diseases. Those were the great days of lily-painting. I have been looking at some old Sears Roebuck catalogues, and they bring everything back so clear.

First you bought a Ruby Safety Reflector for the rear, so that your posterior would glow in another car's brillance. Then you invested thirty-nine cents in some radiator Moto Wings, a popular ornament which gave the Pegasus touch to the machine and did something godlike to the owner. For nine cents you bought a fan-belt guide to keep the belt from slipping off the pulley.

You bought a radiator compound to stop leaks. This was as much a part of everybody's equipment as aspirin tablets are of a medicine cabinet. You bought special oil to prevent chattering, a clamp-on dash light, a patching outfit, a tool box that you bolted to the running board, a sun visor, a steering-column brace to keep the column rigid, and a set of emergency containers for gas, oil, and water—three thin, disc-like cans that reposed in a case on the running board during long, important journeys—red for gas, gray for water, green for oil. It was only a beginning. After the car was about a year old, steps were taken to check the alarming disintegration. (Model T was full of tumors, but they were benign.) A set of anti-rattlers (ninety-eight cents) was a popular panacea. You hooked them on to the gas and spark rods, to the brake pull rod, and to the steering-rod connections. Hood silencers, of black rubber, were applied to the fluttering hood. Shock-absorbers and snubbers gave "complete relaxation." Some people bought rubber pedal pads, to fit over the standard metal pedals. (I didn't like these, I remember.) Persons of a suspicious or pugnacious turn of mind bought a rear-view mirror; but most Model T owners weren't worried by what was coming from behind because they would soon enough see it out in front. They rode in a state of cheerful catalepsy. Quite a large mutinous clique among Ford owners went over to a foot accelerator (you could buy one and screw it to the floor board), but there was a certain madness in these people, because the Model T, just as she stood, had a choice of three foot pedals to push, and there were plenty of moments when both feet were occupied in the routine performance of duty and when the only way to speed up the engine was with the hand throttle.

Gadget bred gadget. Owners not only bought ready-made gadgets, they invented gadgets to meet special needs. I myself drove my car directly from the agency to the blacksmith's, and had the smith affix two enormous iron brackets to the port running board to support an army trunk.

People who owned closed models builded along different lines: they bought ball grip handles for opening doors, window anti-rattlers, and de-luxe flower vases of the cut-glass anti-splash type. People with delicate sensibilities garnished their car with a device called the Donna Lee Automobile Disseminator—a porous vase guaranteed, according to Sears, to fill the car with a "faint clear odor of lavender." The gap between open cars and closed cars was not as great then as it is now: for $11.95, Sears Roebuck converted our touring car into a sedan and you went forth renewed. One agreeable quality of the old Fords was that they had no bumpers, and their fenders softened and wilted with the years and permitted the driver to squeeze in and out of tight places.

Tires were $30 \times 3\frac{1}{2}$, cost about twelve dollars, and punctured readily. Everybody carried a Jiffy patching set, with a nutmeg grater to roughen the tube before the goo was spread on. Everybody was capable of putting on a patch, expected to have to, and did have to.

During my association with Model T's, self-starters were not a prevalent accessory. They were expensive and under suspicion. Your car came equipped with a serviceable crank, and the first thing you learned was how to Get Results. It was a special trick, and until you learned it (usually from another Ford owner, but sometimes by a period of appalling experimentation) you might as well have been winding up an awning. The trick was to leave the ignition switch off, proceed to the animal's head, pull the choke (which was a little wire protruding through the radiator) and give the crank two or three nonchalant upward lifts. Then, whistling as though thinking about something else, you would saunter back to the driver's cabin, turn the ignition on, return to the crank, and this time, catching it on the down stroke, give it a quick spin with plenty of That. If this procedure was followed, the engine almost always responded—first with a few scattered explosions, then with a tumultuous gunfire, that you checked by racing around to the driver's seat and retarding the throttle. Often, if the emergency brake hadn't been pulled all the way back, the car advanced on you the instant the first explosion occurred and you would hold it back by leaning your weight against it. I can still feel my old Ford nuzzling me at the curb, as though looking for an apple in my pocket.

In zero weather, ordinary cranking became an impossibility, except for giants. The oil thickened, and it became necessary to jack up the rear wheels, which, for some planetary reason, eased the throw.

The lore and legend that governed the Ford were boundless. Owners had their own theories about everything; they discussed mutual problems in that wise, infinitely resourceful way old women discuss rheumatism. Exact knowledge was pretty scarce, and often proved less effective than superstition. Dropping a camphor ball into the gas tank was a popular expedient; it seemed to have a tonic effect on both man and machine. There wasn't much to base exact knowledge on. The Ford driver flew blind. He didn't know the temperature of his engine, the speed of his car, the amount of his fuel, or the pressure of his oil (the old Ford lubricated itself by what was amiably described as the "splash system"). A speedometer cost money and was an extra, like a windshield-wiper. The dashboard of the early models was bare save for an ignition key; later models, grown effete, boasted an ammeter which pulsated alarmingly with the throbbing of the car. Under the dash was a box of coils, with vibrators that you adjusted, or thought you adjusted. Whatever the driver learned of his motor, he learned not through instruments but through sudden developments. I remember that the timer was one of the vital organs about which there was ample doctrine. When everything else had been checked, you "had a look" at the timer. It was an extravagantly odd little device, simple in construction, mysterious in function. It contained a roller, held by a spring, and there were four contact points on the inside of the case against which, many people believed, the roller rolled. I have had a timer apart on a sick Ford many times. But I never really knew what I was up to—I was just showing off before God.

There were almost as many schools of thought as there were timers. Some people, when things went wrong, just clenched their teeth and gave the timer a smart crack with a wrench. Other people opened it up and blew on it. There was a school that held that the timer needed large amounts of oil; they fixed it by frequent baptism. And there was a school that was positive it was meant to run dry as a bone; these people were continually taking it off and wiping it. I remember once spitting into a timer; not in anger, but in a spirit of research. You see, the Model T driver moved in the realm of metaphysics. He believed his car could be hexed.

One reason the Ford anatomy was never reduced to an exact science was that, having "fixed" it, the owner couldn't honestly claim that the treatment had brought about the cure. There were too many authenticated cases of Fords fixing themselves—restored naturally to health after a short rest. Farmers soon discovered this, and it fitted nicely with their draft-horse philosophy: "Let'er cool off and she'll snap into it again."

A Ford owner had Number One Bearing constantly in mind. This bearing, being at the front end of the motor, was the one that always burned out, because the oil didn't reach it when the car was climbing hills. (That's what I was always told, anyway.) The oil used to recede and leave Number One dry as a clam flat; you had to watch that bearing like a hawk. It was like a weak heart—you could hear it start knocking, and that was when you stopped to let her cool off. Try as you would to keep the oil supply right, in the end Number One always went out. "Number One Bearing burned out on me and I had to have her replaced," you would say, wisely; and your companions always had a lot to tell about how to protect and pamper Number One to keep her alive.

Sprinkled not too liberally among the millions of amateur witch doctors who drove Fords and applied their own abominable cures were the heaven-sent mechanics who could really make the car talk. These professionals turned up in undreamed-of spots. One time, on the banks of the Columbia River in Washington, I heard the rear end go out of my Model T when I was trying to whip it up a steep incline onto the deck of a ferry. Something snapped; the car slid backward into the mud. It seemed to me like the end of the trail. But the captain of the ferry, observing the withered remnant, spoke up.

"What's got her?" he asked.

"I guess it's the rear end," I replied, listlessly. The captain leaned over the rail and stared. Then I saw that there was a hunger in his eyes that set him off from other men.

"Tell you what," he said, carelessly, trying to cover up his eagerness, "let's pull the son of a bitch up onto the boat, and I'll help you fix her while we're going back and forth on the river."

We did just this. All that day I plied between the towns of Pasco and Kennewick, while the skipper (who had once worked in a Ford garage) directed the amazing work of resetting the bones of my car.

Springtime in the heyday of the Model T was a delirious season. Owning a car was still a major excitement, roads were still wonderful and bad. The Fords were obviously conceived in madness: any car that was capable of going from forward into reverse without any perceptible mechanical hiatus was bound to be a mighty challenging thing to the human imagination. Boys used to veer them off the highway into a level pasture and run wild with them, as though they were cutting up with a girl. Most everybody used the reverse pedal quite as much as the regular foot brake—it distributed the wear over the bands and wore them all down evenly. That was the big trick, to wear all the bands down evenly, so that the final chattering would be total and the whole unit scream for renewal.

The days were golden, the nights were dim and strange. I still recall with trembling those loud, nocturnal crises when you drew up to a signpost and raced the engine so the lights would be bright enough to read destinations by. I have never been really planetary since. I suppose it's time to say goodbye. Farewell, my lovely!

ALFRED KAZIN

FROM THE
SUBWAY
TO THE SYNAGOGUE

". . . It was never learning I associated with that school: only the necessity to succeed, to get ahead of the others in the daily struggle to 'make a good impression' . . ."

ALL my early life lies open to my eye within five city blocks. When I passed the school, I went sick with all my old fear of it. With its standard New York public-school brown brick courtyard shut in on three sides of the square and the pretentious battlements overlooking that cockpit in which I can still smell the fiery sheen of the rubber ball, it looks like a factory over which has been imposed the facade of a castle. It gave me the shivers to stand up in the courtyard again; I felt as if I had been mustered back into the service of those Friday morning "tests" that were the terror of my childhood.

It was never learning I associated with that school: only the necessity to succeed, to get ahead of the others in the daily struggle to "make a good impression" on our teachers, who grimly, wearily, and often with ill-concealed distaste watched against our relapsing into the natural savagery they expected of Brownsville boys. The white, cool, thinly ruled record book sat over us from their desks all day long, and had remorselessly entered into it each day—in blue ink if we had passed, in red ink if we had not—our attendance, our conduct, our "effort," our merits and demerits; and to the last possible decimal point in calculation, our standing in an unending series of "tests"—surprise tests, daily tests, weekly tests, formal midterm tests, final tests. They never stopped trying to dig out of us whatever small morsel of fact we had managed to get down the night before. We had to prove that we were really alert, ready for anything, always in the race. That white thinly ruled record book figured in my mind as the judgment seat; the very thinness and remote blue lightness of its lines instantly showed its cold authority over me; so much space had been left on each page, columns and columns in which to note down everything about us, implacably and forever. As it lay there on a teacher's desk, I stared at it all day long with such fear and anxious propriety that I had no trouble believing that God, too, did nothing but keep such record books, and that on the final day He would face me with an account in Hebrew letters whose phonetic dots and dashes looked strangely like decimal points counting up my every sinful thought on earth.

All teachers were to be respected like gods, and God Himself was the greatest of all school superintendents. Long after I had ceased to believe that our teachers could see with the back of their heads, it was still understood, by me, that they knew everything. They were the delegates of all visible and invisible power on earth—of the mothers who waited on the stoops every day after three for us to bring home tales of our daily triumphs; of the glacially remote Anglo-Saxon principal, whose very name was King; of the incalculably important Superintendent of Schools who would someday rubberstamp his name to the bottom of our diplomas in grim acknowledgment that we had, at last, given satisfaction to him, to the Board of Superintendents, and to our benefactor the City of New York—and so up and up, the government of the United States and to the great Lord Jehovah Himself. My belief in teachers' unlimited wisdom and power rested not so much on what I saw in them—how impatient most of them looked, how wary—but on our abysmal humility, at least in those of us who were "good" boys, who proved by our ready compliance and "manners" that we wanted to get on. The road to a professional future would be shown us only as we pleased *them. Make a good impression the first day of the term, and they'll help you out. Make a bad impression, and you might as well cut your throat.* This was the first article of school folklore, whispered around the classroom the opening day of each term. You made the "good impression" by sitting firmly at your wooden desk, hands clasped; by silence for the greatest part of the live-long day; by standing up obsequiously when it was so expected of you; by sitting down noiselessly when you had answered a question; by "speaking nicely," which meant reproducing their painfully exact enunciation; by "showing manners," or an ecstatic submissiveness in all things; by outrageous flattery; by bringing little gifts at Christmas, on their birthdays, and at the end of the term—the well-known significance of these gifts being that they come not from us, but from our parents, whose eagerness in this matter showed a high level of social consideration, and thus raised our standing in turn.

It was not just our quickness and memory that were always being tested. Above all, in that word I could never hear without automatically seeing it raised before me in gold-plated letters, it was our *character*. I always felt anxious when I heard the word pronounced. Satisfactory as my "character" was, on the whole, except when I stayed too long in the playground reading; outrageously satisfactory, as I can see now, the very sound of the word as our teachers coldly gave it out from the end of their teeth, with a solemn weight on each dark syllable, immediately struck my heart cold with fear—they could not believe I really had it. Character was never something you had; it had to be trained in you, like a technique. I was never very clear about it. On our side *character* meant demonstrative obedience; but teachers already had it—how else could they have become teachers? They had it; the aloof Anglo-Saxon principal whom we remotely saw only on ceremonial occasions in the assembly was positively encased in it; it glittered off his bald head in spokes of triumphant light; the President of the United States had the greatest conceivable amount of it. Character belonged to great adults. Yet we were constantly being driven onto it; it was the great threshold we had to cross. *Alfred Kazin, having shown proficiency in his course of studies and having displayed satisfactory marks of character....* Thus someday the hallowed diploma, passport to my further advancement in high school. But there—I could already feel it in my bones—they would put me through even more doubting tests of character; and after that, if I should be good enough and bright enough, there would be still more. *Character* was a bitter thing, racked with my endless striving to please. The school—from every last stone in the courtyard to the battlements frowning down at me from the walls—was only the stage for a trial. I felt that the very atmosphere of learning that surrounded us was fake—that every lesson, every book, every approving smile was only a pretext for the constant probing and watching of me, that there was not a secret in me that would not be decimally measured into that white record book. All week long I lived for the blessed sound of the dismissal gong at three o'clock on Friday afternoon.

I was awed by this system, I believed in it, I respected its force. The alternative was "going bad." The school was notoriously the toughest in our tough neighborhood, and the dangers of "going bad" were constantly impressed upon me at home and in school in dark whispers of the "reform school" and in examples of boys who had been picked up for petty thievery, rape, or flinging a heavy inkwell straight into a teacher's face. Behind any failure in school yawned the great abyss of a criminal career. Every refractory attitude doomed you with the sound "Sing Sing." Anything less than absolute perfection in school always suggested to my mind that I might fall out of the daily race, be kept back in the working class forever, or—dared I think of it?—fall into the criminal class itself.

I worked on a hairline between triumph and catastrophe. Why the odds should always have felt so narrow I understood only when I realized how little my parents thought of their own lives. It was not for myself alone that I was expected to shine, but for them—to redeem the constant anxiety of their existence. I was the first American child, their offering to the strange new God; I was to be the monument of their liberation from the shame of being—what they were. And that there was shame in this was a fact that everyone seemed to believe as a matter of course. It was in the gleeful discounting of themselves—what do we know? with which our parents greeted every fresh victory in our savage competition for "high averages," for prizes, for a few condescending words of official praise from the principal at assembly. It was in the sickening invocation of "Americanism"—the word itself accusing us of everything we apparently were not. Our families and teachers seemed tacitly agreed that we were somehow to be a little ashamed of what we were. Yet it was always hard to say why this should be so. It was certainly not—in Brownsville!—because we were Jews, or simply because we spoke another language at home, or were absent on our holy days. It was rather that a "refined," "correct," "nice" English was required of us at school that we did not naturally speak, and that our teachers could never be quite sure we would keep. This English was peculiarly the ladder of advancement. Every future young lawyer was known by it. Even the Communists and Socialists on Pitkin Avenue spoke it. It was bright and clean and polished. We were expected to show it off like a new pair of shoes. When the teacher sharply called a question out, then your name, you were expected to leap up, face the class, and eject those new words fluently off the tongue.

There was my secret ordeal: I could never say anything except in the most roundabout way; I was a stammerer. Although I knew all those new words from my private reading—I read walking in the street, to and from the Children's Library on Stone Avenue; on the fire escape and the roof; at every meal when they would let me; read even when I dressed in the morning, propping my book up against the drawers of the bureau as I pulled on my long black stockings—I could never seem to get the easiest words out with the right dispatch, and would often miserably signal from my desk that I did not know the answer rather than get up to stumble and fall and crash on every word. If, angry at always being put down as lazy or stupid, I did get up to speak, the black wooden floor would roll away under my feet, the teacher would frown at me in amazement, and in unbearable loneliness I would hear behind me the groans and laughter: *tuh-tuh-tuh-tuh*.

The word was my agony. The word that for others was so effortless and so neutral, so unburdened, so simple, so exact, I had first to meditate in advance, to see if I could make it, like a plumber fitting together odd lengths and shapes of pipe. I was always preparing words I could speak, storing them away, choosing between them. And often, when the word did come from my mouth in its great and terrible birth, quailing and bleeding as if forced through a thornbush, I would not be able to look the others in the face, and would walk out in the silence, the infinitely echoing silence behind my back, to say it all cleanly back to myself as I walked in the streets. Only when I was alone in the open air, pacing the roof with pebbles in my mouth, as I had read Demosthenes had done to cure himself of stammering; or in the street, where all words seemed to flow from the length of my stride and the color of the houses as I remembered the perfect tranquillity of a phrase in *Beethoven's Romance in F* I could sing back to myself as I walked—only then was it possible for me to speak without the infinite premeditations and strangled silences I toiled through whenever I got up at school to respond with the expected, the exact answer.

It troubled me that I could speak in the fullness of my own voice only when I was alone on the streets, walking about. There was something unnatural about it; unbearably isolated. I was not like the others! At midday, every freshly shocking Monday noon, they sent me away to a speech clinic in a school in East New York, where I sat in a circle of lispers and cleft palates and foreign accents holding a mirror before my lips and rolling difficult sounds over and over. To be sent there in the full light of the opening week, when everyone else was at school or going about his business, made me feel as if I had been expelled from the great normal body of humanity. I would gobble down my lunch on my way to the speech clinic and rush back to the school in time to make up for the classes I had lost. One day, one unforgettable dread day, I stopped to catch my breath on a corner of Sutter Avenue, near the wholesale fruit markets, where an old drugstore rose up over a great flight of steps. In the window were dusty urns of colored water floating off iron chains; cardboard placards advertising hairnets, EX-LAX: a great illustrated medical chart headed THE HUMAN FACTORY, which showed the exact course a mouthful of food follows as it falls from chamber to chamber of the body. I hadn't meant to stop there at all, only to catch my breath; but I so hated the speech clinic that I thought I would delay my arrival for a few minutes by eating my lunch on the steps. When I took the sandwich out of my bag, two bitterly hard pieces of hard salami slipped out of my hand and fell through a grate onto a hill of dust below the steps. I remember how sickeningly vivid an odd thread of hair looked on the salami, as if my lunch were turning stiff with death. The factory whistles called their short, sharp blasts stark through the middle of noon, beating at me where I sat outside the city's magnetic circle. I had never known, I knew instantly I would never in my heart again submit to, such wild passive despair as I felt at that moment, sitting on the steps before THE HUMAN FACTORY, where little robots gathered and shoveled the food from chamber to chamber of the body. They had put me out into the streets, I thought to myself; with their mirrors and their everlasting pulling at me to imitate their effortless bright speech and their stuperfaction that a boy could stammer and stumble on every other English word he carried in his head, they had put me out into the streets, had left me high and dry on the steps of that drugstore staring at the remains of my lunch turning black and grimy in the dust.

DYLAN THOMAS

REMINISCENCES
OF CHILDHOOD

The "... little park ... held within its bor-
ders of old tall trees, notched with our names
and shabby with our climbing, as many
secret places ... as a country somewhere
at the end of the sea ..."

I LIKE very much people telling me about their childhood, but they'll have to be quick or else I'll be telling them about mine.

I was born in a large Welsh town at the beginning of the Great War—an ugly, lovely town (or so it was and is to me), crawling, sprawling by a long and splendid curving shore where truant boys and sandfield boys and old men from nowhere, beachcombed, idled and paddled, watched the dock-bound ships or the ships steaming away into wonder and India, magic and China, countries bright with oranges and loud with lions; threw stones into the sea for the barking outcast dogs; made castles and forts and harbours and race tracks in the sand; and on Saturday summer afternoons listened to the brass band, watched the Punch and Judy, or hung about on the fringes of the crowd to hear the fierce religious speakers who shouted at the sea, as though it were wicked and wrong to roll in and out like that, whitehorsed and full of fishes.

One man, I remember, used to take off his hat and set fire to his hair every now and then, but I do not remember what it proved, if it proved anything at all, except that he was a very interesting man.

This sea-town was my world; outside a strange Wales, coal-pitted, mountained, river-run, full, so far as I knew, of choirs and football teams and sheep and storybook tall hats and red flannel petticoats, moved about its business which was none of mine.

Beyond that unknown Wales with its wild names like peals of bells in the darkness, and its mountain men clothed in the skins of animals perhaps and always singing, lay England which was London and the country called the Front, from which many of our neighbours never came back. It was a country to which only young men travelled.

At the beginning, the only "front" I knew was the little lobby before our front door. I could not understand how so many people never returned from there, but later I grew to know more, though still without understanding, and carried a wooden rifle in the park and shot down the invisible unknown enemy like a flock of wild birds. And the park itself was a world within the world of the sea-town. Quite near where I lived, so near that on summer evenings I could listen in my bed to the voices of older children playing ball on the sloping paper-littered bank, the park was full of terrors and treasures. Though it was only a little park, it held within its borders of old tall trees, notched with our names and shabby from our climbing, as many secret places, caverns and forests, prairies and deserts, as a country somewhere at the end of the sea.

And though we would explore it one day, armed and desperate, from end to end, from the robbers' den to the pirates' cabin, the highwayman's inn to the cattle ranch, or the hidden room in the undergrowth, where we held beetle races, and lit the wood fires and roasted potatoes and talked about Africa, and the makes of motor cars, yet still the next day, it remained as unexplored as the Poles—a country just born and always changing.

There were many secret societies but you could belong only to one; and in blood or red ink, and a rusty pocketknife, with, of course, an instrument to remove stones from horses' feet, you signed your name at the foot of a terrible document, swore death to all the other societies, crossed your heart that you would divulge no secret and that if you did, you would consent to torture by slow fire, and undertook to carry out by yourself a feat of either daring or endurance. You could take your choice: would you climb to the top of the tallest and most dangerous tree, and from there hurl stones and insults at grown-up passers-by, especially postmen, or any other men in uniform? Or would you ring every doorbell in the terrace, not forgetting the doorbell of the man with the red face who kept dogs and ran fast? Or would you swim in the reservoir, which was forbidden and had angry swans, or would you eat a whole old jam jar full of mud?

There were many more alternatives. I chose one of endurance and for half an hour, it may have been longer or shorter, held up off the ground a very heavy broken pram we had found in a bush. I thought my back would break and the half hour felt like a day, but I preferred it to braving the red face and the dogs, or to swallowing tadpoles.

We knew every inhabitant of the park, every regular visitor, every nurse-maid, every gardener, every old man. We knew the hour when the alarming retired policeman came in to look at the dahlias and the hour when the old lady arrived in the Bath chair with six Pekinese, and a pale girl to read aloud to her. I think she read the newspaper, but we always said she read the *Wizard*. The face of the old man who sat summer and winter on the bench looking over the reservoir, I can see clearly now and I wrote a poem long long after I'd left the park and the seatown called:

THE HUNCHBACK IN THE PARK

The hunchback in the park
A solitary mister
Propped between trees and water
From the opening of the garden lock
That lets the trees and water enter
Until the Sunday sombre ball at dark

Eating bread from a newspaper
Drinking water from the chained cup
That the children filled with gravel
In the fountain basin where I sailed my ship
Slept at night in a dog kennel
But nobody chained him up.

Like the park birds he came early
Like the water he sat down
And Mister they called Hey mister
The truant boys from the town
Running when he had heard them clearly
On out of sound

Past lake and rockery
Laughing when he shook his paper
Hunchbacked in mockery
Through the loud zoo of the willow groves
Dodging the park-keeper
With his stick that picked up leaves.

And the old dog sleeper
Alone between nurses and swans
While the boys among willows
Made the tigers jump out of their eyes
To roar on the rockery stones
And the groves were blue with sailors

Made all day until bell-time
A woman figure without fault
Straight as a young elm
Straight and tall from his crooked bones
That she might stand in the night
After the locks and the chains

All night in the unmade park
After the railings and shrubberies
The birds the grass the trees and the lake

And the wild boys innocent as strawberries
Had followed the hunchback
To his kennel in the dark.

And that park grew up with me; that small world widened as I learned its secrets and boundaries, as I discovered new refuges and ambushes in its woods and jungles; hidden homes and lairs for the multitudes of imagination, for cowboys and Indians, and the tall terrible half-people who rode on nightmares through my bedroom. But it was not the only world—that world of rockery, gravel path, playbank, bowling green, bandstands, reservoir, dahlia garden, where an ancient keeper, known as Smoky, was the whiskered snake in the grass one must keep off. There was another world where with my friends I used to dawdle on half holidays along the bent and Devon-facing seashore, hoping for gold watches or the skull of a sheep or a message in a bottle to be washed up with the tide; and another where we used to wander whistling through the packed streets, stale as station sandwiches, round the impressive gasworks and the slaughter house, past by the blackened monuments and the museum that should have been in a museum. Or we scratched at a kind of cricket on the bald and cindery surface of the recreation ground, or we took a tram that shook like an iron jelly down to the gaunt pier, there to clamber under the pier, hanging perilously on to its skeleton legs or to run along to the end where patient men with the seaward eyes of the dockside unemployed capped and mufflered, dangling from their mouths pipes that had long gone out, angled over the edge for unpleasant tasting fish.

Never was there such a town as ours, I thought, as we fought on the sandhills with rough boys or dared each other to climb up the scaffolding of half-built houses soon to be called Laburnum Beaches. Never was there such a town, I thought, for the smell of fish and chips on Saturday evenings; for the Saturday afternoon cinema matinees where we shouted and hissed our threepences away; for the crowds in the streets with leeks in their hats on international nights; for the park, the inexhaustible and mysterious, bushy red-Indian hiding park where the hunchback sat alone and the groves were blue with sailors. The memories of childhood have no order, and so I remember that never was there such a dame school as ours, so firm and kind and smelling of galoshes, with the sweet and fumbled music of the piano lessons drifting down from upstairs to the lonely schoolroom, where only the sometimes tearful wicked sat over undone sums, or to repeat a little crime—the pulling of a girl's hair during geography, the sly shin kick under the table during English literature. Behind the school was a narrow lane where only the oldest and boldest threw pebbles at windows, scuffled and boasted, fibbed about their relations—

"My father's got a chauffeur."

"What's he want a chauffeur for? He hasn't got a car."

"My father's the richest man in the town."

"My father's the richest man in Wales."

"My father owns the world."

And swapped gob-stoppers for slings, old knives for marbles, kite strings for foreign stamps.

The lane was always the place to tell your secrets; if you did not have any, you invented them. Occasionally now I dream that I am turning out of school into the lane of confidences when I say to the boys of my class, "At last, I have a real secret."

"What is it—what is it?"

"I can fly."

And when they do not believe me, I flap my arms and slowly leave the ground only a few inches at first, then gaining air until I fly waving my cap level with the upper windows of the school, peering in until the mistress at the piano screams and the metronome falls to the ground and stops, and there is no more time.

And I fly over the trees and chimneys of my town, over the dockyards skimming the masts and funnels, over Inkerman Street, Sebastopol Street, and the street where all the women wear men's caps, over the trees of the everlasting park, where a brass band shakes the leaves and sends them showering down on to the nurses and the children, the cripples and the idlers, and the gardeners, and the shouting boys: over the yellow seashore, and the stone-chasing dogs, and the old men, and the singing sea.

The memories of childhood have no order, and no end.

ERIC HOFFER

A TIME
OF
JUVENILES

". . . History is made by men who have the restlessness, impressionability, credulity, capacity for make-believe, ruthlessness, and self-righteousness of children . . ."

THERE was a week several years ago during which the newspapers reported an epidemic of student riots spreading from Istanbul to Teheran, Bombay, Saigon, Seoul, Tokyo, and Mexico City. Most of the riots had an anti-American flavor. And I remember how, early one morning, while waiting for the bus that would take me to the waterfront, I saw the headline of still another riot, and heard myself snorting with disgust: "History made by juvenile delinquents!"

The sound of my words had a peculiar effect on me. Inside the bus I did not look at the newspaper but sat staring in front of me. Who makes history? Is it the old? How much of a role did the young play in shaping events? Things were coming together in my mind; I remembered that years ago I had inserted in *The Passionate State of Mind* an aphorism which read: "History is made by men who have the restlessness, impressionability, credulity, capacity for make-believe, ruthlessness, and self-righteousness of children. It is made by men who set their hearts on toys. All leaders strive to turn their followers into children." This insight which came to me from observing two willful godchildren in action had been filed away in my mind and did not affect my thinking. Now I concluded that we can hardly know how things happened in history unless we keep in mind that much of the time it was juveniles who made them happen.

Until relatively recent times man's span of life was short. Throughout most of history the truly old were a rarity. In an excavation of one of the world's oldest cemeteries, the skeletons showed that the average age of the population at death was less than twenty-five, and there is no reason to suppose that the place was unusually unhealthy. Thus it seems plausible that the momentous discoveries and inventions of the Neolithic Age—such as the wheel, calendar, and brickmaking—were the work of an almost child-like population and were probably made in the course of play. Nor is it likely that the ancient myths and legends, with their fairytale pattern and erotic symbolism, were elaborated by burnt-out old men.

The history of less ancient periods, too, reveals the juvenile character of their chief actors. Many observers have remarked on the smallness of the armor which has come down to us from the Middle Ages. Actually, the men who wore this armor were not grown-ups. They were married at thirteen, were warriors and leaders in their late teens, and senile at thirty-five or forty. Without some familiarity with the juvenile mentality and the aberrations of juvenile delinquency it would be difficult to make sense of the romanticism, trickery, and savagery which characterized the Middle Ages. Nor did things change markedly in the sixteenth century. Montaigne tells us that he hardly ever met a man as old as fifty. In the first half of the sixteenth century, Charles V became Holy Roman Emperor at the age of twenty, Francis I became King of France at twenty-one, and Henry VIII King of England at eighteen.

But is juvenile mentality confined to adolescents? Do people automatically grow up as they grow older? Are there not teen-agers of every age? In 1502 Cardinal Giuliano della Rovere was elected Pope at the age of fifty-nine. He took the name of Julius II in honor of Julius Caesar, whom he esteemed the greatest man who ever lived, and whose career he determined to emulate. So on the threshold of old age he put on helmet and cuirass, mounted a horse and set out to become a conqueror. Clearly, the juvenile mentality may persist or reemerge later, even in old age.

In all times there are people who cannot grow up, and there are times when whole societies begin to think and act like juveniles. The twentieth century in particular has seen juvenilization on an almost global scale. No one can fail to discern the juvenile character of communism, fascism, racism (Ku Klux Klan), and the mass movements erupting at present in the underdeveloped parts of the world. Almost all the leaders of the new or renovated countries—de Gaulle, Castro, Sukarno, Nkruma, and the rest— have a pronounced juvenile element in their make-up.

Arthur Koestler suggests that there is in the revolutionary "some defective quality" which keeps him from growing up. The indications are, however, that the present trend toward juvenile behavior has been gathering force for over a century and has affected people who cannot be classed as revolutionaries. Such behavior was rampant on the frontier and in gold-rush camps, and the American go-getter, though he has no quarrel with the status quo, is as much a perpetual juvenile as any revolutionary. Militant nationalism, too, though not primarily revolutionary in character, fosters juvenile manifestations in all sorts of people. Laurens Van der Post calls nationalism "the juvenile delinquency of the contemporary world." Clearly, the childish pattern is not confined to people with "some defective quality" which keeps them from growing up, but may arise or be induced in all types.

To understand the process we must know something about the genesis of the juvenile mentality in the adolescent. We shall not get anywhere by looking for differences in brain structure or the nervous system between adolescent and adult. I know of no demonstrable differences. The reasonable approach is to assume that the adolescent's behavior is induced largely by his mode of existence, by the situation in which he finds himself. This would imply that adults, too, when placed in a similar situation, would behave more or less like juveniles.

Now, the chief peculiarity of the adolescent's existence is its inbetweenness: It is a phase of transition from childhood to manhood, a phase of uprootedness and drastic change. If our assumption is correct, other types of drastic change should evoke a somewhat similar psychological pattern. There should be a family likeness between the adolescents and people who migrate from one country to another, or are converted from one faith to another, or pass from one way of life to another—as when peasants are turned into industrial workers, serfs into free men, civilians into soldiers, and people in undeveloped countries are subjected to rapid modernization.

Let us have a close look at the experience of change. After the second world war, backward countries in Asia and Africa began to modernize themselves in an atmosphere charged with passion and a deafening clamor. As a naïve American I asked myself why the sober, practical task of modernization—of building factories, roads, dams, schools, and so forth—should require the staging of a madhouse. In *The Ordeal of Change* I tried to find answers to this question. My central idea was that drastic change is a profoundly upsetting experience, that when we face the new and unprecedented, our past experience and accomplishments become obsolete and are a hindrance rather than an aid. What Montaigne said of death is also true of the wholly new: "We are all apprentices when we come to it." We are all misfits when we have to fit ourselves to a new situation. And misfits live and breathe in an atmosphere of passion. We used to think that revolutions are the cause of change. Actually it is the other way around: change prepares the ground for a revolution. The difficulties and irritations inherent in the experience of change render people receptive to the appeal of a revolution. Change comes first. Where things have not changed at all there is the least likelihood of revolution.

However, the staging of a madhouse in the process of modernization is not peculiar to backward countries in Asia and Africa. We have been living in an apocalyptic madhouse staged on a global scale by Germany, Russia, and Japan, which set out to industrialize themselves at breakneck speed. There is also more to the experience of drastic change than a state of unfitness—the mass movements, upheavals, and wars which are a by-product of change indicate that the process involves the deeper layers of man's soul. After all, change such as the world has seen during the last hundred years is something wholly unprecedented in human experience. It would be legitimate, therefore, to assume that there is in man's nature a built-in resistance to change. We are not only afraid of the new, but convinced that we cannot really change, that we can adapt ourselves to the new only by getting out of our skin and assuming a new identity. In other words, drastic change generates a need for a new birth and a new identity. And it perhaps depends on the way this need is satisfied whether the process of change runs smoothly or is attended with convulsions and explosions.

It is of interest to have a quick look at the means employed by some ossified primitive societies to tackle the passage from childhood to manhood. In the Congo, boys at the age of fifteen are declared dead, taken into the forest and there subjected to purification, flagellation, and intoxication with palm wine, resulting in anesthesia. The priest-magician (*ngànga*) who is in charge teaches them a special language and gives them special food. Finally come the rites of reintegration in which the novices "pretend not to know how to walk or eat and, in general, act as if they were newly born and must relearn all the gestures of ordinary life."[1] In several Australian tribes the boy is taken violently from his mother who weeps for him. He is subjected to physical and mental weakening to simulate death, and is finally resurrected and taught to live as a man.

The interest of their rites is in their motif of rebirth rather than in any bearing they may have on change in a civilized society. In the modern world change overtakes a whole population, and the denouement is not a return to an immemorial way of life. Here the sense of rebirth and a new identity are created by mass movements or mass migrations. One becomes a member of a glorious Germany, a glorious Japan, a master race, a nation of heroic warriors destined to conquer the world; or one joins a revolutionary or

[1] Arnold van Gennep, *The Rites of Passage* (University of Chicago Press, 1960).

religious movement which envisages a new life; or one actually emigrates to a new country and becomes a new man.

The tale of Moses and the exodus is a luminous example of the difficulties encountered, and the outlandish means that have to be employed, in the realization of drastic change.

Moses wanted to accomplish a relatively simple thing: he wanted to transform the enslaved Hebrews into free men. But being a genuine leader, Moses knew that the task of endowing the liberated slaves with a new identity and immersing them in a new life was not at all simple and required the employment of extravagant means. The exodus from Egypt was the first step. But more vital was the fiction of a chosen people led by a mighty Jehovah to a promised land—the kind of milieu essential for a drastic human transformation.

Now the human transformation which took place during the last hundred years was not the turning of slaves into free men but drastic changes brought about by the Industrial Revolution. Here too the sense of rebirth was generated by exoduses (mass migrations), the fiction of a chosen people, and the vision of a promised land. In Europe, during the second half of the nineteenth century, the wholesale transformation of peasants into industrial workers gave rise not only to nationalist and revolutionary movements but also to mass rushes to the New World, particularly the United States, where the European peasant was literally processed into a new man—made to learn a new language, adopt a new mode of dress, a new diet, and often a new name.

The juvenile, then, is the archetypal man in transition. Juvenile impulses manifest themselves in people of all ages—even the change of retirement may evoke a juvenile pattern in the old. Retired shopkeepers and farmers have made southern California a breeding ground of juvenile cults, utopias, and wild schemes. The Birch movement with its unmistakable flavor of juvenile delinquency was initiated by a retired candy maker and is sustained largely by retired business executives, generals, and admirals.

The significant point is that juvenilization inevitably results in some degree of primitive social behavior. We are up against the great paradox of the twentieth century; namely, that a breakneck technological advance has gone hand in hand with a return to tribalism, charismatic leaders, medicine men, credulity, and tribal wars. The tendency has been to blame the machine. There is a considerable literature on the barbarizing and dehumanizing effects of the machine: how it turns us into robots and slaves, stifles our individuality, and dwarfs our lives. Most of the indictments of the machine come of course from writers, poets, philosophers, and scholars —men of words—who have no firsthand experience of working and living with machines. It should also be noted that long before the advent of the machine age the same types of men of words looked upon common people who did the world's work as soulless robots and automated ghouls. They have always viewed as materialistic the effort to turn matter to the service of man. Anyone who has worked with machines knows that they can be as temperamental and willful as any living thing, and that communion with machines does not blunt our sensibilities. The proficient mechanic is an alert and intuitive human being. On the waterfront one can see how the ability to make a fork-lift or a winch do one's bidding with precision and finesse generates a peculiar exhilaration, so that the skilled lift-driver and winch-driver are as a rule of good cheer, and work as if at play. Even if it were proven beyond a doubt that the assembly line makes robots of workers, it still affects only a small fraction of the population, and cannot be held responsible for the nature of a whole society.

No, it is not the machine as such but drastic change which produces this social primitivism. Where a new identity is found by embracing a mass movement, for example, the reason is obvious: a mass movement absorbs and assimilates the individual into its corporate body, and does so by stripping the individual of his own opinions, tastes, and values. He is thereby reduced to an infantile state, for this is what a new birth really means: to become like a child. And children are primitive beings—they are credulous, follow a leader, and readily become members of a pack. Immigration produces a similar reaction. Like a child, the immigrant has to learn to speak, and how to act and assert himself. Finally, primitivism also follows when people seek a new identity by plunging into ceaseless action and hustling. It takes leisure to mature. People in a hurry can neither grow nor decay; they are preserved in a state of perpetual puerility.

The question is whether this social primitivism is merely an unfortunate by-product or whether it is a vital factor in the process of change. What a society needs above all when it has to adjust itself to wholly new conditions is a high degree of human plasticity. Now, a population rendered juvenile and primitive tends to become a homogeneous, plastic mass. We who have lived through the Stalin-Hitler era know that one of the most striking functions of a mass movement is the inducement of plasticity—the creation of a population that will go through breathtaking somersaults at a word of command, and can be made, in the words of Boris Pasternak, "to hate what it loves and love what it hates."

The True Believer is, then, a plastic human type thrown up by a century of ceaseless change. The adaptation to change has also produced the American hustler, a type as juvenile, primitive, and plastic as the True Believer, but functioning without ideology and the magic of communion. The immigrant, too, having been stripped of his traditions and habits, is easily molded. Finally, there is the plastic type of the warrior. All through history conquerors have learned more willingly and readily from the conquered than the other way around. The conqueror does not see imitation as an act of submission and proof of his inadequacy. It is a fact that nations with a warrior tradition, such as the Japanese and the inheritors of Genghis Khan in Outer Mongolia, find the transition of modernization less difficult than nations of subjected peasants such as Russia and China. There is thus a kernel of practicalness in the preposterous tendency of an Indonesia or an Egypt to cast its people in the role of warriors. It is also plausible that the defeat of forty million Arabs by tiny Israel is rendering the modernization of the Arab world difficult and painful.

To sum up: The throes of the machine age stem not from the machine as such but from the social dislocation caused by the rapid transformation of millions of peasants into urban industrial workers. It was this abrupt change in the life of the European masses in the second half of the nineteenth century which released the nationalist, revolutionary, and racialist movements that are still with us. A similar change in the backward countries of Asia, Africa, and Latin America is now setting off the social tremors that keep our world in a state of perpetual shock.

In instances where large-scale movement of peasants into the cities has taken place without industrialization, the social consequences have been equally explosive, as we have seen in recent decades in Latin America. In largely nonindustrial Argentina, Chile, Cuba, Uruguay, and Venezuela, restless, unemployed townsmen already outnumber countrymen. Here rapid industrialization when it comes will find masses of urbanized peasants ready to be processed into factory workers, and the result is likely to be a considerable easing of social unrest rather than revolution.

The curious thing is that with the coming of automation we may see something like the present Latin American pattern emerging in the advanced industrialized countries. The banishing of workers by automation from factories, warehouses, etc. will fill the cities with millions of unemployed workers waiting for something to happen. Condemned to inaction, and deprived of a sense of usefulness and worth, they will become receptive to extremism, and to political and racial intolerance. Thus it seems that in our present world problems come and go but the by-products remain the same, and the end of The Time of Juveniles is nowhere in sight.

E. B. WHITE

ONCE MORE
TO
THE LAKE

*"...everything was as it had always been ...
the years were a mirage ...there had been
no years between the ducking of this dragonfly and the other one—the one that was
part of memory ..."*

ONE summer, along about 1904, my father rented a camp on a lake in Maine
and took us all there for the month of August. We all got ringworm from
some kittens and had to rub Pond's Extract on our arms and legs night and
morning, and my father rolled over in a canoe with all his clothes on; but
outside of that the vacation was a success and from then on none of us ever
thought there was any place in the world like that lake in Maine. We returned summer after summer—always on August 1st for one month. I have
since become a salt-water man, but sometimes in summer there are days
when the restlessness of the tides and the fearful cold of the sea water and
the incessant wind which blows across the afternoon and into the evening
make me wish for the placidity of a lake in the woods. A few weeks ago this
feeling got so strong I bought myself a couple of bass hooks and a spinner
and returned to the lake where we used to go, for a week's fishing and to
revisit old haunts.

I took along my son, who had never had any fresh water up his nose and
who had seen lily pads only from train windows. On the journey over to
the lake I began to wonder what it would be like. I wondered how time would
have marred this unique, this holy spot—the coves and streams, the hills
that the sun set behind, the camps and the paths behind the camps. I was
sure that the tarred road would have found it out and I wondered in what
other ways it would be desolated. It is strange how much you can remember
about places like that once you allow your mind to return into the grooves
which lead back. You remember one thing, and that suddenly reminds you
of another thing. I guess I remembered clearest of all the early mornings,
when the lake was cool and motionless, remembered how the bedroom
smelled of the lumber it was made of and of the wet woods whose scent
entered through the screen. The partitions in the camp were thin and did
not extend clear to the top of the rooms, and as I was always the first up I
would dress softly so as not to wake the others, and sneak out into the sweet

outdoors and start out in the canoe, keeping close along the shore in the long shadows of the pines. I remembered being very careful never to rub my paddle against the gunwale for fear of disturbing the stillness of the cathedral.

The lake had never been what you would call a wild lake. There were cottages sprinkled around the shores, and it was in farming country although the shores of the lake were quite heavily wooded. Some of the cottages were owned by nearby farmers, and you would live at the shore and eat your meals at the farmhouse. That's what our family did. But although it wasn't wild, it was a fairly large and undisturbed lake and there were places in it which, to a child at least, seemed infinitely remote and primeval.

I was right about the tar: it led to within half a mile of the shore. But when I got back there, with my boy, and we settled into a camp near a farmhouse and into the kind of summertime I had known, I could tell that it was going to be pretty much the same as it had been before—I knew it, lying in bed the first morning, smelling the bedroom, and hearing the boy sneak quietly out and go off along the shore in a boat. I began to sustain the illusion that he was I, and therefore, by simple transposition, that I was my father. This sensation persisted, kept cropping up all the time we were there. It was not an entirely new feeling, but in this setting it grew much stronger. I seemed to be living a dual existence. I would be in the middle of some simple act, I would be picking up a bait box or laying down a table fork, or I would be saying something, and suddenly it would be not I but my father who was saying the words or making the gesture. It gave me a creepy sensation.

We went fishing the first morning. I felt the same damp moss covering the worms in the bait can, and saw the dragonfly alight on the tip of my rod as it hovered a few inches from the surface of the water. It was the arrival of this fly that convinced me beyond any doubt that everything was as it always had been, that the years were a mirage and there had been no years. The small waves were the same, chucking the rowboat under the chin as we fished at anchor, and the boat was the same boat, the same color green and the ribs broken in the same places, and under the floor-boards the same fresh-water leavings and débris—the dead helgramite, the wisps of moss, the rusty discarded fishhook, the dried blood from yesterday's catch. We stared silently at the tips of our rods, at the dragonflies that came and went. I lowered the tip of mine into the water, tentatively, pensively dislodging the fly, which darted two feet away, poised, darted two feet back, and came to rest again a little farther up the rod. There had been no years between the ducking of this dragonfly and the other one—the one that was part of memory. I looked at the boy, who was silently watching his fly, and it was my hands that held his rod, my eyes watching. I felt dizzy and didn't know which rod I was at the end of.

We caught two bass, hauling them in briskly as though they were mackerel, pulling them over the side of the boat in a businesslike manner without any landing net, and stunning them with a blow on the back of the head.

When we got back for a swim before lunch, the lake was exactly where we had left it, the same number of inches from the dock, and there was only the merest suggestion of a breeze. This seemed an utterly enchanted sea, this lake you could leave to its own devices for a few hours and come back to, and find that it had not stirred, this constant and trustworthy body of water. In the shallows, the dark, watersoaked sticks and twigs, smooth and old, were undulating in clusters on the bottom against the clean ribbed sand, and the track of the mussel was plain. A school of minnows swam by, each minnow with its small individual shadow, doubling the attendance, so clear and sharp in the sunlight. Some of the other campers were in swimming, along the shore, one of them with a cake of soap, and the water felt thin and clear and unsubstantial. Over the years there had been this person with the cake of soap, this cultist, and here he was. There had been no years.

Up to the farmhouse to dinner through the teeming, dusty field, the road under our sneakers was only a two-track road. The middle track was missing, the one with the marks of the hooves and the splotches of dried, flaky manure. There had always been three tracks to choose from in choosing which track to walk in; now the choice was narrowed down to two. For a moment I missed terribly the middle alternative. But the way led past the tennis court, and something about the way it lay there in the sun reassured me; the tape had loosened along the backline, the alleys were green with plantains and other weeds, and the net (installed in June and removed in September) sagged in the dry noon, and the whole place steamed with midday heat and hunger and emptiness. There was a choice of pie for dessert, and one was blueberry and one was apple, and the waitresses were the same country girls, there having been no passage of time, only the illusion of it as in a dropped curtain—the waitresses were still fifteen; their hair had been washed, that was the only difference—they had been to the movies and seen the pretty girls with the clean hair.

Summertime, oh summertime, pattern of life indelible, the fadeproof lake, the woods unshatterable, the pasture with the sweetfern and the juniper forever and ever, summer without end; this was the background, and the life along the shore was the design, the cottages with their innocent and tranquil design, their tiny docks with the flagpole and the American flag floating against the white clouds in the blue sky, the little paths over the roots of the trees leading from camp to camp and the paths leading back to the outhouses and the can of lime for sprinkling, and at the souvenir counters at the store the miniature birch-bark canoes and the post cards that showed things looking a little better than they looked. This was the American family at play, escaping the city heat, wondering whether the newcomers in the camp at the head of the cove were "common" or "nice," wondering whether it was true that the people who drove up for Sunday dinner at the farmhouse were turned away because there wasn't enough chicken.

It seemed to me, as I kept remembering all this, that those times and those summers had been infinitely precious and worth saving. There had been jollity and peace and goodness. The arriving (at the beginning of August) had been so big a business in itself, at the railway station the farm wagon drawn up, the first smell of the pine-laden air, the first glimpse of the smiling farmer, and the great importance of the trunks and your father's enormous authority in such matters, and the feel of the wagon under you for the long ten-mile haul, and at the top of the last long hill catching the first view of the lake after eleven months of not seeing this cherished body of water. The shouts and cries of the other campers when they saw you, and the trunks to be unpacked, to give up their rich burden. (Arriving was less exciting nowadays, when you sneaked up in your car and parked it under a tree near the camp and took out the bags and in five minutes it was all over, no fuss, no loud wonderful fuss about trunks.)

Peace and goodness and jollity. The only thing that was wrong now, really, was the sound of the place, an unfamiliar nervous sound of the outboard motors. This was the note that jarred, the one thing that would sometimes break the illusion and set the years moving. In those other summertimes all motors were inboard; and when they were at a little distance, the noise they made was a sedative, an ingredient of summer sleep. They were one-cylinder and two-cylinder engines, and some were make-and-break and some were jump-spark, but they all made a sleepy sound across the lake. The one-lungers throbbed and fluttered, and the twin-cylinder ones purred and purred, and that was a quiet sound too. But now the campers all had outboards. In the daytime, in the hot mornings, these motors made a petulant, irritable sound; at night, in the still evening when the afterglow lit the water, they whined about one's ears like mosquitoes. My boy loved our rented outboard, and his great desire was to achieve singlehanded mastery over it, and authority, and he soon learned the trick of choking it a little (but not too much), and the adjustment of the needle valve. Watching him I would remember the things you could do with the old one-cylinder engine with the heavy flywheel, how you could have it eating out of your hand if you got really close to it spiritually. Motor boats in those days didn't have clutches, and you would make a landing by shutting off the motor at the proper time and coasting in with a dead rudder. But there was a way of reversing them, if you learned the trick, by cutting the switch and putting it on again exactly on the final dying revolution of the flywheel, so that it would kick back against compression and begin reversing. Approaching a dock in a strong following breeze, it was difficult to slow up sufficiently by the ordinary coasting method, and if a boy felt he had complete mastery over his motor, he was tempted to keep it running beyond its time and then reverse it a few feet from the dock. It took a cool nerve, because if you threw the switch a twentieth of a second too soon you would catch the flywheel when it still had speed enough to go up past center, and the boat would leap ahead, charging bull-fashion at the dock.

We had a good week at the camp. The bass were biting well and the sun shone endlessly, day after day. We would be tired at night and lie down in the accumulated heat of the little bedrooms after the long hot day and the breeze would stir almost imperceptibly outside and the smell of the swamp drift in through the rusty screens. Sleep would come easily and in the morning the red squirrel would be on the roof, tapping out his gay routine. I kept remembering everything, lying in bed in the mornings—the small steamboat that had a long rounded stern like the lip of a Ubangi, and how quietly she ran on the moonlight sails, when the older boys played their mandolins and the girls sang and we ate doughnuts dipped in sugar, and how sweet the music was on the water in the shining night, and what it had felt like to think about girls then. After breakfast we would go up to the store and the things were in the same place—the minnows in a bottle, the plugs and spinners disarranged and pawed over by the youngsters from the boys' camp, the fig newtons and the Beeman's gum. Outside, the road was tarred and cars stood in front of the store. Inside, all was just as it had always been, except there was more Coca Cola and not so much Moxie and root beer and birch beer and sarsaparilla. We would walk out with a bottle of pop apiece and sometimes the pop would backfire up our noses and hurt. We explored the streams, quietly, where the turtles slid off the sunny logs and dug their way into the soft bottom; and we lay on the town wharf and fed worms to the tame bass. Everywhere we went I had trouble making out which was I, the one walking at my side, the one walking in my pants.

One afternoon while we were there at that lake a thunderstorm came up. It was like the revival of an old melodrama that I had seen long ago with childish awe. The second-act climax of the drama of the electrical disturbance over a lake in America had not changed in any important respect. This was the big scene, still the big scene. The whole thing was so familiar, the first feeling of oppression and heat and a general air around camp of not wanting to go very far away. In midafternoon (it was all the same) a curious darkening of the sky, and a lull in everything that had made life tick; and then the way the boats suddenly swung the other way at their moorings with the coming of a breeze out of the new quarter, and the premonitory rumble. Then the kettle drum, then the snare, then the bass drum and cymbals, then crackling light against the dark, and the gods grinning and licking their chops in the hills. Afterward the calm, the rain steadily rustling in the calm lake, the return of light and hope and spirits, and the campers running out in joy and relief to go swimming in the rain, their bright cries perpetuating the deathless joke about how they were getting simply drenched, and the children screaming with delight at the new sensation of bathing in the rain, and the joke about getting drenched linking the generations in a strong indestructible chain. And the comedian who waded in carrying an umbrella.

When the others went swimming my son said he was going in too. He pulled his dripping trunks from the line where they had hung all through the shower, and wrung them out. Languidly, and with no thought of going in, I watched him, his hard little body, skinny and bare, saw him wince slightly as he pulled up around his vitals the small, soggy, icy garment. As he buckled the swollen belt suddenly my groin felt the chill of death.

C. NORTHCOTE PARKINSON

INJELITITIS
OR PALSIED
PARALYSIS

*In this selection, Parkinson satirizes the
business world through an elaborate analogy. Posing as a scientist or medical man,
he likens the ineptitude of many organizations to a fatal disease, "injelititis," brought
on by incompetence and jealousy.*

WE FIND everywhere a type of organization (administrative, commercial,
or academic) in which the higher officials are plodding and dull, those less
senior are active only in intrigue against each other, and the junior men
are frustrated or frivolous. Little is being attempted. Nothing is being
achieved. And in contemplating this sorry picture, we conclude that those
in control have done their best, struggled against adversity, and have finally
admitted defeat. It now appears from the results of recent investigation,
that no such failure need be assumed. In a high percentage of the moribund
institutions so far examined the final state of coma is something gained
of set purpose and after prolonged effort. It is the result, admittedly, of a
disease, but of a disease that is largely self-induced. From the first signs
of the condition, the progress of the disease has been encouraged, the causes
aggravated, and the symptoms welcomed. It is the disease of induced inferiority, called Injelititis. It is a commoner ailment than is often supposed,
and the diagnosis is far easier than the cure.

Our study of this organizational paralysis begins, logically, with a description of the course of the disease from the first signs to the final coma.
The second stage of our inquiry concerns symptoms and diagnosis. The third
stage should properly include some reference to treatment, but little is
known about this. Nor is much likely to be discovered in the immediate
future, for the tradition of British medical research is entirely opposed to
any emphasis on this part of the subject. British medical specialists are
usually quite content to trace the symptoms and define the cause. It is the
French, by contrast, who begin by describing the treatment and discuss
the diagnosis later, if at all. We feel bound to adhere in this to the British
method, which may not help the patient but which is unquestionably more
scientific. To travel hopefully is better than to arrive.

The first sign of danger is represented by the appearance in the organization's hierarchy of an individual who combines in himself a high concentration of incompetence and jealousy. Neither quality is significant in itself and most people have a certain proportion of each. But when these two qualities reach a certain concentration—represented at present by the formula I^3J^5—there is a chemical reaction. The two elements fuse, producing a new substance that we have termed "injelitance." The presence of this substance can be safely inferred from the actions of any individual who, having failed to make anything of his own department, tries constantly to interfere with other departments and gain control of the central administration. The specialist who observes this particular mixture of failure and ambition will at once shake his head and murmur, "Primary or idiopathic injelitance." The symptoms, as we shall see, are quite unmistakable.

The next or secondary stage in the progress of the disease is reached when the infected individual gains complete or partial control of the central organization. In many instances this stage is reached without any period of primary infection, the individual having actually entered the organization at that level. The injelitant individual is easily recognizable at this stage from the persistence with which he struggles to eject all those abler than himself, as also from his resistance to the appointment or promotion of anyone who might prove abler in course of time. He dare not say, "Mr. Asterisk is too able," so he says, "Asterisk? Clever perhaps—but is he *sound*? I incline to prefer Mr. Cypher." He dare not say, "Mr. Asterisk makes me feel small," so he says, "Mr. Cypher appears to me to have the better judgment." Judgment is an interesting word that signifies in this context the opposite of intelligence; it means, in fact, doing what was done last time. So Mr. Cypher is promoted and Mr. Asterisk goes elsewhere. The central administration gradually fills up with people stupider than the chairman, director, or manager. If the head of the organization is second-rate, he will see to it that his immediate staff are all third-rate; and they will, in turn, see to it that their subordinates are fourth-rate. There will soon be an actual competition in stupidity, people pretending to be even more brainless than they are.

The next or tertiary stage in the onset of this disease is reached when there is no spark of intelligence left in the whole organization from top to bottom. This is the state of coma we described in our first paragraph. When that stage has been reached the institution is, for all practical purposes, dead. It may remain in a coma for twenty years. It may quietly disintegrate. It may even, finally, recover. Cases of recovery are rare. It may be thought odd that recovery without treatment should be possible. The process is quite natural, nevertheless, and closely resembles the process by which various living organisms develop a resistance to poisons that are at first encounter fatal. It is as if the whole institution had been sprayed with a DDT solution guaranteed to eliminate all ability found in its way. For a period of years this practice achieves the desired result. Eventually, however, individuals develop an immunity. They conceal their ability under a mask of imbecile good humor. The result is that the operatives assigned to the task of ability-elimination fail (through stupidity) to recognize ability when they see it. An individual of merit penetrates the outer defenses and begins to make his way toward the top. He wanders on, babbling about golf and giggling feebly, losing documents and forgetting names, and looking just like everyone else. Only when he has reached high rank does he suddenly throw off the mask and appear like the demon king among a crowd of pantomime fairies. With shrill screams of dismay the high executives find ability right there in the midst of them. It is too late by then to do anything about it. The damage has been done, the disease is in retreat, and full recovery is possible over the next ten years. But these instances of natural cure are extremely rare. In the more usual course of events, the disease passes through the recognized stages and becomes, as it would seem, incurable.

We have seen what the disease is. It now remains to show by what symptoms its presence can be detected. It is one thing to detail the spread of the infection in an imaginary case, classified from the start. It is quite a different thing to enter a factory, barracks, office, or college and recognize the symptoms at a glance. We all know how an estate agent will wander round a vacant house when acting for the purchaser. It is only a question of time before he throws open a cupboard or kicks a baseboard and exclaims, "Dry rot!" (acting for the vendor, he would lose the key of the cupboard while drawing attention to the view from the window). In the same way a political scientist can recognize the symptoms of Injelititis even in its primary stage. He will pause, sniff, and nod wisely, and it should be obvious at once that he *knows*. But how does he know? How can he tell that injelitance has set in? If the original source of the infection were present, the diagnosis would be easier, but it is still quite possible when the germ of the disease is on holiday. His influence can be detected in the atmosphere. It can be detected, above all, in certain remarks that will be made by others, as thus: "It would be a mistake for us to attempt too much. We cannot compete with Toprank. Here in Lowgrade we do useful work, meeting the needs of the country. Let us be content with that." Or again, "We do not pretend to be in the first flight. It is absurd the way these people at Much-Striving talk of their work, just as if they were in the Toprank class." Or finally, "Some of our younger men have transferred to Toprank—one or two even to Much-Striving. It is probably their wisest plan. We are quite happy to let them succeed in that way. An exchange of ideas and personnel is a good thing—although, to be sure, the few men we have had from Toprank have been rather disappointing. We can only expect the people they have thrown out. Ah well, we must not grumble. We always avoid friction when we can. And, in our humble way we can claim to be doing a good job."

What do these remarks suggest? They suggest—or, rather, they clearly indicate—that the standard of achievement has been set too low. Only a low standard is desired and one still lower is acceptable. The directives issuing from a second-rate chief and addressed to his third-rate executives speak only of minimum aims and ineffectual means. A higher standard of competence is not desired, for an efficient organization would be beyond the chief's power to control. The motto, "Ever third-rate" has been inscribed over the main entrance in letters of gold. Third-rateness has become a principle of policy. It will be observed, however, that the existence of higher standards is still recognized. There remains at this primary stage a hint of apology, a feeling of uneasiness when Toprank is mentioned. Neither this apology nor unease lasts for long. The second stage of the disease comes on quickly and it is this we must now describe.

The secondary stage is recognized by its chief symptom, which is Smugness. The aims have been set low and have therefore been largely achieved. The target has been set up within ten yards of the firing point and the scoring has therefore been high. The directors have done what they set out to do. This soon fills them with self-satisfaction. They set out to do something and they have done it. They soon forget that it was a small effort to gain a small result. They observe only that they have succeeded—unlike those people at Much-Striving. They become increasingly smug and their smugness reveals itself in remarks such as this: "The chief is a sound man and very clever when you get to know him. He never says much—that is not his way— but he seldom makes a mistake." (These last words can be said with justice of someone who never does anything at all.) Or this: "We rather distrust brilliance here. These clever people can be a dreadful nuisance, upsetting established routine and proposing all sorts of schemes that we have never seen tried. We obtain splendid results by simple common sense and teamwork." And finally this: "Our canteen is something we are really rather proud of. We don't know how the caterer can produce so good a lunch at the price. We are lucky to have him!" This last remark is made as we sit at a table covered with dirty oilcloth, facing an uneatable, nameless mess on a plate and shuddering at the sight and smell of what passes for coffee. In point of fact, the canteen reveals more than the office. Just as for a quick verdict we judge a private house by inspection of the WC (to find whether there is a spare toilet roll), just as we judge a hotel by the state of the cruet, so we judge a larger institution by the appearance of the canteen. If the decoration is in dark brown and pale green; if the curtains are purple (or absent); if there are no flowers in sight; if there is barley in the soup (with or without a dead fly); if the menu is one of hash and mold; and if the executives are still delighted with everything—why, then the institution is in a pretty bad way. For self-satisfaction, in such a case, has reached the point at which those responsible cannot tell the difference between food and filth. This is smugness made absolute.

The tertiary and last stage of the disease is one in which apathy has taken the place of smugness. The executives no longer boast of their efficiency as compared with some other institution. They have forgotten that any other institution exists. They have ceased to eat in the canteen, preferring now to bring sandwiches and scatter their desks with the crumbs. The bulletin boards carry notices about the concert that took place four years ago, Mr.

Brown's office has a nameplate saying, "Mr. Smith." Mr. Smith's door is marked, "Mr. Robinson," in faded ink on an adhesive luggage label. The broken windows have been repaired with odd bits of cardboard. The electric light switches give a slight but painful shock when touched. The whitewash is flaking off the ceiling and the paint is blotchy on the walls. The elevator is out of order and the cloakroom tap cannot be turned off. Water from the broken skylight drips wide of the bucket placed to catch it, and from somewhere in the basement comes the wail of a hungry cat. The last stage of the disease has brought the whole organization to the point of collapse. The symptoms of the disease in this acute form are so numerous and evident that a trained investigator can often detect them over the telephone without visiting the place at all. When a weary voice answers "Ullo!" (that most unhelpful of replies), the expert has often heard enough. He shakes his head sadly as he replaces the receiver. "Well on in the tertiary phase," he will mutter to himself, "and almost certainly inoperable." It is too late to attempt any sort of treatment. The institution is practically dead.

We have now described this disease as seen from within and then again from outside. We know now the origin, the progress, and the outcome of the infection, as also the symptoms by which its presence is detected. British medical skill seldom goes beyond that point in its research. Once a disease has been identified, named, described, and accounted for, the British are usually quite satisfied and ready to investigate the next problem that presents itself. If asked about treatment they look surprised and suggest the use of penicillin preceded or followed by the extraction of all the patient's teeth. It becomes clear at once that this is not an aspect of the subject that interests them. Should our attitude be the same? Or should we as political scientists consider what, if anything, can be done about it? It would be premature, no doubt, to discuss any possible treatment in detail, but it might be useful to indicate very generally the lines along which a solution might be attempted. Certain principles, at least, might be laid down. Of such principles, the first would have to be this: a diseased institution cannot reform itself. There are instances, we know, of a disease vanishing without treatment, just as it appeared without warning; but these cases are rare and regarded by the specialist as irregular and undesirable. The cure, whatever its nature, must come from outside. For a patient to remove his own appendix under a local anaesthetic may be physically possible, but the practice is regarded with disfavor and is open to many objections. Other operations lend themselves still less to the patient's own dexterity. The first principle we can safely enunciate is that the patient and the surgeon should not be the same person. When an institution is in an advanced state of disease, the services of a specialist are required and even, in some instances, the services of the greatest living authority: Parkinson himself. The fees payable may be very heavy indeed, but in a case of this sort, expense is clearly no object. It is a matter, after all, of life and death.

The second principle we might lay down is this, that the primary stage of the disease can be treated by a simple injection, that the secondary stage can be cured in some instances by surgery, and that the tertiary stage must be regarded at present as incurable. There was a time when physicians used to babble about bottles and pills, but this is mainly out of date. There was another period when they talked more vaguely about psychology; but that too is out of date, most of the psychoanalysts having since been certified as insane. The present age is one of injections and incisions and it behooves the political scientists to keep in step with the Faculty. Confronted by a case of primary infection, we prepare a syringe automatically and only hesitate as to what, besides water, it should contain. In principle, the injection should contain some active substance—but from which group should it be selected? A kill-or-cure injection would contain a high proportion of Intolerance, but this drug is difficult to procure and sometimes too powerful to use. Intolerance is obtainable from the bloodstream of regimental sergeant majors and is found to comprise two chemical elements, namely: (a) the best is scarcely good enough (GG^{nth}) and (b) there is no excuse for anything (NE^{nth}). Injected into a diseased institution, the intolerant individual has a tonic effect and may cause the organism to turn against the original source of infection. While this treatment may well do good, it is by no means certain that the cure will be permanent. It is doubtful, that is to say, whether the infected substance will be actually expelled from the system. Such information as we have rather leads us to suppose that this treatment is merely palliative in the first instance, the disease remaining latent though inactive. Some authorities believe that repeated injections would result in a complete cure, but others fear that repetition of the treatment would set up a fresh irritation, only slightly less dangerous than the original disease. Intolerance is a drug to be used, therefore, with caution.

There exists a rather milder drug called Ridicule, but its operation is uncertain, its character unstable, and its effects too little known. There is little reason to fear that any damage could result from an injection of ridicule, but neither is it evident that a cure would result. It is generally agreed that the injelitant individual will have developed a thick protective skin, insensitive to ridicule. It may well be that ridicule may tend to isolate the infection, but that is as much as could be expected and more indeed than has been claimed.

We may note, finally, that Castigation, which is easily obtainable, has been tried in cases of this sort and not wholly without effect. Here again, however, there are difficulties. This drug is an immediate stimulus but can produce a result the exact opposite of what the specialist intends. After a momentary spasm of activity, the injelitant individual will often prove more supine than before and just as harmful as a source of infection. If any use can be made of castigation it will almost certainly be as one element in a preparation composed otherwise of intolerance and ridicule, with perhaps other drugs as yet untried. It only remains to point out that this preparation does not as yet exist.

The secondary stage of the disease we believe to be operable. Professional readers will all have heard of the Nuciform Sack and of the work generally associated with the name of Cutler Walpole. The operation first performed by that great surgeon involves, simply, the removal of the infected parts and the simultaneous introduction of new blood drawn from a similar organism. This operation has sometimes succeeded. It is only fair to add that it has also sometimes failed. The shock to the system can be too great. The new blood may be unobtainable and may fail, even when procured, to mingle with the blood previously in circulation. On the other hand, this drastic method offers, beyond question, the best chance of a complete cure.

The tertiary stage presents us with no opportunity to do anything. The institution is for all practical purposes dead. It can be founded afresh but only with a change of name, a change of site, and an entirely different staff. The temptation, for the economically minded, is to transfer some portion of the original staff to the new institution—in the name, for example, of continuity. Such a transfusion would certainly be fatal, and continuity is the very thing to avoid. No portion of the old and diseased foundation can be regarded as free from infection. No staff, no equipment, no tradition must be removed from the original site. Strict quarantine should be followed by complete disinfection. Infected personnel should be dispatched with a warm testimonial to such rival institutions as are regarded with particular hostility. All equipment and files should be destroyed without hesitation. As for the buildings, the best plan is to insure them heavily and then set them alight. Only when the site is a blackened ruin can we feel certain that the germs of the disease are dead.

RIXFORD KNIGHT

STREET ELBOW

Humorous understatement and caricature are employed here to expose a problem in semantics—people's inability to communicate.

IT SEEMED to me that while the plumber was right there in the house was naturally a good time to find out why a street elbow was called a street elbow, so I went down cellar and said, "Good morning. How is everything going this morning?" And then I said, "Say—by the way, why is a street elbow called a *street* elbow? I can see why it is an elbow all right. But where does the *street* part come from?"

The plumber explained. He said, "I'll tell you. You see a street elbow has one male and one female end. On a regular elbow both ends are female. Here, let me show you."

I said, "Yes, I understand about that; but what I mean is: why does its having one male and one female end make a *street* elbow of it? Streets don't have one male and one female end that I know of. So why a *street* elbow?"

The plumber said, "Wait now. Just let me show you. Look at this here. See? On this end the threads are on the outside. That's because it is the male end. And on this end the threads are on the inside. That's the female end. Now you take a regular elbow—like this here—the threads are on the inside on both ends. That makes it a regular elbow instead of a street elbow. *You* can see how it is."

I told the plumber I could see what the difference was between a street elbow and a regular elbow. "Only what I can't understand is why they show the difference by calling one a *street* elbow. Why not call it a mixed elbow? Or a hermaphrodite elbow? Or something that would mean something? *Street* doesn't mean anything, so far as I know; that is, not in this connection."

The plumber said, "But it does mean something. Like I've just been telling you: it means a street elbow has one male and one female end. If it had two female ends it would be just a regular elbow."

"Listen," I said, "Take a piece of pipe, now. If you say 'This is a brass pipe,' that means something different from what it does if you say 'This is galvanized pipe.' Anybody would know what you meant. But when you say 'This is a *street* elbow,' that doesn't mean anything except to somebody who already knows what a street elbow is."

"I can't help that," said the plumber. "There's a lot of things people don't know about the plumbing business. But any plumber knows what a street elbow is. You ask any plumber, I don't care who he is, and he will tell you a street elbow has got one male and one female end. That's what makes it a *street* elbow."

I said, "Yes, sure. It is *called* a street elbow. But it could be called a whattentot elbow and it would still have one male and one female end; so why pick on *street* to call it?"

The plumber said, "Well, I've been in the plumbing business for thirty-five years now and a street elbow has always been called a street elbow for as long as I can remember. And my father was in the plumbing business for longer than that and *he* always called it a street elbow, and I guess he ought to know if anybody would."

"Of course he would," I told the plumber. "All I'm saying is, how did they come to be called *street* elbows in the first place? Why did your father or whoever it was pick out *street* as the name to call them?"

"Jeez, I wouldn't know about that," said the plumber. "I suppose they had

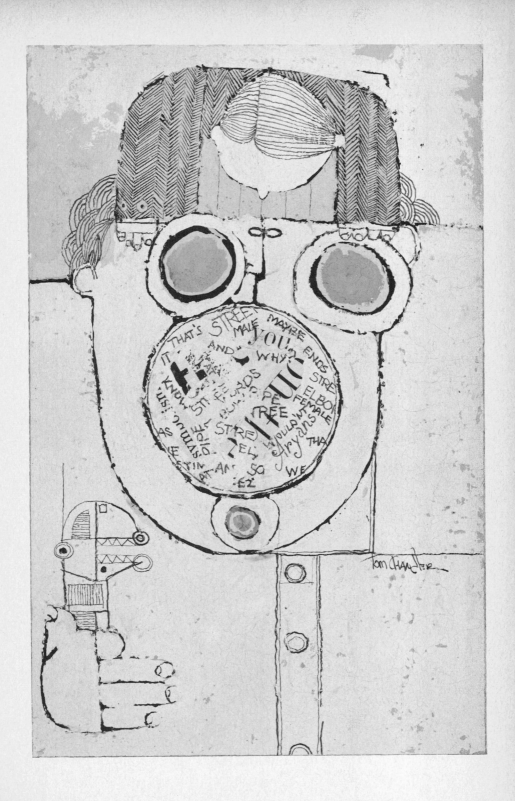

to call them something or nobody would know what anybody else was talking about. Why do you call a pipe a pipe or a house a house or a kitchen a kitchen? You just do, that's all."

"But calling a pipe a pipe or a house a house is altogether different from calling a street elbow a street elbow. The word for house may have come from the ancient Aryans or something and we call it that because they did. There is a reason for it. But I can't see any reason at all for calling this thing a *street* elbow."

"Maybe the ancient Aryans called them street elbows," said the plumber.

"But for cripe sake, the ancient Aryans didn't have street elbows. They didn't have pipes and I doubt if they even had streets; and even if they did, why would they call a piece of curved pipe a *street* elbow unless they called one end of a street the male end and the other end female? Maybe they did. That's what I am trying to find out. Why did somebody start calling this thing a *street* elbow?"

"You mean, why did they call it a *street* elbow?" said the plumber.

"That's it! Why did they call this thing a *street* elbow? Did maybe a man named Street invent it or something?"

The plumber said, "Well, I couldn't say as to that. I never knew of a man named Street in the plumbing business; though of course they might have been, sometime. I don't claim to know everything. Maybe if you were to look in some of those books or something."

I said, "I have already looked in the encyclopedia. All it says is that a street elbow has one male and one female end."

"That's right. The book is right about that," said the plumber.

"But what has that got to do with its being called a *street* elbow? Why call it of all things a *street* elbow?"

The plumber thought that one over. He said, "Y'know, I've been wondering about that myself. Why," he wanted to know, "do they call it a *street* elbow?"

JAMES THURBER

COME ACROSS
WITH
THE FACTS

"...I could tell from Mrs. Quibble's expression that she was seeking for a single sentence with which to destroy me and my subversive attitude toward American education..."

"Do you believe that education in our time and nation is going to improve?" lovely women often ask me at cocktail parties.

"No, ma'am," I always reply, politely. "I think it is going to hell."

"Upon what do you base those dark prognostics?" the ladies, many of whom almost got through high school before they quit to get married, will demand.

"Upon letters that I get from boys and girls in the eighth, ninth, tenth, eleventh and twelfth grades of schools all over the country, asking me— nay, madam, ordering me—to write their term papers for them."

"Don't you want to hear from these children, or what?" asked Mrs. Quibble. (Let's call all these ladies Mrs. Quibble, and put this thing in the past tense, before it drives me crazy.)

"Almost all the letters indicate that we are a nation of tired teachers and apathetic pupils," I said. "I gather that the English teachers cannot interest the children in any writer that isn't living. The youngsters seem to regard all dead writers, from Thackeray to Jim Tully, as equally dull. Dead writers do not send out autographs or autographed photographs. Before long the kids will begin asking a writer for a pencil he has used, or a button from his overcoat, to be sure of getting passing grades."

Mrs. Quibble looked puzzled and skeptical. "You are not making yourself precisive," she said. "You are digressionizing. What is it that's eating you, anyways?"

"May I get you a raspberry ice?" I asked courteously. "You have had too many martinis."

"Don't get cute," she said, with fine hauteur, reaching for another martini. "Give me some instances."

"Let me say first," I said first, "one out of every thirty-two letters shows a trace of originality, even a gleam of ingenuity. If statistics interest you, one out of five girls spells 'all right' 'alright.' "

"Well, if they spell all right, then all right," snapped Mrs. Quibble. "What's eating you, anyhow?"

"That's 'anyhows,' " I said. "Leastways, if it's 'anyways,' then it has to be 'anyhows.' "

"You choose to be egnimatic," said Mrs. Quibble. "As for spelling, my great-grandmother couldn't even read or write."

"And look at her now," I said severely. "Dead and gone and forgotten by everyone on this planet save you."

"Never mind about saving me. You'd better save yourself. You're the one that needs saving," she told me. She reached for a martini on a tray, but I beat her to it.

"What disturbs me most," I said, offering her the olive, which she refused, "is the pervading apathy, the lengthening shadow of lethargy across the land. Almost everybody wants to get through school, or, rather, get *around* it, the easy way. It doesn't surprise me to learn that one can buy themes, theses, dissertations, stand-ins for exams, and even Ph.D. degrees."

"Let's get down to pacific instances about the letters you get from children," said Mrs. Quibble.

"Well, then," I said, "the average letter I get goes like this: 'I have read all your books and liked them very much, and your attitude toward life. Please answer the following questions. 1. What books have you written? 2. What is your attitude toward life? If you will answer this, I will get an A, maybe with a photograph of yourself. You are a Twentieth Century author, and so there is nothing about you in the libary.' One boy ended his letter with, 'Please process this information as soon as possible.' "

"There are worse things than that," Mrs. Quibble said, but she didn't name any. "Do you answer these children?"

"Only the ones that sound intelligent and sincere," I said. "Some of the children write from villages or ghost towns, and I believe them when they say there is no library where they live, or that it has no books that tell you anything about anybody since Tennyson. I have answered boys and girls in places like Wounded Knee, South Dakota, and Dilles Bottom, Ohio, but I refuse to do any research work or writing for New York City children."

"Do you hear from *them*?" my companion wanted to know.

"Once in a while," I said. "I answered one young lazybones and told him he was a liar when he said there was nothing about twentieth-century writers in any New York library. Another New York youngster asked me how to dedicate a book. Since I figured he would never write a book, and probably couldn't tie his tie or shoes without help, I threw his letter away. Then I got another one from him, at once aggrieved and imperious, demanding to know how to dedicate a book. I told him."

"I suppose your letter was full of ironics," said Mrs. Quibble. This time she beat me to the martini on the passing tray.

"I told him that he could dedicate it 'To Mom,' or 'To Madge Mudge,' or

'To Pop,' but I suggested that if he ever did write a book, the most fitting dedication should probably go like this: 'To Miss Gorby, whom, without she had learnt me English, this book never would of been written.'"

"Nobody is as unliterate as that, and you know it," said Mrs. Quibble.

"They ain't, huh?" I said. "You should see my mail, which, without I got so much of it, I might of got more written."

I could tell from Mrs. Quibble's expression that she was seeking for a single sentence with which to destroy me and my subversive attitude toward American education. She found it at last.

"The trouble with you is, you just don't like no children," she said coldly.

"You are wrong, madam," I said icily. "I *do* like no children."

Editor's Note: Mr. Thurber does like children, but he thinks nothing of abusing truth to point up a grammatical outrage.

A.B.C. (*PSEUDONYM*)

HALF
LIFE
BEGINS AT 30

"... Some people laughed, but the idea that brains were like hot atoms spread from engineering to other professions ..."

ALTHOUGH atoms had alarmed most folk, few foresaw that men would start comparing themselves to such wee things. Everyone knows that every second some hot atoms decay. Each species has a half-life, which is whatever period of time it takes for half a batch of that kind of stuff to cool down. Early in the 1960s a few engineers noted that a man's knowledge, similarly, could turn to ashes and suggested that people, too, might have half-lives.

Experienced engineers were being benched, yet high salaries were being offered to youngsters fresh from college. Employers said the reason was that the older men's knowledge was obsolete. Science and technology were racing forward, and half the things a fellow learned in school were liable to be useless to his boss a decade later. Mathematical oracles said, therefore, that the half-life of an engineer's special know-how was only about ten years.

Some people laughed, but the idea that brains were like hot atoms spread from engineering to other professions. It became fashionable to regard wisdom as radioactivity. Bankers, morticians, lawyers, doctors, and even clowns consulted social statisticians about the half-lives of their special skills. It was a way of saving face and keeping clients from beating fees down.

The bankers and morticians both found that they had much longer half-lives than the engineers. The state of their arts didn't change much, and they felt pretty smug about this at first. But the lawyers were surprised to find that they were even worse off than the physicians. An old lawyer's ideas of crime, punishment, and justice were liable to make people regard him as an old fogy, whereas an old doctor who let his patients eat, drink, and smoke as usual was often saluted as a sage. The professional comedians, however, had even longer half-lives than the bankers and morticians.

The revelations of such research embarrassed the public relations men for many professions. Instead of boasting about the durability of their employers' wisdom, they therefore had to crow about how quickly that knowledge decayed.

The remedy for a short half-life was clearly to get a man's mental gas tank refilled periodically. The more often he could do this, the less risk he ran of status slippage. A race began, consequently, to see which profession's practitioners could stand the most frequent replenishment of their know-how.

A few corporation executives, labor leaders, and newspaper reporters had discovered earlier that going back to Harvard, Dartmouth, or Stanford was less work than working. They, however, had not understood half-lives. The engineers began not only to go back to college every tenth year, but also to collect beginners' wages again when they returned to their office suites. The salesmen then got into higher income brackets sooner than the engineers by resuming their schooling every fifth year.

This race for prestige between occupations became even more of a drain on the economy than the race to the moon. Only a few big spenders could have spaceships; this was a contest between classes, in which everyone could participate.

In many fields, naturally, more knowledge was desperately needed so that something or other could be taught to the practitioners scrambling for it.

Fantastic though this crusade for new know-how became, the consequences of it were even more implausible. Everyone knew that when enough of some kinds of radioactive atoms were brought together, they became a critical mass and exploded. But few appreciated, until too late, how truly similar human beings' knowledge might be to the natural radioactivity of atoms.

Whenever and wherever a large mass of seekers for fresh facts was assembled, each man inspired the others. Some hot groups were soon producing new data faster than they could retain them. Some lost more than they could pass on to others. Finally, some of these fertile fellows began simply dumping their discoveries into computers and leaving them there, like so much surplus wheat.

By the 1980s the countryside was peppered with places in which experts were huddling in laboratories and seminars in order to extend their half-lives. These plastic palaces full of specialists and computers were called complexes, and became as hard to get into as college had been for high school graduates a couple of decades earlier. So still more complexes had to be built.

Factories were closed to make way for them. More than half of the nation's trained manpower was always in school, studying or searching for something to study, and the other half was so busy designing and building new complexes that no new factories were built. Never before had so many men known so much and done so little with what they knew.

Production plummeted, and the gross national income shrank. And another group of creative thinkers had to be assembled in a super-complex, to see if its members' knowledge could be updated soon enough to save the marvelous new culture that everyone said was evolving. By then, fortunately, the census bureau's big computers knew what everybody was doing every second of every day and night. So the solution was simple. The super-brains disposed of the production problem by arming those computers in the 1990s to curb the population.

As soon as men became scarcer, they stopped thinking of themselves as hot atoms; wages went up, and people began going back to work and dying happily the old-fashioned way. But by then, alas, what had begun as the century of the common man had decayed into the century of the uncommon man.

PAUL TABORI

THE MARTIAN MEMO

*Here the mythical Martian, so familiar in
writing and cartoons, gives the satirist a
detached, objective observer whose naïve
view of society exposes its ironies and absurdities.*

"SOME astronomers believe it is probable that there is intelligent life
on Mars and that it may have developed much earlier than ours, in which
case Martians may have been civilized for millions of years, as compared
to our thousands. In such an event the Martians' knowledge of science
and nature would be enormously greater than ours, and men from Mars
may already have visited the Earth. Unless they had spent some time
in a large city or landed sufficiently recently to be photographed, we
would have no record of their having been here. Any few men who had
seen them would probably not be believed by anyone else."

—Dr. Lyman Spitzer, Jr., Associate Professor of Astrophysics at Yale
University, in an interview published in the *New York Times*, 1947.

"Pending the submission of my full report to the Council, I offer you the
enclosed memorandum with some reluctance. I have spent only a short
time on this peculiar planet, less than the pitifully brief life span of a
single native. Though I have acquired reasonable proficiency in their
languages and customs, their thought processes and history, there is
still much that puzzles and baffles me. However, at the repeated insistence of the Council, I send you these notes, unavoidably disjointed and
fragmentary. They will, perhaps, give some indication as to the conclusions of the final report which I intend to render immediately upon my
return."

XU

Except for an inconsiderable minority, humans attach far greater importance to their bodies than to their minds. One of the most elaborate games

they play is centered around the proportion of exposure, both in actual physical fact and in the body's so-called artistic representation. The two main categories on the active side of this game are called strip-teasers and artists; their opponent is variously called censor, watch committee, blue-nose, or puritan. The advantage appears to be on the latter's side; there is a limit to exposure, i.e., complete nudity; while there is no limit to what can be forbidden or denounced.

They spend immense amounts of money, time, and energy to darken their skin, if white, by exposure to sunshine and artificial substitutes for the sun. Yet any human who has acquired this color, in various shades of darkness, at birth, is considered to be inferior and suffers grave economic and social disadvantages.

A large proportion of their communal endeavor is devoted to the making of laws to regulate human conduct. Subsequently they employ, at great cost, specialists in the art of breaking the same laws. I have not yet discovered a single law, decree or regulation which these specialists—quaintly called lawyers—have not been able to surmount or frustrate.

Their wise men declare repeatedly that the peculiar convention embodied in certain objects called money represents the root of all evil; but they not only submit to this evil with remarkable docility, they even seek to acquire as much of it as possible. Most of this money is invested with arbitrary value based on precious metals which many of their separate units, called states or countries, are supposed to possess but which only a negligible proportion of the citizens ever see or touch.

They are all afraid of the termination of physical existence, called death —something that is very difficult for us to imagine. But no single human believes, in the depth of his being, that he will ever die. It is something that happens to others all the time but cannot be encompassed by their conscious-ness, which is supposed to end with this so-called death. Their experts in such matters—called priests, clergymen, and, sometimes, philosophers— talk a great deal about life after death but their descriptions and forecasts of this state are based entirely on speculation. However, according to them it is a condition entirely preferable to life before death. Yet anybody volun-tarily proving a preference for this condition—this they call suicide—is considered a weakling or a criminal.

According to them the ideal relationship of the two sexes (there are only two which they acknowledge though an increasing number of them appear to belong to a third one) is the institution called marriage. For a female not to achieve this is considered to be unlucky and even unhappy, while a male who refuses or fails to attain it is more often than not called fortunate. Some are so enthusiastic about it that they make repeated attempts, even four or five times in their ridiculously short existence, to contract such a union. Their convention decrees that males and females, having achieved it, shall "live happily ever after." Yet most of their countries have ample provision for breaking the union. To this, elaborate legal rituals are attached which benefit considerably the strange tribe of lawyers mentioned above.

In several of their countries the leaders have managed the incredible feat of persuading the people that if they undergo immense privations and work as hard as animals, their grandchildren—who may never be born—will be both happy and free. This promise is safely made as there is no way of checking it against fact; what is unbelievable is the readiness with which the people believe it. True, the most fervent believers of this theory are men and women who live outside the countries mentioned.

Their diet is equally fantastic. They will, in their most highly civilized countries, eat any four- or two-legged animal that has horns but not the ones without—i.e., the mammals known as horses and donkeys. They will go to immense lengths to insure that their comestibles are clean and appetizing to look at; they also follow elaborate processes to render them tasteless.

Their females are traditionally afraid of a small animal called a mouse, but are delighted to wear the skins of much larger and fiercer animals upon their bodies.

They are passionate gamblers and are capable of a total suspension of disbelief in face of the most discouraging mathematical odds in pursuit of this passion. The successful gambler is one of their most universally venerated heroes; luck is supposed to equal morality and wisdom.

They spend a great deal more money on punishing the wrongdoer than on rewarding the upright, though what constitutes these two categories varies from place to place. To kill while wearing individual or "civilian" garb is considered a heinous crime; to do the same wearing something called "uniform" and in a collective organization, is looked upon as heroism and patriotism. They are the only living beings on this planet who periodically set out to kill their own species at no visible profit to themselves.

Those who believe least in them, create their own heavens and their own hells. Their greatest curse is the thing they call "sin" in which they have greater faith than in other things called "virtue" and "happiness." "Sin" changes form and color, acquires different penalties and rewards, in each age and in many of their countries. Those who are the most virtuous, according to their poor lights, are most conscious of sin and therefore most ready to attribute it to others. A few have learned that sin is the refusal to live up to the enlightenment which they possess, however rudimentary this may be.

They pay immense amounts of their money to people who can make them laugh or weep. They are light-years away from realizing that perfection can be achieved only by those who are beyond both. Yet sometimes I felt envious of this talent which, as you know, we Martians have lost long ago.

They have some individuals who call themselves pessimists and pretend always to expect the worse. But they still rise in the morning, eat and drink, get married, and produce offspring. To them, the greatest boon to be expected would be the end of the world; yet they do not seem capable of action that would hasten the fulfillment of this desire.

Their stimulants are incredibly crude. The most prevalent is called alcohol. It has, in the end, disastrous effects, yet the revenue of their countries consists to a large extent of tax levied on it. Their other drug is tobacco, which is equally noxious but equally profitable to their governments. These two are permitted, while many others—to name only a few, opium, cocaine, heroin, morphine, and a score more—are outlawed. I met one human who was an anti-alcoholist. He explained that this was not because he did not need it to achieve illusions but because even without it he could reach the unpleasant condition they call a hangover.

It is an essential quality of this planet that for its inhabitants truth is the hardest thing to prove.

What would you think of creatures who, setting out on a journey of a hundred miles (to use their measure of distance) would travel twenty on the first day, return the second day to their starting point, cover forty miles the third day, go back again where they started from and then, on the fifth finally reach their goal? Yet this is, I assure you, a fairly accurate description of what they call "human progress."

They desire success desperately but find no happiness in achieving it. They would not believe anyone who told them that success was getting what you wanted and happiness was wanting what you got. Nor that there is often far less danger in the things they fear than in the things they desire.

Their sympathy is the most natural and amiable form of bias. Whether they talk or keep silent, they cannot escape misunderstanding. Because they are mutually burdensome to each other, they have invented something they call "good manners." Most of their leaders do not really want to lead, only to be followed. Their complex game called "politics" is their art to demand of others all they cannot or will not do themselves. For them it is easier to travel around the world than journey to the core of their minds. They discover the necessity of freedom only when they have lost it.

    . . . And yet I like them.

DEAR MUMMY

The clash of attitudes and personalities, presented through these "letters," revealingly exaggerates the absurdities of some social attitudes that this satirist wishes to condemn.

Mrs. Howard Andrews
Our Place
Crestview, Ohio

Dear Addie,
Your father and I are very disturbed about something we just heard from the Maitlands (they came aboard yesterday for drinks). Ginny said that just before they left for Flat Key, Ann Rossiter called her from Oakdale and said that the Westover girl had given a birthday party that turned into something of a riot. She was very vague about the details, but it seems things got very rough and the house was a shambles. We are very worried because we remembered that Doug had been seeing something of the Westover girl, and we naturally hope he wasn't involved.
    Please let us know what, if anything, happened.

Love,
Mummy

Mr. and Mrs. Curtis Munson
Fool's Paradise
Flat Key, Bahamas

Dearest Mummy,
    It's just like Ginny Maitland to go gabbing away like that upsetting people for no reason. We are all trying to keep the affair in the family, so to speak, and Howie even saw to it that Ed Bates didn't print anything about it in the Oakdale Sentinel.
    Franny Westover *did* give a birthday party for about a hundred kids, and I guess it went on a little late and the boys wanted some fun and threw a few things around. Doug doesn't seem to remember what exactly happened, he said they "twisted" and then someone thought it would be funny if they had

a "book-wetting," so they took all the books in the house and threw them in the swimming pool, and then someone else (I think it was a girl) thought it would be fun to have everyone take off their ordinary clothes and dress in window curtains. Dick Westover was very unpleasant over the phone yesterday (we never liked him anyway) and accused Doug of being one of the boys who cut up the living room rug with pruning shears, but it was a hideous mustard broadloom (that house is in the *worst* taste) and I don't much blame them.

The point is, Daddy, it was a simple case of high spirits and no real harm done. Just to smooth things over, I gave Doug a check for $300 to cover some glassware and the rug business (he swears he didn't burn any curtains).

So please don't worry about it, Doug is a fine boy, really, and those were the nicest kids anyone would want to know, all from the best homes and Yale and Princeton and all that.

Love and Kisses,
Addie

Mrs. Howard Andrews
Our Place
Crestview, Ohio

Dear Addie,
Your father had one of his indigestion attacks after getting your letter, and has asked me to write you.

I need hardly say we were appalled. How is it possible for boys of decent families to destroy the property of other people who are giving them a party? And why weren't there any grownups at the party to stop them? In my days, the parents and older people were always around.

Your Distressed Mother,
Mother

P.S. If I'd been you and Howie I'd have made Doug pay for the damage out of his own pocket and taken away his college tuition for a semester. How else will these spoiled young ruffians ever learn?

Dad

Mrs. Curtis Munson
Fool's Paradise
Andros, Bahamas

Dear Mummy,
Your letter shows how out of touch you two have been with things today. No self-respecting parent would *dream* of being in the house when the kids are having a party, it inhibits them so. Howie and I just engage the band and the caterer and have our own fun somewhere else. Just to be on the safe side, we *did* hire a policeman for Carol's last party to see that the "crashers" didn't get too out of hand. In case you didn't know, it's the custom for a lot of kids to drive to a party they haven't been asked to, and in a way I think it's

very democratic even if they do make a sort of mess of the place. But we always get a house-cleaning crew in the next day to sweep up the broken glass, refinish the furniture, and plant new bushes. It's just part of the expense of entertaining these days.

Also I don't see how you can say Doug is spoiled. He deserved a new Thunderbird for getting into Yale (Howie never thought he'd make it), and as for his speedboat this summer, you couldn't really expect him to take his dates across the lake in an outboard.

Doug is *not* a "ruffian." Why only the other day, Mr. Ballard (he's Vice President of Western Swivel) told Howie that Doug was a natural leader with a real feeling for money.

Love,
Addie

Mrs. Howard Andrews
Our Place
Crestview, Ohio

Dear Addie,
"Natural leaders with a real feeling for money" have been known to land in jail. Doug may too some day if you and Howie don't set him straight before it's too late.

Speaking of which, have you ever bothered to tell the kid about Right and Wrong and Responsibility? Where's his father been all this time? How can you possibly expect kids who drink hard liquor from fourteen on and crash parties and need policemen to keep them in order to turn into decent citizens?

High spirits my hat! Those boys need a flogging or a psychiatric examination. Not that I believe in that stuff, it's mostly mumbo-jumbo, but something must be wrong inside if a boy has to destroy something to feel good.

Love,
Dad

Mrs. Curtis Munson
Fool's Paradise
Eleuthera, Bahamas

Dear Mummy,
I can't write to Dad in his present condition, he just doesn't understand the realities of today.

For one thing, Doug went to Sunday School from the ages of 8 to 10, and then at prep school they had the Lord's Prayer every morning before they banned it. So he's had as good a Christian upbringing as anyone.

For another, Dad seems to forget that when Doug was fifteen he won the D.A.R. prize for the best essay on Why Our Way of Life is the Best Way. So don't talk to me about ethics.

And what does Dad mean asking where Howie's been? Howie's in town every day as he well knows, working so that we can all have a decent standard of living, and it isn't his fault that he doesn't see his son from one end of the week to the other. It's the mother's responsibility anyway, and God knows I've given Doug everything since he was a tiny baby.

What Dad refuses to realize is that it's terribly hard growing up, with the bomb and insecurity and China, and boys like Doug don't know what's going to happen to them so they have to have some outlet somewhere.

Love,
Addie

Telegram to Mrs. Howard Andrews
RE OUTLET HOW ABOUT HONEST WORK OR THE PEACE CORPS?

Dad

Mr. Curtis Munson
Fool's Paradise
St. James, Barbados

Dear Curtis,

Addie has just showed me your letter and telegram, and as she is rather emotional about all this, I thought I'd write to you directly.

My personal view is that the Communists were behind all these so-called riots you read about. I don't doubt that some Harvard red got into that Westover party and planted the whole thing so that it would reflect badly on our society.

Anyway, you have no cause to worry about Doug. He's a fine red-blooded kid with a great sense of humor and a lot of git-up-and-go.

What it all comes down to is, what would you rather have: a free society or a socialist state?

Cordially,
Howie

Miss Frances Westover
Oakdale, Ohio

Dear Fran,

I'm sorry you thought I sounded mad when you phoned me the news yesterday, but you can understand why it was something of a shock, especially as I don't remember a thing that happened that night, any more than you did. Somebody shot the lights out and I couldn't see who the hell I was with.

Honest, I'm really glad it was you and we might as well have a family now as later anyway.

I'll break the news to my old bag next weekend. It'll take her mind off this price-fixing and Dad's company you've probably read about.

Anyway, relax, I'll be calling you.

Your everlovin Doug

Mr. and Mrs. Curtis Munson
Fool's Paradise
Tobago, Trinidad

Dear Dad and Mom,

I know you'll be as happy as I am to know that Doug is engaged to Frances Westover and they hope to be married very soon. She's a darling girl (they're Mainland Steel), and they seem in a romantic daze about each other. So you see, the little Doug who worried you so is now about to be a responsible married man and, of course, some day, the father of a family.

I am hoping that after he finishes college (Howie naturally will see them through that), they'll settle somewhere near us so that the children can grow up in a fine healthy community with people who think alike and have the same values.

Doug will write you himself, I know. In spite of his sometimes casual manner, he is really very fond of you both, even if the generations don't always mix. Young people are more realistic, don't you think?

Lovingly,
Addie

ROLLO MAY

THE MAN
WHO WAS PUT
IN A CAGE

"... And now the man, in his desultory conversations, never used the word 'I' any more. He had accepted the cage. He had no anger, no hate ..."

ONE evening a king of a far land was standing at his window, vaguely listening to some music drifting down the corridor from the reception room in the other wing of the palace. The king was wearied from the diplomatic reception he had just attended, and he looked out of the window pondering about the ways of the world in general and nothing in particular. His eye fell upon a man in the square below—apparently an average man, walking to the corner to take the tram home, who had taken that same route five nights a week for many years. The king followed this man in his imagination—pictured him arriving home, perfunctorily kissing his wife, eating his late meal, inquiring whether everything was right with the children, reading the paper, going to bed, perhaps engaging in the love act with his wife or perhaps not, sleeping, and getting up and going off to work again the next day.

And a sudden curiosity seized the king which for a moment banished his fatigue, "I wonder what would happen if a man were kept in a cage, like the animals at the zoo?"

So the next day the king called in a psychologist, told him of his idea, and invited him to observe the experiment. Then the king caused a cage to be brought from the zoo, and the average man was brought and placed therein.

At first the man was simply bewildered, and he kept saying to the psychologist who stood outside the cage, "I have to catch the tram, I have to get to work, look what time it is, I'll be late for work!" But later on in the afternoon the man began soberly to realize what was up, and then he protested vehemently, "The king can't do this to me! It is unjust, and against the laws." His voice was strong, and his eyes full of anger.

During the rest of the week the man continued his vehement protests. When the king would answer, "Look here, you get plenty of food, you have a good bed, and you don't have to work. We take good care of you—so why are you objecting?" Then after some days the man's protests lessened and then ceased. He was silent in his cage, refusing generally to talk, but the psychologist could see hatred glowing like a deep fire in his eyes.

But after several weeks the psychologist noticed that more and more it now seemed as if the man were pausing a moment after the king's daily reminder to him that he was being taken good care of—for a second the hatred was postponed from returning to his eyes—as though he were asking himself if what the king said were possibly true.

And after a few weeks more, the man began to discuss with the psychologist how it was a useful thing if a man were given food and shelter, and that man had to live by his fate in any case and the part of wisdom was to accept his fate. So when a group of professors and graduate students came in one day to observe the man in the cage, he was friendly toward them and explained to them that he had chosen this way of life, that there are great values in security and being taken care of, that they would of course see how sensible his course was, and so on. How strange! thought the psychologist, and how pathetic—why is it he struggles so hard to get them to approve of his way of life?

In the succeeding days when the king would walk through the court-yard, the man would fawn upon him from behind the bars in his cage and thank him for the food and shelter. But when the king was not in the yard and the man was not aware that the psychologist was present, his expression was quite different—sullen and morose. When his food was handed to him through the bars by the keeper, the man would often drop the dishes or dump over the water and then be embarrassed because of his stupidity and clumsiness. His conversation became increasingly one-tracked; and instead of the involved philosophical theories about the value of being taken care of, he had gotten down to simple sentences like "It is fate," which he would say over and over again, or just mumble to himself, "It is."

It was hard to say just when the last phase set in. But the psychologist became aware that the man's face seemed to have no particular expression: his smile was no longer fawning, but simply empty and meaningless, like the grimace a baby makes when there is gas on its stomach. The man ate his food, and exchanged a few sentences with the psychologist from time to time; his eyes were distant and vague, and though he looked at the psychologist, it seemed that he never really *saw* him.

And now the man, in his desultory conversations, never used the word "I" any more. He had accepted the cage. He had no anger, no hate, no rationalizations. But he was now insane.

That night the psychologist sat in his parlor trying to write a concluding report. But it was very difficult for him to summon up words, for he felt within himself a great emptiness. He kept trying to reassure himself with the words, "They say that nothing is ever lost, that matter is merely changed to energy and back again." But he couldn't help feeling something *had* been lost, something had been taken out of the universe in this experiment, and there was left only a void.

LUCY EISENBERG

WHAT COMPUTERS CAN'T DO

"...Even among those who believe that computers can think, there are few...except for a rabid fringe—who hold that they actually are thinking...."

THERE is a computer at Massachusetts Institute of Technology which goes by the engaging name of Pandemonium. Its creator is Oliver Selfridge, a thirty-nine-year-old mathematician, who is a director of project MAC (Machine-Aided Cognition); and in his spare time a devotee of skiing, Elizabethan madrigals, and organic farming. The task which Selfridge has set for the machine is to recognize letters like R, A, and T. Unfortunately, Pandemonium is somewhat of a dunce.

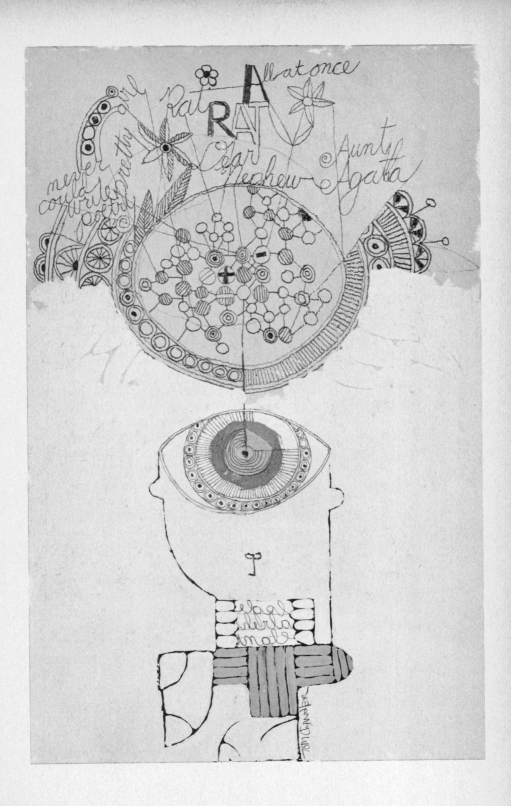

When rat is written out in capitals

RAT

it can identify the letters. But write

Rat

or

or   **RAT**

and Pandemonium is stumped. Many computers can make excuses, such as: THE ABOVE LETTER IS AMBIGUOUS, or, with hubris, THE ABOVE LETTER IS IMPOSSIBLE. But the fact is that Pandemonium is nonplussed by modified forms of R, A, and T. Evidently it lacks a basic intellectual skill called pattern recognition. Children learn this skill in the crib. But it is almost impossible to teach it to a machine.

After twenty years of research, computer experts are forced to admit that recognition is hard to understand and even harder to simulate. This deficiency remains a formidable barrier to building a truly intelligent machine.

A computer is a calculating machine. The basic components of a computer are: the executive, which does rapid arithmetic, and the memory, which stores information. A third component, the control, directs input of data, the order of arithmetical calculations, and the printing of results. As soon as a program (*i.e.*, the rules for input, output, and calculation) is punched onto cards, and the cards are fed into the machine, the control takes over and manages it alone.

Computer programs vary according to their purposes. When, for example, equations are to be evaluated the program contains rules for reducing the equation to simple arithmetical operations. Other programs are tailor-made for different commercial firms. American Airlines, for instance, has recently invested $30 million in a computer that is programmed to handle airplane reservations. The program lists rules for making reservations: for looking up flight information, for calculating the available seats on a plane, and for transmitting information back to the ticket clerks.

Mathematicians, in their wisdom, have also written programs which have no use at all except to simulate such human mental activities as logic, solving theorems, and the peculiar type of thinking we call "playing" a game. Arthur Samuel at IBM has even programmed a computer to play checkers (he has been grooming it for a match sometime against the national checkers champion.) While it is hard to say exactly what *kind* of thinking checkers demands, there is no question that the computer "learns," remembers moves, changes strategies, and improves from game to game.

Another kind of thinking, the ability to handle language, has been simulated by the project MAC computer at M.I.T. A number of programs are stored in the machine, and new data can be introduced by typing into a keyboard which communicates with the control. Bertram Raphael, a doctoral student, has programmed the machine to handle words according to their logical relations. Sitting at the keyboard, he types out questions, which are translated into a code that the machine understands. The computer's answers come back in seconds and are typed out automatically. Here is a typical dialogue (R is Mr. Raphael, C is the computer):

R: Every boy is a person
C: I understand
R: A finger is part of a hand
C: I understand
R: Each person has two hands
C: The above sentence is ambiguous Please rephrase it
R: There are two hands on each person
C: I understand
R: How many fingers does John have Q
C: The above sentence is ambiguous, but I assume (has) means (has as parts) I don't know whether finger is a part of John
R: John is a boy
C: I understand
R: How many fingers does John have Q
C: The above sentence is ambiguous, but I assume (has) means (has as parts) How many fingers per hand Q
R: Each hand has five fingers
C: The above sentence is ambiguous, but I assume (has) means (has as parts) The answer is ten
R: How many automobiles does John have Q
C: The above sentence is ambiguous Please rephrase it
R: Who is President of the United States Q
C: Statement form not recognized

Computers, as Mr. Raphael has shown, can handle words well enough to carry on a simple conversation. They can remember, they can learn, and they also make assumptions. In fact, they can manage most of the skills we associate with thinking.

Yet there is something dissatisfying about the way they think. They are exasperatingly rigid, and their intelligence is narrow in scope. They answer some questions but fail on others which are almost identical. One is hard put to name an intellectual skill which computers cannot perform, yet reluctant to say they really can think. As Oliver Selfridge put it recently, "Even among those who believe that computers *can* think, there are few these days— except for a rabid fringe—who hold that they actually *are* thinking."

Computers can do logical, deductive reasoning. But, Selfridge explained, not all problems are amenable to these processes. To illustrate the point, he pulled out his pen, jotted down this column of letters on a napkin, and asked me to add the next one:

O
T
T
F
F
S

After a minute of silence, he gave me a hint by adding a second column:

O	E
T	O
T	E
F	R
F	E
S	X

I was still baffled. Finally he added another letter:

O	N	E
T		O
T		E
F		R
F		E
S		X

I then saw what the next letter would be.

This problem—which is taken from the British eleven-plus-examination— is the kind that intelligent machines should be able to solve. Yet they fail to do so. This is because they cannot discover the *class* of letter to which the particular letters belong. An even simpler problem in classification is to identify the figures below as triangles:

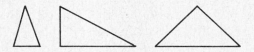

Computers cannot do this either because it requires a type of thinking called cognition or perception, or—by computer experts—pattern recognition.

To name even the simplest object involves pattern recognition. How do we decide that two different shapes are both triangles? Presumably by analyzing the visual images and reducing them to some common pattern. How do we identify the letter A when it is printed in one of twenty type fonts, or written with more or less flourish by hand? Again, by reducing the specimen to a pattern that represents the type. This process of categorization enables us to decide that this shape is a triangle and that shape is an A.

Programmers have generally overlooked pattern recognition in their efforts to design intelligent machines. In effect, they have turned intelligence upside down. They have taught computers to solve mathematical problems, but not to recognize digits as they are normally written. They have taught them to manipulate words like *boy, finger,* and *hand,* but not to identify the objects the words represent. They have programmed computers to take part in conversation, but not to analyze speech into meaningful patterns of sound.

There is nothing wrong with upsetting the normal order of education. Nor is it absolutely necessary (though it would be useful) to build computers which read writing or understand speech. But pattern recognition plays an important role in the growth and development of a child's mind and it is an integral part of thinking.

Over the years computer experts have attempted—with little success—to invent a set of rules for recognizing patterns and program them into a machine. A different approach to the problem would be to wait for biologists to discover the rules the human brain uses to recognize patterns. This avenue of attack is even less promising according to most biologists.

What little is known today about the biology of pattern recognition is based on the work of another M.I.T. scientist, Jerry Lettvin. Trained as a psychiatrist, he worked in the Boston City Hospital, and then went to Chicago where he studied under Warren McCulloch, a philosopher and cybernetician. Later Lettvin turned to research biology, and today he is a professor of neurophysiology at M.I.T. In size, appearance, and mannerisms he reminds one of the comedian Zero Mostel.

Lettvin has studied the first step of pattern recognition; that is, how the eye processes the rays of light which it receives and reduces them to some sort of pattern. He did this by moving bits of black paper across a screen in front of a frog. Then he placed an electrode on the visual center of the frog's brain to record the electrical messages sent to the brain from different cells in the eye.

Through these experiments he discovered that most cells in the eye respond to patterns, and not just to the presence or absence of light, as had previously been thought. Moreover, the cells send messages to the brain only in response to certain *kinds* of patterns: one cell responds if there is a moving edge in the visual field and another if there is a convex edge. The basis for this phenomenon is the complicated network of nerve cells in the eye; because the cells are all "plugged" into each other, a single cell "knows" what is going on in most of its nearest neighbors.

As Lettvin explained, these cells are very useful to the frog, which is more interested in watching bugs than anything else. The frog's eye is built so that it responds immediately to "bug-ish" patterns, *i.e.,* to shapes which are circular and which move. The cell network, he pointed out, is a concrete example of what philosophers since Plato have called an "innate idea." That is to say, there is a mechanism built into the frog's eye which formulates complex ideas like "convex edge" and "moving edge," and passes them on to the brain. Presumably there are similar mechanisms built into the eye of a human being but biologists don't know what they are, and Lettvin himself is not hopeful about unraveling this mystery.

I did not immediately understand the reasons for Lettvin's pessimism. He uses an idiomatic language which is picturesque but also slightly puzzling.

"So you want us to study the brain," he said. "So how are you going to study the brain? You want to put an electrode on a brain cell? Okay, we'll take a frog and put an electrode on its brain, and then we'll bring it things from the world. We'll bring it tabletops and salt shakers and knishes and pretty girls. And then we'll count the number of times that the brain cell fires and we find that it fires 6.5 times for pretty girls. So! Now you know how a frog sees pretty girls?"

Lettvin's point, I discovered, is that it is logically impossible to describe any stimulus completely, whether it is a knish, or a pretty girl, or just a black spot on a white wall. Most biologists are not particularly concerned by this difficulty. But Lettvin is something of a philosopher as well as a research biologist, and he feels the point *is* important, and that it should not be overlooked. Other biologists have repeated Lettvin's work using cats and kittens. But comparable experiments on human beings are not feasible and in fact very little is known about how a man recognizes patterns.

Oliver Selfridge—when he designed Pandemonium—did not try to imitate the exact process whereby a human being recognizes a pattern. Pandemonium was rather an attempt to program a computer to solve a limited problem, but not to fully simulate human thought.

Selfridge simplified the task of letter-recognition by choosing ten particular letters: R A E O T M I L N S. In this way, he avoided ambiguous pairs like O and Q. He then programmed the computer to carry out a series of operations. First, the letter was projected onto an electronic grid for Pandemonium to "see." Next the machine performed twenty-eight little tests, like measuring the height-to-width ratio of a letter, or the number of times the letter intersected a horizontal line. Finally, the machine searched its memory to compare the results of these tests with previous ones. Thus Pandemonium could deduce that the letter with two intersections and a horizontal line, a letter that was wider at the bottom than the top and taller than it was wide, was an A.

"The only trouble with Pandemonium," Selfridge explained, "was that it never really worked." Even with only ten letters, it made mistakes. It could not read cursive writing at all because the letters were not discrete. Rather than struggle on with the problem, Selfridge abandoned Pandemonium temporarily. Other experimenters who continued to work on the problem have met with little success.

A machine that could recognize handwritten letters would have unlimited practical uses: it could, for instance, run a post office by itself. But Selfridge is primarily interested in building a thinking machine and regards letter recognition as only a means to this end. By tackling such limited problems he believes computer experts will discover new principles which will enable them eventually to build a truly intelligent machine. Other experts do not agree. Some feel that until a general *theory* of intelligence is developed there is nothing to be gained by working on any particular problem.

Intelligence, however, is a puzzling phenomenon. Psychologists cannot define it, and neither can the engineers and mathematicians. They can merely judge intelligence by its results. A child is intelligent if he scores well on an IQ test. And a machine would be intelligent if it could score well on Turing's Imitation Game.

The Imitation Game is a hypothetical test designed by Alan Turing, who was a mathematician at Manchester University in England. In Turing's game, an interrogator tries to distinguish between a computer and a man simply by asking a series of questions. He cannot see the respondents because they are hidden by a screen; he cannot hear them because the questions and answers are transmitted by teletype. All he can do is ask questions to X and to Y; at the end of the game, he must decide whether X is a computer or a man. If the computer can deceive the examiner, then, according to Turing, the computer may be said to think.

Turing envisioned the following conversation:

Q: Please write me a sonnet on the subject of the Fourth Bridge.
A: Count me out on this one. I never could write poetry.
Q: Add 34957 to 70764.
A: (Pause about 30 seconds and then give as answer) 105621.
Q: Do you play chess?
A: Yes.
Q: I have K at my K1, and no other pieces. You have only K at K6 and R1. It is your move. What do you play?
A: (after a pause of 15 seconds) R-R8 mate.

No computer in existence today could possible carry on such a conversation. They can add, *or* count John's fingers, *or* play mediocre chess, but none of them can do all these things at once (much less pause artfully so as not to give itself away).

This is not to belittle the remarkable feats that can be performed by computers. Mr. Samuel's checker-playing machine, for instance, can regularly defeat the man who programmed it. But neither it—nor any other existing computer—can decode your Aunt Agatha's inimitable scrawl. This is depressing to computer experts but something of a comfort for the man who has forgotten whatever he once knew about the differential calculus. A human brain, it would seem, is still worth having.

BERTRAND RUSSELL ON THE SINFUL AMERICANS

"...You suffer from what the theologians call 'invincible ignorance.' ..."

THE following correspondence grew out of an article published in this space last January, "A 'Scientific' Formula for Disarmament?" In it John Fischer commented on the tendency of some scientists—including Bertrand Russell, British mathematician and philosopher—to take an oversimplified view of the problems of disarmament and international tensions.

———————————

March 4, 1963

Sirs,

You published an article in your January issue by a Mr. J. Fischer. This article is not sufficiently serious to warrant the time necessary to examine it, but it may be worthwhile to mention that the views attributed to me by Mr. J. Fischer bear no relation to what I have advocated, and it seems clear from the context of his article that he has attributed these false views to me with foreknowledge. I shall charitably assume that this was due to oversight and I shall, therefore, seek to explain briefly what it is I am saying, in sufficiently simple language such as to enable J. Fischer to understand more clearly.

I am contending that human beings live, at the moment, in immediate danger of total annihilation. I do not say this rhetorically, but base the statement upon the fact that rocket bases and nuclear missiles cover our planet and rest upon warning systems of a few minutes. This entire apparatus of global butchery depends upon radar, which is incapable of distinguishing natural phenomena from missiles. Many of *Harper's* readers will be familiar with the kinds of statements made by insurance companies concerning the possibility and likelihood of accidents with regard to airplane flights and automobile transport. We know there will be a mean number of accidents each year, although we cannot say which cars will crash or planes fall. So it is a simple problem of mathematical statistics that with each day the possibility of total annihilation through accident increases to a point of near certainty.

In the Cold War, the two giants competing for power ruthlessly extirpate every semblance of human decency wherever they are able to do so in pursuit of their mad struggle. The United States, for example, imposes intolerable regimes upon Asian, Latin-American, and Middle Eastern countries, and economically exploits the great majority of mankind who live at below-subsistence level to support American profit. Similar things can be said of the Soviet Union, but Americans need reminding of the nature of the society they inhabit. Devil theory, fanaticism, such as was practiced in the Thirty Years' War and evident in the conflicts between Catholics and Protestants, Christians and Moslems, will eliminate life from our planet. The Russians are not devils. Their record is comparable to that of any other nation State, no better, little worse. The American government pursues a policy of genocide. This is a plain statement of fact. You, like Eichmann, acquiesce in this policy and you, like him, have the imperative moral responsibility to demand an end to such a policy. It can be done, if cowardice is put aside for clarity.

Yours faithfully,
Bertrand Russell

March 10, 1963

Dear Lord Russell:

Thank you for your letter of March 4. It is the best possible illustration of my main point in that article to which you refer: that when scientists stray outside of their own field, they are likely to come up with some rather curious notions.

For example, it is a simple, easily verifiable matter of fact that the American nuclear missile does *not* "rest upon warning systems of a few minutes" nor does its apparatus "depend upon radar, which is incapable of distinguishing natural phenomena from missiles." The primary purpose of the Polaris and Minuteman systems is to eliminate dependence upon any sort of warning system, and to make possible a deliberate, slow reaction. If a Russian missile were to land on American territory, therefore, there need be no immediate retaliation. The President could take whatever time might be necessary to find out whether the missile was fired by accident, or whether it was fired as part of a deliberate attack. Moreover, this country has established an elaborate system of safeguards which makes it virtually inconceivable that a missile could ever be fired by accident; and it seems quite probable that the Russians have developed similar systems of their own.

I doubt you will convince very many Americans that their government is pursuing "a policy of genocide," that it "imposes intolerable regimes" upon other countries, or that we are exploiting other peoples "to support American profit." On the contrary, other peoples are exploiting us at the rate of a good many billions of dollars a year given them as foreign aid.

Finally, I was puzzled by your suggestion that the article misrepresented your views. Do you mean that you are *not* advocating unilateral disarmament?

Sincerely,
John Fischer

Dear Mr. Fischer,

You suffer from what the theologians call "invincible ignorance." You also lack acquaintance with elementary logic. *Ad hominem* comment is no help to argument. Even if the absurd contention [were made] that men of particular intelligence are less well equipped to comment on public affairs than men of practiced ignorance, it would still be necessary to examine the remarks of the former on their merit in order to refute their claims. It will not help you to call scientists names. To complain of their training as a means of coping with their contentions is not an argument but a prejudice.

I shall examine the facts since you show so unbelievable an ignorance of them. You assert unabashedly:

> It is a simple, easily verifiable matter of fact that the American nuclear missile system does *not* "rest upon warning systems of a few minutes"; nor does its apparatus "depend upon radar, which is incapable of distinguishing natural phenomena from missiles."

And I thought that the Americans were telling the truth when they justified their blockade of sovereign Cuba by invoking the danger provided by wicked Russian missiles. These missiles were dangerous because they reduced the warning time, said Mr. Kennedy. But perhaps he was following the procedure announced by Mr. Sylvester [1] and "lied in the national interest."

The DEW-Line system and NORAD [2] are a fantasy, I suppose. This radar network is designed to detect oncoming missiles, and the firing of American missiles is said to depend upon the information provided by DEW-Line and NORAD. The warning system upon which SAC works is fifteen minutes. The warning system in Britain is four minutes. All of the rocket bases are primed according to signals expected on radar registering missile attack. Would you claim that SAC and rocket bases abroad are *not* part of the American nuclear missile and bomber system?

So much for that contention. With regard to the reliability of radar, Sir Robert Watson-Watt, who is the inventor of radar, has declared unequivocally that radar can not distinguish natural phenomena from missiles. The Director of Jodrell Bank, Sir Bernard Lovell, has stated that it would not be possible to distinguish on radar between meteorites and missiles. There have been a large number of accidents due to the faultiness of radar. NORAD interpreted the rising of the moon as an invading Russian armada and on the basis of this error the signal to attack was given; only the freak occurrence of an iceberg cutting an underwater cable delayed it sufficiently to cause doubt in the mind of a Canadian commander. [3]

The Mershon National Security Report, published on June 28, 1960, itemizes fifty accidents involving nuclear weapons including twelve major accidents. It predicted accidental nuclear war during the 1960's as a matter

[1] Presumably Arthur Sylvester, Assistant Secretary of Defense for Public Affairs; if so, the words in quotation marks are a misquotation.—J.F.

[2] Presumably references to the Distant Early Warning radar network and the North American Air Defense Command.—J.F.

[3] Where Lord Russell heard these alarming tales is unclear.—J.F.

of statistical probability. It lists the accidents caused by radar and confirms the statements concerning its faulty character made by Watson-Watt and Lovell. So much for the infallibility of radar.

You say categorically that the safeguards taken make it inconceivable that a missile could be fired by accident. In 1958 twelve Nike missiles were fired because of an electrical short circuit. Twenty-four warheads were scattered less than a day before the missiles were to be fitted with hydrogen warheads. The Mershon report lists comparable examples.

As regards the Minuteman missile, Professor Ralph Lapp states: "It might go by accident, it might be tampered with by saboteurs, or fired by fanatics."

After discussing safety precautions concerning ICBMs, President Kennedy stated: "All the safety factors leave a serious loophole in the control of ICBMs."

Lloyd V. Berkner, organizer of the International Geophysical Year, stated:

As large numbers of fast-flying missiles come into the possession of both sides, ready for use, critical command will tend to devolve to lower and lower echelons. To some extent this is already occurring. If we are going to be able to retaliate effectively, it will become less and less practicable to assemble Congress or to call together the Cabinet or even for the President to be consulted when missiles with the ultimate destructive power are seen flying toward us.

As Professor Lapp put it, "In the era of missile warfare, the control of nuclear weapons steadily becomes more diffuse and the danger of war through accident, miscalculation, or madness must rise accordingly."

The President of the American Psychological Association, Dr. Charles E. Osgood, stated: "The maintenance of peace depends upon rational behavior by those in control; yet in the present era of great danger we are more than ever at the mercy of 'the unpredictability of human behavior under stress.'"

On the same subject, Professor Lapp stated: "This unpredictability applies equally to chiefs of state and to lower echelons. But with the diffusion of control of nuclear weapons to more and more hands, the chances of someone breaking under the stress are multiplied."

Stockpiles of nuclear warheads are available at bases of the West German Air Force and may, according to President Kennedy, be turned over to the Germans in emergency! When a B-52 bomber had to jettison a 24-megaton bomb over North Carolina, five of the six "safety" mechanisms had been triggered. One switch separated us from the obliteration of a vast area. So it is that the following men have stated the danger:

Accidental nuclear warfare is extremely likely. —*Lord Hailsham*
Future generations will look back with amazement if war is averted.
—*John Foster Dulles*
These modern weapons are simply too hot to handle and as time goes on, the curve of probability that they will go off will steadily rise. —*Thomas K. Finletter*
If developments continue as they have during the last fifteen years, I believe all-out nuclear war is, in the long run, inevitable. —*Harrison Brown*
Every year, every month lost is not just marking time . . . but a lightning-fast slide to the line separating peace from the blast of rocket nuclear war. —*Andrei Gromyko*

As for genocide, this is a simple matter of definition. The utilization of the nuclear rockets will entail the murder of hundreds of millions. This is genocide.

I shall list the intolerable regimes supported solely by American capital and American guns: Vietnam, South Korea, Thailand, Paraguay, Peru, Chile, Ecuador, Bolivia, Guatemala, Haiti, Formosa, and Spain. There are others. There are even more who are tolerated for just as long as they do not challenge American economic exploitation. Greece, Portugal, and France are tyrannies and all three maintain camps for political prisoners.

I enclose a copy of my article in the *Bulletin of the Atomic Scientists* in which I once again repeat my position as stated in *Commonsense and Nuclear Warfare* and in *Has Man a Future*. It can be found in countless articles and interviews. It is perfectly clear you have never read my writing on the subject and I challenge you to provide the source for the view you attribute to me in your article.

It amuses me to have you suggest that I am unfamiliar with the issues about which I write, and that questions of war and peace are not my province. I have written on social issues since 1896 and on matters of peace and war and international politics for over fifty years.

I can not say whether your ignorance on these matters is real or whether you suppress the facts which alarm you. I can say that it is abominable for a man who edits a journal to be both so ill-informed and so prepared to write on the subjects of which he has no knowledge. This practice spreads ignorance and untruth.

I should wish you to publish this letter along with yours of 10 March.

Yours faithfully,
Bertrand Russell

March 21, 1963

Dear Lord Russell:

Your main trouble, it would appear from your letter of March 15, is a confusion between warning time and reaction time. This is not surprising, since there was a period some years ago when the two concepts were closely related. During that period the American deterrent was made up entirely of bombers, based on highly vulnerable airfields. Consequently it was necessary for them to get off the ground within about fifteen minutes after a radar warning might be received of an enemy attack. (This did not mean, of course, that they had to launch a retaliatory attack of their own on such short notice, but the reaction time was still relatively short: that is, a decision would have to be made within the few hours that a plane could stay in flight.)

Within the last two years, we have been in the process of replacing manned bombers and the early, vulnerable type of missiles such as the Thor, Jupiter, and Titan, with new varieties of missiles which are largely invulnerable to enemy attack. These are the Minutemen, located in "hardened" underground sites scattered over a very wide area, and the Polaris, which can be fired from submarines under water. It is most unlikely that even a massive enemy attack could knock out more than a very small percentage of either the Minuteman or Polaris systems. Consequently, they have become entirely independent of the radar warning network. This network is still maintained, for whatever minor service it might be to unhardened installations and to the civilian population, but the firing of American missiles is *not* dependent upon the information provided by DEW-Line and NORAD as you suggested in your letter of March 15. These new missiles would not need to be fired until after enemy missiles had actually landed on American territory, and if it seemed advisable, any retaliatory action could be delayed for days or weeks until it could be fully determined whether the enemy attack was accidental or intentional.

As the Minuteman and Polaris systems are being completed, the obsolescent bomber bases and early-generation missiles are being taken out of service, both here and abroad. The manufacture of strategic bombers has already been stopped, and—as you may know—American bombers and early-generation missiles have been removed from a number of overseas sites, including Turkey, England, Italy, and Morocco.

Two other misconceptions mentioned in your letter deserve comment:

(1) The Nike missile is a short-range antiaircraft weapon; it is not fitted with a hydrogen warhead. There has never been an accidental explosion of a nuclear weapon.

(2) The statement of Dr. Ralph Lapp's which you quoted about the Minuteman missile was apparently made while this weapon was in the early stage of development. If you are interested in the precautions taken to prevent accidental firing of a Minuteman missile, you might glance through the attached reprint.[4]

Since you seem to speak frequently on these matters, and since you state rather emphatically that you are opposed to the spreading of misinformation, I thought you might want to acquaint yourself with some of the current facts.

Sincerely,
John Fischer

March 24, 1963

Dear Mr. Fischer:

Our controversy has centered on the issue of accidental war and the nature of American policy. You are unable to refute the overwhelming evidence of specific and statistical kind. You are unable to "unwrite" the Mershon Report, the work of the Pugwash scientists whose competence in their fields is real, the statements of Kennedy, Dulles, Gromyko, Hailsham, and scores of others. And you are unwilling to grasp what you would never deny with regard to the data of insurance companies on accidents in many spheres. Insofar as hundreds of millions of lives are involved, I have no compunction in saying to you that you enhance the prospect of annihilation by your journalism.

The electrical failure which detonated Nike missiles in 1958, the in-

[4] Of an article published in *Harper's* in May 1962, entitled "Sixty Ivory Towers Forty Feet Underground."

stance of total mental breakdown such as has been recently recorded for American missile officers, the occurrence of a mad first-strike act by a rebellious commander are all part of the data concerning accidental nuclear war. Kennedy's remarks were directed to "hardened" ICBMs.

The "invulnerability" to hydrogen attack from 100-megaton weapons may delude you but its absurdity deludes few other than military propagandists. The errors on radar which give false evidence of massive attack will provoke reply. The Institute for Strategic Studies assesses the strategic strength for early 1963 on the part of the United States to include over 1,600 medium-range bombers, 600 long-range bombers, 250 medium-range missiles, and 500 long-range missiles. If you think that this arsenal will not come into use should radar show a massive attack, I leave you to your delusion. If the missiles which detonated in 1958 are now said to have been antiaircraft weapons, the claims of the time were lies. The danger is in no way lessened.

Finally, Polaris submarines are increasingly detectable and sinkable. So much so that there is serious consideration of going over to surface vessels. As the day approaches that radar is not felt to give "warning" or "reaction time," the likelihood that either side will feel compelled to strike first will increase. There are many crises brewing in this world, many of them because of the American exploitative policy I have specified, and in each the probability of an error of judgment is high.

Any claim that "accidental war is impossible," any statement that rational acts are guaranteed and American judgment is infallible, are lunatic. I note in this discussion your insensitivity to the issues couched in such grand and pseudo-technical jargon. The issues concern vast suffering and agony, mass murder and devastation. How extraordinary that men so diminished as those who can discuss this without awareness of what they do should escape universal opprobrium. In a long life during which I have often observed the vanity and cruelty of men I can not cite a more cold-blooded parallel.

I should be grateful for your permission to publish this correspondence.

Yours faithfully,
Bertrand Russell

April 3, 1963

Dear Lord Russell:

Our recent correspondence leaves me with a certain feeling of frustration, because we seem to be talking about different things—and because I apparently have failed completely to make my position clear. May I try once more?

(1) I have never suggested that "accidental war is impossible," that rational acts are guaranteed, or that American judgment is infallible. Obviously nothing is impossible and no one is infallible. I do regard accidental war as most unlikely, and I have tried to set forth some of the facts on which this view is based. Your own view—that accidental nuclear war is inevitable, or at least highly probable—seems to me to be based on some facts

which are now obsolete, other "facts" which never existed, and on an almost total misconception of American policy.

(2) So far as I know, we do not disagree on two points: that a nuclear war would be an unparalleled catastrophe, and that every conceivable effort should be made to reach a satisfactory agreement on nuclear disarmament. What reasonable man could believe otherwise?

(3) Where we do differ, apparently, is on what would constitute a "satisfactory" disarmament agreement, and how it might be reached. If I correctly understand your position—as set forth in your letters, your article in the March 1962 issue of the *Bulletin of the Atomic Scientists*, and your other recent writings and speeches—you would like to see Britain abandon nuclear weapons, adopt a position of neutrality, and break up the NATO alliance. This in itself would constitute a considerable degree of unilateral disarmament by the West, and (in my view) would bring war dangerously closer by tempting the Soviet Union to further aggression.

In addition, if your statements have been correctly reported in the British press, you advocate American acceptance of a disarmament agreement that contains no adequate provisions for verification or inspection. This simply would be the equivalent of complete unilateral disarmament by the West, since there is no reason to believe, on the basis of the historical record, that the Soviet Union would keep such an agreement for a moment.

(4) It is also part of this historical record that the United States made the first and most sweeping proposals for nuclear disarmament—offering, *at a time when we had a monopoly of nuclear weapons*, to abolish them and to turn all nuclear technology over to an international agency (the so-called Baruch-Acheson-Lilienthal proposals in 1946). Since that time, American negotiators have persisted, with infinite patience, in trying to reach an agreement that will effectively control or eliminate nuclear arms. So far, apparently, they have been unable to evoke any serious interest from either the Russians or General de Gaulle. Under these circumstances, I am at a loss to know what further steps this country might take.

(5) There is no point in arguing with you about the nature of American society or American policy. Anyone who really believes that "the power of decision" in this country rests "in the hands of semi-literate paranoids compulsively acting out their sick hates and their blind malice"—as you put it in the *Bulletin* article—obviously is beyond persuasion.

On a few subordinate matters, however, I do hope that you might be willing to re-examine the facts. For example, no nuclear weapon, so far as I can discover, was ever detonated by accident; [5] the Nike is and always was, a short-range antiaircraft weapon, and I can find no published suggestion to the contrary; I know of no evidence of "total mental breakdown . . . recently recorded for American missile officers," or of "a mad first-strike act by a rebellious commander." (If you have any such evidence I would be glad to hear of it.) President Kennedy has never proposed that nuclear warheads

[5] It is conceivable, of course, that some such accident may have happened in Russia without the knowledge of the outside world; but there is no reason to believe this might be so.

"be turned over to the Germans in an emergency"; that would be contrary both to treaty obligations and to American law. There is no "serious consideration of going over to surface vessels" as a replacement for the Polaris submarines because they are "increasingly detectable and sinkable." (The suggestion that a European multi-national nuclear force might use surface vessels was advanced because they are cheaper than submarines, not because they are less vulnerable; they are not. And such a force would be intended to supplement, not replace, the Polaris.) All I am suggesting is that you should examine such documents as the so-called "Mershon Report" [6] with the same intellectual vigor that you once applied to the arguments of G. E. Moore and Wittgenstein.

(6) Finally, rising population pressures throughout the world seem to me a greater danger, in the long run, than the existence of nuclear weapons, since if they are not checked they will make war virtually inevitable. Is it too much to hope that you might enlist your considerable energies as a propagandist in this kind of peace movement?

Certainly you have my permission to publish this correspondence, provided it is published in full, including this letter.

Sincerely,
John Fischer

[6] An unofficial document issued by the Mershon Center for Education in National Security, at Ohio State University.

WALTER LIPPMANN

THE NUCLEAR AGE

"... For as long a time as we can see into the future, we shall be living between ... a war that cannot be fought and a peace that cannot be achieved...."

THE age we are living in is radically new in human experience. During the past fifteen years or so there has occurred a profound revolution in human affairs, and we are the first generation that has lived under these new conditions. There has taken place a development in the art of war, and this is causing a revolutionary change in the foreign relations of all the nations of the world. The radical development is, of course, the production of nuclear weapons.

As a scientific phenomenon, the nuclear age began with the explosion at Los Alamos in 1945; but in world relations the nuclear age really began about ten years later. During the 1940s the United States was the only nuclear power in the world. But by the middle fifties and in the years following, the Soviet Union had created an armory of nuclear weapons and had built rockets which have made it, for all practical purposes of diplomacy, a nuclear power equal to the United States. The essential fact about the appearance of two opposed great powers armed with nuclear weapons is that war, which is an ancient habit of mankind, has become mutually destructive. Nuclear war is a way of mutual suicide. The modern weapons are not merely much bigger and more dangerous than any which existed before. They have introduced into the art of warfare a wholly new kind of violence.

Always, in the past, war and the threat of war, whether aggressive or defensive, were usable instruments. They were usable instruments in the sense that nations could go to war for their national purposes. Nations could transform themselves from petty states to great powers by means of war. They could enlarge their territories, acquire profitable colonies, change the religion of a vanquished population, all by means of war. War was the instrument with which the social, political, and legal systems of large areas were changed. Thus, in the old days before the nuclear age began, war was a usable—however horrible and expensive—instrument of national purpose. The reason for that was that the old wars could be won.

In the pre-nuclear age, right down through World War II, the victorious power was an organized state which could impose its will on the vanquished. The United States did that with Germany and with Japan. The damage they had suffered, although it was great, was not irreparable, as we know from the recovery after World War II of West Germany and Japan, as well as the Soviet Union.

But from a full nuclear war, which might well mean a hundred million dead, after the devastation of the great urban centers of the Northern Hemisphere and the contamination of the earth, the water, and the air, there would be no such recovery as we have seen after the two world wars of this century.

The damage done would be mutual. There would be no victor. The United States has the nuclear power to reduce Soviet society to a smoldering ruin, leaving the wretched survivors shocked and starving and diseased. In an interchange of nuclear weapons, it is estimated coolly by experts who have studied the possibility, the Soviet Union would kill between thirty and seventy million Americans.

A war of that kind would not be followed by reconstruction; it would not be followed by a Marshall Plan and by all the constructive things that were done after World War II. A nuclear war would be followed by a savage struggle for existence, as the survivors crawled out of their shelters; and the

American republic would have to be replaced by a stringent military dictatorship, trying to keep some kind of order among the desperate survivors.

To his great credit, President Eisenhower was quick to realize what nuclear war would be. After he and Prime Minister Churchill had studied some of the results of the nuclear tests, President Eisenhower made the historic declaration that there was no longer any alternative to peace.

When President Eisenhower made that statement no one of us, I think, understood its full significance and consequences. We are now beginning to understand them, and here, I venture to say, is the root of the frustration and the confusion which torment us. For while nuclear weapons have made war, the old arbiter of human affairs, an impossible action for a rational statesman to contemplate, we do not have any other reliable way of dealing with issues that used to be resolved by war.

It is enormously difficult to make peace. It is intolerably dangerous and useless to make war about the fundamental issues. That is where our contemporary frustration and confusion originate. We are confronted with an extraordinarily tantalizing and nerve-racking dilemma.

For as long a time as we can see into the future, we shall be living between war and peace, between a war that cannot be fought and a peace that cannot be achieved. The great issues which divide the world cannot be decided by a war that could be won, and they cannot be settled by a treaty that can be negotiated. Our world is divided as it has not been since the religious wars of the seventeenth century, and a large part of the globe is in a great upheaval, the like of which has not been known since the end of the Middle Ages. But the power which used to deal with the divisions and conflicts of the past—namely, organized war—has become an impossible instrument to use.

President Eisenhower and President Kennedy are the only two American Presidents who ever lived in a world like this one. It is a great puzzle to know how to defend the nation's rights and how to promote its interests in the nuclear age. There are no clear guidelines of action because there are no precedents for the situation in which we find ourselves. And as statesmen grope their way from one improvisation and accommodation to another, there are masses of people who are frightened, irritated, impatient, frustrated, and in search of quick and easy solutions.

The nuclear age is only a few years old. But we have already learned one or two things about how to conduct policy in this age. It was once said of a British admiral in World War I that if he made a mistake, he could lose the British Fleet and with it the whole war in an afternoon. Mr. Khrushchev and Mr. Kennedy are in a similar position today. In a few days or so Mr. Khrushchev can lose the Soviet state and the promise of a Communist economy. He can lose all the work of the Five-Year Plans, Seven-Year Plans, and Twenty-Year Plans. In that same time, Mr. Kennedy can lose the Constitution of the United States, the free-enterprise system, and the American way of life, and along with them all the frontiers, old and new. I don't think I am exaggerating. A full nuclear war would produce by far the biggest convulsion which has ever occurred in recorded history. We cannot understand the realities of the Khrushchev-Kennedy encounter, which has been going on since they met at Vienna last June, unless we remind ourselves again and again of what war has become in the nuclear age.

The poor dears among us who say that they have had enough of all this talking and negotiating and now let us drop the bomb have no idea of what they are talking about. They do not know what has happened in the past twenty years. They belong to the past, and they have not been able to realize what a nuclear war would be.

Only a moral idiot with a suicidal mania would press the button for a nuclear war. Yet we have learned that, while a nuclear war would be lunacy, it is nevertheless an ever-present possibility. Why? Because, however lunatic it might be to commit suicide, a nation can be provoked and exasperated to the point of lunacy where its nervous system cannot endure inaction, where only violence can relieve its feelings. This is one of the facts of life in the middle of the twentieth century. The nerves of a nation can stand only so much provocation and humiliation, and beyond the tolerable limits, it will plunge into lunacy. This is as much a real fact as is the megaton bomb, and it is a fact which must be given great weight in the calculation of national policy. It is the central fact in the whole diplomatic problem of dealing with the cold war. There is a line of intolerable provocation beyond which reactions become uncontrollable. It is the business of the governments to find out where that line is and to stay well back of it.

Those who do not understand the nature of war in the nuclear age, those who think that war today is what it was against Mexico or Spain or in the two world wars, regard the careful attempts of statesmen not to carry the provocation past the tolerable limit as weakness and softness and appeasement. It is not any of these things. It is not softness. It is sanity.

But it leaves us with a task: because we cannot make war, because we cannot achieve peace, we must find some other way of meeting the great issues which confront us. For life will go on, and if the answers of the past do not work, other answers must exist and must be found.

The answer lies, I believe, in the nature of the struggle between our Western society and the Communist society.

It is often said that the struggle which divides the world is for the minds and the souls of men. That is true. As long as there exists a balance of power and of terror, neither side can impose its doctrine and its ideology upon the other. The struggle for the minds of men, moreover, is not, I believe, going to be decided by propaganda. We are not going to convert our adversaries, and they are not going to convert us.

The struggle, furthermore, is not going to be ended in any foreseeable time. At bottom it is a competition between two societies, and it resembles more than any other thing in our historical experience the long centuries of conflict between Christendom and Islam. The modern competition between the two societies turns on their respective capacities to become powerful and rich, to become the leaders in science and technology, to see that their people are properly educated and able to operate such a society, to keep their people healthy, and to give them the happiness of knowing that they are able and free to work for their best hopes.

The historic rivalry of the two societies and of the two civilizations which they contain is not going to be decided by what happens on the periphery and in the outposts. It is going to be decided by what goes on in the heart of each of the two societies. The heart of Western civilization lies on the shores of the Atlantic Ocean, and our future depends on what goes on in the Atlantic community. Will this community advance? Can the nations which compose it work together? Can it become a great and secure center of power and of wealth, of light and of leading? To work for these ends is to be engaged truly in the great conflict of our age and to be doing the real work that we are challenged to do. I speak with some hope and confidence. For I believe that in the months to come we shall engage ourselves in the long and complicated, but splendidly constructive, task of bringing together in one liberal and progressive economic community all the trading nations which do not belong to the Communist society.

I dare to believe that this powerful Western economic community will be able to live safely and without fear in the same world as the Soviet Union and that the rising power and influence of the Western society will exert a beneficent magnetic attraction upon eastern Europe. This will happen if we approach it in the right way. Jean Monnet, who is the original founder of this movement, has put it the right way. "We cannot build our future," he has said, "if we are obsessed with fear of Russia. Let us build our own strength and health, not against anyone, but for ourselves, so that we will become so strong that no one will dare attack us, and so progressive and prosperous that we set a model for all other peoples—indeed, for the Russians themselves."

At the same time, the wealth and confidence of the new community will enable the Western society to assist and draw to it the societies of the Southern Hemisphere, where social and economic change is proceeding rapidly.

You will have seen that I do not agree with those who think that in order to defend ourselves and to survive we must put a stop to the progressive movement which has gone on throughout this century. This movement began in the Administration of Theodore Roosevelt. Its purpose was to reform and advance our own social order, and at the same time to recognize that we must live in the world beyond our frontiers. We shall lose all our power to cope with our problems if we allow ourselves to become a stagnant, neurotic, frightened, and suspicious people. Let us not punish ourselves by denying ourselves the hope, by depriving ourselves of the oldest American dream, that we are making a better society on this earth than has ever been made before.

Is all this conservative? Is all this liberal? Is it all progressive? It is, I say, all of these. There is no irreconcilable contradiction among these noble adjectives. Do not Republicans believe in democracy, and do not Democrats believe in a republic? Such labels may describe political parties in England; they do not describe political attitudes in the United States.

Every truly civilized and enlightened man is conservative and liberal and progressive. A civilized man is conservative in that his deepest loyalty is to the Western heritage of ideas which originated on the shores of the Mediterranean Sea. Because of that loyalty he is the indefatigable defender of our own constitutional doctrine, which is that all power, all government, all officials, all parties, and all majorities are under the law—and that none of them is sovereign and omnipotent.

The civilized man is a liberal because the writing and the administration of the laws should be done with enlightenment and compassion, with tolerance and charity, and with affection.

And the civilized man is progressive because the times change and the social order evolves and new things are invented and changes occur. This conservative who is a liberal is a progressive because he must work and live, he must govern and debate in the world, as it is in his own time and as it is going to become.

JOSEPH FLETCHER

THE PATIENT'S RIGHT TO DIE

"...Where can we draw the line between prolonging a patient's life and prolonging his dying? ..."

ON HIS way to the hospital a minister stops at a house near his church to say a word of personal sympathy to a couple sitting on the porch with their family doctor. Upstairs the man's mother is in bed, the victim of a series of small cerebral hemorrhages over the last eleven years. Her voice went two years ago and there is now no sign that she hears anything. Communication has ended. Says the son, with a complex question-asking glance at his wife, "My mother is already dead."

Listening to those telltale words, the doctor shakes his head sympathetically and helplessly. To the minister, that involuntary gesture seems almost a ritual. Earlier that day another doctor did exactly the same thing when the minister told him about his talk with a family whose twenty-year-old son has been lying in the "living death" of complete coma for four years. An auto crash hopelessly shattered his cerebral cortex. Since then only the brain stem has sustained life. All thought and feeling have been erased, and he hasn't moved a single muscle of his body since the accident. But he is in "excellent health" although he feels no stimulus of any kind, from within or without. Once an angular blond youth of sixteen, he is now a baby-faced brunette seemingly ten years old. He is fed through an indwelling nasal tube. He suffers no pain, only reacts by reflex to a needle jab. His mother says, "My son is dead."

Later, at the hospital, the minister visits a woman in her early seventies. He had last seen her at her fiftieth wedding-anniversary party two months earlier. She has now been in the hospital for a week with what was tentatively thought to be "degenerative arthritis." But the diagnosis is bone cancer. Both legs were already fractured when she arrived at the hospital and little bits of her bones are splintering all the time; she has agonizing shaking attacks that break them off. She turns away from her clerical caller and looks at her husband. "I ought to die. Why can't I die?" It is the living that fear death, not the dying.

The minister leaves, somehow feeling guilty, and goes upstairs to Surgical. An intern and a young resident in surgery grab his arms and say, "Come on, join our council of war." They go into an empty room where two staff physicians and the chaplain are waiting. In the next room a man is dying, slowly, in spite of their ingenious attempt to save him from pneumonic suffocation by means of a "tracheotomy," a hole cut in his throat through which an artificial respirator is used. The question is: should they take away the oxygen tank, let the patient go? The chaplain is pulled two ways. One of the doctors is against it, the other joins the resident in favor. The intern says he doesn't "like" it. The visiting clergyman says, "I would." They do. The oxygen is removed, the light turned off, the door closed behind them. Then they send the chaplain to comfort the widow out in the alcove at the end of the hall, saying, "We are doing everything we can."

This heartbreaking struggle over mercy death has become a standard drama in hospital novels—most recently in Richard Frede's *The Interns*. Physicians and clergymen struggle constantly in the most vital, intimate, and highly personal centers of human existence. The "primary events" of birth, procreation, and death, are their daily fare. Ultimate as well as immediate concerns tax their capacity for creative and loving decisions. Squarely and continually confronting them is death, the prospect of nonbeing which lurks out of sight though never wholly out of mind for most of us. Because most people cannot look it in the eye they cling to irrational, phobic, and sentimental attitudes about voluntary death and the medical control of dying. They cannot see death as experienced doctors and ministers do—in perspective, a familiar adversary. This is the case even among psychologists. For example, many aspects were discussed in a recent sympo-

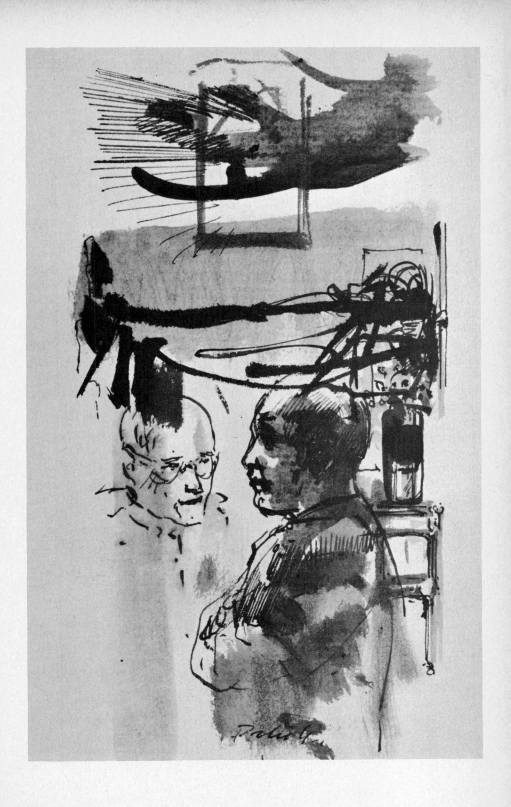

sium, *The Meaning of Death*, at a convention of the American Psychological Association. But nothing whatever was said about the growing problem of dying in dignity. Bad words such as "euthanasia" were unmentioned.

We are, however, becoming somewhat less irrational than our forebears on this subject. At the level of sheer logic, one of the most curious features of the "theological era" of the past is that most people feared and sought to avoid death at any and every cost, except sometimes for honor's sake. Even though they professed to have faith in personal survival after death, it was their Worst Enemy. Nowadays, when faith is waning not only in the prospect of hell but even of heaven, there is a trend toward accepting death as a part of reality, just as "natural" as life. Churchmen, even clergymen, are dropping the traditional faith in personal survival after death, just as many unbelievers do. Curiously, it is the skeptics about immortality who appear to face death more calmly. They seem somehow less inclined to hang on desperately to life at the cost of indescribable and uncreative suffering for themselves and others.

But a painful conflict persists. For instance, not long ago a man came to me deeply depressed about his role, or lack of one, in his mother's death. She had been an invalid for years, requiring his constant care and attention. At last her illness reached a "terminal" stage and she had to be taken to the hospital. One Saturday after work when he arrived in her semi-private room the other patient greeted him by crying out, "I think your mother has just passed away. See. Quick! His immediate reaction was relief that her suffering, and his, were now ended; so he hesitated to act on the other patient's plea to breathe into his mother's mouth in an effort to resuscitate her. Ever since, he had been troubled by a profound sense of guilt. His "conscience" accused him. This conflict is a "lay" version of what many doctors, if not most, feel when they forgo some device that might sustain a patient's life a little longer. Some are comforted when their action, or inaction, is interpreted to them as a refusal to prolong the patient's *death*.

In truth, the whole problem of letting people "go" in a merciful release is a relatively new one. It is largely the result of our fabulous success in medical science and technology. Not long ago, when the point of death was reached, there was usually nothing that could be done about it. Now, due to the marvels of medicine, all kinds of things can keep people "alive" long after what used to be the final crisis. For example, there is the cardiac "pacemaker," a machine that can restart a heart that has stopped beating. Turn off the machine, the heart stops. Is the patient alive? Is he murdered if it is taken away? Does he commit suicide if he throws it out the window? Artificial respirators and kidneys, vital organ transplants, antibiotics, intravenous feeding—these and many other devices have the double effect of prolonging life and prolonging dying. The right to die in dignity is a problem raised more often by medicine's successes than by its failures. Consequently, there is a new dimension in the debate about "euthanasia." The old-fashioned question was simply this: "May we morally do anything to put people mercifully out of hopeless misery?" But the issue now takes a more troubling twist:

"May we morally omit to do any of the ingenious things we *could* do to prolong people's suffering?"

For doctors, this dilemma challenges the Hippocratic oath which commits them to increasingly incompatible duties—to preserve life and to relieve suffering. This conflict of conscience is steadily magnified by the swelling numbers of elderly people. Medical genius and sanitation have resulted in greater longevity for most of our population. In consequence, the predominant forms of illness are now degenerative—the maladies of age and physical failure—not the infectious diseases. Disorders in the metabolic group, renal problems, malignancy, cardio-vascular ills, are chronic rather than acute. Adults in middle life and beyond fill the beds of our hospitals, and the sixty-five-and-over class grows fastest of all. Under these circumstances, many people fear the prospect of senility far more than they fear death.

Unless we face up to the facts with moral sturdiness our hospitals and homes will become mausoleums where the inmates exist in a living death. In this day of "existential" outlook, in its religious and nonreligious versions, we might think twice on Nietzsche's observation, "In certain cases it is indecent to go on living." Perhaps it is a supreme lack of faith and self-respect to continue, as he put it, "to vegetate in a state of cowardly dependence upon doctors and special treatments, once the meaning of life, the right to life has been lost."

Consider an actual case, in a top-flight hospital. After a history of rheumatic heart disease a man was admitted with both mitral and aortic stenosis—a blockage of the heart valves by something like a calcium deposit. The arts and mechanics of medicine at once went into play. First open-heart surgery opened the mitral valve. Then—the patient's heart still sluggish—the operation was repeated. But the failure of blood pressure brought on kidney failure. While the doctors weighed a choice between a kidney transplant and an artificial kidney machine, staphylococcal pneumonia set in. Next antibiotics were tried and failed to bring relief, driving them to try a tracheotomy. Meanwhile the heart action flagged so much that breathing failed even through the surgical throat opening. The doctors then tried oxygen through nasal tubes, and failed; next, they hooked him into an artificial respirator. For a long time, technically speaking, the machine did his breathing. Then, in spite of all their brilliant efforts, he died.

Should they have "let him go" sooner into the Christian heaven or Lucretius' "long good night"? If so, at what point? Would it have been "playing God" to stop before the second operation? Before the tracheotomy? Before the respirator? Only the ignorant imagine that these are easy decisions. In practice they are complex even for those who favor merciful deaths in principle. Doctors as responsible ministers of medicine carry an awesome responsibility. Indeed, by their very use of surgical, chemical, and mechanical devices they are, in a fashion, playing God. In this case from the beginning some of the doctors had little hope, but they felt obliged to do what they could. A few insisted that they had to do everything possible *even if they felt sure they would fail.* Where can we draw the line between prolonging a patient's life and prolonging his dying?

The ugly truth is that sometimes patients *in extremis* try to outwit the doctors and escape from medicine's ministrations. They swallow Kleenex to suffocate themselves, or jerk tubes out of their noses or veins, in a cat-and-mouse game of life and death which is neither merciful nor meaningful. Medical innovation makes it ever easier to drag people back to "life" in merely physiological terms. Yet when these patients succeed in outwitting their medical ministrants, can we say that they have committed suicide in any real sense of the word? Who is actually alive in these contrivances and contraptions? In such a puppetlike state most patients are, of course, too weakened and drugged to take any truly human initiative.

The classical deathbed scene, with its loving partings and solemn last words, is practically a thing of the past. In its stead is a sedated, comatose, betubed object, manipulated and subconscious, if not subhuman. This is why, for example, one desperate woman is trying to guarantee herself a fatal heart attack to avoid anything like her mother's imbecile last years. It is an unnerving experience to any sensitive person to hear an intern on the terminal ward of a hospital say with defensive gallows humor that he has to "go water the vegetables" in their beds.

Families—and their emotional and economic resources—deserve some reckoning too. And finally, all of us are potential patients. Surely we need to give these questions a fresh look, even though the obligation lies heaviest on leaders in medicine and allied fields.

It is an oversimplification to think of the issue any longer as "euthanasia" and decide for or against it. Euthanasia, meaning a merciful or good death, may be achieved by direct or indirect methods. If it is direct, a deliberate action or "mercy-killing" to shorten or end life, it is definitely murder as the law now stands. But indirect euthanasia is another matter, the more complicated and by far the more frequent form of the problem. There are three forms it can take: (1) administering a death-dealing pain-killer, (2) ceasing treatments that prolong the patient's life—or death, if you prefer, and (3) withholding treatment altogether.

An example of the first form is the administration of morphine in doses which are pyramided to toxic, fatal proportions. The doctor has been forced to choose between doing nothing further to alleviate suffering, or giving a merciful dose which kills both the pain and the patient. Usually he chooses the latter course. An example of the second form is the hospital scene described earlier when two doctors, a resident, an intern, a chaplain, and a visiting minister agreed to "pull the plug" and disconnect the bubbling life-prolonging oxygen tank.

To illustrate the third form of indirect euthanasia we might look at this practical problem. A poliomyelitis patient—a young woman—is struck down by an extensive paralysis of the respiratory muscles. Lacking oxygen, her brain suffers irreparable damage from suffocation. She *could* be kept "alive" for months—maybe longer—by artificial respiration through a tracheostomy.

However, is there anything in moral law, either the law of nature, the law of Scripture, or the law of love, that obliges us to use such extraordinary means, such gimmicks? If we forgo their use, and let the patient die of natural asphyxiation, we have "euthanased" in the third, indirect form. Both Protestant and Catholic teachers have favored such a course. Or, to take another case, if a patient with incurable cancer gets pneumonia may we morally withhold antibiotics that would cure the pneumonia and let the patient "go," thus escaping a protracted and pain-ridden death? Roman Catholics are not so sure about this one, but most others are agreed that the best and most loving course would be to withhold the antibiotics.

Some of those who have tried to face these issues—the Euthanasia Societies in America and England, for example—have wanted to restrict both direct and indirect euthanasia to *voluntary* situations where the patient has consented. Such a concept is applicable to people—of whom there are many—who have private understandings with doctor friends and with their families in anticipation of the end. But what of the patient who has never stated his wishes and is past making a mentally competent choice? Under this code mercy would have to be denied no matter how hideous and hopeless his suffering. Yet in modern medical practice most terminal patients are in precisely this submoral condition. Therefore, many moralists are prepared to approve even involuntary forms of indirect euthanasia. Pope Pius XII, for example, said that in deciding whether to use reanimation techniques, if life is ebbing hopelessly, doctors may cease and desist, "to permit the patient, already virtually dead, to pass on in peace." This decision could be made by the family and doctor *for* the patient. In the same vein, the Archbishop of Canterbury (Cosmo, Lord Lang) agreed that "cases arise in which some means of shortening life may be justified." Both of these church leaders of the recent past preferred to leave the decision as to *when* in the physician's hands.

This is probably the wisest policy, provided the doctors do not take a rigid or idolatrous view of their role as "life" savers. Medicine's achievements have created some tragic and tricky questions. Margaret Mead, the anthropologist, in a recent lecture on medical ethics at Harvard Medical School, called for an end to the present policy of pushing the responsibility off on physicians. It is certainly unfair to saddle the doctors with all the initiative and responsibility, to create such a "role image" for them, when pastors and relatives might take it. There is some wisdom, nevertheless, in the Pope's injunction to the family of the dying to be guided by the doctors' advice as to *when* "vital functions" have ceased and only minimal organic functioning continues.

The *direct* ending of a life, with or without the patient's consent, is euthanasia in its simple, unsophisticated, and ethically candid form. This is opposed by many teachers, Roman Catholics, and others. They claim to see a moral difference between deciding to end a life by deliberately doing something and deciding to end a life by deliberately *not* doing something. To many others this seems a very cloudy distinction. What, morally, is the difference between doing nothing to keep the patient alive and giving a fatal dose of a pain-killing or other lethal drug? The intention is the same, either way. A decision *not* to keep a patient alive is as morally deliberate as a decision to *end* a life. As Kant said, if we will the end we will the means. Although differences persist in its application, the *principle* of mercy-death is today definitely accepted, even in religious circles where the pressures of death-fear have been strongest. Disagreements concern only the "operational" or practical question—who does what under which circumstances?

Doctors and laymen have asked lawmakers to legalize *direct* euthanasia, thus far unsuccessfully. While this writer's decision is in favor of the direct method, it may be necessary to settle temporarily for an intermediate step in the law. One distinguished jurist, Glanville Williams, has suggested that since there is little immediate hope of having the direct-method proposal adopted, it might be more practical to try for a law to safeguard the doctors in the *indirect* forms of mercy-death which *they are now practicing anyway*, and which leading moralists of all persuasions could endorse. Such a measure would provide that a medical practitioner is not guilty of any offense if he has sought to speed or ease the death of a patient suffering a painful and fatal disease. Doctors would then have protection under the law, freedom to follow their consciences. To bring this matter into the open practice of medicine would harmonize the civil law with medical morals, which must be concerned with the quality of life, not merely its quantity.

The biggest obstacle to a compassionate and honest understanding of this problem is a superstitious concept of "nature" inherited from an earlier, pre-scientific culture. People often feel that death should be "natural"—that is, humanly uncontrolled and uncontrived. Sometimes they say that God works through nature and therefore any "interference" with nature by controlling what happens *to* people in the way of illness and death—interferes with God's activity. This argument has a specious aura of religious force. For example, one doctor with an eighty-three-year-old patient, paralyzed by a stroke and a half-dozen other ailments, tells the compassionate family that he will do nothing, "leave it to God." But God does not co-operate; their mother goes on gasping. Maybe the doctor needs a better and more creative theology.

For the fact is that medicine itself is an interference with nature. It freely co-operates with or counteracts and foils nature to fulfill humanly chosen ends. As Thomas Sydenham said three hundred years ago, medicine is "the support of enfeebled and the coercion of outrageous nature." Blind, brute nature imposing an agonized and prolonged death is outrageous to the limit, and to bow to it, to "leave things in God's hands" is the last word in determinism and fatalism. It is the very opposite of a morality that prizes human freedom and loving kindness.

The right of spiritual beings to use intelligent control over physical nature rather than submit beastlike to its blind workings, is the heart of many crucial questions. Birth control, artificial insemination, sterilization, and abortion are all medically discovered ways of fulfilling and protecting human values and hopes in spite of nature's failures or foolishnesses. Death control, like birth control, is a matter of human dignity. Without it persons become puppets. To perceive this is to grasp the error lurking in the notion—widespread in medical circles—that life as such is the highest good. This kind of vitalism seduces its victims into being more loyal to the physical spark of mere biological life than to the personality values of self-possession and human integrity. The beauty and spiritual depths of human stature are what should be preserved and conserved in our value system, with the flesh as the means rather than the end. The vitalist fallacy is to view life at any old level as the highest good. This betrays us into keeping "vegetables" going and dragging the dying back to brute "life" just because we have the medical know-how to do it.

Medicine, however, has a duty to relieve suffering equal to preserving life. Furthermore, it needs to re-examine its understanding of "life" as a moral and spiritual good—not merely physical. The morality of vitalism is being challenged by the morality of human freedom and dignity. Natural or physical determinism must give way to the morality of love. Doctors who will not respirate monsters at birth—the start of life—will not much longer have any part in turning people into monsters at the end of life.

JANE JACOBS

VIOLENCE
IN THE
CITY STREETS

"... The safety of the street works best—and with least taint of hostility or suspicion—where people are using and enjoying the city streets voluntarily. ..."

To BUILD city districts that are custom-made for easy crime is idiotic. Yet that is what we do. Today barbarism has taken over many city streets—or people fear it has, which comes to much the same thing in the end.

"I live in a lovely quiet residential area," says a friend of mine who is hunting for another place to live. "The only disturbing sound at night is the occasional scream of someone being mugged."

It does not take many incidents of violence to make people fear the streets. And as they fear them, they use them less, which makes the streets still more unsafe.

This problem is not limited to the older parts of cities. Sidewalk and door-step insecurity are as serious in cities that have made conscientious efforts to rebuild as they are in those cities that have lagged. Nor is it illuminating to tag minority groups, or the poor, or the outcast, with responsibility for city danger. Some of the safest—as well as some of the most dangerous—side-walks in New York, for example, are those along which poor people or minority groups live. And this is true elsewhere.

Deep and complicated social ills underlie delinquency and crime—in suburbs and towns as well as great cities. But if we are to maintain a city society that can diagnose and keep abreast of these profoundly difficult problems, the starting point must be to strengthen the workable forces that now exist for maintaining urban safety and civilization. In fact we do precisely the opposite.

First, we must understand that the public peace—the sidewalk and street peace—of cities is not kept primarily by the police, necessary though they are. It is kept primarily by an intricate, almost unconscious, network of voluntary controls and standards among the people themselves. In some city areas—notably older public-housing projects and streets with very high population turnover—the keeping of public sidewalk law and order is left almost entirely to the police and special guards. Such places are jungles.

Nor can the problem be solved by spreading people out more thinly, trading the characteristics of cities for the characteristics of suburbs. If this were possible, then Los Angeles should be in good shape because superficially it is almost all suburban. It has virtually no districts compact enough to qualify as dense city. Yet Los Angeles' crime figures are flabbergasting. Among the seventeen standard metropolitan areas with populations over a million, Los Angeles stands pre-eminent in crime, especially the crimes associated with personal attack, which make people fear the streets. (Los Angeles, for example, has a forcible rape rate more than twice as high as either of the next two cities, which happen to be St. Louis and Philadelphia, three times as high as the rate for Chicago, and more than four times the rate for New York.)

The reasons for Los Angeles' high crime rates are complex, and at least in part obscure. But of this we can be sure: thinning out a city does not insure safety from crime and fear of crime. This is demonstrable too in cities where pseudo-suburbs or superannuated suburbs are ideally suited to rape, muggings, beatings, holdups, and the like. The all-important question is: How much easy opportunity does any city street offer to crime? It may be that there is some absolute amount of crime in a given city, which will find an outlet somehow (I do not believe this). In any case, different kinds of city streets garner radically different shares of barbarism.

Some city streets afford no such opportunity. The streets of the North End of Boston are outstanding examples. City planners officially consider this area a "slum" but the streets are probably as safe as any place on earth. Although most of the North End's residents are Italian or of Italian descent, the district's streets are heavily and constantly used also by people of every race and background. Some of the strangers from outside work in or close to the district; some come to shop and stroll; many make a point of cashing their paychecks in North End stores and immediately making their big weekly purchases in streets where they know they will not be parted from their money between the getting and the spending.

Frank Havey, director of the North End Union, the local settlement house, says, "In twenty-eight years I have never heard of a single case of rape, mugging, molestation of a child, or other street crime of that sort in the district. And if there had been any, I would have heard of it even if it did not reach the papers." Half-a-dozen times or so in the past three decades, says Havey, would-be molesters have made a try toward luring a child or, late at night, attacking a woman. In every such case the try was thwarted by passers-by, by kibitzers from windows, or shopkeepers.

Meantime, in the Elm Hill Avenue section of Roxbury, a part of inner Boston that is suburban in superficial character, prudent people stay off the streets at night because of the ever-present possibility of street assaults with no kibitzers to protect the victims. For this and other related reasons—dispiritedness and dullness—most of Roxbury has run down. It has become a place to leave.

Roxbury's disabilities, and especially its Great Blight of Dullness, are all too common in other cities too. But differences like these in public safety within the same city are worth noting. The once fine Elm Hill Avenue section's basic troubles are not due to a criminal or a discriminated-against or a poverty-stricken population. Its troubles are due to the fundamental fact that it is physically unsuited to function with vitality as a city district, and so cannot function safely.

Even within supposedly similar parts of supposedly similar places, drastic differences in public safety exist. For example, at Washington Houses, a public-housing project in New York, a tenants' group put up three Christmas trees in mid-December 1958. The biggest tree—a huge one—went into the project's inner "street," a landscaped central mall. Two smaller trees were placed at the outer corners of the project where it abuts a busy avenue and lively cross streets. The first night, the large tree and all its trimmings were stolen. The two smaller ones remained intact, lights, ornaments, and all, until they were taken down at New Year's. The inner mall is *theoretically* the most safe and sheltered place in the project. But, says a social worker who has been helping the tenants' group, "People are no safer in that mall than the Christmas tree. On the other hand, the place where the other trees were safe, where the project is just one corner out of four, happens to be safe for people."

Everyone knows that a well-used city street is apt to be safe. A deserted one is apt to be unsafe. But how does this work, really? And what makes a city street well used or shunned? Why is the inner sidewalk mall in Washington Houses—which is supposed to be an attraction—shunned when the sidewalks of the old city just to its west are not? What about streets that are busy part of the time and then empty abruptly? A city street equipped to make a safety asset out of the presence of strangers, as successful city neighborhoods always do, must have three main qualities:

First, there must be a clear demarcation between public and private spaces. They cannot ooze into each other as they do typically in housing projects where streets, walks, and play areas may seem at first glance to be open to the public but in effect are special preserves. (The fate of Washington Houses' large Christmas tree is a classic example of what happens when the distinction between public and private space is blurred, and the area which should be under public surveillance has no clear practicable limits.)

Second, there must be *eyes* upon the street, eyes belonging to what we might call its natural proprietors. To insure the safety of both residents and strangers, the buildings on a street must be oriented to it. They cannot turn their backs or blank sides on it and leave it blind.

And third, the sidewalk must have users on it fairly continuously, both to add more effective eyes and to induce plenty of people in buildings along the street to watch the sidewalks. Nobody enjoys sitting on a stoop or looking out a window at an empty street. But large numbers of people entertain themselves, off and on, by watching street activity.

In settlements smaller than cities, public behavior (if not crime) is controlled to some extent by a web of reputation, gossip, approval, disapproval, and sanctions. All of these are powerful if people know each other and word travels. But a city's streets must control not only the behavior of city people but also of visitors who want to have a big time away from the gossip and sanctions at home. It is a wonder cities have solved such a difficult problem at all. And yet in many streets they do it magnificently.

The issue of unsafe streets cannot be evaded by trying to make some other features of a locality safe instead—for example, interior courtyards, or sheltered play spaces. The streets of a city are where strangers come and go. The streets must not only defend the city against predatory strangers. They must also insure the safety of the many peaceable strangers who pass through. Moreover no normal person can spend his life in some artificial haven, and this includes children. Everyone must use the streets.

On the surface, we seem to have here some simple aims: To try for streets where the public space is unequivocally public and to see that these public street spaces have eyes on them as continually as possible.

But it is far from simple to accomplish these things. You can't make people use streets without reason. You can't make people watch streets if they do not want to. The safety of the street works best—and with least taint of hostility or suspicion—where people are using and enjoying the city streets voluntarily.

The basic requisite for such surveillance is a substantial quantity of stores and other public places sprinkled along the sidewalks; it is especially important that places frequented during the evening and night be among them. Stores, bars, and restaurants—the chief examples—abet sidewalk safety in different and complex ways.

First, they give people concrete reasons for using the sidewalks.

Second, they draw people along the sidewalks past places which have few attractions in themselves; this influence does not carry very far geographically, so there must be many—and different—enterprises in a city district if they are to give walkers reason for criss-crossing paths and populating barren stretches on the street.

Third, small businessmen and their employees are typically strong proponents of peace and order themselves; they hate broken windows, holdups, and nervous customers. If present in sufficient abundance, they are great street watchers and sidewalk guardians.

Fourth, the activity generated by people on errands, or people aiming for food or drink, in itself attracts more people to the street.

This last point seems incomprehensible to city planners and architectural designers. They operate on the premise that city people seek emptiness, obvious order, and quiet. Nothing could be less true. The love of people for watching activity and other people is evident in cities everywhere. This trait reaches an almost ludicrous extreme on upper Broadway in New York, where the street is divided by a narrow, central mall, right in the middle of traffic. Benches have been placed at the cross-street intersections of this long mall, and on any day when the weather is even barely tolerable they are filled with people watching the pedestrians, the traffic, and each other.

Eventually Broadway reaches Columbia University and Barnard College, one to the right, the other to the left. Here all is obvious order and quiet. No more stores and the activity they generate, almost no more pedestrians— and no more watchers on the benches. I have tried them and can see why. No place could be more boring. Even the students shun it. They do their outdoor loitering, homework, and street watching on the steps overlooking the busiest campus crossing.

It is just so elsewhere. A lively street always has both its users and watchers. Last year I was in the Lower East Side of Manhattan, waiting for a bus on a street full of errand-goers, children playing, and loiterers on the stoops. In a minute or so a woman opened a third floor tenement window, vigorously yoo-hooed at me, and shouted down that "The bus doesn't run here on Saturdays!" Then she directed me around the corner. This woman was one of thousands of New Yorkers who casually take care of the streets. They notice strangers. They observe everything going on. If they need to take action, whether to direct a stranger or to call the police, they do so. Such action usually requires, to be sure, a certain self-assurance about the actor's proprietorship of the street and the support he will get if necessary, and this raises special problems I will not deal with here. But the fundamental thing is the watching itself.

Not everyone in cities helps to take care of the streets, and many a resident or worker is unaware of why his neighborhood is safe. Consider, for example, a recent incident which occurred on the street where I live.

My block is a small one, but it contains a remarkable range of buildings, varying from several vintages of tenements to three- or four-story houses. Some of these have been converted into low-rent flats with stores on the ground floor; some, like ours, have been returned to single-family use. Across the street are some four-story brick tenements with stores below. Half of them were converted twelve years ago into small high-rent elevator apartments.

From my second-story window I happened to see a suppressed struggle going on between a man and a little girl. He seemed to be trying to get her to go with him, by turns cajoling her, and then acting nonchalant. The child was making herself rigid against the wall.

I wondered whether I should intervene, but then it became unnecessary. The wife of the butcher emerged from their shop with a determined look on her face. Joe Cornacchia came out of his delicatessen and stood solidly to the other side. Several heads poked out of the tenement windows above; one was withdrawn quickly, and its owner reappeared a moment later in the doorway behind the man. Two men from the bar next to the butcher shop came to the doorway and waited. On my side of the street, the locksmith, the fruit man, and the laundry proprietor came out of their shops, and other eyes peered from windows. That man did not know it, but he was surrounded. Nobody was going to allow a little girl to be dragged off, even if nobody knew who she was. I am sorry—for dramatic reasons—to have to report that the little girl turned out to be the man's daughter.

Throughout this little drama, perhaps five minutes in all, *no eyes appeared in the windows of the high-rent apartments*. It was the only building of which this was true. When we first moved to our block, I used to hope that soon all the old tenements would be rehabilitated in the same way. I know better now, and am filled with gloom by the recent news that such a transformation is scheduled for the rest of the block. The high-rent tenants, most of whom are so transient [1] we cannot even keep track of their faces, have not the remotest idea of who takes care of their street, or how. A city neighborhood can absorb and protect a substantial number of these birds of passage. But if and when they *become* the neighborhood, the streets will gradually grow less secure, and if things get bad enough they will drift away to another neighborhood which is mysteriously safer.

In some rich neighborhoods, where there is little do-it-yourself surveillance, street watchers are hired. The monotonous sidewalks of residential Park Avenue in New York, for example, are surprisingly little used; their logical users are populating instead the interesting sidewalks of Lexington and Madison Avenues to the east and west, filled with bars, stores, and

---

[1] Some, according to the storekeepers, live on beans and bread and spend their sojourn looking for a place to live where all their money will not go for rent.

restaurants. A network of doormen and superintendents, of delivery boys and nursemaids—a form of *hired* neighborhood—keeps residential Park Avenue supplied with eyes. At night, dog walkers safely venture forth and supplement the doormen. But this street is blank of built-in eyes, and devoid of concrete reasons for using or watching it. If its rents were to slip below the point where they could support a plentiful hired neighborhood of doormen and elevator men, it would become a woefully dangerous street.

Once a street has effective demarcation between private and public spaces and has a basic supply of activity and eyes, it is equipped to handle strangers, in fact the more the merrier.

Strangers can be a safety asset, particularly at night. The street on which I live is fortunate in having a locally supported bar, another around the corner, and a famous one—the White Horse—that draws continuous troops of strangers. (Dylan Thomas used to go there, and mentioned it in his writing.) This bar, indeed, works two distinct shifts. In the morning and early afternoon it is a social gathering place for Irish longshoremen and other craftsmen in the area, as it always was. But beginning in midafternoon it changes to kind of a college bull session combined with a literary cocktail party, and this continues until the early hours of the morning. On a cold winter's night, when the doors of the White Horse open, a solid wave of conversation surges out—very warming. The comings and goings from this bar do much to keep our street reasonably populated until three in the morning, make it safe to come home to. The only instance I know of a beating in our street occurred in the dead hours between the closing of the bar and dawn. (The beating was halted by one of our neighbors who saw it from his window.)

I know a street uptown where a church youth and community center, with many night dances and other activities, performs about the same service as the White Horse bar. Orthodox planning is much imbued with puritanical conceptions of how people should spend their free time. But there is room in cities for many differences in people's tastes, proclivities, and occupations. And these differences are in fact *needed*. Utopians and other compulsive managers of other people's leisure openly prefer one kind of legal enterprise over others—youth centers and restaurants are "better" than bars and poolrooms. This kind of thinking is worse than irrelevant for cities. It is harmful. The greater and more plentiful the range of all legitimate interests—in the strictly legal sense—that city streets and their enterprises can satisfy, the better for the streets and for the safety of the city.

Bars, and indeed all commerce, have a bad name in many city districts precisely because they do draw strangers and the strangers do not work out as an asset.

This is especially true in the dispirited gray belts of great cities and in once-fashionable (or at least once-solid) inner residential areas gone into decline. Because these neighborhoods are so dangerous, and the streets typically so dark, it is commonly believed that their troubles with strangers may result from insufficient street lighting. Good lighting is important, but darkness alone does not account for the gray areas' deep, functional sickness, the Great Blight of Dullness.

Bright lights do give some reassurance to people who need or want to go out. Thus lights induce these people to contribute their own eyes to the upkeep of the street. Moreover, as is obvious, good lighting makes the eyes count for more because their range is greater. Each additional pair of eyes, and every increase in their range, is that much to the good. But unless eyes are there, and unless in the brains behind those eyes is the almost unconscious reassurance of general street support in upholding civilization, lights can do no good. Horrifying public crimes can, and do, occur in well-lighted subway stations when no effective eyes are present (although a few people may be). They virtually never occur in darkened theatres where many people and eyes are present.

To explain the troubling effect of strangers on the streets of gray city areas, it is useful to examine the peculiarities of another and figurative kind of street—the corridors of high-rising public-housing projects which have become standard all over America. The elevators and corridors of these projects are, in a sense, streets piled up in the sky to permit the ground to become deserted parks like the mall at Washington Houses where the tree was stolen.

These interior parts of the building are not only streets in the sense that they serve the comings and goings of residents—few of whom may know each other or recognize, necessarily, who is a resident and who is not. They are streets also in the sense of being accessible to the public. They have been designed in an imitation of upper-class standards for apartment living without upper-class cash for doormen and elevator men. Anyone can go into these buildings, unquestioned, and use the elevator and corridors. These blind-eyed streets, although completely accessible to public use, are closed to public view and thus lack the checks and inhibitions exerted by eye-policed city streets.

The New York Housing Authority some years back experimented with corridors open to public view in a Brooklyn project which I shall call Blenheim Houses although that is not its name. (I do not wish to add to its troubles by advertising it.)

Because the buildings of Blenheim Houses are sixteen stories high, the open corridors cannot really be watched from the ground or from other buildings. But their psychological openness has had some effect. More importantly, the corridors were well designed to induce surveillance from within the buildings themselves. They were equipped to serve as play space, and as narrow porches, as well as passageways. This all turned out to be so lively and interesting that the tenants added still another use: picnic grounds—this in spite of continual pleas and threats from the management which did not *plan* that the balcony corridors should serve as picnic grounds. (One of the main tenets of planners is that the Plan should anticipate everything and then permit no changes.) The tenants are devoted to the balcony-corridors which are, as a result, under intense surveillance. There has been no problem of crime in these corridors nor of vandalism either. Not even light bulbs are stolen or broken.

Nonetheless, Blenheim Houses has a fearsome problem of vandalism and scandalous behavior. The lighted balconies which are, as the manager puts it, "the brightest and most attractive scene in sight," draw strangers, especially teen-agers, from all over Brooklyn. But these strangers do not halt at the visible corridors. They go into other "streets" of the buildings, streets that lack surveillance—the elevators and, more important in this case, the fire stairs and their landings. The housing police run up and down after the malefactors—who behave barbarously and viciously in the blind-eyed, sixteen-story stairways—and the malefactors elude them. It is easy to run the elevators up to a high floor, jam the doors so the elevators cannot be brought down, and then play hell with a building and anyone you can catch. So serious is the problem and apparently so uncontrollable, that the advantage of the safe corridors is all but canceled out—at least in the harried manager's eyes.

What happens at Blenheim Houses is somewhat the same as in dull gray areas of cities. Their pitifully few and thinly spaced patches of life are like the visible corridors at Blenheim Houses. They do attract strangers. But the relatively deserted, blind streets leading from these places are like the fire stairs at Blenheim Houses. They lack the kind of street life which could equip them to handle strangers safely, and the presence of strangers in them is thus an automatic menace.

The temptation in such cases is to blame the balconies—or the commerce or bars that serve as a magnet. A typical train of thought is exemplified in the Hyde Park–Kenwood renewal project now under way in Chicago. This piece of gray area adjoining the University of Chicago contains many splendid houses and grounds, but for thirty years it has been plagued with a frightening street-crime problem, accompanied in recent years by considerable physical decay. The "cause" of Hyde Park–Kenwood's decline has been brilliantly identified, by the city planners, as the presence of "blight." By this they mean that too many of the college professors and other middle-class families steadily deserted this dull and dangerous area and their places were often, quite naturally, taken by those with little economic or social choice among living places.

What does the Hyde Park–Kenwood plan do? It designates and removes these chunks of blight and replaces them with housing projects designed, as usual, to minimize use of the streets. The plan also adds still more empty spaces here and there, blurs even further the district's already poor distinctions between private and public space, and amputates the existing commerce, which is no great shakes.

The early plans for this renewal included, for example, a relatively large imitation-suburban shopping center. But further thought gave the planners a faint glimmer of the realities. A large center—larger than that required for the standard shopping needs of the renewal district's residents—"might draw into the area extraneous people," as one of the architectural planners put it. A small shopping center was thereupon settled on. Large or small matters little.

It matters little because Hyde Park–Kenwood, like all city districts, is, in real life, surrounded by "extraneous" people—hundreds of thousands of them. The area is an embedded part of Chicago. It cannot wish away its location. It cannot bring back its one-time condition, long gone, of semi-suburbia. To plan as if it could, and to evade its deep, functional inadequacies, can have only one of two possible results so far as safety is concerned:

(1) Extraneous people will continue to come into the area as they please, including some who are not at all nice, and the opportunity for street crime will be a little easier, if anything, because of the added emptiness. (2) Or a determined effort can be made to keep extraneous people out of the area. Indeed, according to the *New York Times*, the adjoining University of Chicago—the institution that was the moving spirit in getting the plan under way—took the extraordinary measure of loosing police dogs every night to patrol its campus. The dogs are trained to hold at bay any human in this dangerous un-urban inner keep. The barriers formed by new projects at the edges of Hyde Park–Kenwood, plus extraordinary policing, may be able to keep out strangers. If so, the price will be hostility from the surrounding city and an ever more beleaguered feeling within the fort. And who can be sure, either, that all those thousands rightfully within the fort are trustworthy in the dark?

I do not wish to single out one area, or in this case one plan, as uniquely opprobrious. Hyde Park–Kenwood is significant mainly because the diagnosis and the corrective measures of its plan typify in slightly more ambitious form plans conceived for cities all over the country. And in city after city, we are seeing the results of orthodox city planning of this kind: great cyclone fences are erected to "protect" sequestered projects and developments from their surroundings and special police are hired to chase intruding boys—while the crime rates rise, and people cling to their cars at night. Hyde Park–Kenwood, in short, is not a local aberration but an example of how we are deliberately building unsafe cities.

In this article I have pointed to some lively and well-used city streets and neighborhoods where lives are secure and civilized and public violence and barbarism are rare. I am not suggesting, however, that we should therefore try to imitate routinely and mechanically the districts that do display strength and success as fragments of city life. That would be impossible, and, moreover, even the best city streets and districts can stand improvement, especially in their amenity. But if life in our cities is to be safe and satisfying, we must first be aware of where it now succeeds and fails, and why. Then we shall at least have some idea both of the kind of city we want and the failure of most urban planning today to achieve anything resembling it. And this first step we have not yet begun to take.

ERNEST VAN DEN HAAG

LOVE OR MARRIAGE?

". . . Love has long delighted and distressed mankind, and marriage has comforted us steadily and well. . . ."

IF SOMEONE asks, "Why do people marry?" he meets indignation or astonishment. The question seems absurd if not immoral: the desirability of marriage is regarded as unquestionable. Divorce, on the other hand, strikes us as a problem worthy of serious and therapeutic attention. Yet marriage precedes divorce as a rule, and frequently causes it.

What explains marriage? People divorce often but they marry still more often. Lately they also marry—and divorce, of course—younger than they used to, particularly in the middle classes (most statistics understate the change by averaging all classes). And the young have a disproportionate share of divorces. However, their hasty exertions to get out of wedlock puzzle me less than their eagerness to rush into it in the first place.

A hundred years ago there was every reason to marry young—though middle-class people seldom did. The unmarried state had heavy disadvantages for both sexes. Custom did not permit girls to be educated, to work, or to have social, let alone sexual, freedom. Men were free but since women were not, they had only prostitutes for partners. (When enforced, the double standard is certainly self-defeating.) And, though less restricted than girls shackled to their families, single men often led a grim and uncomfortable life. A wife was nearly indispensable, if only to darn socks, sew, cook, clean, take care of her man. Altogether, both sexes needed marriage far more than now—no TV, cars, dates, drip-dry shirts, cleaners, canned foods—and not much hospital care, insurance, or social security. The family was all-important.

Marriage is no longer quite so indispensable a convenience; yet we find people marrying more than ever, and earlier. To be sure, prosperity makes marriage more possible. But why are the young exploiting the possibility so sedulously? Has the yearning for love become more urgent and widespread?

What has happened is that the physical conveniences which reduced the material usefulness of marriage have also loosened the bonds of family life. Many other bonds that sustained us psychologically were weakened as they were extended: beliefs became vague; associations impersonal, discontinuous, and casual. Our contacts are many, our relationships few: our lives, externally crowded, often are internally isolated; we remain but tenuously linked to each other and our ties come easily undone. One feels lonely surrounded by crowds and machines in an unbounded, abstract world that has become morally unintelligible; and we have so much time now to feel lonely in. Thus one longs, perhaps more acutely than in the past, for somebody to be tangibly, individually, and definitely one's own, body and soul.

This is the promise of marriage. Movies, songs, TV, romance magazines, all intensify the belief that love alone makes life worthwhile, is perpetual, conquers the world's evils, and is fulfilled and certified by marriage. "Science" hastens to confirm as much. Doesn't popular psychology, brandishing the banner of Freud with more enthusiasm than knowledge, tell us, in effect, that any male who stays single is selfish or homosexual or mother-dominated and generally neurotic? and any unmarried female frustrated (or worse, not frustrated) and neurotic? A "normal" person, we are told, must love and thereupon marry. Thus love and marriage are identified with each other and with normality, three thousand years of experience notwithstanding. The yearning for love, attended by anxiety to prove oneself well-adjusted and normal, turns into eagerness to get married.

The young may justly say that they merely practice what their parents preached. For, indeed, the idea that "love and marriage go together like a horse and carriage" has been drummed into their heads, so much that it finally has come to seem entirely natural. Yet, nothing could be less so. Love has long delighted and distressed mankind, and marriage has comforted us steadily and well. Both, however, are denatured—paradoxically enough, by their stanchest supporters—when they are expected to "go together." For love is a very unruly horse, far more apt to run away and overturn the carriage than to draw it. That is why, in the past, people seldom thought of harnessing marriage to love. They felt that each has its own motive power: one primed for a lifelong journey; the other for an ardent improvisation, a voyage of discovery.

Though by no means weaker, the marital bond is quite different from the bond of love. If you like, it is a different bond of love—less taut, perhaps, and more durable. By confusing these two related but in many ways dissimilar bonds, we stand to lose the virtues and gain the vices of both: the spontaneous passion of love and the deliberate permanence of marriage are equally endangered as we try to live up to an ideal which bogs down one and unhinges the other.

Marriage is an immemorial institution which, in some form, exists everywhere. Its main purpose always was to unite and to continue the families of bride and groom and to further their economic and social position. The families, therefore, were the main interested parties. Often marriages were arranged (and sometimes they took place) before the future husbands or wives were old enough to talk. Even when they were grown up, they felt, as did their parents, that the major purpose of marriage was to continue the family, to produce children. Certainly women hoped for kind and vigorous providers and men for faithful mothers and good housekeepers; both undoubtedly hoped for affection, too; but love did not strike either of them as indispensable and certainly not as sufficient for marriage.

Unlike marriage, love has only recently come to be generally accepted as something more than a frenzied state of pleasure and pain. It is a welcome innovation—but easily ruined by marriage; which in turn has a hard time surviving confusion with love. Marriage counselors usually recognize this last point, but people in love seldom consult them. Perhaps their limited clientele colors the views of too many marriage counselors: instead of acknowledging that love and marriage are different but equally genuine relationships, they depict love as a kind of dependable wheel horse that can be harnessed to the carriage of married life. For them, any other kind of love must be an "immature" or "neurotic" fantasy, something to be condemned as Hollywood-inspired, "unrealistic" romanticism. It is as though a man opposed to horse racing—for good reasons perhaps—were to argue that race horses are not real, that all real horses are draft horses. Thus marriage counselors often insist that the only "real" and "true" love is "mature"—it is the comfortable workaday relation Mommy and Daddy have. The children find it hard to believe that there is nothing more to it.

They are quite right. And they have on their side the great literature of the world, and philosophers from Plato to Santayana. What is wrong with Hollywood romance surely is not that it is romantic, but that its romances are shoddy clichés. And since Hollywood shuns the true dimensions of conflict, love in the movies is usually confirmed by marriage and marriage by love, in accordance with wishful fantasy, though not with truth.

Was the love Tristan bore Isolde "mature" or "neurotic"? They loved each other before and after Isolde was married—to King Mark. It never occurred to them to marry each other; they even cut short an extramarital idyll together in the forest. (And Tristan too, while protesting love for Isolde, got married to some other girl.) Dante saw, but never actually met, Beatrice until he reached the nether world, which is the place for permanent romance. Of course, he was a married man.

It is foolish to pretend that the passionate romantic longing doesn't exist or is "neurotic," i.e., shouldn't exist; it is as foolish to pretend that romantic love can be made part of a cozy domesticity. The truth is simple enough, though it can make life awfully complicated: there are two things, love and affection (or marital love), not one; they do not usually pull together as a team; they tend to draw us in different directions, if they are present at the same time. God nowhere promised to make this a simple world.

In the West, love came to be socially approved around the twelfth century. It became a fashionable subject of discussion then, and even of disputation, in formal "courts of love" convoked to argue its merits and to elaborate its true characteristics. Poets and singers created the models and images of love. They still do—though mass production has perhaps affected the quality; what else makes the teen-age crooners idols to their followers and what else do they croon about? In medieval times, as now, manuals were written, codifying the behavior recommended to lovers. With a difference though. Today's manuals are produced not by men of letters, but by doctors and therapists, as though love, sex, and marriage were diseases or therapeutic problems—which they promptly become if one reads too many of these guidebooks (any one is one too many). Today's manuals bear titles like "Married Love" (unmarried lovers can manage without help, I guess); but regardless of title, they concentrate on sex. In handbooks on dating they tell how to avoid it; in handbooks on marriage, how to go about it. The authors are sure that happiness depends on the sexual mechanics they blueprint. Yet, one doesn't make love better by reading a book any more than one learns to dance, or ride a bicycle, by reading about it.

The sexual engineering (or cook-book) approach is profitable only for the writer: in an enduring relationship, physical gratification is an effect and not a cause. If a person does not acquire sexual skill from experience, he is not ready for it. Wherever basic inhibitions exist, no book can remove them. Where they do not, no book is necessary. I have seen many an unhappy relationship in my psychoanalytic practice, but none ever in which sexual technique or the lack of it was more than a symptom and an effect. The mechanical approach never helps.

The troubadours usually took sex and marriage for granted and dealt with love—the newest and still the most surprising and fascinating of all relationships. And also the most unstable. They conceived love as a longing, a tension between desire and fulfillment. This feeling, of course, had been known before they celebrated it. Plato described love as a desire for something one does not have, implying that it is a longing, not a fulfillment. But in ancient Greece, love was regarded diffidently, as rather undesirable, an intoxication, a bewitchment, a divine punishment—usually for neglecting sex. The troubadours thought differently, although, unlike many moderns, they did not deny that love is a passion, something one suffers.[1] But they thought it a sweet suffering to be cultivated, and they celebrated it in song and story.

The troubadours clearly distinguished love and sex. Love was to them a yearning for a psychic gratification which the lover feels only the beloved can give; sex, an impersonal desire anybody possessing certain fairly common characteristics can gratify by physical actions. Unlike love, sex can thrive without an intense personal relationship and may erode it if it exists.

[1] . . . I am in love
And that is my shame.
What hurts the soul
My soul adores,
No better than a beast
Upon all fours.

So says W.B. Yeats. About eight centuries earlier, Chrestien de Troyes expressed the same sentiment.

Indeed, the Romans sometimes wondered if love would not blunt and tame their sexual pleasures, whereas the troubadours fretted lest sex abate the fervor of love's longing. They never fully resolved the contest between love and sex; nor has anyone else. (To define it away is, of course, not to solve it.)

We try to cope with this contest by fusing love and sex. (Every high-school student is taught that the two go together.) This, as Freud pointed out, does not always succeed and may moderate both, but, as he also implied, it is the best we can hope for. In the words of William Butler Yeats, "Desire dies because every touch consumes the myth and yet, a myth that cannot be consumed becomes a specter. . . ."

Romantics, who want love's desiring to be conclusive, though endless, often linked it to death: if nothing further can happen and rival its significance, if one dies before it does, love indeed is the end. But this is ending the game as much as winning it—certainly an ambiguous move. The religious too perpetuate longing by placing the beloved altogether out of physical reach. The "bride of Christ" who retires to a convent longs for her Redeemer—and she will continue to yearn, as long as she lives, for union with a God at once human and divine, incarnating life and love everlasting. In its highest sense, love is a reaching for divine perfection, an act of creation. And always, it is a longing.

Since love is longing, experts in the Middle Ages held that one could not love someone who could not be longed for—for instance, one's wife. Hence, the Comtesse de Champagne told her court in 1174: "Love cannot extend its rights over two married persons." If one were to marry one's love, one would exchange the sweet torment of desire, the yearning, for that which fulfills it. Thus the tension of hope would be replaced by the comfort of certainty. He who longs to long, who wants the tension of desire, surely should not marry. In former times, of course, he married—the better to love someone else's wife.

When sexual objects are easily and guiltlessly accessible, in a society that does not object to promiscuity, romantic love seldom prospers. For example, in imperial Rome it was rare and in Tahiti unknown. And love is unlikely to arouse the heart of someone brought up in a harem, where the idea of uniqueness has a hard time. Love flowers best in a monogamous environment morally opposed to unrestrained sex, and interested in cultivating individual experience. In such an environment, longing may be valued for itself. Thus, love as we know it is a Christian legacy, though Christianity in the main repudiates romantic love where the object is worldly, and accepts passion only when transcendent, when God is the object—or when muted into affection: marital love.

Let me hazard a Freudian guess about the genesis of the longing we call love. It continues and reproduces the child's first feeling for his parent—the original source of unconditioned and unconditional love. But what is recreated is the child's image, the idealized mother or father, young and uniquely beautiful, and not the empirical parent others see. The unconsummated love for this ideal parent (and it could be someone else important in the child's experience) remains as an intense longing. Yet any fulfillment now must also become a disappointment—a substitute, cheating the longing that wants to long. Nonetheless most of us marry and replace the ideal with an imperfect reality. We repudiate our longing or we keep it but shift its object. If we don't, we may resent our partners for helping us "consume the myth," and leaving us shorn of longing—which is what Don Giovanni found so intolerable, and what saddens many a faithful husband.

Sexual gratification, of course, diminishes sexual desire for the time being. But it does more. It changes love. The longing may become gratitude; the desire tenderness; love may become affectionate companionship— "After such knowledge, what forgiveness?" Depending on character and circumstance, love may also be replaced by indifference or hostility.

One thing is certain though: if the relationship is stabilized, love is re- placed by other emotions. (Marriage thus has often been recommended as the cure for love. But it does not always work.) The only way to keep love is to try to keep up—or re-establish—the distance between lovers that was inevitably shortened by intimacy and possession, and thus, possibly, regain desire and longing. Lovers sometimes do so by quarreling. And some per- sonalities are remote enough, or inexhaustible enough, to be longed for even when possessed. But this has disadvantages as well. And the deliberate and artificial devices counseled by romance magazines and marriage manuals ("surprise your husband . . .")—even when they do not originate with the love of pretense—are unlikely to yield more than the pretense of love.

The sexual act itself may serve as a vehicle for numberless feelings: lust, vanity, and self-assertion, doubt and curiosity, possessiveness, anxiety, hostility, anger, or indifferent release from boredom. Yet, though seldom the only motive, and often absent altogether, love nowadays is given as the one natural and moral reason which authorizes and even ordains sexual relations. What we have done is draw a moral conclusion from a rule of popular psychology: that "it is gratifying, and therefore healthy and natural, to make love when you love, and frustrating, and therefore unhealthy and unnatural, not to; we must follow nature; but sex without love is unnatural and therefore immoral."

Now, as a psychological rule, this is surely wrong; it can be as healthy to frustrate as it is to gratify one's desires. Sometimes gratification is very unhealthy; sometimes frustration is. Nor can psychological health be ac- cepted as morally decisive. Sanity, sanitation, and morality are all desirable, but they are not identical; our wanting all of them is the problem, not the solution. It may be quite "healthy" to run away with your neighbor's wife, but not, therefore, right. And there is nothing unhealthy about wishing to kill someone who has injured you—but this does not morally justify doing so. Finally, to say "we must follow nature" is always specious: we follow nature in whatever we do—we can't ever do what nature does not let us do. Why then identify nature only with the nonintellectual, the sensual, or the emotional possibilities? On this view, it would be unnatural to read: literacy is a gift of nature only if we include the intellect and training in nature's realm. If we do, it makes no sense to call a rule unnatural merely because it restrains an urge: the urge is no more natural than the restraint.

The combination of love and sex is no more natural than the separation. Thus, what one decides about restraining or indulging an emotion, or a sexual urge, rests on religious, social, or personal values, none of which can claim to be more natural than any other.

Not that some indulgences and some inhibitions may not be healthier than others. But one cannot flatly say which are good or bad for every man. It depends on their origins and effects in the personalities involved. Without knowing these, more cannot be said—except, perhaps, that we should try not to use others, or even ourselves, merely as a means—at least not habitually and in personal relations. Sex, unalloyed, sometimes leads to this original sin which our moral tradition condemns. Psychologically, too, the continued use of persons merely as instruments ultimately frustrates both the user and the used. This caution, though it justifies no positive action, may help perceive problems; it does not solve them; no general rule can.

What about marriage? In our society, couples usually invite the families to their weddings, although the decision to marry is made exclusively by bride and groom. However, a license must be obtained and the marriage registered; and it can be dissolved only by a court of law. Religious ceremonies state the meaning of marriage clearly. The couple are asked to promise "forsaking all others, [to] keep thee only unto her [him], so long as ye both shall live." The vow does not say, "as long as ye both shall want to," because marriage is a promise to continue even when one no longer wishes to. If marriage were to end when love does, it would be redundant: why solemnly ask two people to promise to be with each other for as long as they want to be with each other?

Marriage was to cement the family by tying people together "till death do us part" in the face of the fickleness of their emotions. The authority of state and church was to see to it that they kept a promise voluntarily made, but binding, and that could not be unmade. Whether it sprang from love did not matter. Marriage differed from a love affair inasmuch as it continued regardless of love. Cupid shoots his arrows without rhyme or reason. But marriage is a deliberate rational act, a public institution making the family independent of Cupid's whims. Once enlisted, the volunteers couldn't quit, even when they didn't like it any longer. That was the point.

The idea that marriage must be synchronous with love or even affection nullifies it altogether. (That affection should coincide with marriage is, of course, desirable, though it does not always happen.) We would have to reword the marriage vow. Instead of saying, "till death do us part," we might say, "till we get bored with each other"; and, instead of "forsaking all others," "till someone better comes along." Clearly, if the couple intend to stay "married" only as long as they want to, they only pretend to be married: they are having an affair with legal trimmings. To marry is to vow fidelity regardless of any future feeling, to vow the most earnest attempt to avoid contrary feelings altogether, but, at any rate, not to give in to them.

Perhaps this sounds grim. But it needn't be if one marries for affection more than for love. For affection, marital love may grow with knowledge and intimacy and shared experience. Thus marriage itself, when accepted as something other than a love affair, may foster affection. Affection differs from love as fulfillment differs from desire. Further, love longs for what desire and imagination make uniquely and perfectly lovable. Possession erodes it. Affection, however,—which is love of a different, of a perhaps more moral and less aesthetic kind—cares deeply also for what is unlovable without transforming it into beauty. It cares for the unvarnished person, not the splendid image. Time can strengthen it. But the husband who wants to remain a splendid image must provide a swan to draw him away, or find a wife who can restrain her curiosity about his real person—something that Lohengrin did not succeed in doing. Whereas love stresses the unique form perfection takes in the lover's mind, affection stresses the uniqueness of the actual person.

One may grow from the other. But not when this other is expected to remain unchanged. And affection probably grows more easily if not preceded by enchantment. For the disenchantment which often follows may turn husband and wife against each other, and send them looking elsewhere for re-enchantment—which distance lends so easily. Indeed, nothing else does.

MARION K. SANDERS

THE NEW AMERICAN FEMALE: DEMI–FEMINISM TAKES OVER

"...they are seeking...to combine the functions of wife and mother with purposeful work outside their homes, which may or may not involve a professional job...."

LIKE the Vice President, the First Lady tailors her job to suit herself—and the President. She is not, however, a free agent, for the Chief Executive's wife is the sole source of copy for the industrious lady reporters who cover the White House. Even if she loafs on the job, they work hard to make her a symbol of contemporary female-ness. Often they succeed. Thus Mamie Eisenhower, in her pink inaugural gown and little-girl bangs, was a kind of corn-fed Queen Victoria beaming upon the bland domesticity that engulfed the nation's postwar brides. Jacqueline Kennedy—an eighteenth-century type like all the Kennedy ladies—was a latter-day Great Whig Hostess. She satisfied an affluent generation's craving for gorgeous entertainments, court hairdressers, riding to hounds, and salons filled with fashionable wits and dandies.

"John Kennedy just didn't understand career women," a warm admirer of the late President said recently. This was natural enough since he scarcely knew any.

Lyndon B. Johnson, on the other hand, is married to one. Miz Johnson— as he and her staff are apt to call her—has, among other things, managed a TV station and parlayed a modest inheritance into a hefty fortune. "Women doers" are high style in Washington and the President has declared war on "male curmudgeonism" in the federal service.

To be sure, Ladybird has turned in her uniform in the pro league. "She works for nothing," the President confessed to a gathering of female eminences. Her amateur standing does not seem to oppress the First Lady. Some weeks ago I trailed her on a dawn-to-dusk safari that started at 6:00 A.M. in the company of a planeload of news-hungry reporters. En route, she chatted individually with each of them. As the day wore on, she made three speeches, presented diplomas to domestic Peace Corps trainees, visited a remedial reading class and toured a rural slum, pausing on the way to accommodate the whims of a rabble of TV cameramen, indigenous small fry, deserving Democrats, and surprised matrons in mink who had never seen anything quite like this before. It was a virtuoso performance, sustained for seventeen hours. When it was over, she flew off to the ranch for "a walk under the sky"—as she put it—and a domestic weekend with a husband whose idea of relaxation is a two-hundred-guest barbecue.

I don't know what the Johnsons talk about in their private moments, if any. But I can vouch that at the White House breakfast table or on the banks of the Pedernales there are no debates about whether or not it is "feminine" for a woman to make political speeches, drive a tractor, or head a government agency.

Perhaps these issues never came up in Texas, which in bygone years was known as fine country for men and dogs but hell on women and horses. Frontiersmen respected the wives and steeds who survived these rigors. It was from Texas in 1875 that Mrs. Sarah W. Hiatt reported to the National Women's party: "There is a great liberality here of sentiment concerning the avocations of women. Though the right of women to the ballot seems to be a new idea to our people, I have never lived in a community where the women are more nearly abreast of men in all the activities of life. . . ."

This "liberality of sentiment" is in the air of Washington today. It is felt particularly by the women who have long toiled in drab obscurity in the old-line government agencies. They have new hairdos and a new gleam in their eyes. The President has given some two thousand of them a long-overdue boost up the civil-service ladder, and is still looking the field over. It is a heady atmosphere according to Ruth Van Cleve, recently appointed director of the Interior Department's Office of Territories. "For years I was just a government lawyer in sensible shoes," she said. "Now I'm a national asset. You should have heard my children cheering the President—and the Virgin Islands—at the Inaugural Parade."

In some instances, the new renown has fallen on already overburdened shoulders. Topflight Negro professional women are in such high demand that the meager available supply is worked overtime. For example, Patricia Harris, a one-time Howard law professor, has been snowed under with speaking engagements, TV appearances, and interracial conferences. In May the President plucked her out of her post on the Commission on the Status of Puerto Rico to make her Ambassador to Luxembourg. Similarly, the Administration robbed Cardozo High School in the District of a highly effective principal to make Bennetta Washington head of the Women's Job Corps. Mrs. Washington is an imaginative administrator who plans to use women volunteers on a scale unprecedented in a government program and has induced the country's leading Catholic, Jewish, Protestant, and Negro women's organizations to work together in this effort.

She believes, she told me recently, that the woman who does responsible community work is quite as much of a national asset as the one who works for pay, if her potentialities are taken seriously and her time and talents are put to rational uses.

On a different level Mrs. Johnson is making the same point when, for example, she takes a trowel in hand to plant a clump of hyacinths on the Mall. The purpose is to lure the garden-club ladies away from their own petunias to discuss perennial borders and window boxes with the inhabitants of a scruffy housing development. Quite a few are actually doing just that.

"It's a good time to be a woman," said Katie Louchheim who is now a State Department official but has also been—simultaneously and seriatim —a wife, mother, poet, and volunteer in politics and civic affairs.

This sanguine view is not shared by the ladies who habitually write about what one man I know calls "The Woman Bit." Indeed the consensus among them seems to be that the Woman problem has reached crisis proportions, comparable to air pollution and urban sprawl. To distinguish these specialists from the experts who write about fashion, home economics, and child rearing, an enterprising New York newspaper has christened this newer art form Feminology. Journalistically, the field is crowded. But so far as I know, Feminology has not yet been exploited as a parlor game. The possibilities are spectacular.

The object, of course, is to solve the Woman problem, and any number can play. Readers of the women's magazines have been well drilled in the basic gambits. For example: If you live in the city, move to the suburbs; if you live in the suburbs, move to the city; if you are a housewife, get a job; if you have a job, have a baby. And so forth.

Drawing up the rules may prove a bit sticky, since our leading Feminologists are at odds about The Solution. On one side is Phyllis McGinley whose sermons in praise of domesticity, or "nesting" as she calls it, have been packaged in a book called *Sixpence in Her Shoe*. Much as she loves her kitchen, I suspect Miss McGinley (in private life Mrs. Charles Hayden) might be willing to compromise. She is a witty and reasonable woman who writes excellent verse when she finishes her ironing. Indeed, her tone is more soothing than evangelical. She seems less eager to win converts to housewifery than to restore a modicum of tranquillity and better cooking to the homes unsettled by her chief adversary. This is Betty Friedan, high priestess of the Salvation Through Job gospel. In the style of Carrie Nation, she flails about at a villain—not the demon rum, but something called *The Feminine Mystique*. This is the title of her book, a shrill, humorless polemic, packed with data mined from the works of psychiatrists, anthropologists and other Feminologists, and interviews with women who are as gabby as they are unhappy.

Naturally, a certain process of self-selection has taken place. Just as an arthritis specialist sees few people who do not have arthritis, Mrs. Friedan specializes in sufferers from what she calls "the problem without a name." (I have not figured out just what this is but believe it has something to do with having so much time on your hands that you enjoy being "depth-interviewed" by Mrs. Friedan.)

Leaving no tome unturned, Mrs. Friedan has come up with the discovery that *"women have outgrown the housewife role"* (italics hers). She has even dug up evidence that career women have better sex lives than homebodies. Such talk would have stunned Susan B. Anthony. But in fact this is simply old-fashioned, hard-line feminism in modern pseudosociological dress.

Mesdames McGinley and Friedan have both made best-sellers of their conflicting theses,* which suggests a certain schizophrenia among female book buyers. On the other hand, this odd ambivalence may mean that a good many women are trying to plot a middle course between the two extreme positions, that they are seeking—in the style of Ladybird Johnson—to combine the functions of wife and mother with purposeful work outside their homes, which may or may not involve a professional job.

This posture—which might be called demi-feminism—is by no means a mass movement. The vast majority of American women are not even fractionally feminists and never were. This is why the Suffragists of yore had trouble recruiting doorbell ringers to circulate their petitions and marchers for their parades.

* As of late spring [1965] 65,000 hardcover copies of *Mystique* had been sold and 700,000 in paperback. *Sixpence* was in its eighth hardcover printing, heading toward the 100,000 mark with a paperback edition still to come.

The average woman was otherwise occupied—chiefly in finding a man to support her and thereafter in keeping him reasonably content with his usually tedious job by baking pies and darning his socks when he came home. Such are still the average female's prime concerns.

This fact has been disguised by the tidings that some twenty-three million American women are currently in the "work force" and that three out of five of them are married. This much-touted statistic creates the illusion of a nation of brisk career women who stack the breakfast dishes, park their children in nursery schools, and charge off each morning to "challenging" jobs.

But what is the case? Of the married women I know in city and suburb, not one in ten has paid employment outside her home, and few are job-hunting. On the business air routes—such as the early-morning flights between New York, Washington, Boston, Detroit, Chicago. and Los Angeles—the stewardesses are often the only women aboard. It would seem that most of the nation's work is being done by men, at least the kind of work that involves traveling by air and carrying an attaché case.

Who then are the twenty-three million? Footnotes to the statistical tables disclose—to those who trouble to read them—that a mere three million are in occupations classed as "technical or professional." Another six million work only intermittently. And most of the remaining fourteen million are in lowly, ill-paid clerical, factory, sales, or service jobs. Of those who are also mothers of young children a dismaying proportion are Negro women.

Undoubtedly they would like to earn more. And they desperately need decent day-care facilities for their young. But above all they yearn for fully employed husbands and a chance to tend their own children and kitchens instead of another woman's. The status of women is a far less burning question in these circles than the status of men.

The Feminologists do not worry much about this female *Lumpenproletariat* who, like their male equivalents, are not much given to buying books. Few of them even see the glossy women's magazines in the beauty parlor. On their days off they put their hair in rollers and head for the supermarket where they can sneak a free peek at *Woman's Day* while waiting at the check-out counter.

The Feminologists' concern is for the Educated Woman, also known as the Trapped Housewife. They find her tormented by doubts as to her worth, plagued by a choice of values and life-styles, each with its own built-in frustrations.

To update my own impressions—which are somewhat different—I decided to confront the Educated Woman in a place where she is currently offered a bewildering variety of choices—Washington, D.C. and its environs. There is, for one thing, no easier spot for a woman to go job-hunting if she has an A.B. degree and a year or two of "experience." Thirty-two likely vocations—ranging from biological scientist to occupational therapist to systems analyst—are listed in the Labor Department's pamphlet *Job Horizons for College Women*. Virtually all these careers can be pursued within the federal

Civil Service, at starting salaries of from five to six thousand a year. Usually too, there are also openings in nearby private foundations, research organizations, and sophisticated industries. In addition, the area is a beehive of energetic volunteer organizations which have been moving into high gear as a result of the civil-rights movement and the anti-poverty programs.

Eight well-schooled young matrons who live in this area agreed not long ago to spend an evening with me discussing the Woman problem. All were in their early or mid-thirties, mothers of two or more children and married to the same husbands they had started out with. Four were professional women—a doctor, an economist, a teacher, and a biochemist. The rest are listed in the census as "housewives." We spent three delightful hours talking about politics, science, segregation, schools, zoning, mental health, and books. As the last one left to relieve her baby-sitter I realized to my chagrin that we had not gotten around to the Woman problem though I had made several conscientious attempts to steer the talk in that direction. Apparently no one was greatly interested.

Realizing that such delicate territory perhaps cannot be probed in a group session, I called next day on one of the housewives who seemed to have a worried look about her. I will call her Jane Jones. "Are you afflicted with the Friedan Syndrome?" I asked.

"I am terribly sorry," she said. "But I don't have time to do much reading outside of my field, which is urban planning. So I have not kept up with all this Feminine Mystique jazz. I have plenty of problems but they all have names. For instance, I am chairman of this committee against discrimination in housing. Some of my best neighbors are bigots. They are also good Democrats and I am Democratic Precinct Chairman. So I have a conflict of roles. What is worse, my husband says I am beginning to talk like one of those girls in the Feiffer cartoons. So what do I do? Escape mechanism. I bake this absolutely divine Viennese apple cake which the children adore—would you care for a piece?"

The telephone rang at this point and I eavesdropped on a dialogue about setting up a nursery school for culturally deprived children and how to go about getting a subsidy from Operation Head Start (a Poverty War project) to enable their culturally deprived mothers to spend a day a week at the school.

Apologizing for the interruption, Jane returned to our conference and launched into a discourse on what might be called the value system of a demi-feminist. Economically, it has a strong patriarchal base. Jane is convinced that when a man stops bringing home the bacon, marriage collapses. She believes also that marriage—with all its flaws—is the best arrangement yet invented for the rearing of a family.

Since her husband's job is arduous, she feels he is entitled to something better than a TV dinner when he gets home. Besides, she likes cooking. As for his duties as a father? "I don't go for this business of demanding that he change the baby and wash dishes," she said. "I think that's *sick* feminism. Why shouldn't he do something pleasant with the children? And I'd rather have him put up shelves in the basement than putter around my kitchen when he's in a domestic mood. Of course, he baby-sits for me when I'm out working."

The Jones family manages nicely on one salary. So Jane is calm about the fact that she is not paid for her "work."

"I used to laugh at all the Worthy Groups my mother belonged to," she said. "But you know if it weren't for the League of Women Voters our school budget would have been hacked to pieces last year. Honestly, this community would fall apart without us do-gooders and the political parties would collapse."

This is equally true in many other sections of the country where decaying political machines have been replaced by lively citizens' organizations. It is strikingly evident in the environs of Washington where many husbands work for the government and are kept out of the partisan fray by the Hatch Act. The grass-roots political work of the area has long been done mainly by women. Nowadays they are not merely stuffing envelopes. They are running for office and often winning.

Jane might be elected to the school board or town council herself next year. But she probably won't try since her husband has had a tempting job offer in the Midwest and may accept. Like the other demi-feminists of her generation she has adapted to the harsh realities of our mobile society. Many factors, of course, are weighed in deciding where the family tent will be pitched—including the quality of schools, the cost of living, and the social and political climate. But in the end what tips the scale is the economic or professional prospect offered the chief breadwinner. Accordingly, Jane has concluded that while the two-job family can work very well (whether or not the wife is paid for her extramural labors), the two-ambition family cannot. Apart from the emotional tension that may be involved, it is not physically feasible for a family to follow two different sets of career opportunities.

Thus it is probably geography more than any other factor that accounts for the meager showing of American women in national affairs. What after all, do you do with your husband and family if you are elected to Congress? This handicap is bipartisan. This spring, for example, Patricia Hutar, the capable assistant chairman of the Republican National Committee, gave notice because of what she called her "home situation." The "situation" consisted of a husband and three-year-old daughter in Chicago. She has been replaced by Mary Brooks, a mobile Idaho widow.

Similarly, the Johnson Administration ran into geographic troubles more than a year ago when the President first started looking for women to place in high federal posts. Lists of likely candidates poured in from local political organizations, women's bar associations, and other professional societies.

"But as we started trying to pin individuals down, the lists evaporated," one of the talent scouts told me. "Most women just don't have movable husbands."

Eventually, the search zeroed in on the reservoir of female talent already resident in and around the capital. And in due course some seventy-five executive appointments were made.

But even in Washington the Important Job did not prove an irresistible lure. There was for example a young woman I will call Doris Smith—another demi-feminist. She is a psychologist, the mother of three, and has a part-time job with a private foundation. Why did she turn down the prestige and higher pay the Administration offered her?

"I don't want to be away from home eight hours a day while the children are so young," she said. "And I don't want the kind of high-pressure work that will be on my mind all the time, even when I'm home."

Doris is the daughter of a married career woman of my vintage. She feels she can do a better job with her children than the nannies and fräuleins to whom we entrusted our young. Whether or not this is so, these spinster mercenaries are a vanished breed. And Doris, in any event, says she produced children because she wanted—and enjoys—the experience of rearing them.

So she has opted for the career of limited ambitions. She has equipped herself with a portable vocation that can be practiced wherever her husband (another peripatetic type) decides to hang his professional hat. She is, of course, well aware that a woman who has to pick up the threads of her professional life in a new community every six or seven years—or who withdraws from her field for a decade or more to be a full-time mother—is not going to climb as high as the man who follows his own star or the woman who does not marry.

"But look at the advantages," Doris said. "A husband is insurance against failure—I mean both financial disaster and social stigma. Men are in a much more exposed position. They have to make irrevocable career decisions before they leave college. And if they fail, who will pay off the mortgage?"

As to her own professional prospects, Doris feels rather like a distinguished woman historian I know who was offered a college presidency a few years ago and turned it down because she did not wish to be parted from her husband, a business executive based in a different part of the country. "I can teach or write where we live," she said. "And I really get more fun out of being Jim's wife than I would out of presiding at a faculty council."

Demi-feminism, of course, makes sense only in a society where it is fun to be a wife. This takes a special and highly adaptable kind of husband—a breed produced in far greater abundance in this country than in most parts of the world. In nations afflicted with socially underdeveloped and spiritually overbearing males, such as Japan, wives badly need a Lucretia Mott to rescue them from their dreary housemaid-concubine status. This is true not only in Asian countries, but also in many parts of Europe where husbands tend to be tightfisted about money and demanding in the home, despite the political "emancipation" of women. Even in Sweden—where because of a labor shortage women are exhorted to take up plumbing, bus driving, and TV repairing—there is a great deal of discussion about "sex roles." This debate does not revolve around the films of Ingmar Bergman or the movie *To Bed or Not to Bed*. The argument is about the extent of the male's as well as the female's parental responsibilities. Much quoted is a report by a Norwegian sociologist (published in a book called *Woman, Her Life and Work*) who has studied sailors' families and found that the father's prolonged absence has an adverse effect on the children, particularly sons.

On a visit to Stockholm last spring, I found bright young women hotly insisting that men should share more in "the work of the home." I was puzzled at first as to why such an obvious point should be so belabored. The reason became clearer after I dined in a middle-class Swedish home where the daughters of the family waited on table and ate in the kitchen while the sons—and of course the hostess and paterfamilias—graced the festive board. Perhaps our most useful export to Scandinavia would be a consignment of dear old American "togetherness."

In this country, in contrast, demi-feminism seems to express the established relationship between the sexes, except in those marginal groups where idleness is fashionable or back-breaking toil a necessity.

This pragmatic philosophy will make increasingly good sense as wider opportunities are opened for women to train and perform as full- and part-time professionals and as volunteers, at a pace and on terms suited to their multiple responsibilities. This requires, in the first instance, a realistic assessment of the unfinished business of our society and the role which women could play in getting it done. Little is accomplished toward that end by much of the cant regularly published about women "as a great wasted national resource." These laments are often coupled with dour comparisons between the 379,000 women engineers in the U.S.S.R. and the 6,000 in this country. In fact, there is little evidence that our slow-growing economy could provide jobs for more engineers of either sex than are currently being produced. Similarly, there is a labor surplus rather than a shortage in several other fields that women are urged to enter. Thus, for example, a data-processing firm in New York acknowledged that it is oversupplied with qualified applicants for programming jobs—an understandable reason for its reluctance to hire part-time workers.[1]

At the same time, administrators and professionals stubbornly resist the large-scale use of women, either as part-time paid workers or effective volunteers in the very fields where their services are desperately needed—notably the schools, hospitals, social agencies, and libraries.

The programs to which Ladybird Johnson is giving energetic support presage change in this situation. This summer, for example, twenty thousand professional, neighborhood, and volunteer workers are to be mobilized to work with preschool children in some three hundred areas. Most of them will be women, and many of them, like Mrs. Johnson, will be chiefly con-

---

[1] These and other illuminating findings are reported by Jane Schwartz in a study of part-time employment published by the Alumnae Advisory Council, 541 Madison Avenue, New York, N.Y.

cerned with getting on with the job, cheerfully willing to assume—as the need and circumstances change—the role of wife, mother, professional, or volunteer. These demi-feminists find it possible, as David Riesman observed in a recent essay, "to lead full multidimensional lives without mounting the barricades at home or abroad." May their tribe increase.

MARYA MANNES

THE
SOPHISTICATED
MAN

"...But they are stereotypes for all that, while the mark of true sophistication is the absence of label...."

IF I SAID that the sophisticated man was what the sophisticated woman wanted, I would be begging trouble. Many a simple girl has yearned for a worldly lover, and many a complicated and polished woman has rushed into the arms of a simple brute. Perhaps I should say that I can remember no time in my life when the sophisticated man was not the object of my interest, if not my search. Unlike some women, I have never had the patience of an educator nor the zeal of a reformer. I prefer the finished product; not a man incapable of growth, but one who has managed to acquire those perceptions, tastes, and attitudes which, to me, constitute sophistication.

What was my yardstick? Well, in younger days when I traveled alone a great deal and had to develop certain techniques against unwanted aggressions, my preliminary judgments were largely visual. If I were standing in the corridor of a wagon-lits, for instance, and saw with the tail of my eye that a male was bearing down on me, I would retreat if he wore any of these things: a pale cloth cap, basket-weave sport shoes, and an ordinary shirt unbuttoned at the neck and exposing, usually, a bristling sprout of hair. These were the days, I am constrained to admit, before what is known as "casual" wear. Now my list of repellents—academically speaking—has formidably increased. It includes plastic raincovers on hats (I have seen them even on Shriner fezzes), jackets pulled down at the shoulder by the straps of heavy cameras, and the pale loose suits, pale hats, and pale ties which mark the American male in all the hotel lobbies, streets, and airports across the country. On the beaches of the North in summer and the South in winter, I would beat a hasty withdrawal from men in matching patterned shorts and jackets or silly hats. And in bucolic parties alfresco, the fellow barbecuing in an apron printed with "Cordon Bleu" or "I Wear the Pants" will have to look elsewhere (which he usually does) for a female companion. I mention these trivialities of attire because I am convinced that the sophisticated man wouldn't be seen dead in them. They are, one and all, emasculators, and if there is anything which the worldly man cossets it is his male dignity. The bareheaded fellow in the khaki shorts and the dark-blue polo shirt has been around.

Now, here we come to the crux of the situation, for I maintain that a man who has never traveled in other countries and been exposed to other societies cannot be sophisticated. I am not speaking of package tours or cruise trips, but of a reasonable familiarity with foreign cities and peoples and arts and customs; an education reading alone cannot provide. For sophistication to me suggests, primarily, a refinement of the senses. The eye that has not appreciated Michelangelo's David in Florence or the cathedral of Chartres is not a sophisticated eye; nor is the tongue that has not tasted the best fettucine in Rome or the best wine in Paris. The hand that has not felt the rough heat of an ancient wall in Siena or the sweating cold of a Salzburg stein of beer is an innocent hand. So are the fingers that have not traveled, in conscious and specific savoring, over the contours of many different women.

Would you recognize this kind of man if you saw him across the room? I think so. He's the one talking with an attractive woman; conservatively dressed, but easy in his clothes. His hair is trimmed close to his head, but not too close. His hands are well-groomed, but not manicured. He does not laugh loudly or often. He is looking directly at the woman he speaks to, but he is not missing the other attractive women as they enter; a flick of the eye does it. For in all ways this man is not obvious. He would no more appear to examine a woman from the ankles up than he would move his head as he read or form the words with his lips. His senses are trained and his reflexes quick. And how did they get that way? From experience, from observation, and from deduction. He puts two and two together without adding on his fingers. He is educated in life.

Now what about that fellow over there—the one in the light-grey suit and the crew cut? He is telling a long story rather loudly to a girl who would rather not be hearing it. He is not, of course, aware of this, since he is not only a little tight but unaccustomed to watching the reactions of women. He will look down the front of her dress but not see the glaze on her eyes. He has not been educated in observation. He is, according to the dictionary, unsophisticated in that he is natural and simple and lacking in experience. And this, again according to the dictionary, is a compliment. For the sophisticated are not only said to be refined to the point of artificiality, but might well—because of this, and in spite of their cleverness—be unsound.

Now Mr. Webster derived his definition from "sophism," which is clearly unpleasant in the company it keeps with fallacy and deceptive reasoning. But Mr. Webster was also an American, and it is no accident that his countrymen have for a long time shared the suspicion that sophisticated people—male or female—were somehow un-American. Open spaces and open people: that's what we've prided ourselves on. The good fellow, the regular guys, the gladhanders, no nonsense about 'em, you know just where they stand; they look you in the eye and talk straight; simple—natural—unaffected. And as for sophisticated women—they're all right for a laugh or a show or a week end, but who would want to marry 'em? No sir, give me the girl next door every time, like home-baked pie.

Sophistication, then, has always seemed something of an import, either from Europe or secondhand from New York. And when women think of sophisticated men, their minds wander from British diplomats to French actors to Italian princes, settling in the end for those American men—mostly in movies—who have made love to British duchesses, French models, or Italian actresses. If examples were wanted, Cary Grant and Henry Fonda would do quite nicely as dream images of the sophisticated male. Most of us, of course, do not meet Cary Grant or Henry Fonda. But we do travel, increasingly. And I would like to issue a warning to those of my countrywomen tempted to believe that a well-cut suit and a well-kept accent can transport them from Crestwood to the world of true values.

Some years ago there was a late-night television program on a local channel called "The Continental." On this a man oozing charm from every pore oiled his way not across the floor but into the hearts, apparently, of thousands of yearning housewives. He did this by looking straight into the camera eye as if it were yours, by raising a glass of wine, to you, of course, and, in an accent drenched with sauce marinara, murmuring sweet nothings of life and love to his unseen, but presumably panting, mistress. Ridiculed as he was by critics and confident husbands, the female response alarmed the sponsors into taking it off. It was not obscene, merely indecent.

Now I am not implying that continentals resemble this man. But they do possess a surface sophistication which may seem like the real thing even when it isn't. Their shirts are of the finest silk, their shoes handmade, and their hair of the proper length. They kiss your hand with the proper lightness, look into your eyes just long enough to create surface tension, their voices are well-modulated, and they do not rush you. They make a flattering show of savoring your intelligence, arriving at your body only at the dessert course of your first meal together. It is then that the tricks begin to show—to anyone, that is, not overcome by Soave and long black lashes. They employ a standard routine which is, precisely because it does not discriminate between you and a hundred other women, the product not of sophistication but of guile. It goes something like this: "You are beautiful, but you have not lived. Let me wake you. Only I can wake you. Most men want to take pleasure—I want to give it." Another very successful variation is the following gambit. The continental: "How can you be so beautiful and so cold!" Mary Jane from

Wilmington: "I'm *not* cold!" The continental, whispering, breathing hard: "Then prove it to me!"

If you prove it to him, you may have some pleasurable moments, but you will discover before long that your Awakener is no more educated in world culture and the refinements of living than the agency man you met in Detroit, and probably less so. He may very well be a haberdasher who has never been out of Italy, thinks all Americans are rich, and lives in a room full of chromos and potted plants. Or he may be a Brazilian cocoa merchant who thinks all American men are uncultured and all American women are hard. These are the common men, adopting a veneer of worldliness that passes for sophistication. They have as I said, picked up some useful techniques. They know that specific flattery—"Your neck is like a column"—is more potent than general flattery—"You look swell"; that the ardent look can be more effective than the hasty grab; and that masculine self-assurance is the best weapon against feminine resistance. They know that a part of this assurance comes from good grooming and correct attire. But they are stereotypes for all that, while the mark of true sophistication is the absence of label.

As for our home-grown stereotypes, their approaches differ only in the crudity of their application and the fact that too often they are impelled by liquor. I have never considered the amorous lurch a compliment, nor the mumbled repetition of certain endearments accompanied by uncertain groping. I am bored by a man so simple, or so unsure, that he can approach a woman only by the chemical solvence of his inhibitions. I am dismayed by a man so unreticent that he can tell me about his wife and himself at our first encounter. This guilelessness, which is considered an American virtue, I find, as a woman, not only dull but immature. Reticence and sophistication go hand in hand, for one of the joys of life is discovery: the gradual peeling of layers. It is a pity, in fact, that the democratization of society has accelerated this process to the degree of Instant Intimacy, or Instimacy. Instead of a relished progression from *vous* to *tu*, from Mister to Jim, it's darling and come to my place in the first hour. Like many time-savers, small pleasures are sacrificed: you travel fast, but you miss the flowers on the roadside. And when you get there, what do you remember of the trip?

No. My sophisticated man does not tip his hand too soon; he savors the moves of the game, and only urgent reasons impel him to quick disclosure.

Now you must have gathered from the foregoing that the S.M. likes women. I would go further and say that he prefers the company of women to men. He is not one for conventions, evenings with the boys, or that post-prandial segregation of the sexes still practiced by hostesses at the peril of their parties. This does not mean that he does not relish conversations with men, but that given a social choice he will favor the inclusion of women.

I have in my life met men of true sophistication in all other spheres who were still naïve in their judgments of women or diffident in their approaches to them. This could be attributed to their mothers, their endocrine balances, a childhood shock, or any one of those causative factors which explain everything and nothing. These are the men who fall in love with maternal women or childish women to avoid the challenge of their equals; or who, in their innocence, cannot discern between the generous woman and the promiscuous one until they are cuckolded. But then, have we not already discussed the men who show sophistication in their treatment of women, but little in other areas? Few of us, men or women, are of the same grain all the way through. Indeed, consistency would discourage that appetite for experience which is the basis of sophistication.

It would seem at first glance that this appetite would make the S.M. less moral than our natural, open, simple man. Again we return to the root of the old American-puritan distrust of him. Yet I maintain that the fine, up-standing, regular, all-American male who married the girl next door and likes steak more than gigot is really no more virtuous; he is merely less fastidious. It is he, on his business trips, who patronizes call girls. The so-phisticated man can gratify his desires without paying for them. It is our unsophisticated big shot who uses his secretaries for more than typing; the wiser fellow keeps business and pleasure separate. It is our simple fellow who gets drunk at conventions and paws the high school drum majorette. Our complex man wouldn't be seen dead with her. The difference is that our regular guy has to prove his virility, while our sophisticated fellow quietly exercises it. He has long since abandoned proving for enjoying.

His enjoyments, as the full use of his senses would indicate, cover a wide range. How a man lives, what he surrounds himself with, is index enough of his sophistication, or lack of it, and there is nothing more revealing than a quiet prowl around his quarters. (I refer, of course, to bachelor quarters; a wife's contributions would complicate the issue.) Does he have flying geese over his mantel and the *Reader's Digest* on his coffee table? Does the one bookshelf in the room feature the works of Harold Robbins, Allen Drury, and *How to Make Two Million Dollars in Real Estate?* Does his record cabinet bulge with Kostelanetz and Gould, but lack Vivaldi or Bach or Fauré or Prokofiev? Then prepare for a simple man and a limited one. His heart may be gold, but his company will be leaden.

I suspect, moreover, the too-neat room, for it can imply a certain barren-ness. The sophisticated man has many passions, and I salute them in the two-foot pile of magazines on his desk which can range from *The Listener* to the *Bulletin of Atomic Scientists* or in the unframed prints, abstract or classical, stacked on available ledges against the wall, awaiting hanging. I am also comforted by the presence in his kitchenette of hunks of cheese, some fruit, and a round loaf of bread, if nothing else. I suspect that his medicine cabinet may be rather full, for the price of sophistication is an awareness so constantly acute that it must be blunted from time to time. I would rather see a collection of pills, in short, than a rowing device.

If I am omitting the lair, or pad, of the beatnik, it is because I would not have gone to it in the first place; this exploration is for the very young. Odd as it may sound, the bearded Zen seeker and café poet is no more sophis-ticated than the glad-handing Shriner. He is merely less organized. They both abide by the conventions of their groups, their horizons equally limited. In the hygienic cheeriness of the Crestview home and the dirty clutter of the beatnik refuge there is the same sterility, the same exclusion of experience. There is in both the self-consciousness of the insecure. They live as they think they should. And it is not, thank heaven, with me.

As revealing as his rooms are the presents a man gives. Like most women I am grateful when anybody gives me anything, but my gratitude increases in direct relation to a man's selectivity. I love cashmere sweaters, but I naturally prefer one in a color that shows the donor's awareness of my own. I love jewels, but I am happier with a handsome piece of junk, that shows not only an appreciation of fashion but of *my* particular fashion, than I would be by a genuine jewel bearing no relation to it. I love perfume but I love it that much more when I know the giver has arrived at his choice after due trial.

I suspect that many of my countrywomen and more of my countrymen may find in my S.M. the portrait of an urban monster—effete, affected, immoral, snobbish, and unreliable. Urbane he certainly is, although I would put an appreciation of the natural world high in his category of perceptions. The man unaware or unmoved by the sea or the sky or the rock or the stream or the flower is not sophisticated; he is merely half-alive. As for the imputed defects, I do not hold them as such. Instead of effete, I would say civilized; instead of affected, effective; instead of immoral, curious; instead of snobbish, superior.

As for unreliable, the sophisticated husband is more aware of the hazards and inconveniences of infidelity than the innocent one, if only because he has been married before.

Some years ago at a large party I met a man whose reputation had preceded him as a brilliant writer and the contented husband of a handsome wife. After fifteen minutes of spirited but impersonal conversation, he took my hand and said very quietly, "I love you." He knew that I knew that he meant it. I knew that he would never leave his wife. We shared a mutual knowledge, separately arrived at.

And that, I think, is the final virtue of sophistication. It is a condition beyond explanation.

LOVE,
DEATH,
SACRIFICE,
AND SO FORTH

"...The atmosphere of the theatre is be-coming electrical with the apprehension of middle-aged ladies who have spent the better parts of their lives in the movies ..."

Tom Garner, in the movie, on the screen, a big broad-shouldered man, a builder of railroads, President of the Chicago & Southwestern, staggers, does not walk, into his room, and closes the door.

You know he is going to commit suicide because he has staggered, and it is a movie, and already a long while has passed since the picture began, and something's got to happen real soon, something big, gigantic, as they say in Hollywood, a suicide or a kiss.

You are sitting in the theatre waiting for what you know is going to happen.

Poor Tom has just learned that the male offspring of his second wife is the product of his grown son by his first wife. Tom's first wife committed suicide when she learned that Tom had fallen in love with the young woman who finally became his second wife. This young woman was the daughter of the President of the Santa Clara Railroad. She made Tom fall in love with her so that her father would go on being President of the Santa Clara. Tom had bought the Santa Clara for nine million dollars. Tom's first wife threw herself beneath a streetcar when she found out about Tom's infatuation. She did it by acting, with her face, her eyes, and lips and the way she walked. You didn't get to see anything sickening, you saw only the motorman's frantic expression while he tried to bring the car to a stop. You heard and saw the steel wheel grinding, the wheel that killed her. You heard people screaming the way they do about violent things, and you got the idea. The worst had happened. Tom's wife Sally had gone to her Maker.

Sally met Tom when he was a trackwalker and she a teacher in a small country school. Tom confessed to her one day that he did not know how to read, write or do arithmetic. Sally taught Tom to read, write, add, subtract, divide and multiply. One evening after they were married she asked him if he wanted to be a trackwalker all his life, and he said that he did. Sally

"Love, Death, Sacrifice, and So Forth," from *The Daring Young Man on the Flying Trapeze* by William Saroyan. Copyright © 1934, 1964 by William Saroyan. Originally published by Random House, 1934. Reprinted by permission of William Saroyan and Laurence Pollinger, Ltd.

asked him if he didn't have at least a little ambition, and Tom said he was satisfied, trackwalking was easy work, they had their little home, and Tom got in a lot of fishing on the side. This hurt Sally, and she began to act. Tom saw that it would mean a lot to Sally if he became ambitious. Sitting at the supper table, he said that he would. A strange look came into his eyes, his face acquired great character. You could almost see him forging ahead in life.

Sally sent Tom to school in Chicago, and she did Tom's work as a trackwalker in order to have money with which to pay for his tuition, a great woman, an heroic wife. You saw her one winter night walking along a railroad track, packing tools and oil cans, snow and desolation all around her. It was sad. It was meant to be sad. She was doing it for Tom, so that he would be able to become a great man. The day Tom announced that he had been made foreman of the construction of the Missouri Bridge, Sally announced she was with child, and Tom said now they could never stop him. With Sally and his baby to inspire him Tom would reach the heights.

Sally gave birth to a son, and while Tom was walking to her bedside you heard symphonic music, and you knew that this was a great moment in Tom's life. You saw Tom enter the dimly lighted room and kneel beside his wife and baby son, and you heard him pray. You heard him say, Our father which art in heaven, thine the glory and the power, forever and forever. You heard two people in the theatre blowing their noses.

Sally made Tom. She took him from the track and sent him to the president's chair. Then Tom became infatuated with this younger and lovelier woman, and Sally threw herself beneath the streetcar. It was because of what she had done for Tom that the suicide was so touching. It was because of this that tears came to the eyes of so many people in the theatre when Sally destroyed herself.

But Sally's suicide did not have any effect on Tom's infatuation for the younger woman, and after a short while he married the girl, being a practical man part of the time, being practical as long as Hollywood wanted him to be practical. Tom's son, a young man just expelled from college for drunkenness, moved into Tom's house, and had an affair with Tom's second wife.

The result was the baby, a good healthy baby, born of the son instead of the father. Tom's son Tommy is an irresponsible but serious and well-dressed young man, and he really didn't mean to do it. Nature did it. You know how nature is, even in the movies. Tom had been away from home so much, attending to business, and his second wife had been so lonely that she had turned to her husband's son, and he had become her dancing partner.

You saw her holding her hand out to the young irresponsible boy, and you heard her ask him significantly if he would like to dance with her. It took him so long to take her hand that you understand the frightening implication instantly. And she was so maddeningly beautiful, extending her hand to him, that you knew you yourself would never have been able to resist her challenge, even under similar circumstances. There was something irresistible about the perfection of her face and figure, lips so kissable, stance so elegant, body so lovely, soul so needful.

It simply had to happen. Man is flesh, and all that.

So the big railroad builder, the man who always had his way, the man who broke the strike and had forty of his men killed in a riot, and a fire, has staggered into his room and closed the door.

And you know the picture is about to end.

The atmosphere of the theatre is becoming electrical with the apprehension of middle-aged ladies who have spent the better parts of their lives in the movies, loving, dying, sacrificing themselves to noble ideals, etc. They've come again to the dark theatre, and a moment of great living is again upon them.

You can feel the spiritual tenseness of all of these ladies, and if you are listening carefully you can actually hear them living fully.

Poor Tom is in there with a terrific problem and a ghastly obligation.

For his honor's sake, for the sake of Hollywood ethics, for the sake of the industry (the third largest in America, I understand), for God's sake, for your sake and my sake, Tom has got to commit suicide. If he doesn't, it will simply mean we have been deceiving ourselves all these years, Shakespeare and the rest of us. We know he'll be man enough to do it, but for an instant we hope he won't, just to see what will happen, just to see if the world we have made will actually smash.

A long while back we made the rules, and now, after all these years, we wonder if they are the genuine ones, or if, maybe, we didn't make a mistake at the outset. We know it's art, and it even looks a little like life, but we know it isn't life, being much too precise.

We would like to know if our greatness must necessarily go on forever being melodramatic.

The camera rests on the bewildered face of Tom's old and faithful secretary, a man who knew Tom as a boy. This is to give you the full implication of Tom's predicament and to create a powerful suspense in your mind.

Then, at a trot, with the same object in view, time hurrying, culminations, ultimates, inevitabilities, Tom's son Tommy comes to the old and faithful secretary and exclaims that he has heard Tom, his father, is ill. He does not know that his father knows. It is a Hollywood moment. You hear appropriate music.

He rushes to the door, to go to his father, this boy who upset the natural order of the universe by having a sexual affair with his father's young wife, and then, bang, the pistol shot.

You know it is all over with the President of the Chicago & Southwestern. His honor is saved. He remains a great man. Once again the industry triumphs. The dignity of life is preserved. Everything is hotsytotsy. It will be possible for Hollywood to go on making pictures for the public for another century.

Everything is precise, for effect. Halt. Symphonic music, Tommy's hand frozen on the door-knob.

The old and faithful secretary knows what has happened, Tommy knows, you know and I know, but there is nothing like seeing. The old and faithful secretary allows the stark reality of the pistol shot to penetrate his old, faithful and orderly mind. Then, since Tommy is too frightened to do so, he forces himself to open the door.

All of us are waiting to see how it happened.

The door opens and we go in, fifty million of us in America and millions more all over the earth.

Poor Tom. He is sinking to his knees, and somehow, even though it is happening swiftly, it seems that this little action, being the last one of a great man, will go on forever, this sinking to the knees. The room is dim, the music eloquent. There is no blood, no disorder. Tom is sinking to his knees, dying nobly. I myself hear two ladies weeping. They know it's a movie, they know it must be fake, still, they are weeping. Tom is man. He is life. It makes them weep to see life sinking to its knees. The movie will be over in a minute and they will get up and go home, and get down to the regular business of their lives, but now, in the pious darkness of the theatre, they are weeping.

All I know is this: that a suicide is not an orderly occurrence with symphonic music. There was a man once who lived in the house next door to my house when I was a boy of nine or ten. One afternoon he committed suicide, but it took him over an hour to do it. He shot himself through the chest, missed his heart, then shot himself through the stomach. I heard both shots. There was an interval of about forty seconds between the shots. I thought afterwards that during the interval he was probably trying to decide if he ought to go on wanting to be dead or if he ought to try to get well.

Then he started to holler. The whole thing was a mess, materially and spiritually, this man hollering, people running, shouting, wanting to do something and not knowing what to do. He hollered so loud half the town heard him.

This is all I know about regular suicides. I haven't seen a woman throw herself under a streetcar, so I can't say about that. This is the only suicide I have any definite information about. The way this man hollered wouldn't please anyone in a movie. It wouldn't make anyone weep with joy.

I think it comes to this: we've got to stop committing suicide in the movies.

GITARS,
FOLK SONGS,
AND HALLS OF IVY

*"... There is no question that the folk renas-
cence is infinitely broader than just topical
or protest songs...."*

ALTHOUGH Peter, Paul, and Mary, The Kingston Trio, and Joan Baez do not
evoke the hysteria caused by The Beatles, "frenzy" is the word used by the
New York Times in assessing the current folk-song revival. The following
statistics support this epithet: more than six million young Americans are
today strumming guitars; the top-selling instrument of 1963 was, in fact,
not the piano, as it had been for most of the twentieth century, but the
guitar; more than eleven million viewers were weekly watchers of this past
season's TV Hootenanny show. For a time, the word "hootenanny" possessed
such magical properties that two Carnegie Hall folk concerts sold out in
advance without prior announcement of a single performer. This year's
Newport Folk Festival outsold its sister Jazz Festival by thirty thousand
admissions. The Hollywood Bowl concert that broke all attendance records
last year was also a gathering of folk singers.

In short, from coast to coast, in coffee houses, concert halls, and college
gyms, Americans are flocking to the sound of lusty young voices accompanied by banjos, guitars, and esoteric instruments like the mountain dul-
cimer, the autoharp, and the Dobro or "Bluegrass" guitar; not infrequently,
by such improvised instruments as washboards, spoons, wine jugs, and
the Brownie Bass—a device made of an overturned washtub, a broomstick
at one side, and a single string stretched from the center of the tub to the
top of the broom handle. The variety of instruments is itself a cue to the
scope of the present revival, which runs the gamut from French love ballads
to Irish rebel songs, country blues to Bluegrass to Israeli horas, indigenous
Appalachian mountain tunes to topical songs of protest. What is most significant, however, is not the magnitude of the renascence but its depth, for
it signalizes an unmistakable shift in the outlook of young people.

Since the end of World War I there have been at least three major folk-
song revivals. The 'twenties were the era of the Great Collectors, yielding
much of the material later popularized. John A. Lomax, Cecil J. Sharp,

John Jacob Niles, and Carl Sandburg were the pioneers in collecting indigenous American songs of the prairie and mountains. More than twenty different collections of Negro spirituals were published, as well as W. C. Handy's famous collection of traditional and original *Blues*, and Sigmund Spaeth's and Dailey Paskman's compilation of old-time minstrel songs.

In many ways the folk revival of the late 'thirties and early 'forties was closer to the present renascence than to that of the 'twenties. Rediscovery of the past was embedded in criticism of the present; if it was nostalgic, it nevertheless looked to the future. And it, too, was informed by the image of the common man, inspired by the New Deal and the rise of the labor unions. This was the era of Josh White, a favorite of FDR and the first entertainer to treat folk tunes as art songs on a nightclub floor. Although bell-like diction and matinee-idol sexuality contributed to White's success, three of his most effective numbers were *The House I Live In*, the painfully humorous *One Meat Ball*, and *Strange Fruit*, the epic protest against lynching. It was also the era of Burl Ives—son of an Illinois tenant farmer—who came to public attention in a Broadway "hootenanny," *Sing Out Sweet Land;* his popular image was formed by such songs as *Blue Tail Fly* and *Wayfarin' Stranger*.

Three seminal figures emerged from the folk revival in the so-called Swing Era. Creator of many earthy blues, Big Bill Broonzy is perhaps best remembered for his biting protest against discrimination: "Now, if you're white/ you're all right/ If you're brown/ Stick aroun'/ But if you're black/ Git back! Git back! Git back!" It was he who gave the classic response when asked whether his songs were truly folk: "Never heard no horse sing 'em!" Another son of an ex-slave, Huddie Ledbetter, became known as Leadbelly because he had "guts of steel and could outwork, outsing, and outlast" every other prisoner on chain gangs where sentences for murder and attempted homicide had consigned him. Freed by the Governor of Texas when he heard his ballad, *Plea for Mercy*, Leadbelly went on to bill himself "King of the Twelve String Guitar." As protégé of curator John A. Lomax, he enriched the folk archives of the Library of Congress with recordings of several hundred songs, including *Good Night Irene*, the chugging *Rock Island Line*, and *Midnight Special*, a great prison blues.

In the 'forties, when Leadbelly lived in Manhattan, he played host for a time to the prolific writer whose songs include *This Land Is Your Land*, regarded as the folk singer's anthem, and *So Long, It's Been Good to Know You*, anthem of the dispossessed dust-bowl farmer. A depressed Woody Guthrie came to draw strength from Leadbelly, as almost twenty years later in 1961 young Bob Dylan, the foremost writer on today's folk scene, journeyed to New York to visit Guthrie, his idol.

Although Guthrie wrote many enchanting children's tunes, like the wonderful *Little Sacka Sugar*, he is remembered for the type of topical song in *Talking Union*, an album he recorded with The Almanacs. In 1949 The Almanacs, sans Guthrie, became The Weavers, a group that rose meteorically with a series of Leadbelly and Guthrie hits (also *Tzena, Tzena* and

On Top of Old Smoky), only to fall victim three years later to the entertainment blacklist of the McCarthy era. A "nearly complete" collection of Woodrow Wilson Guthrie's songs has recently been compiled and edited by Pete Seeger, who worked with Guthrie in The Almanacs and was lead tenor of The Weavers. In a dedication written from a Queens hospital bed where he lies incurably ill, Guthrie describes his goal:

"I am out to sing songs that will prove to you that this is your world and that . . . no matter how hard it's run you down and rolled over you, no matter what color, what size you are, how you are built, I am out to sing songs that make you take pride in yourself and in your work."

Although various folk figures and groups—Harry Belafonte, The Tarriers, The Weavers—emerged in the years between 1945 and the onset of the current revival, World War II seemed to bring an end to the folk trend as it did to the Swing Era. The Big Bands of Goodman, Artie Shaw, etc., were superseded by the Big Ballads of Frank Sinatra and Perry Como. Yielding its functional character as dance music, jazz became small combo bop, and then cool, some say numb, jazz. When the new generation wanted to dance, they had to turn to raucous, driving rock 'n' roll, a vocal amalgam of Negro rhythm-and-blues and white hillbilly music.

The present revival began in 1958 when a group of ex-collegians recorded the ditty of a returning Civil War vet hanged for the murder of his sweetheart. As sung by the Kingston Trio, *Tom Dooley* sold over two million records, propelled the group to stardom, and ignited the generation that had grown up on rock 'n' roll and was now in college. In actuality, rock 'n' roll prepared the ground for the folk craze. Lacking the beauty and poetry of folk song, it embodied its ebullient rhythms, its simple, angular harmonies and its stark, primitive melodies. Moreover, it permitted teen-agers to discharge their feelings of conflict with the older generation and led them to seek new values through folk music.

Look Magazine attributes the rise of folk to the dearth of good show tunes and the confused, concert character of contemporary jazz in a world still dominated by the juvenile sounds of rock 'n' roll. But obviously, the teen-agers and pre-teen-agers who are "sent" by The Beatles do not constitute the audience of folk. Neither is it the choice of the older generation comprising the loyal audiences of Lawrence Welk and Mitch Miller. To the age-group in between, the hootenanny doubtless gets much of its appeal by inviting the audience to participate. And the guitar enthusiasts, tired of being sung to and played at, want to make their own music, as swains once did around the parlor grand.

The largest and most vocal audience for folk material is unquestionably on campus. Folk-song clubs have mushroomed and folk festivals are being held at many colleges and universities, among them, UCLA, Berkeley, and Chicago. Last summer's Newport Folk Festival was inescapably collegiate in make-up. For a number of the youngsters who made up the 45,000 admissions, the trek to Newport represented a major financial outlay, which is one reason that the city fathers provided patrolled sleeping space on the beaches at a dollar a head. On the last morning of the three-day fest, I found myself walking behind four youths attired in sloppy Harvard T-shirts. As a large can of orange juice—it was their breakfast—passed from mouth to mouth, one collegian observed, "You see, I told you guys, you get used to the hunger pains after forty-eight hours." While Newport has become in part a social event for the college crowd, not unlike the journey some centuries ago of the Canterbury pilgrims, it is nevertheless a commitment of the devoted.

This fact has led observers as different as *Variety* and *Time* to read profounder motivations into the folk revival than a mere change of musical taste. "Collegians want songs that deal with what's going on in the world today," the Bible of show biz has said. According to *Time*, "rootless root seekers . . . discern in folk songs the fine basic values of American life." Oscar Brand, who has conducted a WNYC folk program for more than a decade, sees an analogy between folk songs and westerns, since they make it easy to choose between right and wrong. "The youth of today, torn by the insecurity and general immorality of the times," he contends, "have turned to the stability and the simplicity implicit in traditional songs."

The most articulate, the most poetic, and the most popular of the new folk writers is a twenty-three-year-old singer-instrumentalist, "a cross between a beatnik and a choir boy," out of Duluth, Minnesota: Bob Dylan. Reviewing a recent overflow Carnegie Hall concert, *Variety* observed unsympathetically that the future held nothing for Dylan but complaints against the past and present, "complaints against warmongers, Nazis, poverty, injustice, commercial hootenannies, blacklisting, prizefighting, atom fallout, hard-hearted sweethearts, Fabian, and the selling and buying of soap. Nowhere was there one word of hope or remedy." Noting that Dylan was born in the year of Pearl Harbor, the reviewer concluded that, unlike the generation that came back from World War II and Korea seeking serenity and happiness, the younger generation "seems to be in bitter, vocal revolt against the world today."

To date, Dylan has recorded three albums of his charged material in a droll, talking-blues style. All have appeared on best-seller charts. Last year his moving rights-of-man ballad, *Blowin' in the Wind*, was among the Top Ten for many weeks. This came as such a shock to music business pros that a coin-machine trade paper commented: "Dylan has clearly established that his brand of seemingly noncommercial music is in reality a commodity the public wants. Dylan cannot be divorced from the protest issues he sings about. Far more than any other folk singer today, he is a derivative of . . . a time he earnestly believes is corrupt."

Dylan's is scarcely the only voice of protest on the current folk scene. Malvina Reynolds of the San Francisco Bay area has dealt with fallout in a delicately ironic ballad, *What Have They Done to the Rain*. Tom Paxton has written sardonically of war in *The Willing Recruit*. *Where Have All the Flowers Gone*, recently recorded by Marlene Dietrich, is an increasingly popular anti-war ballad by Pete Seeger, whose stirring song, *If I Had a Ham-*

mer, has been a hit for Peter, Paul, and Mary as well as for Trini Lopez. In *Ira Hayes*, recorded by country singer Johnny Cash, Peter La Farge has told the tragic story of the American Indian who helped raise the flag on Iwo Jima.

Among performers who gravitate toward socially oriented material are the Chad Mitchell Trio, who define folk music as "an expression of the times preserved in music," and who feel that their Trio comes closest to being folk when they sing songs like their spoof of *The John Birch Society* and their anti-Nazi version of *The Twelve Days of Christmas*, both of which "express *our* time and involve issues that concern us."

There is no question that the folk renascence is infinitely broader than just topical or protest songs. It seems clear that the folk revival reflects the troubling search of young people for new, positive ideas. As the union and liberal movements of the 'thirties and 'forties once stirred the imagination of the college generation, so today the nationwide campaign against racial inequality has caused a ferment on the campus. The Old Baptist song, *O Ship of Zion*, which became *Union Train* in the depression, has become *Freedom Train* with The Freedom Singers, a quartet of field secretaries of the Student Nonviolent Coordinating Committee. The audiences that applaud The Freedom Singers and join in their songs are not unaware that each member of the group has served a jail sentence for civil-rights activities. In contrast with the era of cool jazz, we are again in a period of commitment and participation.

The high seriousness and dedication of the folk artist and fan lead inevitably to strictures and cults encountered in jazz but not in other areas of popular music. The folk status of The Kingston Trio is questioned by purists, for example, because of the secondary source of their material, and also because of their slick style. The Trio argue:

"After all, what is ethnic? It's what is true in the time and place it's sung. Why should we imitate Leadbelly's inflections when we have so little in common with his background and experience?" Ed McCurdy, whose repertoire runs from romper ditties to the ribald, laughs at the idea that a folk singer must come from the hills and learn tunes at his mother's knee; he suggests that urban performers call themselves "city-type singers," which is close to the identification favored by Peter, Paul, and Mary. "We're urban folk singers," says Peter. "We try to make the music significant for today."

The traditional definition of folk music emphasizes two concepts: unknown origin and oral transmission. Implicit is a third concept: that the subject matter or experience is indigenous to the singer's background. Even today there are a certain number of folk singers who are *ethnic* in this pure sense, such as Jean Ritchie, whose tender, dulcimer-accompanied ballads come out of a Kentucky background she has described in *Singing Family of the Cumberlands*, and Mance Lipscomb, an elderly Brazos Valley sharecropper, who worked the land all his life and functioned as a "songster" on Sundays, accumulating a rich storehouse of reels, breakdowns, drags, shouts, jubilees, and blues. The danger inherent in restricting folk music to ethnic singers is suggested by a recent statement of another country blues singer, Sam Lightnin' Hopkins: "The white boys just don't have the voices for blues. . . . They're afraid to let go of themselves. Afraid it makes them too much like a fool. . . . It isn't white man's music."

With rare exceptions, most purists grant that a singer who immerses himself in material and milieu may develop the ability to re-create a given style. Included among such *reporters* or *interpreters* are the New Lost City Ramblers, a trio of college-bred city slickers, who effectively re-create the "old-timey" string-band music that antedated contemporary Bluegrass. There are also the Greenbrier Boys, another Manhattan-based trio, who have won banjo and band competitions at the Annual Old Time Fiddlers Convention in North Carolina and whose music has been acclaimed as a true re-creation of the spirited style popularized by Lester Flatt and Earl Scruggs of the Foggy Mountain Boys. When he performs Texas songs, Alan Lomax, son of pioneer John Lomax, is an authentic reporter. But his labors as a collector (*Folk Songs of North America*), spanning as they do the past three decades, make him along with Pete Seeger a dean of the current revival.

The largest and the best-known group (also best-rewarded) consists of the *popularizers* or professional performers whose primary interest is to entertain. The spellbinders of folk music, they help build an audience for the "ethnics" and the "authentics." While this group does not lack Negro representation (Odetta, Belafonte, Leon Bibb, etc.) it is preponderantly white and Ivy League. In truth, so many performers of the revival possess college degrees that it has been said: "Once they went to college for the higher education; now they go to join a folk-singing group." This is true of The Brothers Four (University of Washington), The Highwaymen (Wesleyan) and, to press the point, of Joan Baez, who began her career in a Harvard coffee shop. Of course, some singers have come to folk simply by way of jazz, as in the case of Brother John Sellers, who played with Dizzy Gillespie, later sang with Mahalia Jackson, and has forged a style that is a cross between Southern Holy Roller and Northern City Folk.

At the March on Washington in August 1963, as the swelling assemblage waited for the signal to proceed from the Washington to the Lincoln monument, various folk singers entertained the crowd. Among these were Peter, Paul, and Mary; Bob Dylan; Odetta; and Josh White. The first voice heard was that of slender, long-haired, olive-complexioned Joan Baez, regarded as the first lady of folk music at the age of twenty-three. In May she had gone to Birmingham to join the demonstrations against segregation. Yet her repertoire belongs to no one school.

"I don't care very much about where a song came from or why," she has said. "All I care about is how it sounds and the feeling of it. I'm not a pure folk singer. I couldn't be. But I try to be an honest one."

And Seeger has said of the present craze: "No one sector has charge of the situation, not the Right nor the Left, the cynic nor the romanticist, the purist nor the hybridist, the scholar nor the fan, the money-maker nor the money-spurner."

What "has charge" is the kind of values that figure in Joan Baez's approach to her material. The current concern among performers and audiences is with the canons of integrity, honesty, genuine feeling that were dismissed as "corny" not too long ago—most of all, perhaps, by our young people. These values apparently become important when people are trying to move forward, as in the massive effort to eliminate racial inequality. At such critical moments, songs become weapons, editorials, instruments to hearten and inspire. Alongside the popular songs of personal desire and hurt, new songs develop and old songs are revived, expressing communal experience, frustrations, dreams. Nor is this literature a grim one. It has, in fact, a rich vein of humor, described as "a grin with a bite in it," a smile with a thought in it. One can hear it in Malvina Reynolds' brittle satire of suburbia, *Little Boxes*—all the same and all made of ticky-tacky.

Whether one sings, listens, ponders or just beats time, the folk frenzy is a matter for rejoicing, reflecting as it does an affirmative change in the temper of the college generation, a still-to-be-assessed turn from cool spectatorism to active involvement.

MICHAEL CRAIG PATTERSON

CONSCIENCE OF AN OBJECTOR

"... no man has any obligation to fight for something with which he strongly disagrees or which is against his conscience...."

THE sanctity of God and Country has become so inviolate that any disagreements with their dictates are usually assured of instant social reproach. Injustice and misunderstanding always arise when one attempts to compress into a few thousand words the countless impressions that contribute to his convictions, and further harm is done when the bases of a particular position vary measurably among different people. That I am speaking only for myself must be understood in order to differentiate my position from those of other men also assembled under the ambiguous and collective term, "conscientious objector."

My arguments can be broken down into two general areas. The first involves the principle of compulsory military service which, in the United States, is enforced through the Selective Service System. The second involves the acceptance of violence as a method of enforcing decisions or policies. The two will be treated separately in this essay because they exist on separate levels. The problem of compulsory military service involves common law and Constitutional principles, whereas the question of the validity of violence as a problem-solving institution involves personal evaluation of one's ethics, his convictions, and his view of how man and his social order are to exist.

My principal Constitutional objection to compulsory military service lies in its violation of the Thirteenth Amendment. This amendment states that "neither slavery nor involuntary servitude, except as punishment for a crime whereof the prisoner shall be duly convicted," shall exist in the United States. The fact that a person is paid for his services does not destroy the fact that service without desire or permission is involuntary servitude. Nor does the fact that the government considers the service essential for its preservation or the common good give it the right to assume power not granted in the Constitution, and expressly forbidden by the Thirteenth Amendment. Arguments such as that of the Supreme Court in *Arver vs. the United States* in 1918 [1] have no bearing because they are not founded on laws, but on assumptions not universally accepted and lacking confirmation in the Constitution. Constitutional government requires that policies and actions be determined within the framework of the specified limits of government. If a state were able to expand its powers on the basis of assumptions it decides are valid, without first amending its constitution to include the new powers, any claims to its being a limited government would be farcical. Arguments contained in *Arver*, the leading case involving constitutionality of the draft, are attempts to rationalize the existence of an institution which has no legal authorization. While military service itself cannot be considered involuntary servitude, compulsory service governed by universal, predetermined rules contains no element of individual consent, and, since it is not inflicted as punishment for a crime, has no legal justification in the United States.

A second Constitutional objection to the draft system is its violation of the First Amendment. In order for an individual to qualify for conscientious objector status, he must attribute his position to belief in a "... Supreme Being involving duties superior to those arising from any human relation ..." The law states that "essentially political, sociological, or philosophical views or a merely personal moral code" are not sufficient grounds for conscientious objector claims. To require belief in a Supreme Being as the only legitimate grounds for a moral position is absurd, and for the state to demand such

[1] The Court said that no society can survive unless it can require its members to share in military duty, and, consequently, military obligations are inherent in all citizens.

belief as a prerequisite for dissent is clearly a violation of the separation of church and state principle of the First Amendment.[2] The Supreme Court is now in the process of considering the constitutionality of the "Supreme Being clause." However, until the Court's decision is delivered in the case of *United States vs. Seeger*, the clause is still binding.

Also inherent in the First Amendment freedoms is the right for an individual to act according to his conscience. The draft requires an individual to enforce, with violence or threat of violence, policies of the government with which he may have political disagreement or which may be against his conscience. There is little tolerance of dissent within the Armed Forces, and, if an individual is in the service because of conscription, he has no opportunity to question the validity of the cause for which he is required to fight. I contend that no man has any obligation to fight for something with which he strongly disagrees or which is against his conscience. To require him to do so is intolerable.

Similarly, no man or state has the right to order a man to kill anyone. Taking a man's life is a drastic move. If such an action is to occur, it must be because the individual has critically and conscientiously considered the action, not because he "is merely carrying out orders," to quote the Nazi war-crimes prisoners. The soldier is put in a position of being required to kill or maim. If he hasn't considered his actions critically and decided for himself the rectitude of the deeds, he becomes a machine, fighting blindly for a cause with which, upon analysis, he might not agree.

The second major area of argument against military service involves objection to the use of violence as a method of enforcing decisions or policies. Problems that must be considered here are the nature of force, basic assumptions on the part of individuals and governments as to the necessity for violence or war, and the nature of a man's obligations to his country, to other men, and to his convictions. Also to be considered are the paradox of the Bomb, the effectiveness of non-violent techniques for dealing with problems, and the role of conscience.

It is important that the distinction between force and violence be emphasized. Violence is one of the many forms of force. It implies physical coercion and arbitrary destruction leading from unrestrained anger. Force, in addition to violence, includes other means of attaining an end. It lies in words, printed and oral, in the power of example, in law, and in symbols and illusions which the mind can relate to its emotions and its beliefs, and, subsequently, translate into actions. The essence of force lies in its ability to effect either maintenance of something or change. Force can best be seen, perhaps, by visualizing it as a scale. On one end lie the symbols mentioned above which indirectly stimulate action. On the other end lies violence, the most direct, most drastic, most physically brutish level of force. It exists not as a stimulant of action, but as action itself, aimed directly at destruction. Between the two extremes lie the other types of force. The essential point is that the levels of force exist

[2] In denying exemption to non-religious objectors, the regulations also violate the equal protection principle of the "due process clause" of the Fifth Amendment.

in a progressive hierarchy, each level more complex, more physical, and more immediately effective than the preceding level. Man's problem is that he must decide at what level of force in any given situation will he remain without resorting to a more complex, more drastic form.

It is a misconception to believe that violence itself solves problems. The most that can be hoped for when violence is used is postponement of the real issue. For example, wars are fought to combat rival ideologies or nations whose concepts of government or economics threaten one's own. But rather than handling the threat by eliminating the causes which create and nurture the rival system, the warring parties kill humans, destroy cities and countryside, and, at best, remove the existing government. The conditions that encouraged the development of the rival system have not been destroyed by the war, and, in the future, may again produce the same system. We claim to have won World War II; yet we are not certain that a Nazi or Fascist system will not gain support again. All that the War accomplished was to delay the real issue. Ideas can only be fought with reason; bombs leave them unscathed.

Governments and people are too often willing to adopt a more drastic and immediate level of force without considering the ultimate futility of violence and the needless death and destruction whenever violence is employed. One of the results is that war is all too frequently a basic assumption. Sentiments such as "Why must people always be fighting?" and "I wish this were a more peaceful era" become platitudes when they are followed by "Why don't we go in and take care of those troublemakers?" Unfortunately, the phrase "to take care of" generally has military connotations. During a military conflict, one party is wronged and retaliates. Counter-retaliation occurs, and, eventually, the battle escalates far beyond the importance of the original issue. Essential, therefore, is awareness by the government and citizenry that violence is not as desirable and inevitable as may be believed. Another level of force may solve the particular problem if applied more intelligently and for a longer period of time. However, if the inevitability or the rectitude of war is the basic assumption before all other levels of force are tried, the resulting destruction will be absurd.

The issue of where a man's obligations lie is a crucial question. Does he have an absolute obligation to the state whereby he is bound to follow any dictates it may prescribe? Does he have a relative obligation whereby he must do some things demanded by the government and not others, and, if so, at what point can a man veto a state demand and still believe that living in a society requires concessions and compromises for the common good? Or, is man ultimately responsible only to his own beliefs? A rule-of-the-thumb answer is impossible because each viewpoint is considered valid by many people.

To me, man's obligations are relative, not absolute. His intelligence tells him that compromise and concession are required for any social harmony and, paradoxically, for the individual to be free to seek his goals without fear of being killed by some other man also striving toward some end. All just law is, ultimately, a vehicle of mass cooperation designed to increase each man's safety in reaching the end he chooses. However, I hold that a man, whenever his strongest personal convictions are involved and whenever his conscience so requires, can veto any demand made upon him by anyone. A person's strongest convictions often embody the goal toward which he lives, and, since he has compromised many beliefs or desires as a cooperative means toward those goals, he is under no obligation to sacrifice his strongest convictions to the will of any person or government. The tool that must be used to determine at what point he will refuse an external demand must be his conscience. Merely because the state says that an issue is of monumental importance, I am not bound to use violence in support of the government's position. This is not to say that I would not employ another level of force to meet the issue because the issue may be sufficiently important to me to warrant a milder level of force. However, since I regard unwarranted violence as morally wrong, I insist on the right to veto any governmental demand that requires my use of violence whenever my conscience dictates that participation would be contrary to my principles. Therefore, I cannot conscientiously accept any position in the military services until the time that an issue which has proved to be unsolvable by all other levels of force insults my values to the point that my conscience requires violent action.

The advent of atomic and hydrogen bombs has created a paradox that man never before faced. An argument for maintaining the Bomb is its deterrent effect, thus securing the peace against ill-considered military action. However, the result of the Bomb being used either through direct Presidential order in time of war, or through human or mechanical failure would be *total destruction*. The fact that sixteen hundred forty out of sixteen hundred fifty-six arms races throughout history have ended in war, and the other sixteen in economic collapse, lends little credence to the notion that the expansion of arms and overkill potential will result in peace. The paradox of the notion that peace can be maintained by instruments capable of ending all human concepts of civilization is compounded by the absurdity of all other weapons in lieu of the Bomb. Nations can proclaim policies of limited warfare and may attempt to follow such policies, but the knowledge that the Bomb may be pulled out of hiding by a losing side in any war will always be present. I have no solution. I can only refuse to be part of the insanity which has expanded the threat of violence to include destruction of mankind. I can accept violence out of individual self-protection when the individual's person is directly threatened with injury or destruction. But the madness inherent in any instrument capable of total destruction is beyond my tolerance, and, in terms of military service, beyond my cooperation.

The criticism is often made that the rejectors of violence are do-nothings, "content to lie down bravely to die rather than fight valiantly to live." This criticism could not be more in error. Non-violence can frequently be more immediately effective, more successful, and less damaging than any violent technique. In fact, throughout history, it is the non-violent actions and programs which follow a war or take the place of it entirely that insure the ultimate victory or failure of the supposed victor. In terms of contemporary life, I offer as an example of the success of non-violence, the work of Dr. Martin Luther King. Dr. King and the civil rights movement are fighting an enemy strikingly similar to that of Nazi Germany twenty-five years ago. The same hatred, the same madness, the same blind intolerance which characterized the Nazis also characterize the racial and religious bigots of the United States. However, the civil rights battle in America is being fought effectively through reason and peace rather than violence. Incredibly, the brutality extended by the bigots is repelled by such an overwhelming belief in the rectitude of non-violent force that no man, even the most adamant segregationist, if he were honest, would deny the growing victory of the civil rights cause. Reason, tolerance, and the force of example are not passive. Only through their use can a victory be secured. This success is proven, unlike violence, which, instead of victory, leaves random and useless death and destruction.

I have stressed the role of conscience throughout this essay because it is the primary basis of my position. The sanctity of conscience is inviolate. One must be honest with himself, and his actions must reflect that honesty. My refusal to cooperate with the military is absolute until such time when my conscience might dictate the necessity for violence, or, recognizing that I could be in error, until the power of reason persuades me to change my stand. That the reader agree with me is not requested, but that he respect my right to act as my conscience dictates is demanded.

In the month since the first half of this essay was written, the Supreme Court has handed down its decision in the case of *United States vs. Seeger*. I would like, therefore, to comment on that decision and its effect upon my classification and also to mention briefly a few implications and motives behind a conscientious objector position.

The Supreme Court did not declare the "Supreme Being clause" of the Selective Service regulations unconstitutional. It did, however, substantially broaden the Government's recognition of what constitutes a Supreme Being. The Court declared that the Government cannot question the validity of what an individual claims to be his Supreme Being. All that a draft board can question is the sincerity of the registrant's position. To be eligible for conscientious objector classification, the individual must base his position on some *supreme obligation* which he believes he must follow. The Supreme Being need not be an orthodox concept of God; it may be devotion to some supreme obligation such as Truth, Love, Brotherhood, Creator, Over-all Power, or Conscience. The sole distinction is that the belief must occupy ". . . a place in the life of its possessor parallel to that filled by the orthodox belief in God of one who clearly qualifies for the exemption."

I view several inconsistencies inherent in the Court's decision. First, the Selective Service requirement that an individual's political, sociological, or philosophic beliefs or his personal moral code are not sufficient grounds for conscientious objector classification is still in effect. However, religion, to me, is nothing more than constant examination of new ideas and devotion to one's own concept of what is true and beautiful, and I question whether the individual or the state can distinguish obligations derived from a Supreme Being and obligations derived fron one's own beliefs and self-examination. But, by law, beliefs *externally* derived and beliefs *internally* derived must be distinguished. Such distinction is, to me, impossible. One may have a supreme obligation to act in some way, but his belief still comes out of a personal moral code. Second, the Court failed to specify the criteria by which a draft board is to determine the registrant's sincerity. One can hope that the boards will limit their investigations to possible inconsistencies between an individual's actions and statements. But it is possible that a board's inability to grasp an individual's position or concept of Supreme Being will result in doubting his sincerity. In such a case, sincerity is determined by judgment on the validity of the person's concept of Supreme Being, even though such inquiry is forbidden by the Court.

Regardless of its few weaknesses, the Court's decision is a momentous improvement in governmental policy. The protection of the First Amendment is extended so that an individual no longer must profess belief in an orthodox God nor rely upon dogmatic statements about religion in order to assert his right to act according to conscience. I cannot accept many of the implications inherent in the traditional concepts of God, yet the Government recognized my concept of Supreme Being, *i.e.*, conscience, as having a religiously obligatory role in my life, and, in accordance with the Supreme Court's decision and the First Amendment, it did not require me to act contrary to conscience. Prior to the Court's decision, conscientious objectors with positions similar to mine were forced to choose between compromise and prison.

One of the most serious misconceptions that the public has about conscientious objectors is the belief that the objectors are unwilling to fulfill their obligations of citizenship. Many people believe that the objector is perfectly willing to derive the benefits of being a citizen, but is too selfish to contribute to the betterment and success of the society. My refusal to participate in the military indicates both an expression of my values and an assertion of what I believe to be a positive contribution to the values that I feel are latently inherent within the country and mankind. I hold that if acceptance of and participation in war are the only ways to contribute to one's country, patriotism is a negative force leading to little possibility of improving the human condition. Patriotism cannot be blinded by pettiness, nor by the fallacies of viewing one's values strictly by national standards, nor by limiting one's tolerance of others and divergent viewpoints solely to the geographical borders of one's own country. Patriotism extends beyond devotion to country; it embraces devotion to man in general. It requires tolerance of all human beings.

I am not so blind as to believe that mutual respect among all men will remove disagreements or serious conflicts. They will exist, but their solutions must lie not in mass murder and destruction. As I mentioned in Part I, the basic assumption that war is necessary has carried man to the point that he is *now* capable of *total destruction*. Intelligence at the moron level should be sufficient to indicate that maintaining a policy of militarism will leave little hope for the continuance of life. I believe strongly that my refusal to participate in the military, rather than exemplifying unwillingness to fulfill the obligations of citizenship, is a positive attempt to avoid what could very well be man's conclusion. It is also a statement of my belief that war is neither a successful nor an honorable institution. Society, on the level of civil justice, asserts that it is wrong to murder a man because one disagrees with him or sees his plans conflicting with one's own. Yet on the international level, murder is not condemned, and, ironically, an individual must ask permission from the state to refuse to kill and destroy. We have been able to extend human tolerance and patriotism to the national boundaries. Can we not extend them one step further and attempt to build a world wherein the basic assumption that war is necessary and proper is supplanted by the assumption that all men have an inalienable right *to live* and *to be*?

That the federal government was willing to respect my right to place conscience above a government dictate was a significant step toward the ultimate tolerance which I believe is crucial. But the problem is not solved. Not until religious and racial injustices cease, not until the censor refuses to hide dissident viewpoints, and not until all men and countries can pursue their goals without fear of being destroyed by the bombs of a rival can any vision of ultimate tolerance be realized. Men are gradually attaining a greater tolerance for each other; all that I ask, as a conscientious objector, is that they be permitted to continue the task without the fear that some military force will stifle them with a deathly finality.

> I have received permission to refuse to kill and
>   destroy.

> My right to be Commander in Chief of my Being
>   is acknowledged.

> Both the state and I exist—
>   mutually inclusive, mutually exclusive—
>   each recognizing, respecting,
>   and complimenting the other.

> My Being has been distinguished from
>   The Gelatin Mass, and

> The *I* can be asserted and honored.

> Half the battle is won . . .

WILLARD THORP

THE WELL OF ENGLISH, NOW DEFILED

"...what appalls one most is that these elected words of ours ... reveal the preoccupations and the state of mind of the age in which we live...."

WHEN Edmund Spenser paused for a moment in the fourth book of his *Faerie Queene* to refer reverently to an earlier poet, Geoffrey Chaucer, as that "well of English undefiled," he was implying, I gather, that the English of his day had become poisoned with ink-horn terms and Italianate expressions. This allusion ought to comfort me as I begin my discussion of the evidences of defilement in English prose today, and more particularly as English teachers see them in the writing we receive from our students. But I am not much comforted because Spenser and fifty other influential writers of Elizabethan England were busy removing the poison from the well. I am not sure we can again accomplish this kind of sanitary engineering. By 1958 the incidence of poison in the well may have passed the safety mark.

I have been red-penciling student papers for a good many years and I ought by now to have become resigned or cynical. But I am not, and the reason for my present concern is a sinister change in the kind of writing we have lately been getting from our students. It used to be that we could do our duty and even bring about reforms by sprinkling in the margins of themes those cabalistic signs "coh." (for coherence), "sp." (for spelling), and "gr." (for grammar). But these traditional correctives will no longer serve. We are now too often presented with a kind of prose—if that is the name for it—which is inviolable. A red-pencil used against it becomes as impotent as a sword in a folk-tale which has had a spell put on it. Sometimes this prose resembles remotely a bad translation from a foreign language. Sometimes it suggests that the writer has squeezed together under pressure the jagged ends of several assorted ideas. The only name I have for this monstrosity is *No-English*.

The writer of No-English is unconscious of the fact that his pages resemble nothing else under the sun. If you say to him, "This is not English.

"The Well of English, Now Defiled," by Willard Thorp. Originally published September 26, 1958, in *Princeton Alumni Weekly*. Reprinted by permission of Professor Thorp and the Editor, *Princeton Alumni Weekly*.

You must tear this up and try again," he will answer plaintively: "But you know what I *mean*, don't you?" He will be indignant if you reply, "I can *guess*, but only because I know what you are supposed to mean."

Let me read you a few choice samples of No-English. These come, alas, from examination papers in my sophomore course in American literature. I shall save the honor of the writers, though not of Princeton, by withholding the names of the perpetrators.

A change from the optimistic view of the individual man as put forth in trancendentic philosophy to the pessimistic view of man kind frought with invalide morals living a superficial life with no direction such as T. S. Eliot flitting bug-eyed from Antwerp to Brussels to London.

He was a man who had dispared to the nature of man and although he had these tendencies of subjection he soon gained aspirations and broke away from the school of disparants and strove on his own beliefs.

When Twain was writing *Huckleberry Finn* he decided to implement the voyage as a cohesive catalyst. Twain used a general local. Faulkner has a restrictive local, and Thoreau wrote for everybody in the universal.

Huck Finn sets out in a cimilar direction, away from society. He also floats on the sea of life and has periodic relations with the sourrounding society. The Grangerfords put Huck up, for instance, and promptly acquaint him with social disorganization and bitterness.

The American ideal seemed to hang void in the twenties, a shameful thing because Americans must forage ahead. Eliot was not the gung-ho American as Whitman. Whitman was one of the best examples of this "nature into thought" angle.

To one who cares about the well-forged instrument by which those who use English communicate with one another there are, I submit, some very alarming symptoms of decay and defilement in these passages of No-English. Listened to with half an ear they sound impressive, authoritative, and even powerful. Though their authors were composing complete nonsense, they put down these jumbled words with the self-assurance of an advertising copy-writer or an editor of *Time*.

Why is the tide of No-English flooding in with such power that we cannot stand against it? I think I know some of the reasons.

First in importance is the influence of officialese. This is the age of the official statement from government, of communiqués, of press releases from public relations officers. All writing of this sort must sound impressive and authoritative, for it is composed to be believed in without dissent.

I have here a prime example of officialese which originated, I am happy to say, not in America but England.

It will be apparent that the draining away of senior experienced men will be of such proportions for some years to come as to constitute a serious factor to be contended with in providing for the adequate staffing of State departments. The difficulty in this respect is aggravated by the expansion of governmental activities which has been a feature during the last few years, and which seems likely to persist for some time. This expansion has already imposed considerable strain upon the personnel of the public service and, coupled with the progressive wastage in the ranks of the senior officers to which reference has been made, tends to produce conditions which, on occasion, border on the acute. The Commission is giving its particular attention to the problems contained in and engendered by the circumstances already present and those which it is anticipated will develop in future.

These lines of "twisted, pretentious, long-winded and down-at-heel" officialese, can, with a little labor, be shortened to fewer than half the lines. You can always condense officialese by about two-thirds. This is one of the ways you recognize it.

So many senior and experienced officers will leave the service during the next few years that State departments will be short of staff; and the difficulties this will cause will be aggravated if, as seems possible, the State's activities continue to expand. The Commission is giving this matter attention.

My long-suffering ear tells me that my students are more often than not trying to write officialese. And why not? This is the way very important people in our society "reveal" or "announce" what are supposed to be matters of life-or-death. This is the interminable voice of the age—or one of its voices.

The evident desire of the writers of No-English to pack power into their prose I think I can trace to another defiler of the well of English. Almost every magazine an undergraduate picks up is likely to be written in a hot-rod style which bursts with energy in every sentence. Authors who wish to sell their wares to *Time*, *Look*, and *Life*, must write in a 500-horsepower style. And their editors, as well, seem to live in constant fear that if they take the foot off the accelerator the reader will drop off to sleep between sentences or, bored and indifferent, turn on the television set.

Two qualities of *Time*-style exert an especially subtle influence. The supercharged *Time*- or *Newsweek*-sentence teaches the student that his prose should never be quiet. It must always shock with the hotfoot. You cannot imagine, for instance, *Time*'s printing one of the calm and witty essays of E. B. White. It would be as much out of place as a preacher at a jitterbug contest.

The souped-up article also teaches the student-reader that certain words are absolute as definitions or attributes of mind and body. No variations or gradations are possible and so none need be sought. Take, for instance, one of *Time*'s pet words—*paunchy*. As one whose paunchiness is increasingly distressful to him, I resent this word's invariability. There was a time when I had a little *professorial pot;* later I was *stout* (as we used to say, in a politer era); then I became, I suppose, definitely *pot-bellied*. But in *Time*'s view I have always been paunchy and there is no need for other words to describe my long struggle with the flesh, my triumphs and my eventual defeat. That is what I have been—paunchy—from graduation day until this moment. Consider another of *Time*'s favorites—*bug-eyed*. Gone are the possibilities of playing with such fine old words as *startled, a-feared, aghast, agog, spellbound, open-mouthed, thunder-struck*. And neither is there any way of knowing whether the man affected with bug-eyedness inherited his condition or is a hyperthyroid case or is exophthalmic. He is just bug-eyed —that's all.

Much more to be feared than the poison-vials of officialese or of *Time* is the expensively distilled poison of advertising-style. Students cannot escape it—nor can we. Though we have our mental blinders in place as we try to read down the river of text in the middle of the page, a glowing specimen of cheesecake lures us to the left-hand column and the depilatory she is applying, all unconcerned to be in so public a place with almost no clothes on. The poet Karl Shapiro has characterized the alarming magnetic pull of advertising in five lines of his satiric poem "Drug Store."

> And every nook and cranny of the flesh
> Is spoken to by packages with wiles.
> "Buy me, buy me," they whimper and cajole;
> The hectic range of lipstick pouts,
> Revealing the wicked and the simple mouth.

Everywhere we go we are assaulted by the adman. We cannot escape him by taking to the highways or diving into a subway station. He pursues us even in our dreams. His latest horror—subliminal-perception on TV—has just come upon us.

One of the most insidious things about advertising-style is that it burns up the language at a furious rate because there is so much oxygen in it. The new Plymouth, the ad-man says, is *newest, most modern* of the low-price three. Also *biggest*. Its Power-Flow 117 motor is *brilliant*. Its Power-Flite no-clutch transmission is the *finest made*. The next ad-writer for Plymouth is going to find ashes all over his cubicle. What can he dig out of the dictionary which is newer than *newest*, bigger than *biggest*, higher than *highest horsepower in the field*?

In the next place, consider the consumption of debased advertising metaphors which goes on in one issue of *Look* or *Life*. We note that "a new day has dawned for the car owners of America." Can this startling statement mean that the atomic-powered automobile has arrived? Not at all. Firestone is merely marketing a new tire. And how are we to "open the door on tomorrow"? By such exciting experiences as getting married? having a baby? a plane trip to Europe? Certainly not. That "door on tomorrow" will open if you make an itsy-bitsy deposit on a Dodge. And what is this on the next page?—"Like all great ideas, this one's slightly marvelous—yet so simple." Can it be we are about to hear something of the order of magnitude of the second law of thermodynamics or Leibnitz's theory of the monads? We are not so easily fooled. We know instinctively, after years of indoctrination, that this great idea will prove, alas, to be only Sta-Flat's creation of a new girdle, with extra strength where you need it most ("midriff, waist, tummy").

I hope I shall live long enough to watch the ad-men run out of metaphors. It will be a happy day. Writers of strong but simple prose may then have a chance again. When there are no more metaphors for

> Kleenex, Kotex, Gleem, and Lux,
> Schick and Mosco, and Coldeen,
> Zemo, Scripto, Schlitz, and Duz,
> Cutex, Crispies and Bactine

the ad-men will have to go back to their old-fashioned unmetaphorical, harmless style, still used, I'm happy to report, by Sergeant's *Sure-Shot* Capsules: "Stop Worms! Don't neglect worms in your dog! . . . 75¢ at any pet counter."

There is another defiler of modern prose whose poisoning is carried out under the cover of darkness. Consequently I should find it difficult to identify him in a police-court lineup. Professor John Clark of the University of Minnesota declares that the culprit is the second-rate newspaper reporter. I am not sure he is the chief offender, but I am certain that some person or persons unknown have put over on us lately a most peculiar, very limited vocabulary which serves, unfortunately, to cover every situation in modern life. In listing these words—about forty in number—Professor Clark notes that "if an historical novelist of fifty or a hundred years from now should wish to give his readers a fairly realistic illusion of the flavor of everyday American English of the 1950's, he could adopt no more economical means than to sprinkle his dialogue with these expressions."

To prove to myself how constantly these pesky words (and a few others) turn up and how unthinkingly we ourselves resort to them, I tried to see if I could use every one of them in a little descriptive scene from campus life. I can report that it took me less than ten minutes to write this vivid and highly dramatic scene, so easily did these words fall into place. I read it to you, not with pride but with shame of authorship.

A teen-ager dropped into my office today, much worried about his inferiority complex and anxious to adjust. He seemed to think I was a sincere-type professor and had some know-how in inter-personal relations. He said there was a campus-inspired rumor that I am good at human engineering and so thought he'd contact me and get a few constructive angles. First I tried to fit him into some frame of reference and then I processed him by screening him with some questions, and so got the overall picture. (I discovered, by the way, that his mother is a low-grade homemaker.) I then briefed him on the need for grasping our most unique set-up here and seeing how we are geared for modern living. Next I made him the proposition that he be less negative, more relaxed, and mix with a few of the outstanding youth at the top-flight level of our student body. He would be sure, I said, to find them like-minded, percentage-wise. When we finished off, he thanked me for our little streamlined get-together and said he would try to integrate better. I found the experience so educational that I think I'll author an article about it after I've researched the matter further.

I hope my little parable horrifies you as much as it does me. I shall try to restrain my disgust while I point out a number of things to be learned from it.

Some of the offensive expressions are hand-me-downs from pseudo-scientific writing; some derive from the writing of sociologists and psychologists; some emanate from the sales conference and the business convention. Several reveal the codified anxieties of modern life, while others are the slogans of "positive thinking" which are supposed to cure these anxieties. Because these expressions make up an important part of the vocabulary of his time, the modern student is compelled to use them. But what appalls one most is that these elected words of ours—as is always the case—reveal the preoccupations and the state of mind of the age in which we live. And what they reveal is disturbing. While this fictional professor was having his cozy little streamlined interview with this hypothetical student, neither of them was a human being—a person, as Shakespeare once said, with hands, organs, dimensions, senses, affections, passions; fed with food, subject to diseases, warmed and cooled with winter and summer. The student was an intelligence test to be taken and scored; the professor was a machine to grind out medians, percentiles, and normal distribution curves.

I come finally to the chief defiler of undergraduate writing. And I regret to say we professors are certainly the culprits. And what we are doing we do in all innocence and with the most laudable of motives. This is a serious accusation, and I must justify it or shut up.

There is one predicament in our present kind of collegiate education which, I am convinced, confuses the student who desires to write good English, which may, indeed, lead him to believe that there is no necessity for trying to write in the great tradition of English prose. What I am referring to is the tremendous specialization which the subjects in our curriculum have undergone in this century. Because the fields of learning now share very little common ground, they (and we) no longer possess a common language. The historian cannot understand the equations of the physicist and the physicist cannot understand the new vocabulary developed by the sociologist. The professor of literature who lectures about "levels of meaning," the "texture and tension of poverty," the wonderful "ambiguities" in Melville's prose, and the "personal symbolism" in the poetry of Robert Frost, opens the eyes but not the ears of his colleague in chemistry who had no idea literature was *that* difficult. This impenetrability of our particular subjects to the uninitiated does not worry us—as professors—to any great extent. We go our separate ways, happy in our isolation. We rejoice in our own jargon. We suppose, rightly of course, that our colleagues in other fields understand the strange stuff they deliver from the lecture platform.

But I have begun to notice lately that our better students take an unholy pride in the specialized vocabularies they encounter as they move through their academic day. Suppose we imagine what the impact of specialized subjects and the vocabularies by which they are presented may be on a conscientious sophomore who really wishes to comprehend what his lecturers, hour after hour, are telling him. At 8:30 in his physics class he hears this:

BARRIER DESIGN

At atmospheric pressure the mean free path of a molecule is of the order of a ten-thousandth of a millimeter or one-tenth of a micron. To insure true "diffusive" flow of the gas, the diameter of the myriad holes in the barrier must be less than one-tenth the mean free path. Therefore the barrier material must have almost no holes which are appreciably larger than 0.01 micron (4×10^{-7} inch), but must have billions of holes of this size or smaller. These holes must not enlarge or plug up as the result of direct corrosion or dust coming from corrosion elsewhere in the system. The barrier must be able to withstand a pressure "head" of one atmosphere.

At 9:30 our sophomore is in his place in his music class in Elementary Harmony. His professor, whom the student likes very much because he hopes to be a composer, also, some day, has been talking about triads in minor keys. After the late-comers have got to their seats he begins:

When the dominant and sub-mediant triads (V and VI) are connected in the minor mode, the voices have to move along certain *fixed* lines in order to avoid consecutive fifths and octaves and the augmented second. The leading-tone always ascends to the tonic (or descends from it). Two of the upper voices must move in contrary motion to the bases, and the *third is always to be doubled* in the triad on the sixth degree, *in four-part writing.*

Our earnest sophomore has a much-needed coke in the Student Center at 10:30 but at 11:30 he is in the Psychology building, eager to hear Professor Jungfreud talk on "Hedonic Summation." The professor begins:

When two simple stimuli are combined in some total perception, the hedonic tone of the resultant depends upon the sum of the hedonic tones of the two stimuli. We must, however, limit this principle in two ways. (a) It holds only when it can operate without interference by some of the other hedonic laws [I have explained]. (b) It holds only when the relative importances of the different constituents in the sum are determined and taken into account.

After a breather at lunch and fifteen minutes at the pool-table, sophomore Sandy is back in place at 1:30, listening to the Professor of Religion who is talking today on the relations between mysticism and magic. Here is what Sandy gets down—correctly, believe it or not—in his notebook.

To the two dogmas of the "Astral Light" or universal agent and the "power of the will" there is to be added a third: the doctrine of Analogy, or implicit correspondence between appearance and reality, the microcosm of man and the macrocosm of the universe, the seen and the unseen worlds. In this, occultism finds the basis of all its transcendental speculations. *Quod superius sicut quod inferius*—the first words of that Emerald Table which was once attributed to Hermes Trismegistus himself—is an axiom which must be agreeable to all Platonists.

Finally, at 2:30, comes Sandy the seeker's last lecture of the day. The course is American literature and the professor is talking about the pamphleteers of the American Revolution. He does up Tom Paine neatly in the last ten minutes of the hour and concludes by saying: "The opening paragraph of Paine's great propaganda pamphlet, 'The Crisis,' which put heart into Washington's ragged little army in December, 1776, and turned the fortunes of war in our favor, contains one of the most eloquent passages of prose written in the eighteenth century." He quotes Paine's words:

These are the times that try men's souls. The summer soldier and the sunshine patriot will, in this crisis, shrink from the service of their country; but he that stands it *now*, deserves the love and thanks of man and woman. Tyranny, like hell, is not easily conquered; yet we have this consolation with us, that the harder the conflict, the more glorious the triumph. What we obtain too cheap, we esteem too lightly; it is dearness only that gives every thing its value. Heaven knows how to put a proper price upon its goods; and it would be strange indeed if so celestial an article as FREEDOM should not be highly rated.

What does Sandy, the sophomore, think, if he can think at all, after the day's barrage of special terms and concepts; and with the weather warm outside and the crack of ball against bat coming in the window? I very much fear that this is what he thinks: "Why does the old boy ask me to listen to such stuff? What does it *tell* me for sure? I've learned important things today, a lot of them. I know how to control dominant and submediant triads in the minor mode. I've got the real poop on Hedonic Summation, and Professor Underhill certainly came through on the doctrine of analogy in mysticism. What did this jerk Tom Paine say back there that's worth listening to now? It's eloquent, is it; so what?"

Who among Sandy's faculty friends will tell him that although it is important to know all he has learned during the day, and that the beginning of wisdom is the certitude of fact, nevertheless there is something beyond fact which is of the utmost importance for him? If, in his pride of knowledge, he refuses to learn how to communicate his knowledge, his ideals and his aspirations, in language that is simple, sensuous, passionate, direct, honest, precise, varied, strong though quiet, *and* eloquent, he will never bring men to his way of thinking. He will have condemned himself to the prison of the public relations officer or the life of the Madison Avenue adman or to the drudgery, without the final reward, of the narrow specialist-scholar. Sandy deserves to win a better fate. He might become a member of the company of those who have moved men to laudable action. He might, through his skill with words, join, in time, John Milton whose *Areopagitica* still defines the rules of free enquiry, and Jonathan Swift who spoke for the oppressed in Ireland and so for enslaved men everywhere, and Thomas Jefferson, and John Stuart Mill, *and* Tom Paine whose words, Sandy does not realize, were more useful to Washington than ten thousand fighting men.

Who among us is ready to speak sternly to Sandy, our pride and our hope, though he still writes No-English?

THE AMBUSH

". . . He had never been a member of a recognized army. His loyalties were to two things: money and personal friendship. . . ."

THERE were thirteen of us in the three-quarter-ton truck, myself included. I was the only American. We stopped for lunch at a big Jarai montagnard village on Route 7.

Cowboy asked me to go with him to the house of a friend of his. This longhouse, like all the others, was a split-bamboo and thatch building set off the ground about five feet by large upright logs called *t'meh*. The floor extended in front of the longhouse proper to make a porch, against which a notched log leaned for stairs. Cowboy scooted up it with ease. I lumbered after him in considerably less agile fashion.

The lady of the house asked us inside and I ducked under the door. The effect inside was very pleasant. From the windows and through the bamboo walls the light filtered softly. The room was not cluttered. A few woven baskets and gourds hung on the walls. There was a square raised section in the middle of the floor that served as a fireplace, the smoke rising to the roof and slowly working its way out of the thatch.

The lady of the house gave us a friendly smile and offered us the floor to sit on. I leaned my AR-15 up in a corner and threw all my gear down beside it. Then I sat cross-legged on the floor. The split bamboo was resilient and pleasant to sit on.

Cowboy leaned his stuff up in the opposite corner and sat down too. He put his cowboy hat and wraparound shades on the floor beside him.

"Where's your friend?" I asked.

"He work in fields now, come back soon."

I started to ask if he was planting or what. Then I realized that Cowboy probably wouldn't know. He had been a soldier since he was twelve and probably hadn't worked a rice field in his life.

Perhaps warrior would be a better term than soldier for Cowboy. He had never been a member of a recognized army. His loyalties were to two things: money and personal friendship. I believed that personal friendship took precedence over money. I never had cause to change that belief.

He had commanded a Special Forces Strike Force Battalion for a year until he found out that being an interpreter paid roughly three times what a Battalion Commander got. He had been an interpreter for a year and a half. Cowboy was twenty-two years old.

He dived down into his pack and brought up a couple of cans of C's and pulled his canteen out of the carrier. "Let's eat," he said.

I got out two small C-ration cans, sliced ham and bread, and the little C-ration can opener. For reasons nobody now on active duty can remember it is called a P-38. The C rations and a couple of gulps of water made a pretty fair meal.

While we were eating, a little boy, about two, came in the door. He was wearing four bracelets on his left arm, and an anklet on each leg, an earring, and a Hopalong Cassidy T-shirt.

I said, "Hi, kid!"

He ran and grabbed his mother's skirts, looking back over his shoulder in apprehension. I guess he'd never seen anybody that big and blond before.

I rooted around in my pack and came up with a can of cookies and cocoa. I got up and opened the can and tried to give it to the kid. He grabbed his mother's skirts again and buried his head in her legs. I gave her two of the cookies and took one for myself. She smiled at me and gave one of the cookies to the kid. He took it and ran off, unsmiling.

I took the little envelope of cocoa and threw it back into my pack. Then I bent back the lid of the can and turned the edges under in a three-way fold, so it can be used as a cup without cutting your fingers on the edges. I gave it to the lady of the house and she smiled and nodded thanks. Later she would probably weave a wicker holder for it and throw away the lid altogether.

I always feel like some kind of condescending jackass giving my castoffs to the yards. But they take the gift as it is intended. They have marvelous dignity and never beg, but offer the hospitality of their homes, their food and their rice wine.

I went back over and sat down. "What time you think we ought to leave?" I asked Cowboy. I was beginning to think his friend wasn't going to show up.

"'Bout four," he replied.

It was one-thirty. "Okay, listen," I said, "I'm going to flake out for a while." I'd been up late the night before writing some kind of screwy report.

I awakened about three-thirty. Cowboy's friend had returned. He had changed into formal attire to meet the *Capitaine*. He was wearing a loincloth and an old U.S. Army olive-drab dress blouse. I suppose it had been lend-lease to the French and from there to one of the montagnard battalions.

"*Bonjour, Monsieur,*" I said, which almost exhausted my command of the language.

He cut loose a tremendous stream of guttural French, which Cowboy interpreted to mean that he wanted me to join him in some rice wine. My mind skittered desperately at the prospect, but I assented. It would have been uncourteous to do otherwise.

He brought the jug and sat it on the floor. Then he took out a long straw. We did not drink through the straw, but he siphoned off the *ou* into a couple of old Bière La Rue bottles.

The stuff tastes like a combination of sugar, water, and vomit. I tried to chug it down at a gulp, not breathing during the process. I couldn't kill it at once, but had to try again. Then I belched and smiled approval.

Naturally he offered more, but I informed him through Cowboy that I had a delicate stomach condition and could not continue.

Then rather more forcefully than was necessary I said, "Let's get started, Cowboy."

His grin was like a baby wolf's. He got up and put on his wraparound shades and his cowboy hat sat down low on his nose. Then he took out that greatest of all South-east Asian status symbols, a Salem cigarette, and lit it. He held the filter in his teeth, James Dean fashion.

Once he got his image intact we walked out into the sunlight and went down the notched log.

The squad was good, handpicked without regard to rank or unit. Their faces were calm and their eyes were ready.

"Cowboy," I said, "how did you explain these soldiers to the village?"

"I tell them we go hunting."

I looked at Big Stoop with his front teeth out and his thirty-caliber machine gun in his arms. "With that?"

"Oh! They know that the soldier must take what gun he have."

It seemed a poor cover to me, but the montagnards are not used to questioning things. "Okay, let's go."

We went out the bamboo gate and past the long spiked fence, the defensive positions, punji stakes and watchtowers. We turned left to head back toward the rice fields.

Moving through the fields we automatically took up a kind of loose diamond formation, although we still carried our weapons slung. Once across the field we moved into the woods and waited. I unslung my rifle and leaned against a tree. Most of the others did likewise. We faced outward into the trees, weapons ready. I lit a cigarette. After we had waited about ten minutes I asked, "Any idea how soon he come?"

"Maybe ten more minute. He must wait so nobody know we go same."

"Uh huh."

Another cigarette later Cowboy's friend came across the fields carrying a Jarai ax for protective coloration. Once he was in the trees we grinned and shook hands all around again. Then the point man moved out, then Cowboy's friend, Cowboy, me and the rest of the squad.

The way was fairly rough and for the first kilometer I felt it: I had been in camp too long. After that it was fine.

The woods were open and green and the light was golden. We crossed a fair-sized stream, jumping from rock to rock, trying to keep our feet dry. I missed the last rock, slipped and my right leg went in the water up to the knee, making me feel like a graceless fool in front of the yards. That sort of thing never happened to John Wayne.

Once we showed *The Longest Day* at the camp. We didn't have a Cinemascope lens so everything was pretty narrow, but the yards didn't seem to mind. Cowboy drove out in his old three-quarter-ton truck with his wife and little girl and a few inlaws. About halfway through the picture he turned to me and said, "This John Wayne, he is paratrooper, he is cowboy, he is pilot. What he really do?"

I tried to explain what an actor was, but he didn't grasp the concept. I guess he thought all those flicks were documentaries.

Thinking about something else makes walking go easier. After we had gone about two kilometers Cowboy's friend, the agent, pointed at the ground. I went up to look. There was a small trail, a path really. It was covered with a fine grey gravel and wound along a slight rise through the luminous green wood. It looked like the path I had imagined Hansel and Gretel taking when I was a kid; pretty in the daytime, but dark and scary at night.

"He says every day, almost, one squad VC come by here."

"They come by day or by night?" I asked.

"Sometimes day, sometimes night."

"Does he see them?"

"Sometimes. Sometimes they make greeting."

I thought that was jolly.

"This is not a good place for ambush," Cowboy said.

"True. Let's get back away from the trail and walk along until we find a good place."

Cowboy nodded and gave instructions to the squad in Jarai. It sounded like a bad coughing fit.

Keeping the same order, we set off through the woods, moving parallel to the trail. The country was not good for ambushes. There was no commanding terrain. There was very little cover, but there was tall grass and some trees to hide behind. Finally we found a place that was less ridiculous than the rest, and set up.

Cowboy asked if I wanted to position the squad. "You are Captain. I must do as you order."

"You've set this thing up. As far as I'm concerned you're running the show. If I see something I don't like I'll let you know and we'll work it out."

Then I asked how he planned to set up.

"AR's on flanks. Machine gun in middle. All spread out with maybe five meter between each and get cover."

Aside from the automatic rifles and the machine gun, every man in the squad had either a Grease Gun or an M-2 carbine, all automatic weapons. Cowboy and I had AR-15's. An AR-15 looks like a cross between a Buck Rogers ray gun and a king cobra. It is six pounds plus of sudden death. It was a hell of a lot of firepower for thirteen men. We could take on anything up to a VC platoon with ease. Anything bigger than that was bad trouble.

I suggested to Cowboy that he put a one-man outpost out behind us so we wouldn't have any unexpected callers coming in from that way. He agreed.

Cowboy placed each man in position behind the best cover he could find. We were pretty well concealed by some tall grass. I chose a spot by a V-fork tree about fifteen feet from the trail and sat down cross-legged.

I took off my patrol harness and put it on the ground in front of me; then I opened the ammo pouches, took a magazine out of both of them and laid them where they could be reached easily. There were two magazines taped together in a U on the weapon itself, and eight more from the pouches, two hundred rounds in all. Then I unsnapped the snaps on the canteen carrier to avoid making the noise later in the night. The canteen itself was wrapped in a wool sock and would make no metallic noise against its cup when taken out.

Everything was ready. It was five-thirty. I opened a can of peaches with the P-38 and ate them with a dirty plastic spoon from my shirt pocket. By then it was getting dark. I rammed the can into the ground, olive drab side up, so the bright metal of its inside would not show; then turned the selector switch to full automatic and lay the weapon beside me.

You have to sit perfectly still and make no noise. None. So immediately you want a cigarette. You have to cough. Your throat starts to tickle and your nose itches. Your back aches, then your legs, then your shoulders, then your neck. When you do not react to this, but continue to sit still, the mind casts about for thoughts to amuse itself and pass the hours.

The moon rose to our front.

I started to shake uncontrollably. It was not cold and I was not afraid. It was a flat rush of adrenalin and the sudden knowledge that the ambush would go. I have had the same feeling since, and it has failed, and sometimes I have not had it and scored. But this was the first time and I was sure. Then the shaking passed and my mind was coldly detached.

My aching shoulders were hunkered for a long wait. I did not expect to see anything until three o'clock the next morning. The moon was high now and full and gold in the blue-black sky with the clouds turning to silver. The breeze rose and then died and the black silhouettes of armed men were passing quickly, quietly down the trail.

We were all firing. One faded from my sights. Tracers from the thirty-caliber weapons were ricocheting so high I thought the Cong were sending up flares. I fired up one magazine and then another. I kept firing. We all did. I wanted nothing to live out there. I felt nothing, neither elation nor horror, just the cold astringent calm.

I fired up five magazines before I stopped. Then everybody stopped and I called out, "Cowboy, let's check out the stiffs."

"Yes, sir."

We got up and moved onto the trail. The bodies were lying to the left, to the right, on the trail, cut down running. There were six bodies in all. Three had moved through and got away before we opened up. Later we learned that another died in a village the following morning.

I moved from one dark shape to the other, making sure they were dead. I fired a round into the ground by each man to see if he would move. None did. Cowboy moved beside a covering.

When I moved up on the last one, he raised up, his arms extended, eyes wide. He had no weapon. I said, "Good, we got a pris—"

Cowboy stitched him up the middle with his AR-15. He didn't even twitch.

"Goddamn it," I said, "we could have got some good information from that guy."

"Sorry," said Cowboy, "I get, you know, excited."

Nothing to do but shrug it off. I said, "Get their weapons and packs and we'll move out."

Cowboy was looking fearfully down the trail. "Maybe better we just get weapons. Must move fast now."

That sounded okay. When we got a report that the weapons had been picked up, I said, "We'll come back for the packs tomorrow." Cowboy didn't say anything, just moved. He really wanted to get out of there.

We cut straight cross-country through the brush and the creek, moving quietly and taking no known trail. We were back in the village by ten o'clock and the villagers loaned us a half-completed longhouse with a roof on it to sleep in.

I hadn't brought a poncho because I had expected to be all night in an ambush position and didn't want to be comfortable and go to sleep.

I flaked out on the bamboo floor with the yards, but it got cold pretty fast and I couldn't sleep. One of the yards had a spare poncho in the truck. He offered it to me. I declined. He insisted. I rolled up in it and wished for a pillow. Never satisfied.

The next morning we hired some villagers to go with us to carry back the Cong's packs and equipment.

The bodies still lay across the trail in their black shortie pajamas and their black sandals made from old truck-tire treads. Rigor mortis had set in and the ants were marching in straight lines across their bodies. They were so stiff we had to cut most of the equipment off.

I wanted to take the stiffs back with the rest of the gear. I figured it would make quite a stir when we kicked them out in front of the Ops Shack. Cowboy pointed out that there was hardly room for thirteen men, all those packs and six stiffs in the back of a three-quarter-ton truck. Besides, it might make some of the boys a little twitchy. I said okay and we left the stiffs on the trail.

Back at the village we gave each of the porters 20 piasters apiece, which is about twenty cents, and Cowboy slipped his buddy, the agent, one thousand in small, old bills when nobody was looking. Then we thanked everybody, shook hands, exchanged smiles, said *Bonjour,* and *Merci,* a few times, jumped in the truck and drove off.

There was no rush. We stopped for a beer in Cheo Reo and still made it to camp by noon.

LOUDON WAINWRIGHT

A BRAVE
SELF
FAR AT SEA

In each of the following editorials, Loudon Wainwright makes his opinions clear and meaningful through the careful use of statement, explanation, subjective expression, and significant detail.

CONSIDER Robert Manry, the Cleveland copyreader who spent 78 days crossing the Atlantic Ocean in a 13½-foot sailboat. His superb presumption has brightened a brutal summer; his miraculous good luck has provided one small, splendid win in a losing season. In an age whose heroes are named in advance of their heroics, when their missions are measured in terms of significance and progress, Mr. Manry bobbed into the national consciousness only when his trip was nearly over, and his astounding mission contributes nothing to our knowledge of the sea he crossed or the sky he passed under. Yet I think we owe a great debt to Mr. Manry. For by extending himself in such a bold and extravagant way, he somehow dignifies each individual and braces all of us.

One of the things that particularly attracts me about this adventure is the utter self-centeredness of it. "There comes a time," Manry's wife quotes him as saying, "that one must decide, of one's dreams, either to risk everything to achieve them, or sit for the rest of one's life in the backyard." What a beautifully arrogant statement. There isn't a word in it to suggest that Manry considered *anything* more important than the fulfillment of his dreams. He obviously went on from there to decide that all the risks were indeed worth it, including the risk to his wife and children that he would not survive the trip.

The whole thing, I think, comes down to the fact that Manry took himself very seriously. He valued his ideas and did not, like Walter Mitty, confine them to his musings. Surely, at 47 with a nice suburban home and a routine desk job on a city newspaper, Manry before his voyage seemed permanently anchored in the backyard. In comparable positions and at his age, many men dilute their dreams, if they have them, with weekend golf, odd jobs around the house and alcohol. For them it is a paunchy, short-winded period, unsuitable for risks, and the limits of life and their participation in it have by then been clearly defined. But Manry—and I wonder if the fact that he was born in the Himalayan foothills doesn't contribute to his acceptance of the unlikely—refused to acknowledge the limits and instead spent his free time working out a way to break past them. He got this big, scary idea, and although he knew that a lot of people would find it positively nutty, he believed he could bring it off. Applying his own good sense to the preposterous, he practiced for it by sailing in rough water in Lake Erie and outfitting his boat with extra flotation material and a radio distress transmitter. He knew there would be idle times at sea, so he brought along a harmonica too, with a book of instructions.

Perhaps the thing I admire most about Manry is not that he was brave enough to take his chances with the wind and a huge amount of water. Rather it is that he had the courage to be alone, vastly alone, for a long period of time. The value of solitude is unquestionable, and it is also true that we don't get enough of it. Yet I find that my own tolerance for aloneness is limited, that after a few minutes or a few hours of it, I will open the door or come back from the walk and see who's around. Possibly this restlessness in solitude is not entirely the need to reestablish contact with others but also the need to escape a self which is most painfully noticed when one is alone. The self can make good plans, clarify complexity and bolster optimism; it can also surge wildly, issue nightmare demands and forecast the end of hope. To plan to spend almost three months alone under dangerous and uncertain conditions seems to me to reflect this man's extraordinary confidence that he could truly manage himself.

Of course, Manry did have some difficulty with himself. On occasion he had terrifying hallucinations. He imagined there was a monster lurking in the tiny shelter on his sailboat, and he thought that the monster had thrown his son overboard. He had to fight for the realization that the boy was back in Cleveland before he could bring himself to go into the shelter. On another occasion Manry thought he was sailing on "a huge sea mountain" and spent a whole day trying to make his way down it. Yet he let neither these unsettling fantasies nor the harrowing facts that the wind blew his boat flat, that his rudder broke (a spare broke too, and he finally fixed it) or that he was washed overboard six times (five times he had himself tied to the boat and the sixth he caught the rigging) force him to try to hitch a ride from the ships which occasionally passed along his course. Smack in the hair-raising midst of achieving his dream, he would not betray it.

There is one thing, however, that worries me about Robert Manry. Now that he has done it, does he have another dream? Perhaps he doesn't need one. To be sure, he'll be able to get an awful lot of mileage out of this one just by telling people about it and savoring it himself over the years. And if, as seems entirely likely to me, he's a competitive sort of fellow, his is the marvelous kind of complete achievement that can't really be topped. Another man might make the trip next summer on a paper plate, and it would not diminish Manry's deed. Yet will the past and the present—the family, the job at the paper, the house in the suburbs and weekend voyages around Lake Erie—now be enough for him? I have no authority to doubt it, but I do. The liberated Manry self will more likely ask: "What have I done for me lately?" and a good answer will be awfully hard to find.

This raises the question of the advisability of having such dreams at all. Or at least of living to see them accomplished. Perhaps they are more useful held in the brain's escrow as possibilities for the future. Nothing ventured, nothing lost. My own dreams are both private and ill defined. Yet Manry has given me a wonderful new idea, and I am going to carry it out. First I am going to buy a harmonica. Then I am going to take my own boat, which is just about the size of his, out into the ocean. I'll be alone, but I won't be far from land. But I will turn my back on the land and play the harmonica to find out how it sounds.

LOUDON WAINWRIGHT

HOT PURSUIT
OF TURNPIKE
FLYERS

"...Then we were finally gaining on the speeder and the dial showed that we were going 105. Waite slowed a bit, turned on his red light and the siren..."

OVER the years the gloomy forecasts of the National Safety Council have made an anxious holiday driver of me. If I have to take my car out at all on such occasions, I slip into the traffic with distinct reluctance, drive with a feeling that DANGER LURKS EVERYWHERE and dismount in my garage with relief.

This Labor Day I decided to venture out on the road not as a driver but as an observer traveling in a state police car. At the time I couldn't imagine a safer place to be. I chose the Connecticut State Police because it has always struck me as an enlightened and safety-minded force. The highway signs ("The Law Observant Driver Never Meets Our Unmarked Police Car") make good, sensible reading, and the troopers have earned a reputation for strict enforcement of the traffic laws.

The trooper I drove with most of that day and night was Sergeant Don Waite, a gentle-looking man with glasses who is an expert in radar speed enforcement. A veteran cop with 13 years' experience, Waite, I found, drives beautifully at both normal and tremendous speeds. If he had any problem at all, it was that his unmarked sedan wouldn't accelerate fast enough for his specialty, which is pinching speeders. Waite complained cheerfully about this to me early in our acquaintance. His car, he explained, had an ordinary engine and ordinary shock absorbers instead of the more powerful engine and heavy shocks he needed to make a fast, safe arrest. In my ignorance at the time, this seemed like a minor professional quibble.

Waite first took me to a radar position on the Connecticut Turnpike near the town of Westport. The radar car was parked in plain view in the grass center strip in the middle of the six-lane highway, and the detection device, which looks roughly like a small searchlight on a tripod, was directed into the oncoming traffic. Several hundred yards up the road from the radar car were three unmarked chase cars. The radar trooper would simply radio ahead when a speeder flashed by and a chase car would jump out into pursuit. One of the chasers, Trooper John Hughes, invited me along on a trip, and I then discovered how a proper police car accelerates. Radioed about a speeder approaching us at 75, Hughes, good-looking enough to play a trooper on television, got us going that fast in a few seconds, before he even shifted into high. Little more than a minute passed from the time the car appeared on radar until its driver was removing his license from his wallet.

I spent much of the day just cruising up and down a 25-mile stretch of highway in Sergeant Waite's anonymous-looking car. Though the traffic was heavy, law-observant drivers were the overwhelming rule. With bicycles and water skis tied to the tops of jammed station wagons, sleeping children stacked in the back seat, dogs sniffing the breeze out of open windows, they formed a huge, domestic caravan peaceably heading for home. The police radio was very quiet without even reports of minor accidents, and Sergeant Waite had just remarked that it was the calmest holiday he could remember when the 1957 sedan suddenly went by us very fast in the outside lane.

Waite pressed hard on the gas. "He looks like a flyer to me," said Waite, and then he swore as his own car accelerated sluggishly. We had just got in behind the other car at a speed of about 75 when the driver decided abruptly to pull over into a fueling area. We had not followed him long enough to get "a good clock" on his speed, and so we went on down the road and parked near a toll gate. There we spent some time listening to the radio and watching drivers repeatedly miss the wire baskets where they were supposed to drop their quarter tolls. Then, quite unexpectedly, the flyer was back. He went through the toll gate and stopped right in front of the place we were parked with our headlights out. Four people got out of the car, two teenaged boys and their girls, and one boy took over the driving from the other. From the instant the car began to move, it was apparent that the new driver intended to go terribly fast.

The next three or four minutes were as crowded as any I remember. Waite, coldly furious at the way his own car was reacting to the chase, ripped out into the highway, reached out with one hand and grabbed his trooper's hat from the seat beside him and jammed it on his head. We were going 80 and the flyer was pulling away from us. Waite took the radio mike and called ahead in hope that the radar cars were still in position. He got no response, and I tightened my seat belt until my belly disappeared. We were passing other cars now and roaring through 90. We hit a tiny rough spot in the pavement and the car suddenly felt soft as a marshmallow as it swayed along the road. I looked at Waite and he hollered: "He has to be doing 95." Then we were finally gaining on the speeder and the dial showed that we were going 105. Waite slowed a bit, turned on his red light and the siren, and the flyer, who realized only then that he'd been followed, began to brake his car. As we dropped past 60, I kept missing a cigaret with the flame from my lighter. When both cars had stopped rolling, I opened the door and stepped out. My legs, weak from the strain of pushing so hard against the floor, were trembling, and the air was filled with the smell of burning rubber. I heard Waite quite pleasantly ask the young driver, "Do you know you were going 95?" With laudable politeness the boy replied, "Something is wrong with my speedometer, sir."

After Waite had put the driver in jail for the night while his friends raised money for a court appearance the next morning (he was fined $100 for speeding), we found out a bit about what had been happening in the rest of the state over the holiday weekend. The state police had covered 106 accidents involving 8 fatalities (there were 564 deaths nationwide). The closest accident to us had involved Trooper Hughes, whose chase car I'd ridden only a few hours earlier. I pieced together the details from other troopers at the station, and with each new fact I realized how lucky I'd been to be flying down the turnpike with Waite.

Hughes had tried to stop a car which came too fast up a ramp to the highway. The driver attempted to avoid the arrest, sped off the turnpike at the next ramp and turned onto narrow country roads. Hughes, light and siren going, followed, and the two cars raced along at speeds up to 110 miles an hour. Showers of sparks flew from the lead car as its undercarriage bounced off the dips in the road. Eight miles from the start of the chase, the runaway driver lost control and hit a light pole. His car broke completely in half. In seconds, still at top speed, Hughes came on the accident and had to decide whether to hit the wreck, run over a girl who was lying at one end of it or smash into a wall. He chose the wall. Then, with several ribs broken, he climbed out the window of his demolished car and began giving first aid to the five teen-agers from the other. All wound up in the hospital and all, through some miracle of speed and space, will live.

Hearing about it, I felt the beneficiary of a miracle, too. If I'd been sitting next to Hughes, I might have survived with him, but I wonder if I would have arrived at the same instant decision about the direction he must take. I thanked Sergeant Waite and drove my own car home through the early morning dark, eyes straight ahead, seat belt fastened and going not one mile an hour above the limit.

LOUDON WAINWRIGHT

THE FIERY PANGS
OF CONSCIENCE

"... war mutes the individual conscience to the extent that it becomes possible to overlook the daily inhumanities while accepting the broad outlines of a national policy...."

WE CANNOT know what Norman Morrison was thinking in those final moments before he lighted a match to himself last week. Perhaps the despair that led him to suicide in full view of hundreds of homebound office workers outside the Pentagon had obliterated all comprehensible thought. Did he hope that Defense Secretary Robert McNamara would step to his nearby window and see Morrison lurching through his agonized dance of fire? Did he intend to heighten the symbolism of his grotesque way of death by inflicting it on his one-year-old daughter, too? Or had Morrison brought the child along with him from their home in Baltimore in some pathetic hope that her presence would save him from his own violent impulse?

Whatever the answers to these questions, whatever the emotional condition of this 31-year-old Quaker at the time, the purpose of his deranged act seems very clear. Even in the grief of a personal disaster that left her a widow with three small children, Morrison's wife spoke for her husband's intentions. "Norman Morrison," she said, "has given his life today to express his concern over the great loss of life and human suffering caused by the war in Vietnam. He was protesting our government's deep military involvement in this war. He felt that all citizens must speak their convictions about our country's action." Thus, through the protest of his truly pitiful death, Norman Morrison appeared to be demanding that Americans undertake a deeper examination of their consciences.

The condition of the American conscience in regard to Vietnam has surely been the subject of a lot of thinking around the country in recent weeks, and Mr. Morrison's death—however vain, insane or otherwise deplorable most people will find it—will doubtless lead to even more consideration. Not long ago in New York, I watched a march in protest of our presence in Vietnam and, though I happen to believe we cannot withdraw from that country until there has been a reasonable settlement, I found myself quite certain that honest conscience motivated many of the marchers. There were probably people in the parade whose motives were more sinister than peaceful and I was horrified by one group that wore skull masks and carried a big dummy of a mangled Vietnamese baby on a stretcher as a symbol of American brutality. Yet for the most part the paraders seemed a distinctly gentle group, young or old, long haired or well barbered, the great majority of them silent and passive as they moved along the route. And while I knew their protest was being watched with considerable satisfaction by America's professed enemies in Asia, my own conscience was shaken by the abusive treatment they received from the ugly packs of hecklers they met as they passed. Red paint, curses, such compliments as "Traitor!" and here and there a few fists greeted them, and I would describe the police protection as both massive and reluctant. The hecklers, who reminded me of angry, red-neck toughs I have seen in Mississippi, viciously proclaimed their support of American policy, and I hated the idea that I was—somehow—aligned with them.

For the people like the hecklers, of course, the whole business of war is a splendid occasion for forgetting conscience completely. A black and white psychology takes over; in the name of patriotism one can even commit outrages against one's fellow citizens, to say nothing of the enemy. But even for more thoughtful people, war mutes the individual conscience to the extent that it becomes possible to overlook the daily inhumanities while accepting the broad outlines of a national policy. Old-fashioned, declared wars are most ideal for this: the central driving purpose of the country is to win, and virtually all are united in that aim. In a situation like Vietnam, however, where there is no declaration and where a military victory is not the ultimate goal, in a conflict where there are all the actions of war and the innocent victims, too, the conscience can more easily rise and break the silence. As well as by parades and bizarre deaths of individuals like Norman Morrison, it is broken by the dialogues of troubled men.

It would be quite wrong to assume that only those people who protest our being in Vietnam are acting from conscience. Obviously President Johnson calls on his own conscience, and military men I met in Vietnam had given intensive thought to the meaning of carrying out their duties. Many had arrived at the conscientious conclusion that their performance represented the best hope for the survival of the people of South Vietnam. The crews of the

B-52 squadrons shown on the next pages can look down from their planes and see the smoke rising from fires caused by their bombs. Can any protest marcher safely believe that these men are acting heedlessly—without conscience? I think not.

Yet, for me at least, a problem of conscience remains, and it is not unlike the problem that drove Norman Morrison to suicide. On the day of his death Morrison had been discussing with his wife an article he had just read. It was a Catholic priest's account of the bombing of a Vietnamese village, and in it the priest was quoted as saying: "I have seen my faithful burned up in napalm." For the most rational of men, these words must come as a stark shock. Then there was the recent news that an error in communications had resulted in the deaths of 48 innocent villagers when the wrong place got bombed. Among other things, that awful mistake led me to wonder how many helpless people, as opposed to Vietcong soldiers, would have died if we'd hit the *right* place. A story which will appear in this magazine in two weeks deals in part with the death and maiming of children who are caught in the crossfires of this war. Reading the piece and looking at the pictures, I was overwhelmed by conscience. These are not the things we mean to do in Vietnam; yet we are doing them. How do we accomplish a humane objective without committing these offenses against humanity? The dilemma is a dreadful one, and a raw conscience does not always provide the whole answer.

But it does provide a vital base for one, and in that notion, I think, lies the real futility and personal failure of Norman Morrison's suicide. At a time when men must live with their consciences and heed the hard messages they speak, he listened and then chose to die. In the fire both man and conscience perished.

NORMAN COUSINS

WHO KILLED
BENNY PARET?

*"...They come out to see the knockout.
They come out to see a man hurt. If they
think anything else, they're kidding themselves...."*

SOMETIME about 1935 or 1936 I had an interview with Mike Jacobs, the
prize-fight promoter. I was a fledgling reporter at that time; my beat was
education but during the vacation season I found myself on varied assignments, all the way from ship news to sports reporting. In this way I found
myself sitting opposite the most powerful figure in the boxing world.

There was nothing spectacular in Mr. Jacobs' manner or appearance;
but when he spoke about prize fights, he was no longer a bland little man
but a colossus who sounded the way Napoleon must have sounded when
he reviewed a battle. You knew you were listening to Number One. His saying something made it true.

We discussed what to him was the only important element in successful
promoting—how to please the crowd. So far as he was concerned, there
was no mystery to it. You put killers in the ring and the people filled your
arena. You hire boxing artists—men who are adroit at feinting, parrying,
weaving, jabbing, and dancing, but who don't pack dynamite in their fists—
and you wind up counting your empty seats. So you searched for the killers
and sluggers and maulers—fellows who could hit with the force of a baseball bat.

I asked Mr. Jacobs if he was speaking literally when he said people came
out to see the killer.

"They don't come out to see a tea party," he said evenly. "They come
out to see the knockout. They come out to see a man hurt. If they think anything else, they're kidding themselves."

Recently, a young man by the name of Benny Paret was killed in the ring.
The killing was seen by millions; it was on television. In the twelfth round,
he was hit hard in the head several times, went down, was counted out,
and never came out of the coma.

The Paret fight produced a flurry of investigations. Governor Rockefeller

"Who Killed Benny Paret?" by Norman Cousins. Originally published May 5, 1962 in *Saturday
Review*. Reprinted by permission of Norman Cousins and *Saturday Review*.

was shocked by what happened and appointed a committee to assess the responsibility. The New York State Boxing Commission decided to find out what was wrong. The District Attorney's office expressed its concern. One question that was solemnly studied in all three probes concerned the action of the referee. Did he act in time to stop the fight? Another question had to do with the role of the examining doctors who certified the physical fitness of the fighters before the bout. Still another question involved Mr. Paret's manager; did he rush his boy into the fight without adequate time to recuperate from the previous one?

In short, the investigators looked into every possible cause except the real one. Benny Paret was killed because the human fist delivers enough impact, when directed against the head, to produce a massive hemorrhage in the brain. The human brain is the most delicate and complex mechanism in all creation. It has a lacework of millions of highly fragile nerve connections. Nature attempts to protect this exquisitely intricate machinery by encasing it in a hard shell. Fortunately, the shell is thick enough to withstand a great deal of pounding. Nature, however, can protect man against everything except man himself. Not every blow to the head will kill a man—but there is always the risk of concussion and damage to the brain. A prize fighter may be able to survive even repeated brain concussions and go on fighting, but the damage to his brain may be permanent.

In any event, it is futile to investigate the referee's role and seek to determine whether he should have intervened to stop the fight earlier. That is not where the primary responsibility lies. The primary responsibility lies with the people who pay to see a man hurt. The referee who stops a fight too soon from the crowd's viewpoint can expect to be booed. The crowd wants the knockout; it wants to see a man stretched out on the canvas. This is the supreme moment in boxing. It is nonsense to talk about prize fighting as a test of boxing skills. No crowd was ever brought to its feet screaming and cheering at the sight of two men beautifully dodging and weaving out of each other's jabs. The time the crowd comes alive is when a man is hit hard over the heart or the head, when his mouthpiece flies out, when the blood squirts out of his nose or eyes, when he wobbles under the attack and his pursuer continues to smash at him with pole-axe impact.

Don't blame it on the referee. Don't even blame it on the fight managers. Put the blame where it belongs—on the prevailing mores that regard prize fighting as a perfectly proper enterprise and vehicle of entertainment. No one doubts that many people enjoy prize fighting and will miss it if it should be thrown out. And that is precisely the point.

MARTIN GANSBERG

38 WHO SAW MURDER DIDN'T CALL THE POLICE

"... The man explained that he had called the police after much deliberation ... 'I didn't want to get involved,' he sheepishly told the police...."

FOR more than half an hour 38 respectable, law-abiding citizens in Queens watched a killer stalk and stab a woman in three separate attacks in Kew Gardens.

Twice their chatter and the sudden glow of their bedroom lights interrupted him and frightened him off. Each time he returned, sought her out, and stabbed her again. Not one person telephoned the police during the assault; one witness called after the woman was dead.

That was two weeks ago today.

Still shocked is Assistant Chief Inspector Frederick M. Lussen, in charge of the borough's detectives and a veteran of 25 years of homicide investigations. He can give a matter-of-fact recitation on many murders. But the Kew Gardens slaying baffles him—not because it is a murder, but because the "good people" failed to call the police.

"As we have reconstructed the crime," he said, "the assailant had three chances to kill this woman during a 35-minute period. He returned twice to complete the job. If we had been called when he first attacked, the woman might not be dead now."

This is what the police say happened beginning at 3:20 A.M. in the staid, middle-class, tree-lined Austin Street area:

Twenty-eight-year-old Catherine Genovese, who was called Kitty by almost everyone in the neighborhood, was returning home from her job as manager of a bar in Hollis. She parked her red Fiat in a lot adjacent to the Kew Gardens Long Island Rail Road Station, facing Mowbray Place. Like many residents of the neighborhood, she had parked there day after day since her arrival from Connecticut a year ago, although the railroad frowns on the practice.

She turned off the lights of her car, locked the door, and started to walk the 100 feet to the entrance of her apartment at 82-70 Austin Street, which is in a Tudor building, with stores on the first floor and apartments on the second.

The entrance to the apartment is in the rear of the building because the front is rented to retail stores. At night the quiet neighborhood is shrouded in the slumbering darkness that marks most residential areas.

Miss Genovese noticed a man at the far end of the lot, near a seven-story apartment house at 82-40 Austin Street. She halted. Then, nervously, she headed up Austin Street toward Lefferts Boulevard, where there is a call box to the 102nd Police Precinct in nearby Richmond Hill.

She got as far as a street light in front of a bookstore before the man grabbed her. She screamed. Lights went on in the 10-story apartment house at 82-67 Austin Street, which faces the bookstore. Windows slid open and voices punctuated the early-morning stillness.

Miss Genovese screamed: "Oh, my God, he stabbed me! Please help me! Please help me!"

From one of the upper windows in the apartment house, a man called down: "Let that girl alone!"

The assailant looked up at him, shrugged, and walked down Austin Street toward a white sedan parked a short distance away. Miss Genovese struggled to her feet.

Lights went out. The killer returned to Miss Genovese, now trying to make her way around the side of the building by the parking lot to get to her apartment. The assailant stabbed her again.

"I'm dying!" she shrieked. "I'm dying!"

Windows were opened again, and lights went on in many apartments. The assailant got into his car and drove away. Miss Genovese staggered to her feet. A city bus, O-10, the Lefferts Boulevard line to Kennedy International Airport, passed. It was 3:35 A.M.

The assailant returned. By then, Miss Genovese had crawled to the back of the building, where the freshly painted brown doors to the apartment house held out hope for safety. The killer tried the first door; she wasn't there. At the second door, 82-62 Austin Street, he saw her slumped on the floor at the foot of the stairs. He stabbed her a third time—fatally.

It was 3:50 by the time the police received their first call, from a man who was a neighbor of Miss Genovese. In two minutes they were at the scene. The neighbor, a 70-year-old woman, and another woman were the only persons on the street. Nobody else came forward.

The man explained that he had called the police after much deliberation. He had phoned a friend in Nassau County for advice and then he had crossed the roof of the building to the apartment of the elderly woman to get her to make the call.

"I didn't want to get involved," he sheepishly told the police.

Six days later, the police arrested Winston Moseley, a 29-year-old busi-ness-machine operator, and charged him with the homicide. Moseley had

no previous record. He is married, has two children and owns a home at 133-19 Sutter Avenue, South Ozone Park, Queens. On Wednesday, a court committed him to Kings County Hospital for psychiatric observation.

When questioned by the police, Moseley also said that he had slain Mrs. Annie May Johnson, 24, of 146-12 133d Avenue, Jamaica, on Feb. 29 and Barbara Kralik, 15, of 174-17 140th Avenue, Springfield Gardens, last July. In the Kralik case, the police are holding Alvin L. Mitchell, who is said to have confessed that slaying.

The police stressed how simple it would have been to have gotten in touch with them. "A phone call," said one of the detectives, "would have done it." The police may be reached by dialing "0" for operator or SPring 7-3100.

Today witnesses from the neighborhood, which is made up of one-family homes in the $35,000 to $60,000 range with the exception of the two apartment houses near the railroad station, find it difficult to explain why they didn't call the police.

A housewife, knowingly if quite casual, said, "We thought it was a lover's quarrel." A husband and wife both said, "Frankly, we were afraid." They seemed aware of the fact that events might have been different. A distraught woman, wiping her hands in her apron, said, "I didn't want my husband to get involved."

One couple, now willing to talk about that night, said they heard the first screams. The husband looked thoughtfully at the bookstore where the killer first grabbed Miss Genovese.

"We went to the window to see what was happening," he said, "but the light from our bedroom made it difficult to see the street." The wife, still apprehensive, added: "I put out the light and we were able to see better."

Asked why they hadn't called the police, she shrugged and replied: "I don't know."

A man peeked out from a slight opening in the doorway to his apartment and rattled off an account of the killer's second attack. Why hadn't he called the police at the time? "I was tired," he said without emotion. "I went back to bed."

It was 4:25 A.M. when the ambulance arrived to take the body of Miss Genovese. It drove off. "Then," a solemn police detective said, "the people came out."

ANONYMOUS

THE WORLDWIDE PLAGUE OF CITY RIOTS

". . . It was an insurrection of anarchy, an outburst against any kind of system by the people left at the bottom. . . ."

IT IS not just an American tragedy. The riots in Los Angeles have sent the editorial writers reaching for that good old standby from Dreiser. The Communists have seen it less as a tragedy than as a morality play, but have been just as ready to claim that the outbreak was peculiarly American; the Peking *People's Daily* even salutes it as a rebellion against President Johnson's imperialist foreign policy. All this is nonsense. What happened in Los Angeles is pretty certainly going to happen in many other countries, both capitalist and communist, as the conditions that caused it spread to them. This was an American phenomenon only in the sense that the United States is half a generation ahead of the rest of the world in the development of an industrial urban society with the special problems that brings. It has the first taste of both the pleasures and the terrors of this new sort of life.

For the Los Angeles riots were the product of two causes, neither of which is peculiar to America. The first has nothing to do with race. For all the anti-white slogans shouted by some of the rioters, the essential news from Los Angeles is that many of them were moved by something quite unconnected with the color of their skin. "This was no race riot; they were just stealing," one Negro store owner is quoted as saying. That is too simple; they were also, after all, sniping and fire-raising and generally rampaging. But as in Harlem and Rochester last year—quiet so far this year—the majority of the rioters were young people caught up on an explosion of violence against authority—any authority, but usually the police, the authoritarians they have run foul of in their everyday lives. This was an insurrection, but not against the economic order (which is the Marxist fallacy) and not even chiefly against white men's domination (which is going to be the Afro-Asian fallacy). It was an insurrection of anarchy, an outburst against any kind of system by the people left at the bottom.

Outbreaks like this are part of the price we are going to pay for a society

"The Worldwide Plague of City Riots," editorial from *The Economist*, © 1965 by *The Economist*, London. Reprinted by permission. This editorial was reprinted in *Harper's Magazine*, November, 1965.

in which more and more people live in cities and do deadly dull work and waste their leisure. One of the problems of urban-industrial life is that it creates communities of the left-behind. These are the people who do the dullest jobs of all, and are the worst paid, and live in the ugliest parts of crumbling old towns. They have a high rate of illegitimacy and broken marriages. Their religious and cultural roots have been cut. Materially, they are better off than their peasant grandfathers were, but cramming a man with distressful bread has never made him contented—quite the reverse. These people know they are a community of the untalented, because a modern state needs to skim off the people with talent and by and large does skim them off. The rest sit and simmer. They know they are the natural bottom layer; they have been deprived of the social and religious consolations of the old rural life; there is no legal outlet for young male violence; and every now and then they go bang.

Many of the Los Angeles rioters are brothers under the skin to the baffled young men from London and its suburbs who spend their holidays stomping along the beach front at Brighton and Margate, or breaking up bars in Calais and Ostend. Their fathers got into fights at football games or satisfied a dim ancestral prejudice by chasing second-generation Irishmen in Glasgow or Jews in Dalston. They were trying to prove that they belonged to something. The elder sons ripped up railway carriages: it was their way of not belonging.

Now the youth of the bottom layer takes it out on the town—and even the seedy parts of their towns have more than ever before to take it out on. The Swedish police were having trouble a decade ago with young toughs raising hell in the center of Stockholm; in the bad things as well as the good, Sweden is America's closest follower on the march to the sort of society most of us will be living in by the year 2000. The Czech police had a first taste of the problem a year ago when young hooligans disrupted Wenceslas Square in Prague. Not even the Russians are immune. The passionate violence of the riots in Novocherkassk a couple of years ago, which probably killed more people than the Los Angeles riots, can no more be wholly explained by their ostensible cause—a rise in food prices—than the Los Angeles outburst can be wholly explained in racial terms.

What has happened since 1945 is that the youngest members of this community of the left-behind now have better means of transport and a wider range of weapons, at any rate in Western Europe and North America. This makes the violence more noticeable; motorbikes and flickknives on a British south-coast esplanade, or car-drivers lobbing fire bombs into Los Angeles stores, make for bigger headlines, especially in the silly season, than a fists-and-boots brawl outside a back-street pub. But at the same time the frustration that lies behind it all has grown sharper, as the hierarchy of modern industrial society takes clearer shape. For those at the bottom, life presents a still more dismal picture when it is not God who calls men to their stations in life, but the unappealable selection processes of economic life.

Russian sociologists have told Western colleagues that they are deeply worried about this. So they should be. Communism and capitalism are rival mechanisms for supplying material plenty. What neither of them has thought out, and what both are going to run headlong into by the end of the century, is the problem of the needs left unsatisfied by relative abundance: how to make routine work bearable, how to help people use their leisure, how to stop them dying of boredom—or killing from it.

But there is the second factor. If part of what made Los Angeles go bang had nothing to do with race, the other part certainly had. Outbursts like this can and will happen when the frustrated bottom-layer people are racially indistinguishable from those who live around them. When they are picked out by the color of their skin as well, the worst happens. They believe—some of them rightly—that they could have risen out of the ghetto of the left-behind but for their color; they band together with a double grievance. Los Angeles is a model of the most explosive sort of situation that the growingly urbanized, growingly race-mixed world of the 1970s and 1980s will have to cope with.

In one way, it may be a help for a pressured community to be able to identify itself by its color. The white proletariat of America and Europe is leaderless; the best of each generation are plucked away from it to take a comfortable place higher up—in the communist world, where they are absorbed into the ranks of the *apparatchiks*, just as much as in the West. The potential leaders of a colored community, by contrast, stay attached to their community by their color, and may be a force for moderation. But even this hope is a limited one. The potential leaders may not be able to take command of their communities. And if they can take command, they may not stay moderate, or they may be pushed aside if they do. What could Martin Luther King, effective in the disciplined South, do for the troubles of rootless Los Angeles?

The mistake no one should make is to think that this is only someone else's problem. People still talk as if the racial conflict in America were in a category of its own; or as if the only significant race confrontation were the one between black and white men. The whites are certainly going to be in the middle of a rolling race row for years to come, if only because for the last couple of centuries they have been in a position to be beastly to everybody else, and everybody else is now in a mood to get his own back.

But the world's record even this year should explode the idea that this is all there is to it. The week of the Los Angeles riots was also the week when Malaysia broke apart because brown men could not control their dark suspicions of yellow men, and when black and brown men resumed their efforts to slug it out in southern Sudan. All the evidence is that there is potential trouble wherever people of different colors rub shoulders uneasily together. The history of the black-brown dividing line in independent Africa in the last five years—with splits opening up in Sudan, in Mauretania, in Chad, and between Somalia and Kenya—makes a man's heart sink into his boots.

Race is the most visible, and thus the most potent of the things that make one lot of men feel different from another lot; and as long as they feel different, they find it difficult to muck in together in any common venture, whether it is sharing a boardinghouse or running a country. This is lamentable, but it is not much help lamenting it; it is one of the rock-bottom facts of political life. The communist Europeans have been learning the lesson since communities of colored students began to live among them.

Even relatively minor distinctions within what is generally accepted as a single race produce the same effect. Nobody who has listened to the comfortable burghers of Germany or Switzerland talking about their Italian, Greek, and Spanish workers—or the workers talking about them—can help wondering how long it will be before these countries suffer their own minor-key variations on the Los Angeles theme.

Heaven knows how it will work out; certainly no politician, communist or democratic, shows the faintest sign of knowing. It is the most preposterous counsel of despair to argue that each race should henceforth retire to its own corner of the earth, and stay there. The industrialized world needs workers from the developing world to keep up the momentum of economic expansion. It is in the interest of the developing world that this momentum should be kept up, and that communities of white men should live in colored countries to start them on the same way.

The only hope—and it is a thin straw to clutch at—is that as people of different colors mix with each other they will gradually lose the sense of difference that inhibits collaboration between them. There are some people —the ones around the Mediterranean, for instance—who have never felt the sense of difference very keenly, though even that is not true of Palestine or Kabylia. There are others, like the West Indians, who have slowly come to find it a little less important than others find it. There is the East Indian community in Holland, where the Dutch have made a better effort than anyone at integration. It is something. Meanwhile, as the races go on jostling each other, and as the race problem exacerbates the other problems of our industrial society, anyone who points a finger of scorn at the Americans over Los Angeles is calling the same beastly experience down on his own head.

JOHN STEINBECK

WHAT ARE AMERICANS LIKE TODAY?

". . . Because their dignity was intact, they had no need to be overbearing, and because the Cooper boys had never heard that they were inferior, their minds could grow to their true limits. . . ."

WHEN I laid the ground plan of my journey, there were definite questions to which I wanted matching answers. It didn't seem to me that they were impossible questions. I suppose they could all be lumped into the single question: "What are Americans like today?"

In Europe it is a popular sport to describe what the Americans are like. Everyone seems to know. And we are equally happy in this game. How many times have I not heard one of my fellow countrymen, after a three-week tour of Europe, describe with certainty the nature of the French, the British, the Italians, the Germans, and above all the Russians? Traveling about, I early learned the difference between an American and the Americans. They are so far apart that they might be opposites. Often when a European has described the Americans with hostility and scorn he has turned to me and said, "Of course, I don't mean you. I am speaking of those others." It boils down to this: the Americans, the British are that faceless clot you don't know, but a Frenchman or an Italian is your acquaintance and your friend. He has none of the qualities your ignorance causes you to hate.

I had always considered this a kind of semantic deadfall, but moving about in my own country I am not at all sure that is so. Americans as I saw them and talked to them were indeed individuals, each one different from the others, but gradually I began to feel that the Americans exist, that they really do have generalized characteristics regardless of their states, their social and financial status, their education, their religious, and their political convictions. But if there is indeed an American image built of truth rather than reflecting either hostility or wishful thinking, what is this image? What does it look like? What does it do? If the same song, the same joke, the same style sweeps through all parts of the country at once, it must be that all Americans are alike in something. The fact that the same joke, the same style, has no effect in France or England or Italy makes this contention valid. But the more I inspected this American image, the less sure I became of what it is. It appeared to me increasingly paradoxical, and it has been my experience that when paradox crops up too often for comfort, it means that certain factors are missing in the equation.

Now I had moved through a galaxy of states, each with its own character, and through clouds and myriads of people, and ahead of me lay an area, the South, that I dreaded to see and yet knew I must see and hear. I am not drawn to pain and violence. I never gaze at accidents unless I can help, or attend street fights for kicks. I faced the South with dread. Here, I knew, were pain and confusion and all the manic results of bewilderment and fear. And the South being a limb of the nation, its pain spreads out to all America.

I knew, as everyone knows, the true but incomplete statement of the problem—that an original sin of the fathers was being visited on the children of succeeding generations. I have many Southern friends, both Negro and white, many of them of superb minds and characters, and often, when not the problem but the mere suggestion of the Negro-white subject has come up, I have seen and felt them go into a room of experience into which I cannot enter.

Perhaps I, more than most people from the so-called North, am kept out of real and emotional understanding of the agony not because I, a white, have no experience with Negroes but because of the nature of my experience.

In Salinas in California, where I was born and grew and went to school gathering the impressions that formed me, there was only one Negro family. The name was Cooper and the father and mother were there when I was born, but they had three sons, one a little older than I, one my age, and one a year younger, so that in grade school and high school there was always a Cooper in the grade ahead, one in my class, and one in the class below. In a word, I was bracketed with Coopers. The father, universally called Mr. Cooper, ran a little trucking business—ran it well and made a good living. His wife was a warm and friendly woman who was good for a piece of gingerbread any time we wanted to put the hustle on her.

If there was any color prejudice in Salinas I never heard or felt a breath of it. The Coopers were respected, and their self-respect was in no way forced. Ulysses, the oldest, was one of the best pole-vaulters our town ever developed, a tall, quiet boy. I remember the lean grace of his movements in a track suit and I remember envying his smooth and perfect timing. He died in his third year in high school and I was one of his pallbearers, and I think I was guilty of the sin of pride at being chosen. The second son, Ignatius, my classmate, was not my favorite, I discover now, because he was far and away the best student. In arithmetic and later in mathematics he topped our grades, and in Latin he not only was a better student but he didn't cheat. And who can like a classmate like that? The youngest Cooper—the baby— was all smiles. It's odd that I do not remember his first name. He was a musician from the start, and when I last saw him he was deep in composition which seemed, to my partially instructed ear, bold and original and good. But beyond this giftedness, the Cooper boys were my friends.

Now, these were the only Negroes I knew or had contact with in the days of my flypaper childhood, and you can see how little I was prepared for the great world. When I heard, for example, that Negroes were an inferior race, I thought the authority was misinformed. When I heard that Negroes were dirty I remembered Mrs. Cooper's shining kitchen. Lazy? The drone and clop of Mr. Cooper's horse-drawn dray in the street outside used to awaken us in the dawn. Dishonest? Mr. Cooper was one of the very few Salinians who never let a debt cross the fifteenth of the month.

I realize now that there was something else about the Coopers that set them apart from other Negroes I have seen and met since. Because they were not hurt or insulted, they were not defensive or combative. Because their dignity was intact, they had no need to be overbearing, and because the Cooper boys had never heard that they were inferior, their minds could grow to their true limits.

That was my Negro experience until I was well grown, perhaps too far grown to reform the inflexible habits of childhood. Oh, I have seen plenty since and have felt the shattering waves of violence and despair and confusion. I have seen Negro children who really cannot learn, particularly those who in their gelatin plate of babyness have been told they were inferior. And, remembering the Coopers and how we felt about them, I think my main feeling is sorrow at the curtain of fear and anger drawn down between us. And I've just thought of an amusing possibility. If in Salinas anyone from a wiser and more sophisticated world had asked, "How would you like your sister to marry a Cooper?" I think we would have laughed. For it might have occurred to us that a Cooper might not have wanted to marry our sister, good friends though we all were.

Thus it remains that I am basically unfitted to take sides in the racial conflict. I must admit that cruelty and force exerted against weakness turn me sick with rage, but this would be equally true in the treatment of any weak by any strong.

Beyond my failings as a racist, I knew I was not wanted in the South. When people are engaged in something they are not proud of, they do not welcome witnesses. In fact, they come to believe the witness causes the trouble.

In all this discussion of the South I have been speaking only about the violence set loose by the desegregation movements—the children going to school, the young Negroes demanding the questionable privilege of lunch counters, buses, and toilets. But I am particularly interested in the school business, because it seems to me that the blight can disappear only when there are millions of Coopers.

Recently a dear Southern friend instructed me passionately in the theory of "equal but separate." "It just happens," he said, "that in my town there are three new Negro schools not equal but superior to the white schools.

Now wouldn't you think they would be satisfied with that? And in the bus station the washrooms are exactly the same. What's your answer to that?"

I said, "Maybe it's a matter of ignorance. You could solve it and really put them in their places if you switched schools and toilets. The moment they realized that your schools weren't as good as theirs, they would realize their error."

And do you know what he said? He said, "You troublemaking son of a bitch." But he said it smiling.

JOHN STEINBECK

THE CHEERLEADERS

". . . Theirs was the demented cruelty of ego-centric children, and somehow this made their insensate beastliness much more heartbreaking. . . ."

WHILE I was still in Texas, late in 1960, the incident most reported and pictured in the newspapers was the matriculation of a couple of tiny Negro children in a New Orleans school. Behind these small dark mites were the law's majesty and the law's power to enforce—both the scales and the sword were allied with the infants—while against them were three hundred years of fear and anger and terror of change in a changing world. I had seen photographs in the papers every day and motion pictures on the television screen. What made the newsmen love the story was a group of stout middle-aged women who, by some curious definition of the word "mother," gathered every day to scream invectives at children. Further, a small group of them had become so expert that they were known as the Cheerleaders, and a crowd gathered every day to enjoy and to applaud their performance.

This strange drama seemed so improbable that I felt I had to see it. It had the same draw as a five-legged calf or a two-headed foetus at a sideshow, a distortion of normal life we have always found so interesting that we will pay to see it, perhaps to prove to ourselves that we have the proper number of legs of heads. In the New Orleans show, I felt all the amusement of the improbably abnormal, but also a kind of horror that it could be so.

At this time the winter which had been following my track ever since I left home suddenly struck with a black norther. It brought ice and freezing sleet and sheeted the highways with dark ice. I gathered Charley from the good doctor. He looked half his age and felt wonderful, and to prove it he ran and jumped and rolled and laughed and gave little yips of pure joy. It felt very good to have him with me again, sitting up right in the seat beside me, peering ahead at the unrolling road, or curling up to sleep with his head in my lap and his silly ears available for fondling. That dog can sleep through any amount of judicious caresses.

Now we stopped dawdling and laid our wheels to the road and went. We could not go fast because of the ice, but we drove relentlessly, hardly glancing at the passing of Texas beside us. And Texas was achingly endless— Sweetwater and Balinger and Austin. We bypassed Houston. We stopped for gasoline and coffee and slabs of pie. Charley had his meals and his walks in gas stations. Night did not stop us, and when my eyes ached and burned from peering too long and my shoulders were side hills of pain, I pulled into a turnout and crawled like a mole into my bed, only to see the highway writhe along behind my closed lids. No more than two hours could I sleep, and then out into the bitter cold night and on and on. Water beside the road was frozen solid, and people moved about with shawls and sweaters wrapped around their ears.

Other times I have come to Beaumont dripping with sweat and lusting for ice and air-conditioning. Now Beaumont with all its glare of neon signs was what they called froze up. I went through Beaumont at night, or rather in the dark well after midnight. The blue-fingered man who filled my gas tank looked in at Charley and said, "Hey, it's a dog! I thought you had a nigger in there." And he laughed delightedly. It was the first of many repetitions. At least twenty times I heard it—"Thought you had a nigger in there." It was an unusual joke—always fresh—and never Negro or even Nigra, always Nigger or rather Niggah. That word seemed terribly important, a kind of safety word to cling to lest some structure collapse.

And then I was in Louisiana, with Lake Charles away to the side in the dark, but my lights glittered on ice and glinted on diamond frost, and those people who forever trudge the roads at night were mounded over with cloth against the cold. I dogged it on through La Fayette and Morgan City and came in the early dawn to Houma, which is pronounced Homer and is in my memory one of the pleasantest places in the world. There lives my old friend Doctor St. Martin, a gentle, learned man, a Cajun who has lifted babies and cured colic among the shell-heap Cajuns for miles around. I guess he knows more about Cajuns than anyone living, but I remembered with longing other gifts of Doctor St. Martin. He makes the best and most subtle martini in the world by a process approximating magic. The only part of his formula I know is that he uses distilled water for his ice and distills it himself to be sure. I have eaten black duck at his table—two St. Martin martinis and a brace of black duck with a burgundy delivered from the bottle as a baby might be delivered, and this in a darkened house where the shades have been closed at dawn and the cool night air preserved. At that table with its silver soft and dull, shining as pewter, I remember the raised glass of the grape's holy blood, the stem caressed by the doctor's strong artist fingers, and even now I can hear the sweet little health and welcome in the singing language of Acadia which once was French and now is itself. This picture filled my frosty windshield, and if there had been traffic would have made me a dangerous driver. But it was pale yellow frozen dawn in Houma and I knew that if I stopped to pay my respects, my will and my determination would drift away on the particular lotus St. Martin purveys and we would be speaking of timeless matters when the evening came, and another evening. And so I only bowed in the direction of my friend and scudded on toward New Orleans, for I wanted to catch a show of the Cheerleaders.

Even I know better than to drive a car near trouble, particularly Rocinante, with New York license plates. Only yesterday a reporter had been beaten and his camera smashed, for even convinced voters are reluctant to have their moment of history recorded and preserved.

So, well on the edge of town I drove into a parking lot. The attendant came to my window. "Man, oh man, I thought you had a nigger in there. Man, oh man, it's a dog. I see that big old black face and I think it's a big old nigger."

"His face is blue-gray when he's clean," I said coldly.

"Well I see some blue-gray niggers and they wasn't clean. New York, eh?"

It seemed to me a chill like the morning air came into his voice. "Just driving through," I said. "I want to park for a couple of hours. Think you can get me a taxi?"

"Tell you what I bet. I bet you're going to see the Cheerleaders."

"That's right."

"Well, I hope you're not one of those trouble-makers or reporters."

"I just want to see it."

"Man, oh man, you going to see something. Ain't those Cheerleaders something? Man, oh man, you never heard nothing like it when they get going."

I locked Charley in Rocinante's house after giving the attendant a tour of the premises, a drink of whisky, and a dollar. "Be kind of careful about opening the door when I'm away," I said. "Charley takes his job pretty seriously. You might lose a hand." This was an outrageous lie, of course, but the man said, "Yes, sir. You don't catch me fooling around with no strange dog."

The taxi driver, a sallow, yellowish man, shriveled like a chickpea with the cold, said, "I wouldn't take you more than a couple of blocks near. I don't go to have my cab wrecked."

"Is it that bad?"

"It ain't is it. It's can it get. And it can get that bad."

"When do they get going?"

He looked at his watch. "Except it's cold, they been coming in since dawn. It's quarter to. You get along and you won't miss nothing except it's cold."

I had camouflaged myself in an old blue jacket and my British navy cap on the supposition that in a seaport no one ever looks at a sailor any more than a waiter is inspected in a restaurant. In his natural haunts a sailor has no face and certainly no plans beyond getting drunk and maybe in jail for fighting. At least that's the general feeling about sailors. I've tested it. The most that happens is a kindly voice of authority saying, "Why don't you go back to your ship, sailor? You wouldn't want to sit in the tank and miss your tide, now would you, sailor?" And the speaker wouldn't recognize you five minutes later. And the Lion and Unicorn on my cap made me even more anonymous. But I must warn anyone testing my theory, never try it away from a shipping port.

"Where you from?" the driver asked with a complete lack of interest.

"Liverpool."

"Limey, huh? Well, you'll be all right. It's the goddamn New York Jews cause all the trouble."

I found myself with a British inflection and by no means one of Liverpool. "Jews—what? How do they cause trouble?"

"Why, hell, mister. We know how to take care of this. Everybody's happy and getting along fine. Why, I *like* niggers. And them goddamn New York Jews come in and stir the niggers up. They just stay in New York there wouldn't be no trouble. Ought to take them out."

"You mean lynch them?"

"I don't mean nothing else, mister."

He let me out and I started to walk away. "Don't try to get too close, mister," he called after me. "Just you enjoy it but don't mix in."

"Thanks," I said, and killed the "awfully" that came to my tongue.

As I walked toward the school I was in a stream of people all white and all going in my direction. They walked intently like people going to a fire after it has been burning for some time. They beat their hands against their hips or hugged them under coats, and many men had scarves under their hats and covering their ears.

Across the street from the school the police had set up wooden barriers to keep the crowd back, and they paraded back and forth, ignoring the jokes called to them. The front of the school was deserted but along the curb United States marshals were spaced, not in uniform but wearing armbands to identify them. Their guns bulged decently under their coats but their eyes darted about nervously, inspecting faces. It seemed to me that they inspected me to see if I was a regular, and then abandoned me as unimportant.

It was apparent where the Cheerleaders were, because people shoved forward to try to get near them. They had a favored place at the barricade directly across from the school entrance, and in that area a concentration of police stamped their feet and slapped their hands together in unaccustomed gloves.

Suddenly I was pushed violently and a cry went up: "Here she comes. Let her through. . . . Come on, move back. Let her through. Where you been? You're late for school. Where you been, Nellie?"

The name was not Nellie. I forget what it was. But she shoved through the dense crowd quite near enough to me so that I could see her coat of imitation fleece and her gold earrings. She was not tall, but her body was ample and full-busted. I judge she was about fifty. She was heavily powdered, which made the line of her double chin look very dark.

She wore a ferocious smile and pushed her way through the milling people, holding a fistful of clippings high in her hand to keep them from being crushed. Since it was her left hand I looked particularly for a wedding ring, and saw that there was none. I slipped in behind her to get carried along by her wave, but the crush was dense and I was given a warning too. "Watch it, sailor. Everybody wants to hear."

Nellie was received with shouts of greeting. I don't know how many Cheerleaders there were. There was no fixed line between the Cheerleaders and the crowd behind them. What I could see was that a group was passing newspaper clippings back and forth and reading them aloud with little squeals of delight.

Now the crowd grew restless, as an audience does when the clock goes past curtain time. Men all around me looked at their watches. I looked at mine. It was three minutes to nine.

The show opened on time. Sound of sirens. Motorcycle cops. Then two big black cars filled with big men in blond felt hats pulled up in front of the school. The crowd seemed to hold its breath. Four big marshals got out of each car and from somewhere in the automobiles they extracted the littlest Negro girl you ever saw, dressed in shining starchy white, with new white shoes on feet so little they were almost round. Her face and little legs were very black against the white.

The big marshals stood her on the curb and a jangle of jeering shrieks went up from behind the barricades. The little girl did not look at the howling crowd but from the side the whites of her eyes showed like those of a frightened fawn. The men turned her around like a doll, and then the strange procession moved up the broad walk toward the school, and the child was even more a mite because the men were so big. Then the girl made a curious hop, and I think I know what it was. I think in her whole life she had not gone ten steps without skipping, but now in the middle of her first skip the weight bore her down and her little round feet took measured, reluctant steps between the tall guards. Slowly they climbed the steps and entered the school.

The papers had printed that the jibes and jeers were cruel and sometimes obscene, and so they were, but this was not the big show. The crowd was waiting for the white man who dared to bring his white child to school. And here he came along the guarded walk, a tall man dressed in light gray, leading his frightened child by the hand. His body was tensed as a strong leaf spring drawn to the breaking strain; his face was grave and gray, and his eyes were on the ground immediately ahead of him. The muscles of his cheeks stood out from clenched jaws, a man afraid who by his will held his fears in check as a great rider directs a panicked horse.

A shrill, grating voice rang out. The yelling was not in chorus. Each took a turn and at the end of each the crowd broke into howls and roars and whistles of applause. This is what they had come to see and hear.

No newspaper had printed the words these women shouted. It was indicated that they were indelicate, some even said obscene. On television the sound track was made to blur or had crowd noises cut in to cover. But now I heard the words, bestial and filthy and degenerate. In a long and unprotected life I have seen and heard the vomitings of demoniac humans before. Why then did these screams fill me with a shocked and sickened sorrow?

The words written down are dirty, carefully and selectedly filthy. But there was something far worse here than dirt, a kind of frightening witches' Sabbath. Here was no spontaneous cry of anger, of insane rage.

Perhaps that is what made me sick with weary nausea. Here was no principle good or bad, no direction. These blowzy women with their little hats and their clippings hungered for attention. They wanted to be admired. They simpered in happy, almost innocent triumph when they were applauded. Theirs was the demented cruelty of egocentric children, and somehow this made their insensate beastliness much more heartbreaking. These were not mothers, not even women. They were crazy actors playing to a crazy audience.

The crowd behind the barrier roared and cheered and pounded one another with joy. The nervous strolling police watched for any break over the barrier. Their lips were tight but a few of them smiled and quickly unsmiled. Across the street the U.S. marshals stood unmoving. The gray-clothed man's legs had speeded for a second, but he reined them down with his will and walked up the school pavement.

The crowd quieted and the next cheer lady had her turn. Her voice was the bellow of a bull, a deep and powerful shout with flat edges like a circus barker's voice. There is no need to set down her words. The pattern was the same; only the rhythm and tonal quality were different. Anyone who has been near the theater would know that these speeches were not spontaneous. They were tried and memorized and carefully rehearsed. This was theater. I watched the intent faces of the listening crowd and they were the faces of an audience. When there was applause, it was for a performer.

My body churned with weary nausea, but I could not let an illness blind me after I had come so far to look and to hear. And suddenly I knew something was wrong and distorted and out of drawing. I knew New Orleans, I have over the years had many friends there, thoughtful, gentle people, with a tradition of kindness and courtesy. I remembered Lyle Saxon, a huge man of soft laughter. How many days I have spent with Roark Bradford, who took Louisiana sounds and sights and created God and the Green Pastures to which He leadeth us. I looked in the crowd for such faces of such people and they were not there. I've seen this kind bellow for blood at a prize fight, have orgasms when a man is gored in the bull ring, stare with vicarious lust at a highway accident, stand patiently in line for the privilege of watching any pain or any agony. But where were the others—the ones who would be proud they were of a species with the gray man—the ones whose arms would ache to gather up the small, scared black mite?

I don't know where they were. Perhaps they felt as helpless as I did, but they left New Orleans misrepresented to the world. The crowd, no doubt, rushed home to see themselves on television; and what they saw went out all over the world, unchallenged by the other things I know are there.

ERIC SEVAREID

ON ILLUSIONS
ABOUT
AMERICA

This is the first of five excerpts from a collection of informal essays by the experienced news analyst, Eric Sevareid. Each deals with an important and timely issue.

WE ARE seeing the end of our adolescence. In its reincarnation as guardian, advisor and donor to half the world the United States is emerging from its teens. A certain glow begins to fade. The hard, gray thoughts of maturity take possession and there is some danger of the cynicism that is itself immature.

In our relations with allied, neutral and client countries we are like the half-boy, half-man who is chagrined to learn that his own best image of himself is not really shared by others, that many he has helped feel no particular gratitude or even obligation and that some he has trusted return the trust only when the occasion serves them.

We will persevere, no doubt, learning that we can re-make very little of the world in our own image, losing many illusions about others and ourselves. But one thing we dare not lose—our essential self-confidence, now shaken under strong assault from within and without. Every other consequential country save Russia and possibly China has already lost this. Not one of them really knows where it is going or how to get there.

In a profound sense the United States is alone in this world. Most Americans who grasp this hard fact have only recently grasped it, as it has dawned upon them that our major alliance *may* be pulled apart, beginning with loss of faith and will among the Germans; as they learn that the neutrals are not going to be "won over" to our side; as they learn that bringing internal stability to a long list of backward countries is a much, much more difficult, drawn-out and expensive task than ever faintly imagined by the advisors who inserted that paragraph called "Point Four" in Mr. Truman's inaugural speech of January 1949.

It is time we ceased clutching illusions to our breast. We have to let them go if our hands are to be free. Some were of a self-denigrating nature, in any case, and it ought to be a pleasure to let them go, a source of greater confidence. Such, at least, have been my own sensations as various items of impediments sloughed off during the two past years in Europe, Africa and Latin America. A few may be worth the mention:

Americans are materialistic. We are, in fact, as furiously moralistic and idealistic as any people left on earth. We are swamped by the materials, but their simple possession fills no hollow in our souls, as it seems to do with the French. For pure money and possession lust I think I would put the black Africans first.

We are status seekers. The most ironclad pecking orders of my observance exist among Africans and Arabs. The average well-off Latin American is so riven by class and status that he wants nothing to do with the poor, even in his thoughts. Some members of my English shooting syndicate, which hunted on Wednesdays, were young businessmen who felt obliged to demonstrate that they could afford a mid-week day off, which they could not. One stock broker carried the *Financial Times* in his cartridge case and consulted it between flights of partridge.

America is a conformist society. The reason for our fantastic profusion of laws and regulations is the fantastic variety of our manners, ambitions and desires. The true conformist societies, of course, are the primitive societies.

We have neglected Latin America. The neglecters of Latin America are Latin Americans. Somewhere between $5 and $10 billion owned by Latin businessmen is salted away in New York, London and Swiss banks, while their governments demand grants and soft-currency loans from us as a matter of ecclesiastical right.

Europeans understand the Communist threat more clearly than we. Less clearly, if anything, because we have to measure it in its worldwide framework. Not even the able British diplomatic establishment possess Russian experts of the eminence of Charles Bohlen or George Kennan. No European provincial city boasts a hard-working citizens group comparable to the Foreign Policy Study organization in Cleveland or in a dozen other American towns. No academic centers of Russian study in Europe are superior to those at Harvard or Columbia.

America is too impatient. We have been, in my reluctant judgment, far too patient with allies, neutrals and clients alike. This has won us no affection and now is losing us respect.

Goodness without power is impotent in this world. Power itself is impotent when there is no belief in the will to use it, if need be.

ON PROGRESS

"... true progress reached the end of its cable some years ago and is now recoiling ... smashing masses of human beings back towards medieval conditions of life...."

ONE way to go quietly insane is to think hard about the concept of eternity. Another way, for anyone living in a megalopolis like New York, is to think hard about "progress."

The eerie sensation comes over one that true progress reached the end of its cable some years ago and is now recoiling upon us, an unstoppable juggernaut smashing masses of human beings back toward medieval conditions of life.

The streets are littered with cigarette and cigar butts, paper wrappings, particles of food and dog droppings. How long before they become indistinguishable from the gutters of medieval towns when slop pails were emptied from the second-story windows?

Thousands of New York women no longer attend evening services in their churches. They fear assault as they walk the few steps from bus or subway station to their apartment houses. The era of the medieval footpad has returned, and, as in the dark ages, the cry for help brings no assistance, for even grown men know they would be cut down before the police could arrive.

A thousand years ago in Europe acres of houses and shops were demolished and their inhabitants forced elsewhere so that great cathedrals could be built. For decades the building process soaked up all available skilled labor; for decades the townspeople stepped around pits in the streets, clambered over ropes and piles of timber, breathed mortar dust and slept and woke to the crashing noise of construction. The cathedrals, when finished, stood half-empty six days a week, but most of them at least had beauty. Today the ugly office skyscrapers go up, shops and graceful homes are obliterated, their inhabitants forced away and year after year New Yorkers step around the pits, stumble through the wooden catwalks, breathe the fine mist of dust, absorb the hammering noise night and day and telephone in vain for carpenter or plumber. And the skyscrapers stand empty two days and seven nights a week. This is progress.

At the rush hour men outrun old women for the available cab; the strong bodily crush back the weak for a place to stand in suffocating bus or subway car, no less destructive of human dignity than a cattle wagon in the time of Peter the Great. When the buses and subway cars began they represented progress.

Great parking garages are built, immediately filled with cars; the traffic remains as before, and that is progress. The renowned New York constructionist, Robert Moses, builds hundreds of miles of access highways, and they are at once crammed bumper to bumper with automobiles as long as locomotives, carrying an average of about two human beings apiece. Parkinson's general law applies here too, for vehicles will always increase in direct proportion to the increase in spaces to hold them. So skyscrapers and boxlike apartment houses will increase as the money to build them increases. So footpads will increase as the number of possible victims increases. But it's progress.

I am not surprised that the English writer, Mervyn Jones, concludes after traveling throughout Russia and the United States that ordinary Americans and ordinary Russians are remarkably alike in at least two respects—in the sheer physical misery they are forced to endure in their cities and in the sheer ugliness of jumbled signs and billboards being spread across their once fair countryside.

They are alike in a third respect. As Jones writes in *Horizon* magazine, both peoples complain remarkably little. Russians don't complain because they don't expect government authorities to listen. American dwellers in our megalopolises don't complain because they have long since abandoned hope. Their authorities may listen, but they know their authorities are helpless. A city like New York is ungovernable.

The secret, terrible fact is that progress, in all measurable terms of human effort, grace and self-respect ended some years ago in the great ant-hill cities. The juggernaut of time and effort has turned around and is now destroying the recent progressive past.

ON GOING
TO THE
MOON

*"... What is at stake is not only the
new marvels to be found, but also the
profound transfiguration of the source of
the search. ..."*

Two years ago, in May 1961, President Kennedy sent his special message
to the Congress in which he said that he himself believed we "should go
to the moon." It has taken two years to develop the beginnings of a national
debate on the question among Congressmen, scientists and editorialists.

I say the "beginnings" of a debate because, on its public plane at least,
the argument has not yet come into its true focus. The true question is not
whether we should try to land men on the moon—the nature of this political
world as well as the nature of man's curiosity and the unquenchable spirit
of science make it inevitable that we try—but how we go about it. The real
argument is going on in semi-private between the Cold Warriors, including
the military, who want a "crash" program, and certain scientists, deeply
aware of the difficulties and dangers, who fear the atmosphere of a "race"
in this delicate operation. They discount the lasting value of the prestige
attendant upon being first.

They would like to see the whole psychology of strain and rush, of looking
over our shoulder, rooted out of this endeavor. They believe that with this
step toward the moon we have reached the point where haste will not only
make enormous financial waste, but very probably produce failure and
human tragedy.

Congressmen now expressing doubts about the moon program are being
contemptuously assailed as pinch-penny mossbacks living in the last century. This comes a bit gratuitously from partisans of the President, since
he himself, in his message of two years ago, urged every citizen and Con-
gressman to "consider the matter carefully in making their judgment,"
because, he said, "it is a heavy burden and there is no sense in agreeing or
desiring that the United States take an affirmative position in outer space
unless we are prepared to do the work and bear the burdens to make it
successful."

Only now are many of us, including the worried members of Congress, beginning faintly to comprehend the order of magnitude of the efforts and the burdens to come. A new and fathomless world of human endeavor is swimming into our ken. It is natural and not necessarily a sign of stodgy un-imaginativeness that practical men instinctively and immediately try to estimate the practical costs involved; indeed, they must. And the more they try the more dismayed they feel.

They have a few present facts to go on: they know that the budgets for NASA have been doubling every year for the past five years. They know that a successful moon landing in this decade would cost at least $30 billion and maybe more. They see that of the 400,000 qualified specialists now working in "R and D"—research and development—60,000 work on NASA projects, and that this percentage must sharply rise, raising the gravest questions about scientific priorities in the American society of the future.

They see what our present budgets for normal military preparedness are and they see no way to reduce them substantially. Now they see, dimly on the horizon, a second realm of uncontrollable expenditure which can match and even surpass normal defense expenditures as the years go by. Space is limitless and there are only staging points in its "conquest"—there is no stopping place.

Being practical men of the present, with present and practical responsibilities, of course they feel dismay. What is a vision to some men is a specter to others. The immediate specter these men see is a permanently growing federal debt, a permanently unbalanced budget, a permanent level of extremely high taxes.

This is only the beginning. Anyone has only to let out his imagination a short notch to see the ultimate possibilities—to see humanity's push into space transforming this society, dominating its intellectual pursuits, absorbing its resources, altering the training of its youth and its moral and religious concepts, upsetting the priorities for its social and humanitarian efforts on terra firma.

Those who scold the worriers say that to cancel the moon voyage would be as if Ferdinand and Isabella had canceled Columbus' voyage, which opened the New World. They are more right than they know. What is at stake are not only the new marvels to be found, but also the profound transfiguration of the source of the search.

After the voyage of Columbus the Old World was never the same in political, economic, military, social, religious or intellectual terms. After the first men walk upon the moon Old Earth will never be the same and the change will begin in the two societies, Russia and America, now competing for the cataclysmic honor of commencing the alteration.

ERIC SEVAREID

ON THE NEGRO PASSION

*"...If the Negro passion of today is not a
true people's revolution, it is as close to one
as we have ever known in our land...."*

BY ITS dominant voices, its most unforgettable faces and its chief acts of
bravery does a generation recognize itself and history mark it.

For America, this postwar period is surely the era of the Negro passion.
The most moving voices are now those of Negroes; the most searing, lasting
words are put on paper by Negro writers; their music is the American music
most penetrating and persuasive to other parts of the world. No cause is
now so fundamental to the health and integrity of this society as the Negro
cause; of no other leaders are so much stamina and courage demanded as
are now required of Negro leaders.

They are bound to win, somehow, not only because their present aims are
so limited and unarguable, but because they have succeeded in involving
us all, whoever we are, wherever we live within the nation's frontiers. They
have caught the attention of the whole American people and, more than
that, they have caught up the conscience of the whole people, however many
of us may try to deny this to ourselves. A newspaper or television picture
of a snarling police dog set upon a human being is recorded in the permanent
photoelectric file of every human brain.

This generation is not likely to find surcease from the Negro passion; its
source springs and the resistance to it are too deeply grounded for easy
resolution, and its present outburst too long delayed. Its more violent manifestations are not going to be confined to the Deep South. The head of black
steam building up in places like New York, Washington and Chicago are
finding outlets too few and too small, at the present rate, for the permanent
avoidance of combustion.

Because this unfolding drama involves the automatic reflexes of the
instinctive sense of justice, because it involves namable, hearable, count-
able individual persons of flesh and blood, it is going to dwarf the general
and social pageants of this domestic era, whether they be the struggles to
rationalize the inchoate megalopolis, to preserve the open spaces, to eradicate a disease, to "conquer" space, or whatever.

The time is coming, soon, when the Negro passion will truly dominate American politics. It is going to change the prism through which we consider the problems of far-off nations; romanticism will have to give way to realism. Liberalism of the academic or cafe-society brand—the motivations of those who rhapsodize over the Peace Corpsmen in Ethiopia or journey 6,000 miles to sit at the feet of Dr. Schweitzer, but who would never dream of visiting the night police court in their own city and observing the tragedy of the American Negro—such impulses are going to lose their present status in the hierarchy of the virtues. There will be a noticeable dearth of hiding places for those professing belief either in their religion or the American Constitution.

An education in the facts of life and history is in store for those pained by the messy contradictions built in to the Negro passion. Those bewildered at the Negro uprising ("after all, they had made a lot of progress") may learn that this is one of the eternal lessons from past rebellions against oppression. It is not when the oppression is most complete that these revolutions begin to revolve, but when concessions are given, hopes are born, light is glimpsed at the end of the dark tunnel. It is when an oppressed people feels close to its goal, not far off from it, that their action becomes frenetic.

Those who are cynical or upset by the moral duality in the Negro phenomenon, by the spectacle of lofty courage and self-sacrifice among the Negro leaders, side by side with the spectacle of spreading crime and moral squalor in the slum-bound masses of the Negro poor, may learn that the first is a direct reflection of the second—its natural, not its unnatural, partner. Desperation, like war, ennobles some among its victims and debases others. No true people's revolution was ever neat, clean or devoid of sad anomalies.

If the Negro passion of today is not a true people's revolution, it is as close to one as we have ever known in our land.

ERIC SEVAREID

ON
BIRTH
CONTROL

*"...The Malthusian law is in operation;
people are living to the edge of the available
food supply, then dying...."*

A FEW months ago, I was talking with a United Nations medical scientist
as we slapped mosquitoes in the dank heat of a hotel lobby in northeastern
Brazil, the biggest area of human blight in the Western Hemisphere. He had
been making the rounds of the local dietetic experts and inspecting the "re-
hydration centers," where vacant-eyed peasant mothers walk in every day
carrying babies already half dead from malnutrition and gastric diseases.

He said, "I'm getting so I wake up in the morning with the thought that
should never pass through the mind of anybody with the job of helping human creatures. I wake up thinking, 'What are we saving the children *for?'*
They just go back to the mud hut in the ocean of sugar cane on the feudal
estates to die a little later from the swamp water they must drink."

These are pictures indelibly stamped on the mind of Westerners who
travel through Latin America and Asia in these years of the mid-twentieth
century. Such a traveler has a choice of obsessions these days. He may return with a burning urge that America plunge into these places and these
miseries with all its energy, money and talent; he may feel the opposite urge
that we get out completely and leave the mass tragedies to God and nature;
he may, in thinking about certain regimes and bosses, indulge the fantasy
wish for a return to judicious assassination as a diplomatic stratagem. But
for many the obsession easiest to come by is the desire to shake by the
shoulders all those ignorant of the need to check the rate of human births
and all those who wish it to be ignored.

Americans who do not travel in these regions speak and write of "what
will happen" if the world increase in population continues at the present
rate of 50 millions a year; if India, "that dust of people," as De Gaulle has
called it, continues to add 8 million more human beings each year; if Pakistan grows at a rate which has added 18 million people in the last ten years;

"On Birth Control," (excerpt from "The Poor Nations Ye Have With Ye Always") from *This
Is Eric Sevareid* by Eric Sevareid. Copyright © 1964 by Eric Sevareid. Used by permission of
McGraw-Hill Book Company.

if Latin America makes its projected leap from 200 million to 300 million in fifteen years; if the intense overcrowding continues in the small and increasingly desperate West Indian islands.

But "what will happen" is already happening in some of these areas and in others. The Malthusian law is in operation; people are living to the edge of the available food supply, then dying. We speculate about how many tens of millions might die in an atomic war and whether cultures could survive such a shock. But nature, with the help of human science, has already loosed a war on the world, tens of millions are dying now, and it seems to me a present question whether many ancient cultures and social structures may not crumble before this storm of life is brought under control.

For India and Pakistan, for parts of Latin America, North Africa and the mid-East, there is, so I have come to believe, no chance of the stable economic growth and progress in enlightenment that our foreign-aid programs are designed to help achieve, without direct recourse to birth-control practices on a massive scale. I am aware that such a statement gives offense to many, that many intelligent Americans believe highly intensified efforts in irrigation and scientific farming, land ownership reform, industrialization and education can and will be the successful as well as the morally superior alternative. I can only say that from what I have seen I cannot share this belief. After a half generation of extraordinary effort, India's long-run prospects seem no better than they were when the effort began, even with the direct encouragement of birth control by methods now widely practiced in Western countries. Nasser's ten years of effort with land sharing, irrigation and industrialization ought to have transformed Egypt, but each year some 400,000 additional Egyptians wipe out the over-all gain with the regularity of a tide blurring over castles of sand.

He has hoped, he told me in August, that eventually education will bring about smaller families. Yet educational structures and standards are themselves diluted and blunted by the same tidal wave, as one sees in Brazil, where one-half the total population is now under nineteen years of age and where, even in the booming areas of modern prosperity, children must attend school in two and three shifts a day.

The arguments on the morality of artificial birth control are as familiar as they are fierce and sincere. But there are signs that the premises involved may be slowly shifting. In our own country there are Catholic intellectuals now making a sharper distinction between what is morally wrong and what is legally wrong. There is developing a new round of argument on the morality of the new "oral pill" for women, with some prospect of a broader area of agreement on the whole subject, so painful for so many on both sides of the discussion.

It is not beyond possibility that history will one day record the invention of a safe, effective anti-birth pill, cheap and simple enough for use by the most ignorant Asia peasant, as this century's great contribution toward peace and order, more important than any missile, "anti" or otherwise.

STORIES

The story is an art form, deliberately shaped to convey features of human experience that the artist has found important. As a form of fiction, the story can convey an astonishingly wide range of experience, far more than was possible a century or even a half-century ago, when various social objections to fiction narrowed the artist's freedom and the reader's responses. In a way, fiction provides the most indispensable kind of experience: we cannot live long enough to discover for ourselves the many fresh viewpoints on human life that fictional writing organizes and brings to us. If we draw on the carefully seasoned, freshly original vision of the artist, a person who feels and thinks on a very high level of sensitivity, we can gain a kind of "literary experience" that gives greater richness, meaning, and wisdom for our own lives. Fortunately, educated people in all ages have recognized this unique value in literature; education in the humanist tradition of the last four centuries has placed its main emphasis on the works of the great literary artists.

Fiction appeals to a wide range of emotional and artistic sensitivity in its readers. It asks us to appreciate the exciting side of language, its power to bring up images and convey feeling. Fiction gives us living models to react toward, letting us decide how we feel about human situations involving "character types," "unforgettable personalities," or people in time of great crisis. We are asked to look at inner thoughts and fundamental motivations, to learn to evaluate people and judge their values and ideas. We also learn the nature of the society in which they lived, and in this way, we get a fresh perspective on our own society.

The art of the short story, now reaching a new zenith in our century, differs somewhat from that of the novel. In the first place, the short story is a far older form. Most "novels" in earlier ages were collections of short stories, sometimes with a central or unifying theme, or a "frame tale" within which one or more characters told short tales to make up a whole novel. Short fiction has also been a medium for parody and satire, forms which are more difficult to manage in novel-length fiction because they require a quick, positive impact on the reader for maximum effect.

A major feature of the novel is that it requires *development* of character, plot, and theme, whereas most short stories can be made quite forceful with a single episode, type characters, and a comparatively less complicated theme. The novel requires a more elaborate background, sometimes an historical framework, and characters showing the growth or change essential to the purpose of the story. The short story, on the other hand, must achieve its iffects in a short space with the greatest economy of devices. Both forms are very important in modern literature, for they carry equally profound "messages" or revelations of the nature of humanity.

An Approach to Analysis

The student who is looking for a way to analyze a story or for a topic for writing about it may find it useful to examine his reading in a pattern of questions like the following, which may show most of a story's main features. Read the story thoroughly once, preferably without interruption. If possible, wait a day to let the ideas simmer, then read the story again rapidly, looking for the answers to these questions:

a. What is the "central incident"? Are there any minor episodes that contribute to the plot?

b. Who are the characters? Do they seem to remain the same or do they change in any way during the story? How are they described to the reader or differentiated from each other?

c. What is the setting of the story? Is the time, location, or social setting of the story significantly different from that of your own experience? Do the differences help to explain the characters' actions?

d. Are there any special features or peculiarities in the language? Examine the dialogue, use of metaphor or figurative language, the unfamilar terms and expressions. How does the writer express his *attitude* toward his subject and toward his reader?

e. Is the meaning stated in an obvious way or implied? If the meaning appears clear to you after the second reading, you are close to deciding the author's dominant theme or idea, which, along with the author's attitude, is the basic factor in analyzing the story.

A careful exploration along these lines will raise the important issues that lie close to the heart of what makes a story appealing.

WALTER VAN TILBURG CLARK

HOOK

". . . Denied the joy of space, without which the joy of loneliness was lost, the joy of battle and killing, the blood lust, became his whole concentration. . . ."

HOOK, the hawks' child, was hatched in a dry spring among the oaks beside the seasonal river, and was struck from the nest early. In the drouth his single-willed parents had to extend their hunting ground by more than twice, for the ground creatures upon which they fed died and dried by the hundreds. The range became too great for them to wish to return and feed Hook, and when they had lost interest in each other they drove Hook down into the sand and brush and went back to solitary courses over the bleaching hills.

Unable to fly yet, Hook crept over the ground, challenging all large movements with recoiled head, erected, rudimentary wings, and the small rasp of his clattering beak. It was during this time of abysmal ignorance and continual fear that his eyes took on the first quality of a hawk, that of being wide, alert and challenging. He dwelt, because of his helplessness, among the rattling brush which grew between the oaks and the river. Even in his thickets and near the water, the white sun was the dominant presence. Except in the dawn, when the land wind stirred, or in the late afternoon, when the sea wind became strong enough to penetrate the half-mile inland to this turn in the river, the sun was the major force, and everything was dry and motionless under it. The brush, small plants and trees alike husbanded the little moisture at their hearts; the moving creatures waited for dark, when sometimes the sea fog came over and made a fine, soundless rain which relieved them.

The two spacious sounds of his life environed Hook at this time. One was the great rustle of the slopes of yellowed wild wheat, with over it the chattering rustle of the leaves of the California oaks, already as harsh and individually tremulous as in autumn. The other was the distant whisper of the foaming edge of the Pacific, punctuated by the hollow shoring of the waves. But these Hook did not yet hear, for he was attuned by fear and hunger to the small, spasmodic rustlings of live things. Dry, shrunken, and nearly starved, and with his plumage delayed, he snatched at beetles, dragging in the sand to catch them. When swifter and stronger birds and animals did not reach them first, which was seldom, he ate the small, silver fish left in the mud by the failing river. He watched, with nearly chattering beak, the quick, thin lizards pause, very alert, and raise and lower themselves, but could not catch them because he had to raise his wings to move rapidly, which startled them.

Only one sight and sound not of his world of microscopic necessity was forced upon Hook. That was the flight of the big gulls from the beaches, which sometimes, in quealing play, came spinning back over the foothills and the river bed. For some inherited reason, the big, ship-bodied birds did not frighten Hook, but angered him. Small and chewed-looking, with his wide, already yellowing eyes glaring up at them, he would stand in an open place on the sand in the sun and spread his shaping wings and clatter his bill like shaken dice. Hook was furious about the swift, easy passage of gulls.

His first opportunity to leave off living like a ground owl came accidentally. He was standing in the late afternoon in the red light under the thicket, his eyes half-filmed with drowse and the stupefaction of starvation, when suddenly something beside him moved, and he struck, and killed a field mouse driven out of the wheat by thirst. It was a poor mouse, shriveled and lice ridden, but in striking, Hook had tasted blood, which raised nest memories and restored his nature. With started neck plumage and shining eyes, he tore and fed. When the mouse was devoured, Hook had entered hoarse adolescence. He began to seek with a conscious appetite, and to move more readily out of shelter. Impelled by the blood appetite, so glorious after his long preservation upon the flaky and bitter stuff of bugs, he ventured even into the wheat in the open sun beyond the oaks, and discovered the small trails and holes among the roots. With his belly often partially filled with flesh, he grew rapidly in strength and will. His eyes were taking on their final change, their yellow growing deeper and more opaque, their stare more constant, their challenge less desperate. Once during this transformation, he surprised a ground squirrel, and although he was ripped and wing-bitten and could not hold his prey, he was not dismayed by the conflict, but exalted. Even while the wing was still drooping and the pinions not grown back, he was excited by other ground squirrels and pursued them futilely, and was angered by their dusty escapes. He realized that his world was a great arena for killing, and felt the magnificence of it.

The two major events of Hook's young life occurred in the same day. A little after dawn he made the customary essay and succeeded in flight. A little before sunset, he made his first sustained flight of over two hundred yards, and at its termination struck and slew a great buck squirrel whose thrashing and terrified gnawing and squealing gave him a wild delight. When he had gorged on the strong meat, Hook stood upright, and in his eyes was the stare of the hawk, never flagging in intensity but never swelling beyond containment. After that the stare had only to grow more deeply challenging and more sternly controlled as his range and deadliness increased. There was no change in kind. Hook had mastered the first of the three hungers which are fused into the single, flaming will of a hawk, and he had experienced the second.

The third and consummating hunger did not awaken in Hook until the following spring, when the exultation of space had grown slow and steady in him, so that he swept freely with the wind over the miles of coastal foothills, circling, and ever in sight of the sea, and used without struggle the warm currents lifting from the slopes, and no longer desired to scream at the range of his vision, but intently sailed above his shadow swiftly climbing to meet him on the hillsides, sinking away and rippling across the brush-grown canyons.

That spring the rains were long, and Hook sat for hours, hunched and angry under their pelting, glaring into the fogs of the river valley, and killed only small, drenched things flooded up from their tunnels. But when the rains had dissipated, and there were sun and sea wind again, the game ran plentiful, the hills were thick and shining green, and the new river flooded about the boulders where battered turtles climbed up to shrink and sleep. Hook then was scorched by the third hunger. Ranging farther, often forgetting to kill and eat, he sailed for days with growing rage, and woke at night clattering on his dead tree limb, and struck and struck and struck at the porous wood of the trunk, tearing it away. After days, in the draft of a coastal canyon miles below his own hills, he came upon the acrid taint he did not know but had expected, and sailing down it, felt his neck plumes rise and his wings quiver so that he swerved unsteadily. He saw the unmated female perched upon the tall and jagged stump of a tree that had been shorn by storm, and he stooped, as if upon game. But she was older than he, and wary of the gripe of his importunity, and banked off screaming, and he screamed also at the intolerable delay.

At the head of the canyon, the screaming pursuit was crossed by another male with a great wing-spread, and the light golden in the fringe of his plumage. But his more skillful opening played him false against the ferocity of the twice-balked Hook. His rising maneuver for position was cut short by Hook's wild, upward swoop, and at the blow he raked desperately and tumbled off to the side. Dropping, Hook struck him again, struggled to clutch, but only raked and could not hold, and, diving, struck once more in passage, and then beat up, yelling triumph, and saw the crippled antagonist side-slip away, half-tumble once, as the ripped wing failed to balance, then steady and glide obliquely into the cover of brush on the canyon side. Beating hard and stationary in the wind above the bush that covered his competitor, Hook waited an instant, but when the bush was still, screamed again, and let himself go off with the current, reseeking, infuriated by the burn of his own wounds, the thin choke-thread of the acrid taint.

On a hilltop projection of stone two miles inland, he struck her down, gripping her rustling body with his talons, beating her wings down with his wings, belting her head when she whimpered or thrashed, and at last clutching her neck with his hook and, when her coy struggles had given way to stillness, succeeded.

In the early summer, Hook drove the three young ones from their nest, and went back to lone circling above his own range. He was complete.

———————————

Throughout that summer and the cool, growthless weather of the winter, when the gales blew in the river canyon and the ocean piled upon the shore, Hook was master of the sky and the hills of his range. His flight became a lovely and certain thing, so that he played with the treacherous currents of the air with a delicate ease surpassing that of the gulls He could sail for hours, searching the blanched grasses below him with telescopic eyes, gaining height against the wind, descending in mile-long, gently declining swoops when he curved and rode back, and never beating either wing. At the swift passage of his shadow within their vision, gophers, ground squirrels and rabbits froze, or plunged gibbering into their tunnels beneath matted turf. Now, when he struck, he killed easily in one hard-knuckled blow. Occasionally, in sport, he soared up over the river and drove the heavy and weaponless gulls downstream again, until they would no longer venture inland.

There was nothing which Hook feared now, and his spirit was wholly belligerent, swift and sharp, like his gaze. Only the mixed smells and incomprehensible activities of the people at the Japanese farmer's home, inland of the coastwise highway and south of the bridge across Hook's river, troubled him. The smells were strong, unsatisfactory and never clear, and the people, though they behaved foolishly, constantly running in and out of their built-up holes, were large, and appeared capable, with fearless eyes looking up at him, so that he instinctively swerved aside from them. He cruised over their yard, their gardens, and their bean fields, but he would not alight close to their buildings.

But this one area of doubt did not interfere with his life. He ignored it, save to look upon it curiously as he crossed, his afternoon shadow sliding in an instant over the chicken-and-crate-cluttered yard, up the side of the unpainted barn, and then out again smoothly, just faintly, liquidly rippling over the furrows and then over the stubble of the grazing slopes. When the season was dry, and the dead earth blew on the fields, he extended his range to satisfy his great hunger, and again narrowed it when the fields were once more alive with the minute movements he could not only see but anticipate.

Four times that year he was challenged by other hawks blowing up from behind the coastal hills to scud down his slopes, but two of these he slew in mid-air, and saw hurtle down to thump on the ground and lie still while he circled, and a third, whose wing he tore, he followed closely to earth and beat to death in the grass, making the crimson jet out from its breast and neck into the pale wheat. The fourth was a strong flier and experienced fighter, and theirs was a long, running battle, with brief, rising flurries of striking and screaming, from which down and plumage soared off.

Here, for the first time, Hook felt doubts, and at moments wanted to drop away from the scoring, burning talons and the twisted hammer strokes of the strong beak, drop away shrieking, and take cover and be still. In the end, when Hook, having outmaneuvered his enemy and come above him, wholly in control, and going with the wind, tilted and plunged for the death rap, the other, in desperation, threw over on his back and struck up. Talons locked, beaks raking, they dived earthward. The earth grew and spread under them amazingly, and they were not fifty feet above it when Hook, feeling himself turning toward the underside, tore free and beat up again on heavy, wrenched wings. The other, stroking swiftly, and so close to down that he lost wing plumes to a bush, righted himself and planed up, but flew on lumberingly between the hills and did not return. Hook screamed the triumph, and made a brief pretense of pursuit, but was glad to return, slow and victorious, to his dead tree.

In all these encounters Hook was injured, but experienced only the fighter's pride and exultation from the sting of wounds received in successful combat. And in each of them he learned new skill. Each time the wounds healed quickly, and left him a more dangerous bird.

In the next spring, when the rains and the night chants of the little frogs were past, the third hunger returned upon Hook with a new violence. In this quest, he came into the taint of a young hen. Others too were drawn by the unnerving perfume, but only one of them, the same with which Hook had fought his great battle, was a worthy competitor. This hunter drove off two, while two others, game but neophytes, were glad enough that Hook's impatience would not permit him to follow and kill. Then the battle between the two champions fled inland, and was a tactical marvel, but Hook lodged the neck-breaking blow, and struck again as they dropped past the treetops. The blood had already begun to pool on the gray, fallen foliage as Hook flapped up between branches, too spent to cry his victory. Yet his hunger would not let him rest until, late in the second day, he drove the female to ground among the laurels of a strange river canyon.

When the two fledglings of this second brood had been driven from the nest, and Hook had returned to his own range, he was not only complete, but supreme. He slept without concealment on his bare limb, and did not open his eyes when, in the night, the heavy-billed cranes coughed in the shallows below him.

The turning point of Hook's career came that autumn, when the brush in the canyons rustled dryly and the hills, mowed close by the cattle, smoked under the wind as if burning. One mid-afternoon, when the black clouds were torn on the rim of the sea and the surf flowered white and high on the rocks, raining in over the low cliffs, Hook rode the wind diagonally across the river mouth. His great eyes, focused for small things, stirring in the dust and leaves, overlooked so large and slow a movement as that of the Japanese farmer rising from the brush and lifting the two black eyes of his shotgun. Too late Hook saw and, startled, swerved, but wrongly. The surf muffled the reports, and nearly without sound, Hook felt the minute whips of the first shot, and the astounding, breath-taking blow of the second.

Beating his good wing, tasting the blood that quickly swelled into his beak, he tumbled off with the wind and struck into the thickets on the far side of the river mouth. The branches tore him. Wild with rage, he thrust up and clattered his beak, challenging, but when he had fallen over twice, he knew that the trailing wing would not carry, and then heard the boots of the hunter among the stones in the river bed and, seeing him loom at the edge of the bushes, crept back among the thickest brush and was still. When he saw the boots stand before him, he reared back, lifting his good wing and cocking his head for the serpent-like blow, his beak open but soundless, his great eyes hard and very shining. The boots passed on. The Japanese farmer, who believed that he had lost chickens, and who had cunningly observed Hook's flight for many afternoons, until he could plot it, did not greatly want a dead hawk.

When Hook could hear nothing but the surf and the wind in the thicket, he let the sickness and shock overcome him. The fine film of the inner lid dropped over his big eyes. His heart beat frantically, so that it made the plumage of his shot-aching breast throb. His own blood throttled his breathing. But these things were nothing compared to the lightning of pain in his left shoulder, where the shot had bunched, shattering the airy bones so the pinions trailed on the ground and could not be lifted. Yet, when a sparrow lit in the bush over him, Hook's eyes flew open again, hard and challenging, his good wing was lifted and his beak strained open. The startled sparrow darted piping out over the river.

Throughout that night, while the long clouds blew across the stars and the wind shook the bushes about him, and throughout the next day, while the clouds still blew and massed until there was no gleam of sunlight on the sand bar, Hook remained stationary, enduring his sickness. In the second evening, the rains began. First there was a long, running patter of drops upon the beach and over the dry trees and bushes. At dusk there came a heavier squall, which did not die entirely, but slacked off to a continual, spaced splashing of big drops, and then returned with the front of the storm. In long, misty curtains, gust by gust, the rain swept over the sea, beating down its heaving, and coursed up the beach. The little jets of dust ceased to rise about the drops in the fields, and the mud began to gleam. Among the boulders of the river bed, darkling pools grew slowly.

Still Hook stood behind his tree from the wind, only gentle drops reaching him, falling from the upper branches and then again from the brush. His eyes remained closed, and he could still taste his own blood in his mouth, though it had ceased to come up freshly. Out beyond him, he heard the storm changing. As rain conquered the sea, the heave of the surf became a hushed sound, often lost in the crying of the wind. Then gradully, as the night turned toward morning, the wind also was broken by the rain. The crying became fainter, the rain settled toward steadiness, and the creep of the waves could be heard again, quiet and regular upon the beach.

At dawn there was no wind and no sun, but everywhere the roaring of the vertical, relentless rain. Hook then crept among the rapid drippings of the bushes, dragging his torn sail, seeking better shelter. He stopped often and stood with the shutters of film drawn over his eyes. At midmorning he found a little cave under a ledge at the base of the sea cliff. Here, lost without branches and leaves about him, he settled to await improvement.

When, at midday of the third day, the rain stopped altogether, and the sky opened before a small, fresh wind, letting light through to glitter upon a tremulous sea, Hook was so weak that his good wing trailed also to prop him upright, and his open eyes were lusterless. But his wounds were hardened, and he felt the return of hunger. Beyond his shelter, he heard the gulls flying in great numbers and crying their joy at the cleared air. He could even hear, from the fringe of the river, the ecstatic and unstinted bubblings and chirpings of the small birds. The grassland, he felt, would be full of the stirring anew of the close-bound life, the undrowned insects clicking as they dried out, the snakes slithering down, heads half erect, into the grasses where the mice, gophers and ground squirrels ran and stopped and chewed and licked themselves smoother and drier.

With the aid of this hunger, and on the crutches of his wings, Hook came down to stand in the sun beside his cave, whence he could watch the beach. Before him, in ellipses on tilting planes, the gulls flew. The surf was rearing again, and beginning to shelve and hiss on the sand. Through the white foam-writing it left, the long-billed pipers twinkled in bevies, escaping each wave, then racing down after it to plunge their fine drills into the minute double holes where the sand crabs bubbled. In the third row of breakers two seals lifted sleek, streaming heads and barked, and over them, trailing his spider legs, a great crane flew south. Among the stones at the foot of the cliff, small red and green crabs made a little, continuous rattling and knocking. The cliff swallows glittered and twanged on aerial forays.

The afternoon began auspiciously for Hook also. One of the two gulls which came squabbling above him dropped a freshly caught fish to the sand. Quickly Hook was upon it. Gripping it, he raised his good wing and cocked his head with open beak at the many gulls which had circled and come down at once toward the fall of the fish. The gulls sheered off, cursing raucously. Left alone on the sand, Hook devoured the fish and, after resting in the sun, withdrew again to his shelter.

In the succeeding days, between rains, he foraged on the beach. He learned to kill and crack the small green crabs. Along the edge of the river mouth, he found the drowned bodies of mice and squirrels and even sparrows. Twice he managed to drive feeding gulls from their catch, charging upon them with buffeting wing and clattering beak. He grew stronger slowly, but the shot sail continued to drag. Often, at the choking thought of soaring and striking and the good, hot-blood kill, he strove to take off, but only the one wing came up, winnowing with a hiss, and drove him over onto his side in the sand. After these futile trials, he would rage and clatter. But gradually he learned to believe that he could not fly, that his life must now be that of the discharged nestling again. Denied the joy of space, without which the joy of loneliness was lost, the joy of battle and killing, the blood lust, became his whole concentration. It was his hope, as he charged feeding gulls, that they would turn and offer battle, but they never did. The sandpipers, at his approach, fled peeping, or, like a quiver of arrows shot together, streamed out over the surf in a long curve. Once, pent beyond bearing, he disgraced himself by shrieking challenge at the businesslike heron which flew south every evening at the same time. The heron did not even turn his head, but flapped and glided on.

Hook's shame and anger became such that he stood awake at night. Hunger kept him awake also, for these little leavings of the gulls could not sustain his great body in its renewed violence. He became aware that the gulls slept at night in flocks on the sand, each with one leg tucked under him. He discovered also that the curlews and the pipers, often mingling, likewise slept, on the higher remnant of the bar. A sensation of evil delight filled him in the consideration of protracted striking among them.

There was only half of a sick moon in a sky of running but far-separated clouds on the night when he managed to stalk into the center of the sleeping gulls. This was light enough, but so great was his vengeful pleasure that there broke from him a shrill scream of challenge as he first struck. Without the power of flight behind it, the blow was not murderous, and this newly discovered impotence made Hook crazy, so that he screamed again and again as he struck and tore at the felled gull. He slew the one, but was twice knocked over by its heavy flounderings, and all the others rose above him, weaving and screaming, protesting in the thin moonlight. Wakened by their clamor, the wading birds also took wing, startled and plaintive. When the beach was quiet again, the flocks had settled elsewhere, beyond his pitiful range, and he was left alone beside the single kill. It was a disappointing victory. He fed with lowering spirit.

Thereafter, he stalked silently. At sunset he would watch where the gulls settled along the miles of beach, and after dark he would come like a sharp shadow among them, and drive with his hook on all sides of him, till the beatings of a poorly struck victim sent the flock up. Then he would turn vindictively upon the fallen and finish them. In his best night, he killed five from one flock. But he ate only a little from one, for the vigor resulting from occasional repletion strengthened only his ire, which became so great at such a time that food revolted him. It was not the joyous, swift, controlled hunting anger of a sane hawk, but something quite different, which made him dizzy if it continued too long, and left him unsatisfied with any kill.

Then one day, when he had very nearly struck a gull while driving it from a gasping yellowfin, the gull's wing rapped against him as it broke for its running start, and, the trailing wing failing to support him, he was knocked over. He flurried awkwardly in the sand to regain his feet, but his mastery of the beach was ended. Seeing him, in clear sunlight, struggling after the chance blow, the gulls returned about him in a flashing cloud, circling and pecking on the wing. Hook's plumage showed quick little jets of irregularity here and there. He reared back, clattering and erecting the good wing, spreading the great, rusty tail for balance. His eyes shone with a little of the old pleasure. But it died, for he could reach none of them. He was forced to turn and dance awkwardly on the sand, trying to clash bills with each tormentor. They banked up squealing and returned, weaving about him in concentric and overlapping circles. His scream was lost in their clamor, and he appeared merely to be hopping clumsily with his mouth open. Again he fell sideways. Before he could right himself, he was bowled over, and a second time, and lay on his side, twisting his neck to reach them and clappering in blind fury, and was struck three times by three successive gulls, shrieking their flock triumph.

Finally he managed to roll to his breast, and to crouch with his good wing spread wide and the other stretched nearly as far, so that he extended like a gigantic moth, only his snake head, with its now silent scimitar, erect. One great eye blazed under its level brow, but where the other had been was a shallow hole from which thin blood trickled to his russet gap.

In this crouch, by short stages, stopping repeatedly to turn and drive the gulls up, Hook dragged into the river canyon and under the stiff cover of the bitter-leafed laurel. There the gulls left him, soaring up with great clatter of their valor. Till nearly sunset Hook, broken spirited and enduring his hardening eye socket, heard them celebrating over the waves.

When his will was somewhat replenished, and his empty eye socket had stopped the twiching and vague aching which had forced him often to roll ignominiously to rub it in the dust, Hook ventured from the protective lacings of his thicket. He knew fear again, and the challenge of his remaining eye was once more strident, as in adolescence. He dared not return to the beaches, and with a new, weak hunger, the home hunger, enticing him, made his way by short hunting journeys back to the wild wheat slopes and the crisp oaks. There was in Hook an unwonted sensation now, that of the ever-neighboring possibility of death. This sensation was beginning, after his period as a mad bird on the beach, to solidify him into his last stage of life. When, during his slow homeward passage, the gulls wafted inland over him, watching the earth with curious, miserish eyes, he did not cower, but neither did he challenge, either by opened beak or by raised shoulder. He merely watched carefully, learning his first lessons in observing the world with one eye.

At first the familiar surroundings of the bend in the river and the tree with the dead limb to which he could not ascend, aggravated his humiliation, but in time, forced to live cunningly and half-starved, he lost much of his savage pride. At the first flight of a strange hawk over his realm, he was wild at his helplessness, and kept twisting his head like an owl, or spinning in the grass like a small and feathered dervish, to keep the hateful beauty of the wind-rider in sight. But in the succeeding weeks, as one after another coasted his beat, his resentment declined, and when one of the raiders, a haughty yearling, sighted his upstaring eye, and plunged and struck him dreadfully, and failed to kill him only because he dragged under a thicket in time, the second of his great hungers was gone. He had no longer the true lust to kill, no joy of battle, but only the poor desire to fill his belly.

Then truly he lived in the wheat and the brush like a ground owl, ridden with ground lice, dusty or muddy, ever half-starved, forced to sit for hours by small holes for petty and unsatisfying kills. Only once during the final months before his end did he make a kill where the breath of danger recalled his valor, and then the danger was such as a hawk with wings and eyes would scorn. Waiting beside a gopher hole, surrounded by the high, yellow grass, he saw the head emerge, and struck, and was amazed that there writhed in his clutch the neck and dusty coffin-skull of a rattlesnake. Holding his grip, Hook saw the great, thick body slither up after, the tip an erect, strident blur, and writhe on the dirt of the gopher's mound. The weight of the snake pushed Hook about, and once threw him down, and the rising and falling whine of the rattles made the moment terrible, but the vaulted mouth, gaping from the closeness of Hook's grip, so that the pale, envenomed sabers stood out free, could not reach him. When Hook replaced the grip of his beak with the grip of his talons, and was free to strike again and again at the base of the head, the struggle was over. Hook tore and fed on the fine, watery flesh, and left the tattered armor and the long, jointed bone for the marching ants.

When the heavy rains returned, he ate well during the period of the first escapes from flooded burrows, and then well enough, in a vulture's way, on the drowned creatures. But as the rains lingered, and the burrows hung full of water, and there were no insects in the grass and no small birds sleeping in the thickets, he was constantly hungry, and finally unbearably hungry. His sodden and ground-broken plumage stood out raggedly about him, so that he looked fat, even bloated, but underneath it his skin clung to his bones. Save for his great talons and clappers, and the rain in his down, he would have been like a handful of air. He often stood for a long time under some bush or ledge, heedless of the drip, his one eye filmed over, his mind neither asleep or awake, but between. The gurgle and swirl of the brimming river, and the sound of chunks of the bank cut away to splash and dissolve in the already muddy flood, became familiar to him, and yet a torment, as if that great, ceaselessly working power of water ridiculed his frailty, within which only the faintest spark of valor still glimmered. The last two nights before the rain ended, he huddled under the floor of the bridge on the coastal highway, and heard the palpitant thunder of motors swell and roar over him. The trucks shook the bridge so that Hook, even in his famished lassitude, would sometimes open his one great eye wide and startled.

After the rains, when things became full again, bursting with growth and sound, the trees swelling, the thickets full of song and chatter, the fields, turning green in the sun, alive with rustling passages, and the moonlit nights strained with the song of the peepers all up and down the river and in the pools in the fields, Hook had to bear the return of the one hunger left him. At times this made him so wild that he forgot himself and screamed challenge from the open ground. The fretfulness of it spoiled his hunting, which was not entirely a matter of patience. Once he was in despair, and lashed himself through the grass and thickets, trying to rise when that virgin scent drifted for a few moments above the current of his own river. Then, breathless, his beak agape, he saw the strong suitor ride swiftly down on the wind over him, and heard afar the screaming fuss of the harsh wooing in the alders. For that moment even the battle heart beat in him again. The rim of his good eye was scarlet, and a little bead of new blood stood in the socket of the other. With beak and talon, he ripped at a fallen log, and made loam and leaves fly from about it.

But the season of love passed over to the nesting season, and Hook's love hunger, unused, shriveled in him with the others, and there remained in him only one stern quality befitting a hawk, and that the negative one, the remnant, the will to endure. He resumed his patient, plotted hunting, now along a field of the Japanese farmer, but ever within reach of the river thickets.

Growing tough and dry again as the summer advanced, inured to the family of the farmer, whom he saw daily, stooping and scraping with sticks in the ugly, open rows of their fields, where no lovely grass rustled and no life stirred save the shameless gulls, which walked at the heels of the workers, gobbling the worms and grubs they turned up, Hook became nearly content with his shard of life. The only longing or resentment to pierce him was that which he suffered occasionally when forced to hide at the edge of the mile-long bean field from the wafted cruising and the restive, down-bent gaze of one of his own kind. For the rest, he was without flame, a snappish, dust-colored creature, fading into the grasses he trailed through, and suited to his petty ways.

At the end of that summer, for the second time in his four years, Hook underwent a drouth. The equinoctial period passed without a rain. The laurel and the rabbit-brush dropped dry leaves. The foliage of the oaks shriveled and curled. Even the night fogs in the river canyon failed. The farmer's red cattle on the hillside lowed constantly, and could not feed on the dusty stubble. Grass fires broke out along the highways, and ate fast in the wind, filling the hollows with the smell of smoke, and died in the dirt of the shorn hills. The river made no sound. Scum grew on its vestigial pools, and turtles died and stank among the rocks. The dust rode before the wind, and ascended and flowered to nothing between the hills, and every sunset was red with the dust in the air. The people in the farmer's house quarreled, and even struck one another. Birds were silent, and only the hawks flew much. The animals lay breathing hard for very long spells, and ran and crept jerkily. Their flanks were fallen in, and their eyes were red.

At first Hook gorged at the fringe of the grass fires on the multitudes of tiny things that came running and squeaking. But thereafter there were the blackened strips on the hills, and little more in the thin, crackling grass. He found mice and rats, gophers and ground-squirrels, and even rabbits, dead in the stubble and under the thickets, but so dry and fleshless that only a faint smell rose from them, even on the sunny days. He starved on them. By early December he had wearily stalked the length of the eastern foothills, hunting at night to escape the voracity of his own kind, resting often upon his wings. The queer trail of his short steps and great horned toes zigzagged in the dust and was erased by the wind at dawn. He was nearly dead, and could make no sound through the horn funnels of his clappers.

Then one night the dry wind brought him, with the familiar, lifeless dust, another familiar scent, troublesome, mingled and unclear. In his vision-dominated brain he remembered the swift circle of his flight a year past, crossing in one segment, his shadow beneath him, a yard cluttered with crates and chickens, a gray barn and then again the plowed land and the stubble. Traveling faster than he had for days, impatient of his shrunken sweep, Hook came down to the farm. In the dark wisps of cloud blown among the stars over him, but no moon, he stood outside the wire of the chicken run. The scent of fat and blooded birds reached him from the shelter, and also within the enclosure was water. At the breath of the water, Hook's gorge contracted, and his tongue quivered and clove in its groove of horn. But there was the wire. He stalked its perimeter and found no opening. He beat it with his good wing, and felt it cut but not give. He wrenched at it with his beak in many places, but could not tear it. Finally, in a fury which drove the thin blood through him, he leaped repeatedly against it, beating and clawing. He was thrown back from the last leap as from the first, but in it he had risen so high as to clutch with his beak at the top wire. While he lay on his breast on the ground, the significance of this came upon him.

Again he leapt, clawed up the wire, and, as he would have fallen, made even the dead wing bear a little. He grasped the top and tumbled within. There again he rested flat, searching the dark with quick-turning head. There was no sound or motion but the throb of his own body. First he drank at the chill metal trough hung for the chickens. The water was cold, and loosened his tongue and his tight throat, but it also made him drunk and dizzy, so that he had to rest again, his claws spread wide to brace him. Then he walked stiffly, to stalk down the scent. He trailed it up the runway. Then there was the stuffy, body-warm air, acrid with droppings, full of soft rustlings as his talons clicked on the board floor. The thick, white shapes showed faintly in the darkness. Hook struck quickly, driving a hen to the floor with one blow, its neck broken and stretched out stringily. He leaped the still pulsing body, and tore it. The rich, streaming blood was overpowering to his dried senses, his starved, leathery body. After a few swallows, the flesh choked him. In his rage, he struck down another hen. The urge to kill took him again, as in those nights on the beach. He could let nothing go. Balked of feeding, he was compelled to slaughter. Clattering, he struck again and again. The henhouse was suddenly filled with the squawking and helpless rushing and buffeting of the terrified, brainless fowls.

Hook reveled in mastery. Here was game big enough to offer weight against a strike, and yet unable to soar away from his blows. Turning in the midst of the turmoil, cannily, his fury caught at the perfect pitch, he struck unceasingly. When the hens finally discovered the outlet, and streamed into the yard, to run around the fence, beating and squawking, Hook followed them, scraping down the incline, clumsy and joyous. In the yard, the cock, a bird as large as he, and much heavier, found him out and gave valiant battle. In the dark, and both earthbound, there was little skill, but blow upon blow, and only chance parry. The still squawking hens pressed into one corner of the yard. While the duel went on, a dog, excited by the sustained scuffling, began to bark. He continued to bark, running back and forth along the fence on one side. A light flashed on in an uncurtained window of the farmhouse, and streamed whitely over the crates littering the ground.

Enthralled by his old battle joy, Hook knew only the burly cock before him. Now, in the farthest reach of the window light, they could see each other dimly. The Japanese farmer, with his gun and lantern, was already at the gate when the finish came. The great cock leapt to jab with his spurs and, toppling forward with extended neck as he fell, was struck and extinguished. Blood had loosened Hook's throat. Shrilly he cried his triumph. It was a thin and exhausted cry, but within him as good as when he shrilled in mid-air over the plummeting descent of a fine foe in his best spring.

The light from the lantern partially blinded Hook. He first turned and ran directly from it, into the corner where the hens were huddled. They fled apart before his charge. He essayed the fence, and on the second try, in his desperation, was out. But in the open dust, the dog was on him, circling, dashing in, snapping. The farmer, who at first had not fired because of the chickens, now did not fire because of the dog, and, when he saw that the hawk was unable to fly, relinquished the sport to the dog, holding the lantern up in order to see better. The light showed his own flat, broad, dark face as sunken also, the cheekbones very prominent, and showed the torn-off sleeves of his shirt and the holes in the knees of his overalls. His wife, in a stained wrapper, and barefooted, heavy black hair hanging around a young, passionless face, joined him hesitantly, but watched, fascinated and a little horrified. His son joined them too, encouraging the dog, but quickly grew silent. Courageous and cruel death, however it may afterward sicken the one who has watched it, is impossible to look away from.

In the circle of the light, Hook turned to keep the dog in front of him. His one eye gleamed with malevolence. The dog was an Airedale, and large. Each time he pounced, Hook stood ground, raising his good wing, the pinions newly torn by the fence, opening his beak soundlessly, and, at the closest approach, hissed furiously, and at once struck. Hit and ripped twice by the whetted horn, the dog recoiled more quickly from several subsequent jumps and, infuriated by his own cowardice, began to bark wildly. Hook maneuvered to watch him, keeping his head turned to avoid losing the foe on the blind side. When the dog paused, safely away, Hook watched him quietly, wing partially lowered, beak closed, but at the first move again lifted the wing and gaped. The dog whined, and the man spoke to him encouragingly. The awful sound of his voice made Hook for an instant twist his head to stare up at the immense figures behind the light. The dog again sallied, barking, and Hook's head spun back. His wing was bitten this time, and with a furious side-blow, he caught the dog's nose. The dog dropped him with a yelp, and then, smarting, came on more warily, as Hook propped himself up from the ground again between his wings. Hook's artificial strength was waning, but his heart still stood to the battle, sustained by a fear of such dimension as he had never known before, but only anticipated when the arrogant young hawk had driven him to cover. The dog, unable to find any point at which the merciless, unwinking eye was not watching him, the parted bead waiting, paused and whimpered again.

"Oh, kill the poor thing," the woman begged.

The man, though, encouraged the dog again, saying, "Sick him; sick him."

The dog rushed bodily. Unable to avoid him, Hook was bowled down, snapping and raking. He left long slashes, as from the blade of a knife, on the dog's flank, but before he could right himself and assume guard again, was caught by the good wing and dragged, clattering, and seeking to make a good stroke from his back. The man followed them to keep the light on them, and the boy went with him, wetting his lips with his tongue and keeping his fists closed tightly. The woman remained behind, but could not help watching the diminished conclusion.

In the little, palely shining arena, the dog repeated his successful maneuver three times, growling but not barking, and when Hook thrashed up from the third blow, both wings were trailing, and dark, shining streams crept on his black-fretted breast from the shoulders. The great eye flashed more furiously than it ever had in victorious battle, and the beak still gaped, but there was no more clatter. He faltered when turning to keep front; the broken wings played him false even as props. He could not rise to use his talons.

The man had tired of holding the lantern up, and put it down to rub his arm. In the low, horizontal light, the dog charged again, this time throwing the weight of his forepaws against Hook's shoulder, so that Hook was crushed as he struck. With his talons up, Hook raked at the dog's belly, but the dog conceived the finish, and furiously worried the feathered bulk. Hook's neck went limp, and between his gaping clappers came only a faint chittering, as from some small kill of his own in the grasses.

In this last conflict, however, there had been some minutes of the supreme fire of the hawk whose three hungers are perfectly fused in the one will; enough to burn off a year of shame.

Between the great sails the light body lay caved and perfectly still. The dog, smarting from his cuts, came to the master and was praised. The woman, joining them slowly, looked at the great wingspread, her husband raising the lantern that she might see it better.

"Oh, the brave bird," she said.

JAMES JOYCE

THE BOARDING HOUSE

"...She dealt with moral problems as a cleaver does with meat...."

MRS. MOONEY was a butcher's daughter. She was a woman who was quite able to keep things to herself: a determined woman. She had married her father's foreman and opened a butcher's shop near Spring Gardens. But as soon as his father-in-law was dead Mr. Mooney began to go to the devil. He drank, plundered the till, ran head-long into debt. It was no use making him take the pledge: he was sure to break out again a few days after. By fighting his wife in the presence of customers and by buying bad meat he ruined his business. One night he went for his wife with the cleaver and she had to sleep in a neighbour's house.

After that they lived apart. She went to the priest and got a separation from him with care of the children. She would give him neither money nor food nor house-room; and so he was obliged to enlist himself as a sheriff's man. He was a shabby stooped little drunkard with a white face and a white moustache and white eyebrows, pencilled above his little eyes, which were pink-veined and raw; and all day long he sat in the bailiff's room, waiting to be put on a job. Mrs. Mooney, who had taken what remained of her money out of the butcher business and set up a boarding house in Hardwicke Street, was a big imposing woman. Her house had a floating population made up of tourists from Liverpool and the Isle of Man and, occasionally, *artistes* from the music halls. Its resident population was made up of clerks from the city. She governed the house cunningly and firmly, knew when to give credit, when to be stern and when to let things pass. All the resident young men spoke of her as *The Madam*.

Mrs. Mooney's young men paid fifteen shillings a week for board and lodgings (beer or stout at dinner excluded). They shared in common tastes and occupations and for this reason they were very chummy with one another. They discussed with one another the chances of favourites and outsiders. Jack Mooney, the Madam's son, who was clerk to a commission agent in Fleet Street, had the reputation of being a hard case. He was fond of using soldiers' obscenities: usually he came home in the small hours. When he met his friends he had always a good one to tell them and he was always sure to be on to a good thing—that is to say, a likely horse or a likely *artiste*. He was also handy with the mits and sang comic songs. On Sunday nights there would often be a reunion in Mrs. Mooney's front drawing-room. The music-hall *artistes* would oblige; and Sheridan played waltzes and polkas and vamped accompaniments. Polly Mooney, the Madam's daughter, would also sing. She sang:

> "I'm a . . . naughty girl.
> You needn't sham:
> You know I am."

Polly was a slim girl of nineteen; she had light soft hair and a small full mouth. Her eyes, which were grey with a shade of green through them, had a habit of glancing upwards when she spoke with anyone, which made her look like a little perverse madonna. Mrs. Mooney had first sent her daughter to be a typist in a corn-factor's office but, as a disreputable sheriff's man used to come every other day to the office, asking to be allowed to say a word to his daughter, she had taken her daughter home again and set her to do housework. As Polly was very lively the intention was to give her the run of the young men. Besides, young men like to feel that there is a young woman not very far away. Polly, of course, flirted with the young men but Mrs. Mooney, who was a shrewd judge, knew that the young men were only passing the time away: none of them meant business. Things went on so for a long time and Mrs. Mooney began to think of sending Polly back to type-writing when she noticed that something was going on between Polly and one of the young men. She watched the pair and kept her own counsel.

Polly knew that she was being watched, but still her mother's persistent silence could not be misunderstood. There had been no open complicity between mother and daughter, no open understanding but, though people in the house began to talk of the affair, still Mrs. Mooney did not intervene. Polly began to grow a little strange in her manner and the young man was evidently perturbed. At last, when she judged it to be the right moment, Mrs. Mooney intervened. She dealt with moral problems as a cleaver deals with meat: and in this case she had made up her mind.

It was a bright Sunday morning of early summer, promising heat, but with a fresh breeze blowing. All the windows of the boarding house were open and the lace curtains ballooned gently towards the street beneath the raised sashes. The belfry of George's Church sent out constant peals and worshippers, singly or in groups, traversed the little circus before the church, revealing their purpose by their self-contained demeanour no less than by the little volumes in their gloved hands. Breakfast was over in the boarding house and the table of the breakfast-room was covered with plates on which lay yellow streaks of eggs with morsels of bacon-fat and bacon-rind. Mrs. Mooney sat in the straw arm-chair and watched the servant Mary remove the breakfast things. She made Mary collect the crusts and pieces of broken bread to help to make Tuesday's bread-pudding. When the table was cleared, the broken bread collected, the sugar and butter safe under lock and key, she began to reconstruct the interview which she had had the night before with Polly. Things were as she had suspected: she had been frank in her questions and Polly had been frank in her answers. Both had been somewhat awkward, of course. She had been made awkward by her not wishing to receive the news in too cavalier a fashion or to seem to have connived and Polly had been made awkward not merely because allusions of that kind always made her awkward but also because she did not wish it to be thought that in her wise innocence she had divined the intention behind her mother's tolerance.

Mrs. Mooney glanced instinctively at the little gilt clock on the mantelpiece as soon as she had become aware through her revery that the bells of George's Church had stopped ringing. It was seventeen minutes past eleven: she would have lots of time to have the matter out with Mr. Doran and then catch short twelve at Marlborough Street. She was sure she would win. To begin with she had all the weight of social opinion on her side: she was an outraged mother. She had allowed him to live beneath her roof, assuming that he was a man of honour, and he had simply abused her hospitality. He was thirty-four or thirty-five years of age, so that youth could not be pleaded as his excuse; nor could ignorance be his excuse since he was a man who had seen something of the world. He had simply taken advantage of Polly's youth and inexperience: that was evident. The question was: What reparation would he make?

There must be reparation made in such case. It is all very well for the man: he can go his ways as if nothing had happened, having had his moment of pleasure, but the girl has to bear the brunt. Some mothers would be content to patch up such an affair for a sum of money; she had known cases cases of it. But she would not do so. For her only one reparation could make up for the loss of her daughter's honour: marriage.

She counted all her cards again before sending Mary up to Mr. Doran's room to say that she wished to speak with him. She felt sure she would win. He was a serious young man, not rakish or loud-voiced like the others. If it had been Mr. Sheridan or Mr. Meade or Bantom Lyons her task would have been much harder. She did not think he would face publicity. All the lodgers in the house knew something of the affair; details had been invented by some. Besides, he had been employed for thirteen years in a great Catholic wine-merchant's office and publicity would mean for him, perhaps, the loss of his job. Whereas if he agreed all might be well. She knew he had a good screw for one thing and she suspected he had a bit of stuff put by.

Nearly the half-hour! She stood up and surveyed herself in the pier-glass. The decisive expression of her great florid face satisfied her and she thought of some mothers she knew who could not get their daughters off their hands.

Mr. Doran was very anxious indeed this Sunday morning. He had made two attempts to shave but his hand had been so unsteady that he had been obliged to desist. Three days' reddish beard fringed his jaws and every two or three minutes a mist gathered on his glasses so that he had to take them off and polish them with his pocket-handkerchief. The recollection of his confession of the night before was a cause of acute pain to him; the priest had drawn out every ridiculous detail of the affair and in the end had so magnified his sin that he was almost thankful at being afforded a loophole of reparation. The harm was done. What could he do now but marry her or run away? He could not brazen it out. The affair would be sure to be talked of and his employer would be certain to hear of it. Dublin is such a small city: everyone knows everyone else's business. He felt his heart leap warmly in his throat as he heard in his excited imagination old Mr. Leonard calling out in his rasping voice: "Send Mr. Doran here, please."

All his long years of service gone for nothing! All his industry and diligence thrown away! As a young man he had sown his wild oats, of course; he had boasted of his free-thinking and denied the existence of God to his companions in public-houses. But that was all passed and done with . . . nearly. He still bought a copy of *Reynolds's Newspaper* every week but he attended to his religious duties and for nine-tenths of the year lived a regular life. He had money enough to settle down on; it was not that. But the family would look down on her. First of all there was her disreputable father and then her mother's boarding house was beginning to get a certain fame. He had a notion that he was being had. He could imagine his friends talking of the affair and laughing. She *was* a little vulgar; some times she said "I seen" and "If I had've known." But what would grammar matter if he really loved her? He could not make up his mind whether to like her or despise her for what she had done. Of course he had done it too. His instinct urged him to remain free, not to marry. Once you are married you are done for, it said.

While he was sitting helplessly on the side of the bed in shirt and trousers she tapped lightly at his door and entered. She told him all, that she had made a clean breast of it to her mother and that her mother would speak with him that morning. She cried and threw her arms round his neck, saying:

"O Bob! Bob! What am I to do? What am I to do at all?"

She would put an end to herself, she said.

He comforted her feebly, telling her not to cry, that it would be all right, never fear. He felt against his shirt the agitation of her bosom.

It was not altogether his fault that it had happened. He remembered well, with the curious patient memory of the celibate, the first casual caresses her dress, her breath, her fingers had given him. Then late one night as he was undressing for bed she had tapped at his door, timidly. She wanted to relight her candle at his for hers had been blown out by a gust. It was her bath night. She wore a loose open combing jacket of printed flannel. Her white instep shone in the opening of her furry slippers and the blood glowed warmly behind her perfumed skin. From her hands and wrists too as she lit and steadied her candle a faint perfume arose.

On nights when he came in very late it was she who warmed up his dinner. He scarcely knew what he was eating feeling her beside him alone, at night, in the sleeping house. And her thoughtfulness! If the night was anyway cold or wet or windy there was sure to be a little tumbler of punch ready for him. Perhaps they could be happy together. . . .

They used to go upstairs together on tiptoe, each with a candle, and on the third landing exchange reluctant good-nights. They used to kiss. He remembered well her eyes, the touch of her hand and his delirium. . . .

But delirium passes. He echoed her phrase, applying it to himself: *"What am I to do?"* The instinct of the celibate warned him to hold back. But the sin was there; even his sense of honour told him that reparation must be made for such a sin.

While he was sitting with her on the side of the bed Mary came to the door and said that the missus wanted to see him in the parlour. He stood up to put on his coat and waistcoat, more helpless than ever. When he was dressed he went over to her to comfort her. It would be all right, never fear. He left her crying on the bed and moaning softly: *"O my God!"*

Going down the stairs his glasses became so dimmed with moisture that he had to take them off and polish them. He longed to ascend through the roof and fly away to another country where he would never hear again of his trouble, and yet a force pushed him downstairs step by step. The implacable faces of his employer and of the Madam stared upon his discomfiture. On the last flight of stairs he passed Jack Mooney who was coming up from the pantry nursing two bottles of *Bass.* They saluted coldly; and the lover's eyes rested for a second or two on a thick bulldog face and a pair of thick short arms. When he reached the foot of the staircase he glanced up and saw Jack regarding him from the door of the return-room.

Suddenly he remembered the night when one of the music-hall *artistes,* a little blond Londoner, had made a rather free allusion to Polly. The reunion had been almost broken up on account of Jack's violence. Everyone tried to quiet him. The music-hall *artiste,* a little paler than usual, kept smiling and saying that there was no harm meant: but Jack kept shouting at him that if any fellow tried that sort of a game on with his sister he'd bloody well put his teeth down his throat, so he would.

Polly sat for a little time on the side of the bed, crying. Then she dried her eyes and went over to the looking-glass. She dipped the end of the towel in the water-jug and refreshed her eyes with the cool water. She looked at herself in profile and readjusted a hairpin above her ear. Then she went back to the bed again and sat at the foot. She regarded the pillows for a long time and the sight of them awakened in her mind secret, amiable memories. She rested the nape of her neck against the cool iron bed-rail and fell into a revery. There was no longer any perturbation visible on her face.

She waited on patiently, almost cheerfully, without alarm, her memories gradually giving place to hopes and visions of the future. Her hopes and visions were so intricate that she no longer saw the white pillows on which her gaze was fixed or remembered that she was waiting for anything.

At last she heard her mother calling. She started to her feet and ran to the banisters.

"Polly! Polly!"

"Yes, mamma?"

"Come down, dear. Mr. Doran wants to speak to you."

Then she remembered what she had been waiting for.

JAMES THURBER

THE CATBIRD SEAT

"...She had begun chipping at the cornices of the firm's edifice and now she was swinging at the foundation stones with a pickaxe...."

MR. MARTIN bought the pack of Camels on Monday night in the most crowded cigar store on Broadway. It was theatre time and seven or eight men were buying cigarettes. The clerk didn't even glance at Mr. Martin, who put the pack in his overcoat pocket and went out. If any of the staff at F & S had seen him buy the cigarettes, they would have been astonished, for it was generally known that Mr. Martin did not smoke, and never had. No one saw him.

It was just a week to the day since Mr. Martin had decided to rub out Mrs. Ulgine Barrows. The term "rub out" pleased him because it suggested nothing more than the correction of an error—in this case an error of Mr. Fitweiler. Mr. Martin had spent each night of the past week working out his plan and examining it. As he walked home now he went over it again. For the hundredth time he resented the element of imprecision, the margin of guesswork that entered into the business. The project as he had worked it out was casual and bold, the risks were considerable. Something might go wrong anywhere along the line. And therein lay the cunning of his scheme. No one would ever see in it the cautious, painstaking hand of Erwin Martin, head of the filing department at F & S, of whom Mr. Fitweiler had once said, "Man is fallible but Martin isn't." No one would see his hand, that is, unless it were caught in the act.

Sitting in his apartment, drinking a glass of milk, Mr. Martin reviewed his case against Mrs. Ulgine Barrows, as he had every night for seven nights. He began at the beginning. Her quacking voice and braying laugh had first profaned the halls of F & S on March 7, 1941 (Mr. Martin had a head for dates). Old Roberts, the personnel chief, had introduced her as the newly appointed special adviser to the president of the firm, Mr. Fitweiler. The woman had appalled Mr. Martin instantly, but he hadn't shown it. He had given her his dry hand, a look of studious concentration, and a faint smile. "Well," she had said, looking at the papers on his desk, "are you lifting the oxcart out of the ditch?" As Mr. Martin recalled that moment, over his milk, he squirmed slightly. He must keep his mind on her crimes as a special adviser, not on her peccadillos as a personality. This he found difficult to do, in spite of entering an objection and sustaining it. The faults of the woman as a woman kept chattering on in his mind like an unruly witness. She had, for almost two years now, baited him. In the halls, in the elevator, even in his own office, into which she romped now and then like a circus horse, she was constantly shouting these silly questions at him. "Are you lifting the oxcart out of the ditch? Are you tearing up the pea patch? Are you hollering down the rain barrel? Are you scraping around the bottom of the pickle barrel? Are you sitting in the catbird seat?"

It was Joey Hart, one of Mr. Martin's two assistants, who had explained what the gibberish meant. "She must be a Dodger fan," he had said. "Red Barber announces the Dodger games over the radio and he uses those expressions—picked 'em up down South." Joey had gone on to explain one or two. "Tearing up the pea patch" meant going on a rampage; "sitting in the catbird seat" meant sitting pretty, like a batter with three balls and no strikes on him. Mr. Martin dismissed all this with an effort. It had been annoying, it had driven him near to distraction, but he was too solid a man to be moved to murder by anything so childish. It was fortunate, he reflected as he passed on to the important charges against Mrs. Barrows, that he had stood up under it so well. He had maintained always an outward appearance of polite tolerance. "Why, I even believe you like the woman," Miss Paird, his other assistant, had once said to him. He had simply smiled.

A gavel rapped in Mr. Martin's mind and the case proper was resumed. Mrs. Ulgine Barrows stood charged with willful, blatant, and persistent attempts to destroy the efficiency and system of F & S. It was competent, material, and relevant to review her advent and rise to power. Mr. Martin had got the story from Miss Paird, who seemed always able to find things out. According to her, Mrs. Barrows had met Mr. Fitweiler at a party, where she had rescued him from the embraces of a powerfully built drunken man who had mistaken the president of F & S for a famous retired Middle Western football coach. She had led him to a sofa and somehow worked upon him a monstrous magic. The aging gentleman had jumped to the conclusion there and then that this was a woman of singular attainments, equipped to bring out the best in him and in the firm. A week later he had introduced her into F & S as his special adviser. On that day confusion got its foot in the door. After Miss Tyson, Mr. Brundage, and Mr. Bartlett had been fired and Mr. Munson had taken his hat and stalked out, mailing in his resignation later, old Roberts had been emboldened to speak to Mr. Fitweiler. He mentioned that Mr. Munson's department had been "a little disrupted" and hadn't they perhaps better resume the old system there? Mr. Fitweiler had said certainly not. He had the greatest faith in Mrs. Barrows' ideas. "They require a little seasoning, a little seasoning, is all," he had added. Mr. Roberts had given it up. Mr. Martin reviewed in detail all the changes wrought by Mrs. Barrows. She had begun chipping at the cornices of the firm's edifice and now she was swinging at the foundation stones with a pickaxe.

Mr. Martin came now, in his summing up, to the afternoon of Monday, November 2, 1942—just one week ago. On that day, at 3 P.M., Mrs. Barrows had bounced into his office. "Boo!" she had yelled. "Are you scraping around the bottom of the pickle barrel?" Mr. Martin had looked at her from under his green eyeshade, saying nothing. She had begun to wander about the office, taking it in with her great, popping eyes. "Do you really need *all* these filing cabinets?" she had demanded suddenly. Mr. Martin's heart had jumped. "Each of these files," he had said, keeping his voice even, "plays an indispensable part in the system of F & S." She had brayed at him, "Well, don't tear up the pea patch!" and gone to the door. From there she had bawled, "But you sure have got a lot of fine scrap in here!" Mr. Martin could no longer doubt that the finger was on his beloved department. Her pickaxe was on the upswing, poised for the first blow. It had not come yet; he had received no blue memo from the enchanted Mr. Fitweiler bearing nonsensical instructions deriving from the obscene woman. But there was no doubt in Mr. Martin's mind that one would be forthcoming. He must act quickly. Already a precious week had gone by. Mr. Martin stood up in his living room, still holding his milk glass. "Gentlemen of the jury," he said to himself, "I demand the death penalty for this horrible person."

The next day Mr. Martin followed his routine, as usual. He polished his glasses more often and once sharpened an already sharp pencil, but not even Miss Paird noticed. Only once did he catch sight of his victim; she swept past him in the hall with a patronizing "Hi!" At five-thirty he walked home, as usual, and had a glass of milk, as usual. He had never drunk anything stronger in his life—unless you could count ginger ale. The late Sam Schlosser, the S of F & S, had praised Mr. Martin at a staff meeting several years before for his temperate habits. "Our most efficient worker neither drinks nor smokes," he had said. "The results speak for themselves." Mr. Fitweiler had sat by, nodding approval.

Mr. Martin was still thinking about that red-letter day as he walked over to the Schrafft's on Fifth Avenue near Forty-Sixth Street. He got there, as he always did, at eight o'clock. He finished his dinner and the financial page of the *Sun* at a quarter to nine, as he always did. It was his custom after dinner to take a walk. This time he walked down Fifth Avenue at a casual pace. His gloved hands felt moist and warm, his forehead cold. He transferred the Camels from his overcoat to a jacket pocket. He wondered, as he did so, if they did not represent an unnecessary note of strain. Mrs. Barrows smoked only Luckies. It was his idea to puff a few puffs on a Camel (after the rubbing-out), stub it out in the ashtray holding her lipstick-stained Luckies, and thus drag a small red herring across the trail. Perhaps it was not a good idea. It would take time. He might even choke, too loudly.

Mr. Martin had never seen the house on West Twelfth Street where Mrs. Barrows lived, but he had a clear enough picture of it. Fortunately, she had bragged to everybody about her ducky first-floor apartment in the perfectly darling three-story red-brick. There would be no doorman or other attendants; just the tenants of the second and third floors. As he walked along, Mr. Martin realized that he would get there before nine-thirty. He had considered walking north on Fifth Avenue from Schrafft's to a point from which it would take him until ten o'clock to reach the house. At that hour people were less likely to be coming in or going out. But the procedure would have made an awkward loop in the straight thread of his casualness, and he had abandoned it. It was impossible to figure when people would be entering or leaving the house, anyway. There was a great risk at any hour. If he ran into anybody, he would simply have to place the rubbing-out of Ulgine Barrows in the inactive file forever. The same thing would hold true if there were someone in her apartment. In that case he would just say that he had been passing by, recognized her charming house, and thought to drop in.

It was eighteen minutes after nine when Mr. Martin turned into Twelfth Street. A man passed him, and a man and a woman, talking. There was no one within fifty paces when he came to the house, halfway down the block. He was up the steps and in the small vestibule in no time, pressing the bell under the card that said "Mrs. Ulgine Barrows." When the clicking in the lock started, he jumped forward against the door. He got inside fast, closing the door behing him. A bulb in a lantern hung from the hall ceiling on a chain seemed to give a monstrously bright light. There was nobody on the stair, which went up ahead of him along the left wall. A door opened down the hall in the wall on the right. He went toward it swiftly, on tiptoe.

"Well, for God's sake, look who's here!" bawled Mrs. Barrows, and her braying laugh rang out like the report of a shotgun. He rushed past her like a football tackle, bumping her. "Hey, quit shoving!" she said, closing the door behind them. They were in her living room, which seemed to Mr. Martin to be lighted by a hundred lamps. "What's after you?" she said. "You're as jumpy as a goat." He found he was unable to speak. His heart was wheezing in his throat. "I—yes," he finally brought out. She was jabbering and laughing as she started to help him off with his coat. "No, no," he said. "I'll put it here." He took it off and put it on a chair near the door. "Your hat and gloves, too," she said. "You're in a lady's house." He put his hat on top of the coat. Mrs. Barrows seemed larger than he had thought. He kept his gloves on. "I was passing by," he said. "I recognized—is there anyone here?" She laughed louder than ever. "No," she said, "we're all alone. You're as white as a sheet, you funny man. Whatever *has* come over you? I'll mix you a toddy." She started toward a door across the room. "Scotch-and-soda be all right? But say, you don't drink, do you?" She turned and gave him her amused look. Mr. Martin pulled himself together. "Scotch-and-soda will be all right," he heard himself say. He could hear her laughing in the kitchen.

Mr. Martin looked quickly around the living room for the weapon. He had counted on finding one there. There were andirons and a poker and something in a corner that looked like an Indian club. None of them would do. It couldn't be that way. He began to pace around. He came to a desk. On it lay a metal paper knife with an ornate handle. Would it be sharp enough? He reached for it and knocked over a small brass jar. Stamps spilled out of it and it fell to the floor with a clatter. "Hey," Mrs. Barrows yelled from the kitchen, "are you tearing up the pea patch?" Mr. Martin gave a strange laugh. Picking up the knife, he tried its point against his left wrist. It was blunt. It wouldn't do.

When Mrs. Barrows reappeared, carrying two highballs, Mr. Martin, standing there with his gloves on, became acutely conscious of the fantasy he had wrought. Cigarettes in his pocket, a drink prepared for him—it was all too grossly improbable. It was more than that; it was impossible. Somewhere in the back of his mind a vague idea stirred, sprouted. "For heaven's sake, take off those gloves," said Mrs. Barrows. "I always wear them in the house," said Mr. Martin. The idea began to bloom, strange and wonderful. She put the glasses on a coffee table in front of a sofa and sat on the sofa. "Come over here, you odd little man," she said. Mr. Martin went over and sat beside her. It was difficult getting a cigarette out of the pack of Camels, but he managed it. She held a match for him, laughing. "Well," she said, handing him his drink, "this is perfectly marvelous. You with a drink and a cigarette."

Mr. Martin puffed, not too awkwardly, and took a gulp of the highball. "I drink and smoke all the time," he said. He clinked his glass against hers. "Here's nuts to that old windbag, Fitweiler," he said, and gulped again. The stuff tasted awful, but he made no grimace. "Really, Mr. Martin," she said, her voice and posture changing, "you are insulting our employer." Mrs. Barrows was now all special adviser to the president. "I am preparing a bomb," said Mr. Martin, "which will blow the old goat higher than hell." He had only a little of the drink, which was not strong. It couldn't be that. "Do you take dope or something?" Mrs. Barrows asked coldly. "Heroin," said Mr. Martin. "I'll be coked to the gills when I bump that old buzzard off." "Mr. Martin!" she shouted, getting to her feet. "That will be all of that. You must go at once." Mr. Martin took another swallow of his drink. He tapped his cigarette out in the ashtray and put the pack of Camels on the coffee table. Then he got up. She stood glaring at him. He walked over and put on his hat and coat. "Not a word about this," he said, and laid an index finger against his lips. All Mrs. Barrows could bring out was "Really!" Mr. Martin put his hand on the doorknob. "I'm sitting in the catbird seat," he said. He stuck his tongue out at her and left. Nobody saw him go.

Mr. Martin got to his apartment, walking, well before eleven. No one saw him go in. He had two glasses of milk after brushing his teeth, and he felt elated. It wasn't tipsiness, because he hadn't been tipsy. Anyway, the walk had worn off all effects of the whiskey. He got in bed and read a magazine for a while. He was asleep before midnight.

Mr. Martin got to the office at eight-thirty the next morning, as usual. At a quarter to nine, Ulgine Barrows, who had never before arrived at work before ten, swept into his office. "I'm reporting to Mr. Fitweiler now!" she shouted. "If he turns you over to the police, it's no more than you deserve!" Mr. Martin gave her a look of shocked surprise. "I beg your pardon?" he said. Mrs. Barrows snorted and bounced out of the room, leaving Miss Paird and Joey Hart staring after her. "What's the matter with that old devil now?" asked Miss Paird. "I have no idea," said Mr. Martin, resuming his work. The other two looked at him and then at each other. Miss Paird got up and went out. She walked slowly past the closed door of Mr. Fitweiler's office. Mrs. Barrows was yelling inside, but she was not braying. Miss Paird could not hear what the woman was saying. She went back to her desk.

Forty-five minutes later, Mrs. Barrows left the president's office and went into her own, shutting the door. It wasn't until half an hour later that Mr. Fitweiler sent for Mr. Martin. The head of the filing department, neat, quiet, attentive, stood in front of the old man's desk. Mr. Fitweiler was pale and nervous. He took his glasses off and twiddled them. He made a small, bruffing sound in his throat. "Martin," he said, "you have been with us more than twenty years." "Twenty-two, sir," said Mr. Martin. "In that time," pursued the president, "your work and your—uh—manner have been exemplary." "I trust so, sir," said Mr. Martin. "I have understood, Martin," said Mr. Fitweiler, "that you have never taken a drink or smoked." "That is correct, sir," said Mr. Martin. "Ah, yes." Mr. Fitweiler polished his glasses. "You may describe what you did after leaving the office yesterday, Martin," he said. Mr. Martin allowed less than a second for his bewildered pause. "Certainly, sir," he said. "I walked home. Then I went to Schrafft's for dinner. Afterward I walked home again. I went to bed early, sir, and read a magazine for a while. I was asleep before eleven." "Ah, yes," said Mr. Fitweiler again. He was silent for a moment, searching for the proper words to say to the head of the filing department. "Mrs. Barrows," he said finally, "Mrs. Barrows has worked hard, Martin, very hard. It grieves me to report that she has suffered a severe breakdown. It has taken the form of a persecution complex accompanied by distressing hallucinations." "I am very sorry, sir," said Mr. Martin. "Mrs. Barrows is under the delusion," continued

Mr. Fitweiler, "that you visited her last evening and behaved yourself in an—uh—unseemly manner." He raised his hand to silence Mr. Martin's little pained outcry. "It is the nature of these psychological diseases," Mr. Fitweiler said, "to fix upon the least likely and most innocent party as the—uh—source of persecution. These matters are not for the lay mind to grasp, Martin. I've just had my psychiatrist, Doctor Fitch, on the phone. He would not, of course, commit himself, but he made enough generalizations to substantiate my suspicions. I suggested to Mrs. Barrows, when she had completed her—uh—story to me this morning, that she visit Doctor Fitch, for I suspected a condition at once. She flew, I regret to say, into a rage, and demanded—uh—requested that I call you on the carpet. You may not know, Martin, but Mrs. Barrows had planned a reorganization of your department —subject to my approval, of course, subject to my approval. This brought you, rather than anyone else, to her mind—but again that is a phenomenon for Doctor Fitch and not for us. So, Martin, I am afraid Mrs. Barrows' usefulness here is at an end." "I am dreadfully sorry, sir," said Mr. Martin.

It was at this point that the door to the office blew open with the suddenness of a gas-main explosion and Mrs. Barrows catapulted through it. "Is the little rat denying it?" she screamed. "He can't get away with that!" Mr. Martin got up and moved discreetly to a point beside Mr. Fitweiler's chair. "You drank and smoked at my apartment," she bawled at Mr. Martin, "and you know it! You called Mr. Fitweiler an old windbag and said you were going to blow him up when you got coked to the gills on your heroin!" She stopped yelling to catch her breath and a new glint came into her popping eyes. "If you weren't such a drab, ordinary little man," she said. "I'd think you'd planned it all. Sticking your tongue out, saying you were sitting in the catbird seat, because you thought no one would believe me when I told it! My God, it's really too perfect!" She brayed loudly and hysterically, and the fury was on her again. She glared at Mr. Fitweiler. "Can't you see how he has tricked up, you old fool? Can't you see his little game?" But Mr. Fitweiler had been surreptitiously pressing all the buttons under the top of his desk and employees of F & S began pouring into the room. "Stockton," said Mr. Fitweiler, "you and Fishbein will take Mrs. Barrows to her home. Mrs. Powell, you will go with them." Stockton, who had played a little football in high school, blocked Mrs. Barrows as she made for Mr. Martin. It took him and Fishbein together to force her out of the door into the hall, crowded with stenographers and office boys. She was still screaming imprecations at Mr. Martin, tangled and contradictory imprecations. The hubbub finally died down the corridor.

"I regret that this has happened," said Mr. Fitweiler. "I shall ask you to dismiss it from your mind, Martin." "Yes, sir," said Mr. Martin, anticipating his chief's "That will be all" by moving to the door. "I will dismiss it." He went out and shut the door, and his step was light and quick in the hall. When he entered his department he had slowed down to his customary gait, and he walked quietly across the room to the W20 file, wearing a look of studious concentration.

THE GUY WHO OWNED THE PITCHER'S MOUND

*"'...Do you know what Ritchie sold him?
He sold him the damn* pitcher's mound, *that's
what! ...'"*

"HARRINGTON!" Hemphill yelled at me over the phone, "he's going to sue!"

"Who's going to sue?" I asked.

"The guy who owns the pitcher's mound!" One thing about Hemphill. He never got excited unless something really earthshaking had happened.

"Who?" I asked for the second time. But the second reply was equally cryptic so I resigned myself to a late afternoon drive across town to find out what was causing dear old L.H. so much pain.

Lester Hemphill—Growlface he is called affectionately (affectionately behind his back)—owns the first-place American League baseball team. As a sideline he also owns the world wide Hemphill Hotel empire. Quite incidental is the fact that there are Hemphill Hotels in all eight American League cities.

And I am Roger Harrington, Hemphill's legal advisor and owner of thirty-five shares of stock in Hemp's ball club.

The first time we met, Growlface had said incredulously, "How in blazes did you get to be a lawyer with a name like Roger Harrington?"

"By going to lawschool," I replied. Growlface must have stared at me for a full fifteen seconds before he broke into gales of laughter.

"Hey, Richie," he said, turning his attention to a young man sitting at a nearby desk. "This guy got to be a lawyer by going to lawschool! Get it?" Richie laughed obediently and went back to his own work, leaving Hemp alone to revel in what he thought was the finest of dry humor. The first time I went on a road trip with the team I was introduced to seven other major league team owners the same way. Growlface never did ask me *what* lawschool I had gone to.

Anyway, that gives you some idea of Lester "Growlface" Hemphill, a shrewd man with a dollar but incoherent when excited. He had bought his ball club ten years ago when it had just finished its third consecutive season in last place. But this year he had a winner. "Predictions!" he had screamed at the reporters during spring training. "I just bought hotels in the two top National League cities. That oughta be prediction enough!"

Hemp greeted me at the front door of his house looking as though the stock market had crashed—right on his head.

"Who owns the pitcher's mound?" I asked.

"He just left," Hemp replied, explaining everything.

I tried a new approach. "When did he buy it?" Growlface slumped down into an easy chair and prepared to tell all. I don't think he was too sure of what had happened himself.

"You know Richie, the fellow who works in the front office? Well, Richie has been leasing out some of the warehouses that I own around the ballpark. So last week he came running into my office while I'm busy talking to Hong Kong and he told me that this pipsqueak—"

"—What pipsqueak?"

"Gerald Perkins. Anyway, Richie told me this long story about why Gerald Perkins never rents; he just buys. So Gerald Perkins wanted to buy a little space along with a right of entry and I said o.k. sell and get to blazes out. Well do you know what he bought?" Hemp said, shaking his finger at me. "Do you know what Richie sold him? He sold him the damn *pitcher's mound*, that's what!" That's Hemphill. *Usually* a smart man with a dollar. "Well? You went to lawschool. What do I do?"

"How much does Gerald Perkins want?"

"Want! He doesn't want money. I tried to give him the Honolulu Hemphill and he wouldn't take it. All he wants is to do his sunbathing on the pitcher's mound between two and four each afternoon, and he says he's going to sue if we disturb him." Growlface was in tears. "Harrington, this is our big year. I've been working for this for ten seasons. I even bought hotels in Milwaukee and Pittsburgh just for the World Series and now we can't even play in our own stadium. One game ahead of the Yanks with three games to go . . ." Hemp's voice trailed off and we both sat in silence, wondering not about what to do, but about the possibility that this was just a horrible, dark nightmare.

"Tomorrow's an open date, isn't it?"

"It's open, yes," Hemp mumbled.

"Well, I'll get hold of Tanker Connolly and tell him to call a practice. Better to have a showdown with this crackpot in private than before thirty thousand fans. And I'll get Richie—"

"I fired Richie," Hemp interjected.

"—and go over the sale papers with him. I'll see you tomorrow at the park."

Richie and I met a half hour later in the club offices. We checked the papers for hours trying to find out just how binding the sale was. Unfortunately it proved to be all too legal and binding.

"But is the pitcher's mound really necessary?" Richie asked with amazing insight into the game. When I convinced him that it was he suggested murder, and I figured we had had enough for one night.

I had to work my way through a dozen Burns men to get into the park the next afternoon but it was well worth the effort just to catch a glimpse of the scene inside. Tanker Connolly, the team manager, was hitting grounders to the infield. One of the coaches was hitting flyballs to the outfield. And the pitcher's mound? It was surrounded by a twelve-foot high wire screen and inside, comfortably settled on a chaise-lounge, was a scrawny, bespectacled young man in yellow bathing trunks, deeply engrossed in a paperback. Growlface was pacing up and down the first base line, stopping each time he reached a small gathering of coaches and pitchers who were idly standing by with hands clamped in their uniform pockets.

"Ten years," I heard Hemphill sob as I approached. "Ten years," and he went on pacing the baseline. The fielding practice stopped and all eyes suddenly became aware of Hemp and me as we mumbled "good mornings" and strolled out to the mound for the stadium summit meeting. Perkins kept right on reading as though he were on a desert island, and I began to think that Richie's idea of murder might not be so bad after all. Finally he took off his horn rimmed glasses with great effort and peered over his book at us.

"What can I do for you gentlemen?" Perkins asked.

"You know damn well what you can do!" Hemphill screamed through the cage and Perkins jumped back frightened.

"Mr. Perkins," I said, "the owner and I do not know why you have done what you have. Evidently it was not for money."

"Of course it was not for money Mr., er, Mr.—"

"Roger Harrington. I am the team's lawyer. Now would you mind telling us why you bought the pitcher's mound? Is this some sort of deal to cost us the pennant?"

"Don't be silly," Perkins replied with a laugh. "I am a loyal fan. I, well I sort of . . . Mr. Harrington," he said softly as he motioned for me to stick my head inside the cage. "Could you send that brute away? I tried to reason with him at his home last night, but all he could say was, 'You own the what!' " I signaled to Hemphill and he left.

"Now, Mr. Perkins."

"First of all, I hope you do believe that I *am* a loyal and trustworthy fan. Why, I've had a season ticket here for years."

"Then why have you put us in this position?"

"Because, Mr. Harrington, I want to pitch."

"YOU WHO?"

"I want to pitch against the New York Yankees tomorrow. It's well, sort of a repressed desire." By the looks of his physique, it was decidedly repressed. "I mean, this is only a last resort. I've been to a dozen tryout camps but they all said I didn't have it. Mr. Harrington, you're not listening."

"Oh yes. Now about this matter of pitching. You realize, of course, that we are only one game ahead of the Yankees and have just three games left to play.

"You don't think I've got it either."

"Well, Perkins, you just don't have the experience."

"Mr. Harrington, I am losing my patience with the major leagues. The day I sign a contract you may have your mound back again. Until then, kindly stay away." And with that he went back to his reading. "Just a dollar-a-year," he called after me as I walked away.

Hemp heard this last statement and decided that all was resolved for the best. "Whatever he wants," Hemp said, "I'll buy him two."

"He wants to pitch against the Yankees tomorrow."

Hemp called a staff meeting immediately. It lasted for two hours.

"He can't do this to us," Hemp said at two-thirty; and a half hour later, "If I ever get my hands on Richie I'll, I'll . . . RHAWWW!"

"He can't pitch," Tanker moaned at three-thirty.

"Lets go home," I said at four-thirty, and the meeting broke up.

About eight-thirty that evening a very defeated Hemphill phoned me. "Harry," he said in a weak voice, "if we, I mean, well, he could have a contract and a uniform and still not pitch. I mean, we could *lie* to him." He must have been afraid that I was going to jump down his throat; he sounded like a little boy suggesting that his mother let him stay up an hour past bedtime. "I mean we wouldn't let him play."

"I'm sure Tanker Connolly wouldn't."

"Yeh, sure, Tanker wouldn't, would he? Harry? He wouldn't, would he?"

"No Hemp. I'm sure he wouldn't. Shall I sign Mr. Perkins into the big leagues?"

"Sign him, Harry, and tell him we'll use him in relief. That's it, in relief. O-h-h-h-h-h misery! Relief!"

Perkins was very understanding when I roused him from his sleep by turning on the night lights. In fact, he was quite overjoyed at the thought of signing a contract until he detected a bit of hedging on my part. I told him all kinds of lies about why we couldn't change our pitching rotation and let him start the game. But we could probably use him in relief, I said.

"Probably, Mr. Harrington?" he asked quite demandingly.

"Uh, definitely," I replied, and he handed me the contract.

"Yoohoo!" he called from beneath the mosquito netting as I left. "Would you please turn off those lights."

Bravado is the word to describe the team atmosphere the next day. Lou Parker was warming up to pitch against nine terrible New York Yankees while Tanker Connolly was getting ready to face Gerald Perkins.

"Are you right handed or left?" Tanker asked meekly.

"Actually I'm a little better left than right," Perkins replied, and Tanker, who had been instructed to handle Gerald with kid gloves, forced a sigh of relief and mumbled something about being short of lefthanders.

"All right gang," Connolly said moments later as the umpire motioned for the team to take the field, "let's play good defense and work up a big lead. A helluva big lead!" And Perkins trudged off happily to the bullpen, probably wondering why the other five relief pitchers had so little to talk about.

The game went well for us. The Yanks managed to get two runs on Elston

Howard's fourth inning home run, but we came back with four runs in the bottom half of the inning. New York couldn't touch Parker after that, and as the ninth inning opened the score was still four to two. McDougald popped up to open the Yankee ninth. Richardson looked at a third strike for out number two. And then it happened.

"Mr. Connolly," Perkins announced over the intercom from the bullpen, "I am coming in to pitch the final out."

"Why you blankety-blank, you stay right where you are," Tanker yelled back, but Perkins was already on his way in. Growlface sat dumbfounded. Tanker kept on talking into the phone.

"Do something!" Growlface said.

"Run out and tell Parker he's got a sore arm," I screamed.

"You got a sore arm!" Tanker shouted as he raced out to the mound. Then he waved Perkins in, but Perkins had already reached second base. Parker stood with one foot on the rubber, shaking his head in disbelief. Connolly kept nodding his head and his lips were pronouncing some very ungentlemanly explanations. Parker flipped the ball to Perkins, rubbed his left arm gingerly and walked off towards the dugout. A click came over the public address system.

"Your attention please. For New York. Dale Long batting for Ryne Duren. Long for Duren."

"Boooooooooooooo!" screamed a little white-haired lady from a box seat near first base.

". . . and for the hometeam, Gerald Perkins now pitching in place of Lou Parker. Perkins for Parker."

"Whoooooooooooo?" the white-haired lady screamed.

Tanker came back from the mound and walked straight through the dugout into the locker room. A coach came out of the Yankee dugout and said a few words to Long, evidently telling him how to hit Perkins. Long nodded and went up to the plate. Growlface picked up a fungo and started tapping it against the cement floor.

Perkins took a big, pumping windup and threw the first pitch with all the force that his 115 pounds would allow. It floated across the plate beautifully for a strike.

"Watchout for that changeup," the coach yelled in from third base.

Perkins shook off one signal from the catcher, then nodded approval at a second one and threw another floater. Long laced it between short and third for a base hit.

Tony Kubek came out of the Yankee dugout and went up to face the terrible Perkins. Kubek looked at a couple of pitches and then hit a double to left center. Two outs, runners on second and third. Growlface started tapping the legs of the water cooler with his bat. Mickey Mantle stepped up to the plate, batting righthanded against lefthanded Perkins. Perk waved the catcher out for a conference. Growlface called for Tanker Connolly to go out and yank Perkins from the game, but Connolly had hidden in a locker. Mantle stepped in and Perkins let fly with his fastest pitch.

"B-a-a-a-a-w-w-w-l-l-l one!"

"He's still throwin' that butterfly ball," Long shouted in from third. Perkins wound and threw another soft one.

"B-a-a-a-a-w-w-w-l-l-l two!"

It took Perkins exactly four pitches to walk Mantle. Growlface sent one of his coaches out to try to convince Perkins that he should get out. Three pitchers were warming up in the bullpen. The fans were booing. The white-haired lady was throwing popcorn onto the field. Hector Lopez came to bat as Hemp's emissary returned from the mound.

"What did he say?" Hemp asked with eagerness.

"He said his arm never felt better." Growlface bashed the water cooler with his bat.

Two outs, the bases loaded and hardhitting Lopez at bat. Perkins stared in at Dusty Turner, the catcher, to get a signal but Turner just shrugged his shoulders. Perkins threw the first pitch wide. He tried a second time to get a signal from Turner, and this time Dusty obliged by pointing at home plate. Perkins shook his head in disagreement and threw the next pitch into the dirt for ball two.

By now everybody in the stadium was screaming, some at Connolly, some at Perkins, and some were just praying in loud voices. Perkins got ready to throw to Lopez and then he backed off the mound. He stared at Lopez for a few seconds and then turned and motioned his outfielders back, only to find that they already stood within a few feet of the wall.

"What's he doing that for?" Hemp asked.

"I think," said one of the players, "I think he just woke up and realized where he was. He looks frightened to death."

Frightened or not, Gerald threw the next pitch and Lopez smashed it to leftcenter. Ted Kennedy came over, chasing the drive into the deepest part of the park. The Yankee manager hit his head on the dugout roof as he came running to the top step. Four Yankee baserunners were hurtling at top speed around the base paths. Kennedy dove through the air and snared the ball with the web of his glove. Growlface fainted. The game was over and the Yankees beaten.

Three hours later, Hemp, Tanker and I were still staring at each other in Hemp's office. The reporters had long since given up banging on the door, and the room was quiet except for the faint noise of an occasional passing automobile.

"Maybe the team lynched him," Tanker mumbled.

There was a gentle tapping at the door. "Please. May I come in?" It was Gerald. I rushed to the door in hopes of avoiding violence. "Please, Mr. Harrington," Gerald said through the partially opened door, "I'd like to come in." He was still wearing his uniform, except for his spikes, and he was nervously wringing his hat.

"Mr. Hemphill, I'd like to apologize." Hemphill, who had been eyeing the entrance with quiet curiosity, nearly jumped across the room.

"You'd like to WHAT?" he said.

"Apologize, sir. You see, I've never really done anything in my life except dream about what I'd like to do. I've got so much money that I can afford to dream and I've got so little talent that all I *can* do is dream."

"You don't have to tell me about your talent," Tanker interjected.

"Wait a minute, Tanker," Hemphill said, still eyeing Perkins curiously. "Just what do you mean by 'apologize?' "

Perkins was still wringing his hat and there were tears in his eyes. "Well, Mr. Hemphill, I've caused a lot of trouble, even though we . . . er . . . that is, even though the team won the game. I guess the best I can do is give you your pitcher's mound back. You don't have to pay me, of course."

"And?"

"And nothing sir. I'll just go away quietly so that you won't get any bad publicity." Perkins turned and started towards the door. He was a sad sight in his ill-fitting uniform.

"Wait a minute, Gerald," Hemp said softly. "Don't go yet." Perkins stopped and turned. "I guess we all know how you felt. You just wanted to be a big leaguer so badly that you, well, let's just say you went to extremes. Isn't that it?"

Perkins mumbled a "yes."

"That's not such an odd thing," Hemp continued. "Let's face it, if I were good enough to play on this ball club I wouldn't have had to buy the damn thing ten years ago!" Hemp laughed, and even Gerald managed a little smile. "Well, Perk, if you wanta be a big leaguer so bad then you might as well be one with this club."

"How do you mean?"

"Well I don't mean to have you get anywhere near that mound again. But after all, anybody who's smart enough to buy the field out from under a team deserves some kind of a position with that team. Right, Harrington?" he asked, but he didn't wait for my answer. "Right," he said in complete self-agreement. "And I can think of no better position than the one Richie had before I fired him. Right? Right. Well, what do you say, Perk?"

Perkins looked at all three of us as if he were taking a vote and then excitedly answered, "Yes." He stuck out his hand only to have it crushed by Hemphill's and kept on saying, "Yes, yes, yes, yes!"

Hemphill re-introduced Perkins to both Connolly and myself but in the midst of the festivities a puzzled look came across his face. "Perk," Hemp said, "there's just one thing bothering me. Just what got into your head out there before that last pitch when you started waving outfielders back?"

"Well," Perkins said, "you might say that I suddenly decided I wasn't cut out to be a pitcher."

"Sure, Gerald, but *why* did you decide this?"

Perkins shrugged very knowingly. "I knew it the minute I realized I didn't know how to pitch to Lopez."

"Lopez?" Tanker said, interrupting. "How about Mantle? You knew how to pitch to Mantle?"

"Sure thing," Perk replied. "Just walk him. After all, first base was open."

Tanker groaned, but Hemp kept on staring at Perkins. Then he burst into laughter and slapped Tanker on the back.

"You hear that, Tanker," he said. "First base was open! Get it?" And with that Hemp threw his arm around Perk, who was undoubtedly the happiest man in the major leagues, and led him into his new office.

But he never did ask him how he'd pitch to Mantle with the bases loaded.

FRANK O'CONNOR

FIRST CONFESSION

"...The woman was really interesting about hell, but my attention was all fixed on the half-crown...."

ALL the trouble began when my grandfather died and my grandmother— my father's mother—came to live with us. Relations in the one house are a strain at the best of times, but, to make matters worse, my grandmother was a real old countrywoman and quite unsuited to the life in town. She had a fat, wrinkled old face, and, to Mother's great indignation, went round the house in bare feet—the boots had her crippled, she said. For dinner she had a jug of porter and a pot of potatoes with—sometimes—a bit of salt fish, and she poured out the potatoes on the table and ate them slowly, with great relish, using her fingers by way of a fork.

Now, girls are supposed to be fastidious, but I was the one who suffered most from this. Nora, my sister, just sucked up to the old woman for the penny she got every Friday out of the old-age pension, a thing I could not do. I was too honest, that was my trouble; and when I was playing with Bill Connell, the sergeant-major's son, and saw my grandmother steering up the path with the jug of porter sticking out from beneath her shawl I was mortified. I made excuses not to let him come into the house, because I could never be sure what she would be up to when we went in.

When Mother was at work and my grandmother made the dinner I wouldn't touch it. Nora once tried to make me, but I hid under the table from her and took the bread-knife with me for protection. Nora let on to

be very indignant (she wasn't, of course, but she knew Mother saw through her, so she sided with Gran) and came after me. I lashed out at her with the bread-knife, and after that she left me alone. I stayed there till Mother came in from work and made my dinner, but when Father came in later Nora said in a shocked voice: "Oh, Dadda, do you know what Jackie did at dinnertime?" Then, of course, it all came out; Father gave me a flaking; Mother interfered, and for days after that he didn't speak to me and Mother barely spoke to Nora. And all because of that old woman! God knows, I was heart-scalded.

Then, to crown my misfortunes, I had to make my first confession and communion. It was an old woman called Ryan who prepared us for these. She was about the one age with Gran; she was well-to-do, lived in a big house on Montenotte, wore a black cloak and bonnet, and came every day to school at three o'clock when we should have been going home, and talked to us of hell. She may have mentioned the other place as well, but that could only have been by accident, for hell had the first place in her heart.

She lit a candle, took out a new half-crown, and offered it to the first boy who would hold one finger—only one finger!—in the flame for five minutes by the school clock. Being always very ambitious I was tempted to volunteer, but I thought it might look greedy. Then she asked were we afraid of holding one finger—only one finger!—in a little candle flame for five minutes and not afraid of burning all over in roasting hot furnaces for all eternity. "All eternity! Just think of that! A whole lifetime goes by and it's nothing, not even a drop in the ocean of your sufferings." The woman was really interesting about hell, but my attention was all fixed on the half-crown. At the end of the lesson she put it back in her purse. It was a great disappointment; a religious woman like that, you wouldn't think she'd bother about a thing like a half-crown.

Another day she said she knew a priest who woke one night to find a fellow he didn't recognize leaning over the end of his bed. The priest was a bit frightened—naturally enough—but he asked the fellow what he wanted, and the fellow said in a deep, husky voice that he wanted to go to confession. The priest said it was an awkward time and wouldn't it do in the morning, but the fellow said that last time he went to confession, there was one sin he kept back, being ashamed to mention it, and now it was always on his mind. Then the priest knew it was a bad case, because the fellow was after making a bad confession and committing a mortal sin. He got up to dress, and just then the cock crew in the yard outside, and—lo and behold!—when the priest looked round there was no sign of the fellow, only a smell of burning timber, and when the priest looked at his bed didn't he see the print of two hands burned in it? That was because the fellow had made a bad confession. This story made a shocking impression on me.

But the worst of all was when she showed us how to examine our conscience. Did we take the name of the Lord, our God, in vain? Did we honour our father and our mother? (I asked her did this include grandmothers and she said it did.) Did we love our neighbours as ourselves? Did we covet our neighbour's goods? (I thought of the way I felt about the penny that Nora got every Friday.) I decided that, between one thing and another, I must have broken the whole ten commandments, all on account of that old woman, and so far as I could see, so long as she remained in the house I had no hope of ever doing anything else.

I was scared to death of confession. The day the whole class went I let on to have a toothache, hoping my absence wouldn't be noticed; but at three o'clock, just as I was feeling safe, along comes a chap with a message from Mrs. Ryan that I was to go to confession myself on Saturday and be at the chapel for communion with the rest. To make it worse, Mother couldn't come with me and sent Nora instead.

Now, that girl had ways of tormenting me that Mother never knew of. She held my hand as we went down the hill, smiling sadly and saying how sorry she was for me, as if she were bringing me to the hospital for an operation.

"Oh, God help us!" she moaned. "Isn't it a terrible pity you weren't a good boy? Oh, Jackie, my heart bleeds for you! How will you ever think of all your sins? Don't forget you have to tell him about the time you kicked Gran on the shin."

"Lemme go!" I said, trying to drag myself free of her. "I don't want to go to confession at all."

"But sure, you'll have to go to confession, Jackie," she replied in the same regretful tone. "Sure, if you didn't, the parish priest would be up to the house, looking for you. 'Tisn't, God knows, that I'm not sorry for you. Do you remember the time you tried to kill me with the breadknife under the table? And the language you used to me? I don't know what he'll do with you at all, Jackie. He might have to send you up to the bishop."

I remember thinking bitterly that she didn't know the half of what I had to tell—if I told it. I knew I couldn't tell it, and understood perfectly why the fellow in Mrs. Ryan's story made a bad confession; it seemed to me a great shame that people wouldn't stop criticizing him. I remember that steep hill down to the church, and the sunlit hillsides beyond the valley of the river, which I saw in the gaps between the houses like Adam's last glimpse of Paradise.

Then, when she had manoeuvred me down the long flight of steps to the chapel yard, Nora suddenly changed her tone. She became the raging malicious devil she really was.

"There you are!" she said with a yelp of triumph, hurling me through the church door. "And I hope he'll give you the penitential psalms, you dirty little caffler."

I knew then I was lost, given up to eternal justice. The door with the coloured-glass panels swung shut behind me, the sunlight went out and gave place to deep shadow, and the wind whistled outside so that the silence within seemed to crackle like ice under my feet. Nora sat in front of me by the confession box. There were a couple of old women ahead of her, and then a miserable-looking poor devil came and wedged me in at the other side, so that I couldn't escape even if I had the courage. He joined his hands and rolled his eyes in the direction of the roof, muttering aspirations in an anguished tone, and I wondered had he a grandmother too. Only a grandmother could account for a fellow behaving in that heartbroken way, but he was better off than I, for he at least could go and confess his sins; while I would make a bad confession and then die in the night and be continually coming back and burning people's furniture.

Nora's turn came, and I heard the sound of something slamming, and then her voice as if butter wouldn't melt in her mouth, and then another slam, and out she came. God, the hypocrisy of women! Her eyes were lowered, her head was bowed, and her hands were joined very low down on her stomach, and she walked up the aisle to the side altar looking like a saint. You never saw such an exhibition of devotion; and I remembered the devilish malice with which she had tormented me all the way from our door, and wondered were all religious people like that, really. It was my turn now. With the fear of damnation in my soul I went in, and the confessional door closed of itself behind me.

It was pitch-dark and I couldn't see priest or anything else. Then I really began to be frightened. In the darkness it was a matter between God and me, and He had all the odds. He knew what my intentions were before I even started; I had no chance. All I had ever been told about confession got mixed up in my mind, and I knelt to one wall and said: "Bless me, father, for I have sinned; this is my first confession." I waited for a few minutes, but nothing happened, so I tried it on the other wall. Nothing happened there either. He had me spotted all right.

It must have been then that I noticed the shelf at about one height with my head. It was really a place for grown-up people to rest their elbows, but in my distracted state I thought it was probably the place you were supposed to kneel. Of course, it was on the high side and not very deep, but I was always good at climbing and managed to get up all right. Staying up was the trouble. There was room only for my knees, and nothing you could get a grip on but a sort of wooden moulding a bit above it. I held on to the moulding and repeated the words a little louder, and this time something happened all right. A slide was slammed back; a little light entered the box, and a man's voice said: "Who's there?"

"'Tis me, father," I said for fear he mightn't see me and go away again. I couldn't see him at all. The place the voice came from was under the moulding, about level with my knees, so I took a good grip of the moulding and swung myself down till I saw the astonished face of a young priest looking up at me. He had to put his head on one side to see me, and I had to put mine on one side to see him, so we were more or less talking to one another upside-down. It struck me as a queer way of hearing confessions, but I didn't feel it my place to criticize.

"Bless me, father, for I have sinned; this is my first confession," I rattled off all in one breath, and swung myself down the least shade more to make it easier for him.

"What are you doing up there?" he shouted in an angry voice, and the strain the politeness was putting on my hold of the moulding, and the shock of being addressed in such an uncivil tone, were too much for me. I lost my grip, tumbled, and hit the door an unmerciful wallop before I found myself flat on my back in the middle of the aisle. The people who had been waiting stood up with their mouths open. The priest opened the door of the middle box and came out, pushing his biretta back from his forehead; he looked something terrible. Then Nora came scampering down the aisle.

"Oh, you dirty little caffler!" she said. "I might have known you'd do it. I might have known you'd disgrace me. I can't leave you out of my sight for one minute."

Before I could even get to my feet to defend myself she bent down and gave me a clip across the ear. This reminded me that I was so stunned I had even forgotten to cry, so that people might think I wasn't hurt at all, when in fact I was probably maimed for life. I gave a roar out of me.

"What's all this about?" the priest hissed, getting angrier than ever and pushing Nora off me. "How dare you hit the child like that, you little vixen?"

"But I can't do my penance with him, father," Nora cried, cocking an outraged eye up at him.

"Well, go and do it, or I'll give you some more to do," he said, giving me a hand up. "Was it coming to confession you were, my poor man?" he asked me.

" 'Twas, father," said I with a sob.

"Oh," he said respectfully, "a big hefty fellow like you must have terrible sins. Is this your first?"

" 'Tis, father," said I.

"Worse and worse," he said gloomily. "The crimes of a lifetime. I don't know will I get rid of you at all today. You'd better wait now till I'm finished with these old ones. You can see by the looks of them they haven't much to tell."

"I will, father," I said with something approaching joy.

The relief of it was really enormous. Nora stuck out her tongue at me from behind his back, but I couldn't even be bothered retorting. I knew from the very moment that man opened his mouth that he was intelligent above the ordinary. When I had time to think, I saw how right I was. It only stood to reason that a fellow confessing after seven years would have more to tell than people that went every week. The crimes of a lifetime, exactly as he said. It was only what he expected, and the rest was the cackle of old women and girls with their talk of hell, the bishop, and the penitential psalms. That was all they knew. I started to make my examination of conscience, and barring the one bad business of my grandmother it didn't seem so bad.

The next time, the priest steered me into the confession box himself and left the shutter back the way I could see him get in and sit down at the further side of the grille from me.

"Well, now," he said, "what do they call you?"

"Jackie, father," said I.

"And what's a-trouble to you, Jackie?"

"Father," I said, feeling I might as well get it over while I had him in good humour, "I had it all arranged to kill my grandmother."

He seemed a bit shaken by that, all right, because he said nothing for quite a while.

"My goodness," he said at last, "that'd be a shocking thing to do. What put that into your head?"

"Father," I said, feeling very sorry for myself, "she's an awful woman."

"Is she?" he asked. "What way is she awful?"

"She takes porter, father," I said, knowing well from the way Mother talked of it that this was a mortal sin, and hoping it would make the priest take a more favourable view of my case.

"Oh, my!" he said, and I could see he was impressed.

"And snuff, father," said I.

"That's a bad case, sure enough, Jackie," he said.

"And she goes round in her bare feet, father," I went on in a rush of self-pity, "and she knows I don't like her, and she gives pennies to Nora and none to me, and my da sides with her and flakes me, and one night I was so heart-scalded I made up my mind I'd have to kill her."

"And what would you do with the body?" he asked with great interest.

"I was thinking I could chop that up and carry it away in a barrow I have," I said.

"Begor, Jackie," he said, "do you know you're a terrible child?"

"I know, father," I said, for I was just thinking the same thing myself. "I tried to kill Nora too with a bread-knife under the table, only I missed her."

"Is that the little girl that was beating you just now?" he asked.

"'Tis, father."

"Someone will go for her with a bread-knife one day, and he won't miss her," he said rather cryptically. "You must have great courage. Between ourselves, there's a lot of people I'd like to do the same to but I'd never have the nerve. Hanging is an awful death."

"Is it, father?" I asked with the deepest interest—I was always very keen on hanging. "Did you ever see a fellow hanged?"

"Dozens of them," he said solemnly. "And they all died roaring."

"Jay!" I said.

"Oh, a horrible death!" he said with great satisfaction. "Lots of the fellows I saw killed their grandmothers too, but they all said 'twas never worth it."

He had me there for a full ten minutes talking, and then walked out the chapel yard with me. I was genuinely sorry to part with him, because he was the most entertaining character I'd ever met in the religious line. Outside, after the shadow of the church, the sunlight was like the roaring of waves on a beach; it dazzled me; and when the frozen silence melted and I heard the screech of trams on the road my heart soared. I knew now I wouldn't die in the night and come back, leaving marks on my mother's furniture. It would be a great worry to her, and the poor soul had enough.

Nora was sitting on the railing, waiting for me, and she put on a very sour puss when she saw the priest with me. She was mad jealous because a priest had never come out of the church with her.

"Well," she asked coldly, after he left me, "what did he give you?"

"Three Hail Marys," I said.

"Three Hail Marys," she repeated incredulously. "You mustn't have told him anything."

"I told him everything," I said confidently.

"About Gran and all?"

"About Gran and all."

(All she wanted was to be able to go home and say I'd made a bad confession.)

"Did you tell him you went for me with the bread-knife?" she asked with a frown.

"I did to be sure."

"And he only gave you three Hail Marys?"

"That's all."

She slowly got down from the railing with a baffled air. Clearly, this was beyond her. As we mounted the steps back to the main road she looked at me suspiciously.

"What are you sucking?" she asked.

"Bullseyes."

"Was it the priest gave them to you?"

" 'Twas."

"Lord God," she wailed bitterly, "some people have all the luck! 'Tis no advantage to anybody trying to be good. I might just as well be a sinner like you."

A & P

*"...You never know for sure how girls'
minds work (do you really think it's a mind
in there or just a little buzz like a bee in a
glass jar?)..."*

IN WALKS these three girls in nothing but bathing suits. I'm in the third
checkout slot, with my back to the door, so I don't see them until they're over
by the bread. The one that caught my eye first was the one in the plaid green
two-piece. She was a chunky kid, with a good tan and a sweet broad soft-
looking can with those two crescents of white just under it, where the sun
never seems to hit, at the top of the backs of her legs. I stood there with my
hand on a box of HiHo crackers trying to remember if I rang it up or not. I
ring it up again and the customer starts giving me hell. She's one of these
cash-register-watchers, a witch about fifty with rouge on her cheekbones
and no eyebrows, and I know it made her day to trip me up. She'd been watching cash registers for fifty years and probably never seen a mistake before.

By the time I got her feathers smoothed and her goodies into a bag—she
gives me a little snort in passing, if she'd been born at the right time they
would have burned her over in Salem—by the time I get her on her way the
girls had circled around the bread and were coming back, without a push-
cart, back my way along the counters, in the aisle between the checkouts
and the Special bins. They didn't even have shoes on. There was this chunky
one, with the two-piece—it was bright green and the seams on the bra were
still sharp and her belly was still pretty pale so I guessed she just got it (the
suit)—there was this one, with one of those chubby berryfaces, the lips all
bunched together under her nose, this one, and a tall one, with black hair
that hadn't quite frizzed right, and one of these sunburns right across under
the eyes, and a chin that was too long—you know, the kind of girl other girls
think is very "striking" and "attractive" but never quite makes it, as they
very well know, which is why they like her so much—and then the third one,
that wasn't quite so tall. She was the queen. She kind of led them, the other

two peeking around and making their shoulders round. She didn't look around, not this queen, she just walked straight on slowly, on these long white prima-donna legs. She came down a little hard on her heels, as if she didn't walk in her bare feet that much, putting down her heels and then letting the weight move along to her toes as if she was testing the floor with every step, putting a little deliberate extra action into it. You never know for sure how girls' minds work (do you really think it's a mind in there or just a little buzz like a bee in a glass jar?) but you got the idea she had talked the other two into coming in here with her, and now she was showing them how to do it, walk slow and hold yourself straight.

She had on a kind of dirty-pink—beige maybe, I don't know—bathing suit with a little nubble all over it, and what got me, the straps were down. They were off her shoulders looped loose around the cool tops of her arms, and I guess as a result the suit had slipped a little on her, so all around the top of the cloth there was this shining rim. If it hadn't been there you wouldn't have known there could have been anything whiter than those shoulders. With the straps pushed off, there was nothing between the top of the suit and the top of her head except just *her,* this clean bare plane of the top of her chest down from the shoulder bones like a dented sheet of metal tilted in the light. I mean, it was more than pretty.

She had sort of oaky hair that the sun and salt had bleached, done up in a bun that was unravelling, and a kind of prim face. Walking into the A & P with your straps down, I suppose it's the only kind of face you *can* have. She held her head so high her neck, coming up out of those white shoulders, looked kind of stretched, but I didn't mind. The longer her neck was, the more of her there was.

She must have felt in the corner of her eye me and over my shoulder Stokesie in the second slot watching, but she didn't tip. Not this queen. She kept her eyes moving across the racks, and stopped, and turned so slow it made my stomach rub the inside of my apron, and buzzed to the other two, who kind of huddled against her for relief, and then they all three of them went up the cat-and-dog-food-breakfast-cereal-macaroni-rice-raisins-seasonings-spreads-spaghetti-soft-drinks-crackers-and-cookies aisle. From the third slot I look straight up this aisle to the meat counter, and I watched them all the way. The fat one with the tan sort of fumbled with the cookies, but on second thought she put the package back. The sheep pushing their carts down the aisle—the girls were walking against the usual traffic (not that we have one-way signs or anything)—were pretty hilarious. You could see them, when Queenie's white shoulders dawned on them, kind of jerk, or hop, or hiccup, but their eyes snapped back to their own baskets and on they pushed. I bet you could set off dynamite in an A & P and the people would by and large keep reaching and checking oatmeal off their lists and muttering "Let me see, there was a third thing, began with A, asparagus, no, ah, yes, applesauce!" or whatever it is they do mutter. But there was no doubt, this jiggled them. A few houseslaves in pin curlers even looked around after pushing their carts past to make sure what they had seen was correct.

You know, it's one thing to have a girl in a bathing suit down on the beach, where what with the glare nobody can look at each other much anyway, and another thing in the cool of the A & P, under the fluorescent lights, against all those stacked packages, with her feet paddling along naked over our checkerboard green-and-cream rubber-tile floor.

"Oh Daddy," Stokesie said beside me. "I feel so faint."

"Darling," I said. "Hold me tight." Stokesie's married, with two babies chalked up on his fuselage already, but as far as I can tell that's the only difference. He's twenty-two, and I was nineteen this April.

"Is it done?" he asks, the responsible married man finding his voice. I forgot to say he thinks he's going to be manager some sunny day, maybe in 1990 when it's called the Great Alexandrov and Petrooshki Tea Company or something.

What he meant was, our town is five miles from a beach, with a big summer colony out on the Point, but we're right in the middle of town, and the women generally put on a shirt or shorts or something before they get out of the car into the street. And anyway these are usually women with six children and varicose veins mapping their legs and nobody, including them, could care less. As I say, we're right in the middle of town, and if you stand at our front doors you can see two banks and the Congregational church and the newspaper store and three real-estate offices and about twenty-seven old freeloaders tearing up Central Street because the sewer broke again. It's not as if we're on the Cape; we're north of Boston and there's people in this town haven't seen the ocean for twenty years.

The girls had reached the meat counter and were asking McMahon something. He pointed, they pointed, and they shuffled out of sight behind a pyramid of Diet Delight peaches. All that was left for us to see was old McMahon patting his mouth and looking after them sizing up their joints. Poor kids, I began to fell sorry for them, they couldn't help it.

Now here comes the sad part of the story, at least my family says it's sad, but I don't think it's so sad myself. The store's pretty empty, it being Thursday afternoon, so there was nothing much to do except lean on the register and wait for the girls to show up again. The whole store was like a pinball machine and I didn't know which tunnel they'd come out of. After a while they come around out of the far aisle, around the light bulbs, records at discount of the Caribbean Six or Tony Martin Sings or some such gunk you wonder they waste the wax on, sixpacks of candy bars, and plastic toys done up in cellophane that fall apart when a kid looks at them anyway. Around they come, Queenie still leading the way, and holding a little gray jar in her hand. Slots Three through Seven are unmanned and I could see her wondering between Stokes and me, but Stokesie with his usual luck draws an old party in baggy gray pants who stumbles up with four giant cans of pineapple juice (what do these bums *do* with all that pineapple juice? I've often asked myself) so the girls come to me. Queenie puts down the jar and I take it into my fingers icy cold. Kingfish Fancy Herring Snacks in Pure Sour Cream: 49¢. Now her hands are empty, not a ring or a bracelet, bare as

God made them, and I wonder where the money's coming from. Still with that prim look she lifts a folded dollar bill out of the hollow at the center of her nubbled pink top. The jar went heavy in my hand. Really, I thought that was so cute.

Then everybody's luck begins to run out. Lengel comes in from haggling with a truck full of cabbages on the lot and is about to scuttle into that door marked MANAGER behind which he hides all day when the girls touch his eye. Lengel's pretty dreary, teaches Sunday school and the rest, but he doesn't miss that much. He comes over and says, "Girls, this isn't the beach."

Queenie blushes, though maybe it's just a brush of sunburn I was noticing for the first time, now that she was so close. "My mother asked me to pick up a jar of herring snacks." Her voice kind of startled me, the way voices do when you see the people first, coming out so flat and dumb yet kind of tony, too, the way it ticked over "pick up" and "snacks." All of a sudden I slid right down her voice into her living room. Her father and the other men were standing around in ice-cream coats and bow ties and the women were in sandals picking up herring snacks on toothpicks off a big glass plate and they were all holding drinks the color of water with olives and sprigs of mint in them. When my parents have somebody over they get lemonade and if it's a real racy affair Schlitz in tall glasses with "They'll Do It Every Time" cartoons stencilled on.

"That's all right," Lengel said. "But this isn't the beach." His repeating this struck me as funny, as if it had just occurred to him, and he had been thinking all these years the A & P was a great big sand dune and he was the head lifeguard. He didn't like my smiling—as I say he doesn't miss much —but he concentrates on giving the girls that sad Sunday-school-superintendent stare.

Queenie's blush is no sunburn now, and the plump one in plaid, that I liked better from the back—a really sweet can—pipes up, "We weren't doing any shopping. We just came in for the one thing."

"That makes no difference," Lengel tells her, and I could see from the way his eyes went that he hadn't noticed she was wearing a two-piece before. "We want you decently dressed when you come in here."

"We *are* decent," Queenie says suddenly, her lower lip pushing, getting sore now that she remembers her place, a place from which the crowd that runs the A & P must look pretty crummy. Fancy Herring Snacks flashed in her very blue eyes.

"Girls, I don't want to argue with you. After this come in here with your shoulders covered. It's our policy." He turns his back. That's policy for you. Policy is what the kingpins want. What the others want is juvenile delinquency.

All this while, the customers had been showing up with their carts but, you know, sheep, seeing a scene, they had all bunched up on Stokesie, who shook open a paper bag as gently as peeling a peach, not wanting to miss a word. I could feel in the silence everybody getting nervous, most of all Lengel, who asks me, "Sammy, have you rung up their purchase?"

I thought and said "No" but it wasn't about that I was thinking. I go through the punches, 4, 9, GROC, TOT—it's more complicated than you think, and after you do it often enough, it begins to make a little song, that you hear words to, in my case "Hello *(bing)* there, you *(gung)* hap-py *pee-*pul *(splat)*!" —the *splat* being the drawer flying out. I uncrease the bill, tenderly as you may imagine, it just having come from between the two smoothest scoops of vanilla I had ever known were there, and pass a half and a penny into her narrow pink palm, and nestle the herrings in a bag and twist its neck and hand it over, all the time thinking.

The girls, and who'd blame them, are in a hurry to get out, so I say "I quit" to Lengel quick enough for them to hear, hoping they'll stop and watch me, their unsuspected hero. They keep right on going, into the electric eye; the door flies open and they flicker across the lot to their car, Queenie and Plaid and Big Tall Goony-Goony (not that as raw material she was so bad), leaving me with Lengel and a kink in his eyebrow.

"Did you say something, Sammy?"

"I said I quit."

"I thought you did."

"You didn't have to embarrass them."

"It was they who were embarrassing us."

I started to say something that came out "Fiddle-de-doo." It's a saying of my grandmother's, and I know she would have been pleased.

"I don't think you know what you're saying," Lengel said.

"I know you don't," I said. "But I do." I pull the bow at the back of my apron and start shrugging it off my shoulders. A couple customers that had been heading for my slot begin to knock against each other, like scared pigs in a chute.

Lengel sighs and begins to look very patient and old and gray. He's been a friend of my parents for years. "Sammy, you don't want to do this to your Mom and Dad," he tells me. It's true, I don't. But it seems to me that once you begin a gesture it's fatal not to go through with it. I fold the apron, "Sammy" stitched in red on the pocket, and put it on the counter, and drop the bow tie on top of it. The bow tie is theirs, if you've ever wondered. "You'll feel this for the rest of your life," Lengel says, and I know that's true, too, but remembering how he made that pretty girl blush makes me so scrunchy inside I punch the No Sale tab and the machine whirs "pee-pul" and the drawer splats out. One advantage to this scene taking place in summer, I can follow this up with a clean exit, there's no fumbling around getting your coat and galoshes, I just saunter into the electric eye in my white shirt that my mother ironed the night before, and the door heaves itself open, and outside the sunshine is skating around on the asphalt.

I look around for my girls, but they're gone, of course. There wasn't anybody but some young married screaming with her children about some candy they didn't get by the door of a powder-blue Falcon station wagon. Looking back in the big windows, over the bags of peat moss and aluminum lawn furniture stacked on the pavement, I could see Lengel in my place in the slot, checking the sheep through. His face was dark gray and his back stiff, as if he'd just had an injection of iron, and my stomach kind of fell as I felt how hard the world was going to be to me hereafter.

DAVID WAGONER

THE
ESCAPE
ARTIST

". . . The flashgun went off, and the reporter came over to lean against the bars. 'Only one hour?' Danny nodded. . . ."

IN THE corridor outside the newspaper office he checked his empty pockets for the last time, tried brushing the wrinkles out of his sport coat, took ten deep breaths, and after running in place for a few seconds till the blood pulsed under his brain like a river under a canoe, he walked in fast. His reflection trailed him for a moment in the plate glass—the long profile he had hopes for, the sharp chin and nose he was going to cut down with a Vandyke as soon as he could make it grow—and he went right to the first desk, in the flesh, himself included, not a daydream or a diagram. He felt only part of the stomach-fluttering, knee-twitching hesitation he'd been afraid of during the months since he'd known he was finally going to get himself out of the sticks and into the big city, into his Doom and Destiny— the grand words went up like balloons in his head—into a place where his life could start happening, after all the rehearsals.

The middle-aged woman behind the desk kept on licking a stack of envelopes. She said, "Yes?" with a bad taste in her mouth.

He looked beyond her at the rows of desks where men bustled back and forth, where telephones, typewriters, and a clacking band of teletype machines kept up a steady racket. "I'd like to see the city editor." He could feel the energy pulsing up from his shoes. It was like standing on a massage machine in a dime store.

"Is it about a job?"

"No, I've got a story for him."

She acted bored. "What about, sonny?"

"I'll tell him."

She hesitated, then shrugged, got up, and began shuffling down one of the aisles toward the busiest-looking desk of all—three telephones, four kinds of in-and-out baskets, a sheaf of clippings, a nest of paper towels soaking up spilled coffee, and a dark thin man practically lying down in a padded swivel chair, interlocked fingers supporting the back of his neck.

The woman spoke inaudibly for a moment, and the thin man motioned him nearer with his chin. "What you got?"

Waiting till the woman had gone, he took a deep breath and pressed it down against his diaphragm. He felt light in the head and light on his feet. He was traveling light, and he was on his own. It was about time. He said, "I'd like to issue a formal challenge to the police department: I'll let them lock me up in any combination of their regular restraints, as long as they're in good working order, and lock me in any solitary cell without a guard, and I'll set myself free within an hour without damaging any city property. And I'll submit to a complete search before and after."

"What's your name?" The thin man's eyes were lazy and cynical.

"Danny Masters."

"Address?"

"I'm just passing through."

The thin man's long face grew longer. "Through what, a phase?"

"You heard what I said. I meant it."

"Kid, what've you been reading, some old pulp magazines?"

"Do you want the story, sir? There's another paper in town."

The man laughed twice, high in his nose. "Can you really pick a lock?"

"I'll repeat the challenge if you didn't hear it."

Taking one foot off the desk, the thin man let his chair straighten up. "You sound like your own lawyer. Come on, what you been reading?"

Danny turned to go.

"Now wait a minute." The man was out of his chair and sitting on a corner of the desk, smiling. "How old are you?"

"Seventeen in the fall."

"And fifteen last spring." The man began swinging his leg. His eyes were going around the office quickly. "You staying somewhere in town?"

"Not if I can help it."

"Ever done anything like this before?"

"I can open any handcuff or any lock or get out of any rope-tie."

"What you need is a little self-confidence, kid." The man was signaling to somebody across the room. "Who taught you all that?"

"It runs in the family, and— What difference does it make? Try me."

"I mean, I haven't heard of an escape artist since before flagpole sitters." The man was looking pleased with himself, and he signaled again impatiently. "Just stay put a minute, okay?"

Danny nodded, and the man hurried between rows and went into an inner office, coming out again fast, talking to an old man in a blue suit. After an argument, they stopped and spoke to a sour-looking man who'd been typing;

then all three of them came toward him. He stood still and kept his hands down.

The city editor was saying, "What difference does it make, damn it? It's a good story either way." He sat on his own desk. "This is Danny Masters."

The old man looked suspicious. "How you feeling, son?"

"I'm fine, thank you."

"Got a little blood on your nose. You in good health?"

Danny fished out his handkerchief. "My nose bleeds sometimes."

"Who're your parents, son?"

"I don't have any." He could feel his face freezing, pulling itself tight across his cheekbones, and he knew exactly the kind of stupid smile it would make—his upper lip rising off his teeth like a curtain—the kind that made people say, What are you scared of? or, What's eating you?

"Was this your own idea? Anybody put you up to it?"

"All my own."

The old man shrugged at the city editor. "There's probably some way we can get sued." He turned to the sour-faced man who had a pencil behind one ear and a crooked necktie. "What do you think, Sam?"

"Is he advertising something?"

Danny said, "No."

The old man pursed his lips. "They might make you look pretty funny."

"I don't think so."

Looking steadily at him, the old man said, "And you'd actually go through with it? You wouldn't—uh, chicken out?"

"No."

The city editor put his hand on the nearest phone. "I can call Fritz and ask. Give them something to do on a dull evening. If they say so, it's still a pretty good story. 'Police Turn Down Teenage Challenger.'"

After another pause the old man said, "Now don't get in too much of a rush." He looked Danny over, then gave a grudging half-smile. "See that green filing cabinet over in the corner? It's locked. Let's see what you can do with it."

Danny looked at their amused faces, at several others nearby, at a kid his own age gawking from beside the water cooler. He picked up a thin metal ruler from the city editor's desk and started walking, and if people left enough keys to the city lying around like that, he wouldn't even have to use his own.

Sitting sideways in the front seat, the reporter said, "How'd you happen to take this up instead of something else?"

"What's so strange about it?" Danny sat deeper in the back seat as the car changed lanes with a sudden swerve, wishing he could think instead of having to talk. He needed to grope ahead to make sure he had everything figured out right, but his forehead felt stuffed full of other people's language.

"Most young guys want something secure. Respectable."

"I'm respectable."

"Sure." The reporter held his pad of copy paper against the top of the front seat. "Who would you say influenced you most to get into this racket?"

"I knew a locksmith."

"He taught you things, huh? He still got a license?"

"He's dead."

"You sure you weren't just practicing up in case you caught a severe case of reform school maybe?"

Danny looked out the window.

The reporter said, "Ever tried to bust out of anything before?"

"Yes."

"How'd it make you feel?"

"Like I wanted to get loose." He hesitated, seeing the reporter taking notes, but went on anyway. "Then I felt free of—everybody. Everything."

"What did you do, your friends tie you up and like that?"

"Sometimes."

The reporter was keeping a straight face. "You know, the police use real handcuffs and complicated stuff like Cicero corsets. It isn't like getting tied up in an alley or picking Grandma's dresser drawer. I mean, they aren't using Mickey Mouse locks in the jail anymore. How did you feel the times you couldn't get loose?"

"It hasn't happened yet. I'll tell you when it happens."

The reporter glanced at the photographer. "We've got a live one."

"Uh-huh."

The reporter said, "Every cowboy movie, the crooks hog-tie the good guy and in five minutes he's loose, so what's so hard about it? The crooks walk in and out of jail like it was the men's john."

"If it's so easy and boring, how come people are paying to watch? Because it's what they wish *they* could do." Danny looked out the window. "So enjoy me. I'm a good story."

The reporter chuckled flatly, once. "Got anything against cops?"

"They're always saying No. I like people who say Yes."

Squinting at him as the car turned, the reporter said, "How would you say an escape artist is different from just plain folks, kid?"

"They just dream about it, but he does it."

The photographer said, "What I'd like to do is pull a disappearing act out of this goddamn silly job. Can you show me how, kid?"

"Yes." He felt his attention sliding backward into himself like a bolt going into a strike.

The policemen crisscrossing importantly from door to door and around corners on both sides of the booking counter seemed in unnaturally sharp focus, outlined so definitely against the cement and plaster they were like targets in a shooting gallery. And no matter how many times Danny blinked, the corridor walls and the polished floor hurt his eyes.

The reporter said, "Okay, wait a minute." He talked to one of the desk sergeants, crowding a man in a ripped undershirt out of the way.

People were in trouble all around him: a man in an old sweater sitting on a bench with his head in his hands, dripping blood onto the floor from some-where on his face; a kid just out of his teens in black pegged pants standing white-faced with his shoulder against the wall while a policeman smiled at him; a groggy-looking man with a hump of white bandage plastered over one ear like a seashell. Everybody had broken something or other, a nose, a win-dow, a law, and now they were being shoved into cells to wait for a judge to decide what thing of theirs he could break to get back at them. A Negro with a greasy shopping bag in his lap stared straight ahead, his eyes popping as if he'd already been hanged. Danny felt his own life locked inside him, keeping as quiet as it could while it aged. Nobody should be able to break anybody else open and clean out the insides. That was why getting away was im-portant, getting out, getting loose, because they had to make you hold still long enough so they could crack you.

The reporter came back and said, "All right, Fritz is coming but we're not supposed to make a fuss. No pictures except when he says so."

Checking the battery case on his belt, the photographer said, "Like hell."

"How you doing, kid?"

Danny nodded at the reporter without looking at him, and that was why they were always trying to pin you down to one room, the smaller the better, because they could find you then could leave you and come back and still find you as if you were a piece of furniture or something in a zoo.

A rough-looking, sad-faced man in a rumpled suit came toward them out of one of the side offices and listened to the reporter talk for a moment with-out taking his eyes from Danny. He said, "First of all, is it just a gag?"

The reporter and the photographer answered at the same time, and after a short pause the man said, "Danny Masters. Masters." He seemed to think for a moment, then shook his head.

Danny simply waited for them to put him in whatever they considered the worst place. You had to expect a certain amount of confusion. Especially when you were causing it yourself.

Fritz nudged him. "So you're going to make us look sick by busting out of our toy jail here? Well, we could use a little more bad publicity." He looked sourly at the photographer.

"Don't blame me, Fritz. I don't pick my assignments."

Touching the reporter on the shoulder, Fritz said, "Ordinarily you know what I'd tell you to do with an idea like this one?"

"It wasn't my baby either, and you must've said Yes to somebody."

Fritz shrugged. "I figured maybe I could earn a favor."

And now, apparently, everybody was supposed to go down the hallway be-cause that's where Fritz was leading the reporter. Instead, Danny paused to look at the tinted photos of policemen killed on duty since the 'twenties, all with level mouths, full faces, and small dark eyes staring into the lens as if into a peephole at somebody fouling up the works.

The photographer took his arm. "Let's get organized. Stall around, and the mayor'll come downstairs and have his face in it."

The others were waiting at the turn in the corridor, beyond the rows of shut office doors on one side and the single small door with a button next to it on the other, and there at the bend the hard part began, the place where they could keep him if he wasn't who he thought he was. The floor was absolutely clean, no stains, no cracks, no chips in the wall. He wiped his feet on the cement as if on a welcome mat.

A sign saying *No Guns In Jail* hung over a row of dead-latched cubicles the size of safety-deposit boxes, and Fritz was locking his pistol in one of them. Beyond him a heavyset turnkey with close-cropped gray hair was holding open the door in the wall of upright bars that separated the cellblock from the station, and Danny had his first glance at the kind of lock he'd have to handle. He went right on seeing it even after he quit looking at it.

Fritz said, "Your boy acts like he was stuffed. What's the matter?"

The reporter shrugged. "I just work here."

"Maybe I should give him a saliva test." Fritz smiled and his jowls creased once on each side of his mouth. Then he went past the turnkey, nodding at him, and said, "Come on in." The reporter followed.

As Danny passed through the door he touched the downward-hooked locking dog with his forefinger as if telling it something, and a flashgun went off behind him. The photographer was walking toward him when he looked back, and the door latched behind them both with a firm collision of iron.

The corridor was fifty feet long with two pairs of left-and-right side aisles. Each of the barred cell doors was concave so a man standing in the bulge could see every part of the cell. The locks were the same make as the one on the outer door, the turnkey was carrying only two keys on the ring at his belt, and everything looked possible as long as they didn't get worried about him.

The reporter said, "How about the drunk tank?"

"What's the matter, don't you like this kid?" Fritz squeezed Danny's arm till it hurt. "Want him to lose his virtue?"

The lock cases on some of the cells were painted red, and they stopped at one to look in at three men sitting at a table eating out of plastic bowls.

Fritz said, "Hi, sport."

One man held still, but two spoons kept going.

"I said Hi."

"Hello, Captain." The man had an Ozark twang. "Sir."

Danny kept from meeting the eyes of the men gawking at him from both sides, in every doorway. A man who looked like an Indian wearing blue-and-white striped coveralls came wheeling a covered dinner wagon around a corner and stopped with a clatter when he saw them.

The turnkey said, "Go on."

Eyes lowered, the Indian pushed the wagon past them toward the outer door. The smell of stew floated behind.

Fritz glanced at the photographer. "Want some? You can be a one-man delegation from the Amalgamated Judges of Horseflesh."

"No thanks."

The rest of the smells were antiseptic, and the concrete floor had a sheen on it that reflected the caged ceiling lights. Everything, including the bars and the horizontal spacers across them, was painted a pale green like a schoolroom, and Danny knew it was time to be younger, even scared.

Fritz said, "See how the floor's shinier down the middle than the sides? By the time a citizen gets back this far, kid, he's usually in so much trouble, all he can do is shuffle." He headed into the first side aisle on the left.

Danny said, "Looks like a very strong place." He let a slight quaver get into it. "Very well constructed."

Fritz smiled over his shoulder. "Like it?"

"How many inside at the moment?" The reporter had his pad out.

"I don't know. Sully?"

The turnkey, who was following, said, "Twenty-eight, sir."

"We try to keep them close together." Fritz motioned back at the main corridor. "Easier to keep clean. The kid can have a nice quiet place to himself." He stepped around a waste can with a push broom upside down in it and swung open a cell door with a red lock case. "Want to try this for size?"

The tension in his stomach let go slightly because it wasn't a canvas-padded maximum-security cell, which might have taken him all night. It was smaller than any of the others he'd seen—a single iron bunk, a wash-bowl with push buttons instead of external fixtures, a seatless john—and the ceiling was a foot lower than the others, a single steel plate with two venti-lator grids cut directly into it.

The photographer said, "Can't we use a different one? I'll have a hard time keeping the john out of the shots."

Before they could change their minds, Danny stepped inside and bent as if to sit on the bunk.

In a harsh voice Fritz said, "Out, kid." When Danny hesitated, he said, "Out here. We'll have to take a little look at you before you set up shop."

He came out again and stood still while Fritz got behind him and peeled off the sport coat, fumbling through the pockets before handing it to the turn-key. The flashgun went off.

The reporter said, "How you feeling, Danny boy?"

Fritz said, "Keep going, kid. I hope you wear a good class of underwear so our friend here won't have to airbrush his prints too much."

The reporter said, "I thought you weren't worried, Fritz. What the hell are you going to do, X-ray him?"

"You can say for publication I'm a brave, confident cop, but I don't throw myself in the lake just to get a laugh."

Danny took off his shirt and handed it over, seeing his bare chest quiver once like a horse's flank. His mind was going faster now. He didn't let it show in his face, but he could feel the speed in his fingers.

Fritz said, "Shoes."

"He'll catch cold." The reporter sounded as if he halfway meant it.

"Get your story and shut up."

Danny slipped out of them without stooping, and Fritz shoved them toward the turnkey with his foot. The man had draped the shirt over the push broom, and now he put the shoes at a neat 45-degree angle at the foot of the waste can. The photographer backed down the corridor and the flashgun went off again.

Fritz said, "Pants."

Danny let them fall to his ankles and stepped out, shifting sideways far enough to get another look at the outside of the lock.

The reporter circled and tried to catch his eye. "Nervous? Any reactions? Like to repeat the challenge for the benefit of posterity?"

"You already took it down."

"Yeah, but I didn't get to see Fritz's face while you were saying it."

Fritz said, "Well at least he came prepared for a little fun: no wallet, no I.D., no keys, no money. Aren't you guys going to pay him something for earning his Junior Horse's Ass Merit Badge right out in front of you like this?"

"He's just natural-born show folks, Fritz." The reporter was scribbling on his pad. "Anything for a little free space."

The flashgun went off again, and Fritz said, "Now I'm going to have to ask you to drop your shorts, kid, like it or not. You don't have to cough, I just don't want to miss anything obvious like adhesive tape because if you start sawing away at our nice bars here, it can get expensive."

He kept his eyes straight ahead while he lowered his shorts, feeling his face redden. The flashgun didn't go off.

"All right, you can keep them on. Turn around."

He pulled up the shorts and faced Fritz.

"Open your mouth. Stick out your tongue. Lift it. Show me your teeth." He did as he was told.

The reporter said, "When was the last time you had a jailbreak?"

Ignoring him, Fritz said, "Okay, now the socks." He waited, then said, "Let's see the soles of your feet."

Danny balanced on one foot at a time.

The turnkey put the socks inside the shoes, and Fritz said, "In."

"Wait a minute." The photographer didn't sound quite as bored. "Don't you have an Oregon boot or some leg-irons or some goddamn chains or something? If I have to shoot it this way, he looks like he's on latrine duty in scout camp."

"Leg-irons? What do you think this is, Russia?"

"At least some handcuffs then, for godsake."

Fritz reached toward his left hip under his coat, then stopped and held out his hand to the turnkey. "Give me yours, Sully." When the man hesitated, Fritz said, "Well, I don't want mine scratched up either." He glanced at Danny who was waiting inside the doorway. "Kid, if you hack these up on the bunk or so much as nick them, you'll be scrubbing out the drunk tank with a toothbrush."

Danny nodded, then watched the pair of glistening Pratt handcuffs go ratcheting into place around his wrists.

"Any other hot ideas?" Fritz looked around. "You want him strung upside down?"

The flashgun went off twice, and then the turnkey was swinging the door shut. It latched with a deep clank. The flat, oval-handled brass bit key went into the lock, turned once, then turned again.

Fritz said, "This is what's called a felon's cell, double-locked like an old maid's back door."

"Look noble, kid." The photographer was crouching near the floor. "You want to gnash your teeth, Fritz?"

"No thanks."

The flashgun went off, and the reporter came over to lean against the bars. "Only one hour?"

Danny nodded.

"I'm just trying to figure out how many cups of coffee we can manage."

Fritz said, "If you want more time, it's okay by me. The main object's for the kid to learn something, isn't it. Let him have two or three lessons."

Trying to look sheepish, Danny said, "One hour."

Then Fritz was helping herd the others down the corridor, joking through the back talk, but he stopped at the mouth and let the turnkey take the newspapermen out of sight toward the entrance to the block.

Danny waited at the right edge of the cell door where he could see as far as possible, making no moves. After a moment the turnkey came back into the side corridor alone, spoke briefly to Fritz, then followed him to Danny's cell again, unlocking it with a double clockwise turn.

Fritz said, "Thanks, Sully. Can you see me?"

"No, sir."

"That's the spirit."

The turnkey went toward the main corridor.

Grabbing hold of the central swivel between handcuffs, Fritz pulled Danny through the door. He spoke in a low voice. "Sorry to interrupt your valuable time, but we have to have a little discussion."

His bare feet slid from the cold steel floor of the cell to the equally cold concrete, and gooseflesh traveled up his legs and arms like a shock.

Fritz tugged him toward the dead end of the corridor and stopped at the last closed solid cell door on the right. He pushed the cover back from the safety-glass judas window and yanked Danny toward it. "Take a good look."

A young man was sitting on the floor of the otherwise empty padded cell, resting his back against one of the bulging vertical humps of green-painted canvas and looking straight at the window. He had two black eyes, like a burglar wearing a mask in a cartoon, and he had on socks, shorts, and a bloody white shirt. When he smiled, the inside of his mouth looked redder than his lips.

In his ear Fritz whispered, "This is an old friend of mine. He tried to bust out of an interrogation room, and unfortunately for him he thought he'd hit somebody on the way out. I have to do a lot of things I don't like in this job, but I don't mind taking care of characters like this. I want to impress something on your mind, kid. I don't quite know what you think you're doing, but I want to show you a bad example just in case. In an hour the boys will take some more pictures of you bawling in your cell with a snotty nose, and they'll write down your deathless observations on the subject of bragging, and then they'll forget about you. After that, it won't matter what color your eyes are or how many teeth you've got." He paused. "You listening?"

"What's this man charged with?"

Fritz smiled. "Booze, as a rule. And don't waste my time. I'm giving you facts. Lot of sick boys around town, and they all wind up here, kid."

The man in the cell got up off the floor and came to the inside of the small window, grinning to show his pink teeth. He was talking rapidly, inaudibly.

Fritz said, "And they all wind up talking to themselves. What's your hometown?"

Danny shut his mouth. The window cover fell back into place, cutting off the prisoner in the middle of a series of slow, silent four-letter words.

Fritz said, "It's Iron City, isn't it."

After a few seconds, Danny realized his eyes hadn't stayed still enough. "What was your old man's name?"

"I never had an old man." He was cold, and he could see his clothes hung over the push broom like a scarecrow. And they liked to make you uncomfortable too; it was all part of their pleasure to take away any chance you had to be dignified. Like the time in the locker room being painted with Merthiolate or the time the laundry fell off his bike on the playground and everybody danced with it.

"Masters." Fritz was smiling uncertainly. "You look like him."

Danny kept his eyes on the open door of his cell, waiting for the pressure on the handcuffs to steer him toward it.

Fritz hauled him a few steps, then stopped again. "Was Harry Masters your old man? I remember it was—" he pushed Danny's chin aside to look at his profile. "I think I'll take a run through the files." He led him the rest of the way to the cell, palmed him inside, then shut the door and looked at Danny through the bars. "You've got more than one funny idea in your head, don't you, kid. Country boys get hungry and they start trying to speed everything up. Your pockets get to starving and you start seeing double at the crotch, and the first thing you know, you have to catch up and get ahead and stay ahead and make sure everybody sees you doing it. Then you have to start showing everybody they're just around to get pushed. I saw your old man try it, and I'm telling you he got pushed back so hard it knocked the wind out of him. Permanently. He was behind the times too, kid. He got to thinking he was a gangster, only there wasn't any gang. I'm not sure what the hell you think *you* are, but maybe we'll find out later." He beckoned down the corridor. "You wouldn't be thinking about hurting anybody, would you?"

Danny kept his eyes on the wall, and the turnkey came and double-locked the door again.

Fritz said, "They didn't shoot him back in here, you know. He got as far as the outside hall, which is pretty good for a country boy at that."

The turnkey said, "They're raising hell out there 'cause we're not letting him alone like he said. I told them I—"

"All right, all right." The two men started along the corridor, and Fritz looked back. "When you get back in here for something real, kid, remember there's no reporters around for miles. Everybody takes their time over things."

Then they were finally going: they turned the corner and didn't come back. He waited an extra minute, then took the flat, two-inch fork-bladed spring-steel pick from between his right lower lip and the gum where it had cut him slightly from talking so much and, with a metallic taste in his mouth, bent it nearly in half and took three seconds apiece to spring the left and right cuffs, not in the keyway but straight down the throat.

He checked the corridor and couldn't see or hear anything, no chains rattling or gunfire, nothing from the ventilators or through the hard walls.

From between his left lower lip and the gum he extracted the plain single-point pick without a handle he'd had to choose out of all the possibilities, knelt on his bare knees behind the blank back of the lock case, and, wedging the handcuff pick longways in the crack of the door, broke it in half. And it wasn't any school locker or ignition lock at the wrecking yard or any simple cabinet deadlatch that could be slipped with a hairpin, and it wasn't the door in the dentist's waiting room that a celluloid bookmark or a putty knife could open. He took a deep breath, then with the pick in one hand and the broken half in the other, reached through separate gaps in the bars till he was embracing the doorcasing. He felt his way in with the pick and pressed up the first of the four oversized pin tumblers, using the thin tough broken piece as a shim to follow between the plug and the case.

And they'd been using these locks too long, nothing was tight anymore, and their whole heavyweight jail was falling apart by a hundredth of an inch just because they didn't understand what was supposed to hold it together. He had the fourth pin out of the way and held there in less than a minute, and then because the action of the bolt was so heavy, he removed the pick and used one of the free tongues of the handcuffs for more leverage. He turned the plug as slowly as he could, wishing he'd thought to take off his shorts and use them as a muffler, but it was too late now, he couldn't let the follower slip out of the breaks in the pins. The first turn sounded like a rock falling into a full bathtub, but he didn't wait to find out whether anybody had heard it. He finished the second turn, and if the cell had been triple- or quadruple-locked, he could have kept right on going. He pushed the handle down, and the door went ajar. He stood up and waited.

Now with a full view of the corridor, he could see no one was sticking his head around the corner or using a shoplifter's mirror. He put his clothes on fast because he didn't want to be sneezing, and he hurried to the dead end in his stocking feet. He pushed back the window cover, waited till the man got to his feet again, then held his fingers to his lips. He stood slightly aside and gestured at the empty corridor. The man smiled and nodded.

The lock was identical with the other, though it was mounted in a solid sliding door, and it was keyed the same and double-locked—as he found out when he repeated the process, having even less trouble now that he could see what he was doing. He could hear the rattle of what sounded like pans and silverware, but the turnkey didn't show up. He slid the door half open.

The man came toward him slowly, suspiciously, looking in all directions including behind. Blood was caked in the corners of his mouth, and he was limping on both bare feet which were streaked blue across the insteps.

Danny held up his finger again and motioned for the man to follow, but the other shook his head and made a throat-cutting gesture. When Danny signaled impatience with both hands, the man hobbled reluctantly as far as the other cell door but stopped there. His eyes seemed panicky.

Giving up, Danny shooed him into the open felon's cell and managed to latch the door almost silently. He bent to double-lock it again while the man tried to get his head between the bars to watch.

The man said, "Well, I'll be damned."

Shushing him violently, Danny stood up and put all the picks in the same shirt pocket. He held the open cuffs tightly so they wouldn't rattle.

Mouthing the words like a mute, the man said, "Good luck." He spat out some blood and smiled. His spindly, slightly bowed legs were quivering.

Danny leaned close to his ear and whispered, "If you hear me bang three times"—he motioned with the handcuffs against the bars—"make a racket."

The man nodded, and Danny picked up his shoes in his free hand and started toward the mouth of the corridor. He wasn't thinking. Sometimes it was like talking, just a waste of attention, but when you could get your whole body doing it, there was no name for it, the feeling of being led yet knowing it was your own choice. It was what could always save you, always set you free: yourself going ahead of yourself and knowing what to do.

When he came to the last empty cell on the right, its door half-open, he paused to listen. The dinner wagon was being wheeled nearby, and then the key clicked and turned just around the corner toward the main entrance. He heard a few muttered words. It was either more dinner or they were picking up the empties, and he ducked through the open door and flattened himself in the near corner. After a moment he heard the wagon moving again.

From the mouth of the side aisle a voice said, "Him too?"

"Nah, that's just some kind of stunt."

When the wagon rattled forward Danny took one glance through the bars and saw the Indian pushing the shiny portable steam table further along the main corridor. The turnkey strolled with him on the near side.

After they passed the mouth, Danny slipped out of the cell and crossed to the opposite wall of his own corridor, sliding along it to the corner. He went to his hands and knees and peeked from near the floor. They had stopped again, short of the second side aisle, and he pulled his head back and looked at most of the corridor between him and the main entrance.

Forty feet of glistening, bare space—no cover except the concave doorways of the cells, usable only if the guys inside would keep quiet.

Then he saw the young man with a dark beard staring at him motionlessly from inside a cell on the far side of the main corridor. His sport shirt was open at the throat, and one of the pockets of his jeans had been ripped halfway down his leg. Danny braced one foot like a sprinter, then held still, watching the man steadily. Suddenly teeth showed through the beard in a wide white smile.

The man started whistling tunelessly, and Danny peeked up the corridor again. They hadn't gone into one of the other branches, they had turned around and were coming down the opposite side. If he had to hit somebody or make a fuss before he was through the outer door, he didn't have a chance.

With a thick Ozark twang the bearded man started singing, "Well, we've all had our dinner, let's have some dessert." He bent at the waist to laugh.

Danny jerked his thumb toward the invisible wagon and raised his eyebrows in a question.

After hawking and spitting into a nearby basin, the bearded man sang, "The Injun's a trusty, he'd give you his shirt."

From up the corridor the Indian said, "Horseshit."

The turnkey said something, and the bearded man started signaling to the cell opposite him, making a shushing gesture, pointing in Danny's direction, then toward the main entrance. He was making other signs like the deaf-and-dumb code, and Danny crossed swiftly into the open cell again, wedging himself into the forward corner as the wagon neared the mouth.

In a slow, drawling, off-key, nasal baritone the bearded man sang, "Jes' wait for the word, boy, it won't be long now."

The turnkey said, "Pipe down."

"Here comes the old covered wagon." The bearded man was half-talking with a loud fake heartiness.

"I said shut up."

The bearded man said, "Hey, Tonto, what did you guys do out on the prairie when the settlers got crouched in behind them covered wagons?"

The Indian said, "Nothin'."

"That's it, that's how the West was won, people doing nothing."

The turnkey said, "Any more noise out of you, sport, and you can do a little time in the stand-up."

"I'm just passing the word along, Sully. When you've got the word, you just naturally got to pass it along *right now.*"

And Danny came out of the cell bent over, on his toes, holding the handcuffs and his shoes against his stomach. The wagon was past the mouth, the Indian was slouched behind it, the turnkey was on the far side facing the bearded man. Danny went to his knees against the warm stainless steel flank of the wagon.

The Indian jerked his head in surprise but didn't change expression, and the turnkey said, "I'll tell you what the word is: quiet."

"What the hell, Sully, it's after hours upstairs. The mayor and all the big shots are out drinking a little dinner. They ain't nobody to bother."

"Bothers me, sport."

"Well, you're a no-account old cop, so what's the difference?"

A gangling, tired-looking man was leaning against the bars of a cell only a few feet from him, and Danny met his eyes, then glanced away embarrassed. He wasn't used to having this many people know what he was doing. Being alone was almost as important as knowing how. He looked ahead at the main entrance and the empty hall beyond it. No telling how long it would stay empty.

The turnkey said, "Come again?"

Breaking into a loud twang, the bearded man chanted. "You're a no-account cop, and I'll sing what I please. If you don't like—"

A key turned in a lock, and from around the edge of one rubber-rimmed wheel Danny saw the cell door swinging open and feet shuffling in it.

The bearded man sang, "If you don't like my music you can—" He stopped with a deep grunt.

The turnkey said, "All right."

There was a brief scuffle, the feet rearranged themselves, and the door clanged shut again.

"You want to do it nice, or you just want to wake up there later?"

"Okay, okay, okay," The bearded man sounded subdued.

The feet started to go deeper along the corridor, and Danny moved to the front corner of the wagon. He ducked and raised one elbow when he felt the hand touch his back, but it was the Indian motioning him to hold still, the straight blue-black hair hanging down in a cowlick almost over one eye.

The bearded man and the turnkey were wrangling and moving further away. The Indian nudged him, and Danny went to the front of the wagon, his cheek against the warm metal. It bumped him like a signal, and when he looked back, using the legs of the Indian's coveralls as a shield, the corridor was empty. The voices were coming out of the side aisle he'd just come from, but he didn't wait to worry. He ran for the main entrance.

Men stood watching from all the remaining cell doors, three on each side, and they didn't make any noise as he went by. Maybe the word had been sent back and forth across the corridor like stitches or they'd heard the newspapermen talking. He only needed a little time now, but the eyes of one old man standing in the last cell door on the left stopped him. He had a red face and a mismatched blue suit.

Danny's socks skidded on the concrete as he stopped. He whispered. "Do you want out? Do you want to come with me?"

The red-faced man looked at the short fat man next to him, looked back into the empty cell, then looked at Danny again. "Who, me?"

"What're you in for?" Danny glanced back along the corridor: the turnkey was still out of sight, and the Indian was coming toward him with the wagon.

"For living."

"Do you want out or don't you?" Not daring to waste any more time, he knelt at the main lock, which was the same type as the others but keyed differently. It only slowed his work with the pick and shim momentarily.

The red-faced man whispered, "I'm in on a D and D, son, I don't want any trouble, I'm getting out tomorrow."

Danny began to hunt for the break in the last pin. The Indian was wheeling the wagon close, turning it to block him from sight. The turnkey would have to come running in order to stop him now because he was going, he was going and knew how to go, where, when, and how far, and he was right on top of the process each step of the way, he was the man with the power, and the word *kid* wasn't fitting him anymore, that key wouldn't even go into the lock. The follower split the last pin, and he started to turn the plug with the tongue of one handcuff.

From up the corridor the turnkey said, "What're you waiting there for?"

The Indian said, "Who?"

"Come on, pick up these trays back here."

"They didn't want to." The Indian's voice was deep, sullen, and stupid-sounding. He came around on Danny's side of the wagon and leaned on it.

"Who didn't want to what, for chrissakes?"

Danny hit the side of the wagon three loud blows with the handcuffs down near one of the Indian's feet, and the man jerked with surprise, looking down.

The turnkey shouted, "You kick any more city property, Redskin, I'll—" In a loud hollow high voice like some kind of hound dog, a man started singing in the distance, using the same tune the bearded man had used but even further off-key. Danny put on his shoes and got ready.

Joining in, the bearded man's deeper voice came out of the side aisle, and it was impossible to understand either one of them.

The Indian said, "Now."

Danny unlatched the door, held it open politely, and looked back. When the Indian shook his head, he ducked through, squeezed it shut, then ratcheted the handcuffs tight from the last bar in the door to the first bar past the jamb, shoved the follower into the keyways of the cuffs, and broke off a fragment in each.

He took five quick steps to the turn in the corridor and, while peeking around it down the long hall to the brighter area of the booking counter, which was nearly deserted, he listened to the growing commotion behind him. It wasn't loud yet, but some kind of alarm was liable to go off at any second.

Standing erect, he stamped the clean place on the floor once, and there wasn't going to be any shooting, nobody floundering around on the shiny disinfected concrete trying to spit blood as fast as it was coming, because there was another way if you could learn it, teach your hands how to do things for themselves, including things nobody else could do or even think of, so in spite of the fact that all fathers were dead except the lousy ones, you could find out how to congratulate yourself, pat yourself on the back, give yourself a break, and forgive yourself for being wrong.

He began walking purposefully to the small door with the button beside it, not caring who happened to glance his way from the booking area because Fritz had made this a piece of private enterprise. Nobody else had any reason to worry about a "kid," and using the six-inch alcove of the door as much as possible, he could stay out of sight of the men behind the counter. The ones in front of it wouldn't holler at him. And it was no use trying any of the side rooms because the windows were bound to have protective screens bolted over them.

The door was locked, of course, and he flattened himself in the slight alcove, unlatched his right shoe-sole while the alarm bell went off in the cell block, and took out the flat playing-card-sized picking gun. He put its thin arm into the keyway, used one of his picks as a torque wrench, and began pulling the trigger. On the seventh snap, the plug turned in the core, and he was inside somewhere-or-other in the dark with the door shut behind him in time to breathe twice before he heard the feet passing in a hurry toward the cells. The reporter was asking muffled questions and sounded happy.

He felt around the yard-square area in front of the elevator, found but didn't use a light switch, then slid the brass cage door far enough aside to let himself in. All elevators made some racket, and after finding the control panel he waited a moment to let things develop in the cell block—the turnkey trying to open his own handcuffs, maybe, or Fritz trying to find which of the cells Danny was hiding in, or the man with the black eyes getting ready to pose for pictures and answer funny questions, and everybody having a good time except Fritz.

He flipped the snap switch below the buttons and turned on the overhead light long enough to punch number two. The cables and drive wheels hummed almost silently, the cab went up, and he could feel the cage growing longer from corner to opposite corner in the dark, disappearing up the magician's sleeve, but the canary wasn't going to get killed or even rumpled if he could help it. The only problem would be dodging a watchman or floor mopper in some distant wing of the building while he chose a window with enough shrubbery under it. From here on, whatever he did would never have been done before, not in the whole history of fathers.

JOHN STEINBECK

HOW
MR. HOGAN
ROBBED A BANK

*"... The Hogans lived at 215 East Maple
Street, in a brown-shingle house with white
trim—there are two. . . ."*

ON THE Saturday before Labor Day, 1955, at 9:04½ A.M., Mr. Hogan robbed a
bank. He was forty-two years old, married, and the father of a boy and a girl,
named John and Joan, twelve and thirteen respectively. Mrs. Hogan's name
was Joan and Mr. Hogan's was John, but since they called themselves Papa
and Mama that left their names free for the children, who were considered
very smart for their ages, each having jumped a grade in school. The Hogans
lived at 215 East Maple Street, in a brown-shingle house with white trim—
there are two. 215 is the one across from the street light and it is the one
with the big tree in the yard, either oak or elm—the biggest tree in the whole
street, maybe in the whole town.

John and Joan were in bed at the time of the robbery, for it was Saturday.
At 9:10 A.M., Mrs. Hogan was making the cup of tea she always had. Mr. Hogan went to work early. Mrs. Hogan drank her tea slowly, scalding hot, and
read her fortune in the tea leaves. There was a cloud and a five-pointed star
with two short points in the bottom of the cup, but that was at 9:12 and the
robbery was all over by then.

The way Mr. Hogan went about robbing the bank was very interesting.
He gave it a great deal of thought and had for a long time, but he did not discuss it with anyone. He just read his newspaper and kept his own counsel.
But he worked it out to his own satisfaction that people went to too much
trouble robbing banks and that got them in a mess. The simpler the better,
he always thought. People went in for too much hullabaloo and hanky-
panky. If you didn't do that, if you left hanky-panky out, robbing a bank
would be a relatively sound venture—barring accidents, of course, of an improbable kind, but then they could happen to a man crossing the street or
anything. Since Mr. Hogan's method worked fine, it proved that his thinking
was sound. He often considered writing a little booklet on his technique
when the how-to rage was running so high. He figured out the first sentence,
which went: "To successfully rob a bank, forget all about hanky-panky."

Mr. Hogan was not just a clerk at Fettucci's grocery store. He was more like the manager. Mr. Hogan was in charge, even hired and fired the boy who delivered groceries after school. He even put in orders with the salesmen, sometimes when Mr. Fettucci was right in the store too, maybe talking to a customer. "You do it, John," he would say and he would nod at the customer, "John knows the ropes. Been with me—how long you been with me, John?"

"Sixteen years."

"Sixteen years. Knows the business as good as me. John, why he even banks the money."

And so he did. Whenever he had a moment, Mr. Hogan went into the storeroom on the alley, took off his apron, put on his necktie and coat, and went back through the store to the cash register. The checks and bills would be ready for him inside the bankbook with a rubber band around it. Then he went next door and stood at the teller's window and handed the checks and bankbook through to Mr. Cup and passed the time of day with him too. Then, when the bankbook was handed back, he checked the entry, put the rubber band around it, and walked next door to Fettucci's grocery and put the bankbook in the cash register, continued on to the storeroom, removed his coat and tie, put on his apron, and went back into the store ready for business. If there was no line at the teller's window, the whole thing didn't take more than five minutes, even passing the time of day.

Mr. Hogan was a man who noticed things, and when it came to robbing the bank, this trait stood him in good stead. He had noticed, for instance, where the big bills were kept right in the drawer under the counter and he had noticed also what days there were likely to be more than other days. Thursday was payday at the American Can Company's local plant, for instance, so there would be more then. Some Fridays people drew more money to tide them over the weekend. But it was even Steven, maybe not a thousand dollars difference, between Thursdays and Fridays and Saturday mornings. Saturdays were not terribly good because people didn't come to get money that early in the morning, and the bank closed at noon. But he thought it over and came to the conclusion that the Saturday before a long weekend in the summer would be the best of all. People going on trips, vacations, people with relatives visiting, and the bank closed Monday. He thought it out and looked, and sure enough the Saturday morning before Labor Day the cash drawer had twice as much money in it—he saw it when Mr. Cup pulled out the drawer.

Mr. Hogan thought about it during all that year, not all the time, of course, but when he had some moments. It was a busy year too. That was the year John and Joan had the mumps and Mrs. Hogan got her teeth pulled and was fitted for a denture. That was the year when Mr. Hogan was Master of the Lodge, with all the time that takes. Larry Shield died that year—he was Mrs. Hogan's brother and was buried from the Hogan house at 215 East Maple. Larry was a bachelor and had a room in the Pine Tree House and he played pool nearly every night. He worked at the Silver Diner but that closed at nine and so Larry would go to Louie's and play pool for an hour. Therefore, it was a surprise when he left enough so that after funeral expenses there were twelve hundred dollars left. And even more surprising that he left a will in Mrs. Hogan's favor, but his double-barreled twelve-gauge shotgun he left to John Hogan, Jr. Mr. Hogan was pleased, although he never hunted. He put the shotgun away in the back of the closet in the bathroom, where he kept his things, to keep it for young John. He didn't want children handling guns and he never bought any shells. It was some of that twelve hundred that got Mrs. Hogan her dentures. Also, she bought a bicycle for John and a doll buggy and walking-talking doll for Joan—a doll with three changes of dresses and a little suitcase, complete with play makeup. Mr. Hogan thought it might spoil the children, but it didn't seem to. They made just as good marks in school and John even got a job delivering papers. It was a very busy year. Both John and Joan wanted to enter the W. R. Hearst National "I Love America" Contest and Mr. Hogan thought it was almost too much, but they promised to do the work during their summer vacation, so he finally agreed.

During that year, no one noticed any difference in Mr. Hogan. It was true, he was thinking about robbing the bank, but he only thought about it in the evening when there was neither a Lodge meeting nor a movie they wanted to go to, so it did not become an obsession and people noticed no change in him.

He had studied everything so carefully that the approach of Labor Day did not catch him unprepared or nervous. It was hot that summer and the hot spells were longer than usual. Saturday was the end of two weeks heat without a break and people were irritated with it and anxious to get out of town, although the country was just as hot. They didn't think of that. The children were excited because the "I Love America" Essay Contest was due to be concluded and the winners announced, and the first prize was an all-expense-paid two days trip to Washington, D.C., with every fixing—hotel room, three meals a day, and side trips in a limousine—not only for the winner, but for an accompanying chaperone; visit to the White House—shake hands with the President—everything. Mr. Hogan thought they were getting their hopes too high and he said so.

"You've got to be prepared to lose," he told his children. "There're probably thousands and thousands entered. You get your hopes up and it might spoil the whole autumn. Now I don't want any long faces in this house after the contest is over."

"I was against it from the start," he told Mrs. Hogan. That was the morning she saw the Washington Monument in her teacup, but she didn't tell anybody about that except Ruth Tyler, Bob Tyler's wife. Ruthie brought over her cards and read them in the Hogan kitchen, but she didn't find a journey. She did tell Mrs. Hogan that the cards were often wrong. The cards had said Mrs. Winkle was going on a trip to Europe and the next week Mrs. Winkle got a fishbone in her throat and choked to death. Ruthie, just thinking out loud, wondered if there was any connection between the fishbone and the ocean voyage to Europe. "You've got to interpret them right." Ruthie did say she saw money coming to the Hogans.

"Oh, I got that already from poor Larry," Mrs. Hogan explained.

"I must have got the past and future cards mixed," said Ruthie. "You've got to interpret them right."

Saturday dawned a blaster. The early morning weather report on the radio said "Continued hot and humid, light scattered rain Sunday night and Monday." Mrs. Hogan said, "Wouldn't you know? Labor Day." And Mr. Hogan said, "I'm sure glad we didn't plan anything." He finished his egg and mopped the plate with his toast. Mrs. Hogan said, "Did I put coffee on the list?" He took the paper from his handkerchief pocket and consulted it. "Yes, coffee, it's here."

"I had a crazy idea I forgot to write it down," said Mrs. Hogan. "Ruth and I are going to Altar Guild this afternoon. It's at Mrs. Alfred Drake's. You know, they just came to town. I can't wait to see their furniture."

"They trade with us," said Mr. Hogan. "Opened an account last week. Are the milk bottles ready?"

"On the porch."

Mr. Hogan looked at his watch just before he picked up the bottles and it was five minutes to eight. He was about to go down the stairs, when he turned and looked back through the opened door at Mrs. Hogan. She said, "Want something, Papa?"

"No," he said. "No," and he walked down the steps.

He went down to the corner and turned right on Spooner, and Spooner runs into Main Street in two blocks, and right across from where it runs in, there is Fettucci's and the bank around the corner and the alley beside the bank. Mr. Hogan picked up a handbill in front of Fettucci's and unlocked the door. He went through to the storeroom, opened the door to the alley, and looked out. A cat tried to force its way in, but Mr. Hogan blocked it with his foot and leg and closed the door. He took off his coat and put on his long apron, tied the strings in a bowknot behind his back. Then he got the broom from behind the counter and swept out behind the counters and scooped the sweepings into a dustpan; and, going through the storeroom, he opened the door to the alley. The cat had gone away. He emptied the dustpan into the garbage can and tapped it smartly to dislodge a piece of lettuce leaf. Then he went back to the store and worked for a while on the order sheet. Mrs. Clooney came in for a half a pound of bacon. She said it was hot and Mr. Hogan agreed. "Summers are getting hotter," he said.

"I think so myself," said Mrs. Clooney. "How's Mrs. standing up?"

"Just fine," said Mr. Hogan. "She's going to Altar Guild."

"So am I. I just can't wait to see their furniture," said Mrs. Clooney, and she went out.

Mr. Hogan put a five-pound hunk of bacon on the slicer and stripped off the pieces and laid them on wax paper and then he put the wax-paper-covered squares in the cooler cabinet. At ten minutes to nine, Mr. Hogan went to a shelf. He pushed a spaghetti box aside and took down a cereal box, which he emptied in the little closet toilet. Then, with a banana knife, he cut out the Mickey Mouse mask that was on the back. The rest of the box he took to the toilet and tore up the cardboard and flushed it down. He went into the store then and yanked a piece of string loose and tied the ends through the side holes of the mask and then he looked at his watch—a large silver Hamilton with black hands. It was two minutes to nine.

Perhaps the next four minutes were his only time of nervousness at all. At one minute to nine, he took the broom and went out to sweep the sidewalk and he swept it very rapidly—was sweeping it, in fact, when Mr. Warner unlocked the bank door. He said good morning to Mr. Warner and a few seconds later the bank staff of four emerged from the coffee shop. Mr. Hogan saw them across the street and he waved at them and they waved back. He finished the sidewalk and went back in the store. He laid his watch on the little step of the cash register. He sighed very deeply, more like a deep breath than a sigh. He knew that Mr. Warner would have the safe open now and he would be carrying the cash trays to the teller's window. Mr. Hogan looked at the watch on the cash register step. Mr. Kenworthy paused in the store entrance, then shook his head vaguely and walked on and Mr. Hogan let out his breath gradually. His left hand went behind his back and pulled the bow-knot on his apron, and then the black hand on his watch crept up on the four-minute mark and covered it.

Mr. Hogan opened the charge account drawer and took out the store pistol, a silver-colored Iver Johnson .38. He moved quickly to the storeroom, slipped off his apron, put on his coat, and stuck the revolver in his side pocket. The Mickey Mouse mask he shoved up under his coat where it didn't show. He opened the alley door and looked up and down and stepped quickly out, leaving the door slightly ajar. It is sixty feet to where the alley enters Main Street, and there he paused and looked up and down and then he turned his head toward the center of the street as he passed the bank window. At the bank's swinging door, he took out the mask from under his coat and put it on. Mr. Warner was just entering his office and his back was to the door. The top of Will Cup's head was visible through the teller's grill.

Mr. Hogan moved quickly and quietly around the end of the counter and into the teller's cage. He had the revolver in his right hand now. When Will Cup turned his head and saw the revolver, he froze. Mr. Hogan slipped his toe under the trigger of the floor alarm and he motioned Will Cup to the floor with the revolver and Will went down quick. Then Mr. Hogan opened the cash drawer and with two quick movements he piled the large bills from the tray together. He made a whipping motion to Will on the floor, to indicate that he should turn over and face the wall, and Will did. Then Mr. Hogan stepped back around the counter. At the door of the bank, he took off the mask, and as he passed the window he turned his head toward the middle of the street. He moved into the alley, walked quickly to the storeroom, and entered. The cat had got in. It watched him from a pile of canned goods cartons. Mr. Hogan went to the toilet closet and tore up the mask and flushed it. He took off his coat and put on his apron. He looked out into the store and then moved to the cash register. The revolver went back into the charge account drawer. He punched No Sale and, lifting the top drawer, distributed the stolen money underneath the top tray and then pulled the tray forward and closed the register, and only then did he look at his watch and it was 9:07½.

He was trying to get the cat out of the storeroom when the commotion boiled out of the bank. He took his broom and went out on the sidewalk. He heard all about it and offered his opinion when it was asked for. He said he didn't think the fellow could get away—where could he get to? Still, with the holiday coming up—

It was an exciting day. Mr. Fettucci was as proud as though it were his bank. The sirens sounded around town for hours. Hundreds of holiday travelers had to stop at the roadblocks set up all around the edge of town and several sneaky-looking men had their cars searched.

Mrs. Hogan heard about it over the phone and she dressed earlier than she would have ordinarily and came to the store on her way to Altar Guild. She hoped Mr. Hogan would have seen or heard something new, but he hadn't. "I don't see how the fellow can get away," he said.

Mrs. Hogan was so excited, she forgot her own news. She only remembered when she got to Mrs. Drake's house, but she asked permission and phoned the store the first moment she could. "I forgot to tell you. John's won honorable mention."

"What?"

"In the 'I Love America' Contest."

"What did he win?"

"Honorable mention."

"Fine. Fine—Anything come with it?"

"Why, he'll get his picture and his name all over the country. Radio too. Maybe even television. They've already asked for a photograph of him."

"Fine," said Mr. Hogan. "I hope it don't spoil him." He put up the receiver and said to Mr. Fettucci, "I guess we've got a celebrity in the family."

Fettucci stayed open until nine on Saturdays. Mr. Hogan ate a few snacks from cold cuts, but not much, because Mrs. Hogan always kept his supper warming.

It was 9:05, or :06, or :07, when he got back to the brown-shingle house at 215 East Maple. He went in through the front door and out to the kitchen where the family was waiting for him.

"Got to wash up," he said, and went up to the bathroom. He turned the key in the bathroom door and then he flushed the toilet and turned on the water in the basin and tub while he counted the money. Eight thousand three hundred and twenty dollars. From the top shelf of the storage closet in the bathroom, he took down the big leather case that held his Knight Templar's uniform. The plumed hat lay there on its form. The white ostrich feather was a little yellow and needed changing. Mr. Hogan lifted out the hat and pried the form up from the bottom of the case. He put the money in the form and then he thought again and removed two bills and shoved them in his side pocket. Then he put the form back over the money and laid the hat on top and closed the case and shoved it back on the top shelf.

Finally he washed his hands and turned off the water in the tub and the basin.

In the kitchen, Mrs. Hogan and the children faced him, beaming. "Guess what some young man's going on?"·

"What?" asked Mr. Hogan.

"Radio," said John. "Monday night. Eight o'clock."

"I guess we got a celebrity in the family," said Mr. Hogan.

Mrs. Hogan said, "I just hope some young lady hasn't got her nose out of joint."

Mr. Hogan pulled up to the table and stretched his legs. "Mama, I guess I got a fine family," he said. He reached in his pocket and took out two five-dollar bills. He handed one to John. "That's for winning," he said. He poked the other bill at Joan. "And that's for being a good sport. One celebrity and one good sport. What a fine family!" He rubbed his hands together and lifted the lid of the covered dish. "Kidneys," he said. "Fine."

And that's how Mr. Hogan did it.

LEE TRAUX

A MAN ALONE

"...He would go...around and between the insidious, unanswerable challenge of the sprawled legs and crowding shoulders and, once outside, straight through the city to Eva...."

ALAN Greene met Eva in the Stadtgarten on Sunday afternoon. Two blond soldiers had approached her, at once brash and uncertain, innocent and condescending, and were rejected by her turned head and furious dachshund. They retreated, barking back at the dog, and Alan had been embarrassed for them.

She does not know Americans, he thought, and when they had gone he left his bench by the war memorial statue, glad for the excuse to apologize for them. He spoke in stumbling German as her stern look softened and she quieted the quivering dog. "Hans does not like Americans yet," she said in fine English.

She was quite tall and very pretty and her hair was cut nearly as short as the ducktails he had seen on many German boys. Perhaps if the blond soldiers had not been together she would have let herself be picked up. He would be careful. Politeness first, always politeness. He pretended she was a girl from Columbia, feeling her out, trying to interpret the little signs. But he liked her immediately, hating again the precautions he had learned so carefully. He asked her to meet him next Sunday at the same place. She will not be there, he thought afterwards, but it will be a week's anticipation.

The following Sunday was September and the mists of early morning were not yet dissipated by the sun when he left the nearly deserted mess hall and went back to his room. Most of the men were still in their bunks, snores and heavy breathing coming from the orderly row of olive-drab cocoons. Alan stepped out of his fatigue pants and sat on the edge of his bunk looking at his shins. He thought of Eva's Nordic pale leg next to his own dark one and laughed at his imagination. He rubbed the spot he had been looking at, which had begun to itch.

"I do not glisten," he thought, remembering a painful time long ago. "It is sort of salt and pepper." He grinned and lay back, sliding under the coarse wool blanket which scratched him pleasantly.

Next to him a pink face, nearly buried in the covers, began to hum "Dixie."

"I thought you were still unconscious, Brad," Alan said. The song was a private joke between them.

"Oh, I'm not going to get up, but I'd like to know what I'm missing for breakfast," said Brad.

"You're missing fried eggs, private," said Alan. He was suddenly very glad he had eaten.

"Do me a great favor, Greene, and hand me that water and the aspirins on the table. I'm afraid to move my head." He extended his hand cautiously from the covers to receive the glass. "Thank you, I'll save your life some time."

"Evil time Saturday night," said Alan.

"Yeah. I was up at the club. It was nickel night." Brad crunched two tablets and swallowed water laboriously, sinking horizontal again with a feeble gasp. "I put the water and aspirins on the table last night in preparation, but they were just a little out of reach. They ought to close that place. Did you drop in?"

"I missed the fun," said Alan.

"Just as well. Some of your boys and my boys took the place apart about twelve-thirty."

"My boys . . . ?" Alan hoped Brad would not stop talking.

"Sorry . . . ." Brad grinned. "You know, booze, town ladies and the primeval passions make a volatile mixture. A hell of a bunch of regulars there on nickel night. Much nastiness."

"I was at the library until one o'clock," said Alan.

But Brad had finished speaking. He yawned. "Well, wake me up at two. I've got to take a nap this afternoon."

Alan swung his feet up on the bunk and stretched. The library was bright neon and silence and emptiness late on a Saturday night, only a quarter of a mile from the Enlisted Men's Club, straight down the cobblestone street between looming rows of gasoline trucks. It was secluded, back from the road, too far for him to have heard the MP's go by.

He began to think of meeting Eva in the city, and he wondered if she would be there. He grew drowsy in the quietly stirring room and slept until eleven, his mind skirting dreams he could not remember.

She was in the park, waiting without the dog. He watched from the gate for a while to be sure it was Eva, then he walked quickly to her. Her eyes flickered an instant and then she knew him.

"You are right on time," she said. "I was afraid you would not recognize me."

"You're easy to spot," he said, smiling.

"And you are also," she said. "You are more polite than most American soldiers. It was very kind of you to apologize for the two last Sunday. Soldiers everywhere have a terrible reputation."

"Yes, I am an ambassador of good will to the conquered nation." Immediately he was sorry he said it.

"That is a very good thing to be when others are not," said Eva.

He must remember she was not any white girl he could have known at Columbia. The talk of girls had been different there: facetious banter and urgent abstractions, always with the same self-confidence.

"Come on," she said, "let's leave the Stadtgarten. You have seen it many times."

"I really come here only to watch the pigeons," he said. "They remind me of New York."

"Kirchendorf would fit into your Central Park, but there are some points of interest." She shrugged. "A few are left anyway. There is also much rebuilding." She pointed to the clocktower at the entrance to the garden. It was meshed in scaffolding, a toy erector set above the trees. "They are making it taller this time," she said.

"It's going to be Gothic again," said Alan.

"Yes," said Eva. "It is very steep."

She turned, indifferent, and started slowly toward the gate. They walked between rows of late summer flowers, passing the fountain and the people who seemed part of the gauntlet benches, and out beyond the wall into the city. The noise of motor scooters and cars was raucous in the narrow street. Eva indicated certain buildings and talked as if she were guiding a tourist.

"That one was very important in the war," she said, waving toward a gray façade recessed from the street front by many steps and a columned overhang. "It was Gestapo headquarters. I was never allowed to go near it again after I once wandered up to the guard in front. He was very nice but my mother was afraid when she saw him talking to me. For her all soldiers were monsters, even those of her own country."

"You made yourself conspicuous. That is always a dangerous thing to do."

"But I was only five years old," she said, laughing suddenly at him.

He was glad she did not know he had been serious. He would not be weak in front of her.

"I don't think your mother should have been afraid," he said.

"Oh yes, she had reason to be. You are right, it is not a good thing to stand out in war."

"Well, I don't really know anything about it," he said, and he wondered if she thought he was lying.

They began to walk again toward the center of the city and the hub of the narrow side streets.

"Would you like to hear Bavarian music?" she asked him suddenly. "It is fun, like country music in the United States. I know of a place where soldiers do not go, but we will have to take the streetcar."

"Lead the way," said Alan, "I'm still a stranger here." He thought of the places the soldiers did go. He had walked by the Rendezvous Club occasionally on his way into town. The blaring hillbilly music on the jukebox must have reminded them of a thousand neon-lit places in the South and Midwest he had never seen, places he had been afraid of.

"No one stays in his house on Sunday afternoon," said Eva as they turned onto Kaiserstrasse, wide and crowded with pedestrians. New glass and concrete fronts of department stores replaced the somber side-street shops and apartments. The large Coca-Cola sign that had surprised him on his first walk through the city still covered the fence in front of the lot where bricks and sand waited for Monday and the start of construction. From the main street, catastrophic with stores and restaurants and theaters showing American movies and the whine of small vehicles discharging the stifling smell of low-octane exhaust, the city burgeoned out in the direction they had come into the neat wooded area beginning at the park. Once, walking alone in the outskirts, he had come on an athletic club with a great open soccer field, interrupting the trees where he had expected only a deepening of shadows. The land had been lived on a long time; every path led somewhere.

The sidewalk was crowded near the trolley stop and Eva kept close to him, once clinging to his arm as she was jostled by a small man in a double-breasted suit. She spoke to him curtly and he replied, slurring in the accent of the town which Alan could not understand. An ancient green coach appeared and grated before them, succumbing painfully to friction. They climbed on and went to the hard, straight seats. Two white soldiers boarded behind them and slumped across the aisle watching them covertly. Eva did not look at them once during the whole trip.

That evening, after the long streetcar ride back, she said good-by to him on the sidewalk in front of the gray apartment building at 22 Goethestrasse where she lived alone.

"I must go early to work tomorrow," she said.

"It was really fun, Eva. Everyone was so darned happy." The band wore Lederhosen and green alpine hats and played very loudly. He remembered toasting people and being toasted back as the "Schwarz Amerikaner," and rocking to the thumping, squeaking music. Eva sat close to him and seemed to enjoy it, but she wanted to go just when the excitement was greatest.

"There's nothing like it in the States," he said. He was still dizzy from the Mosel wine and strong beer.

"Wait until you see Fasching season," she said. "The whole city goes crazy."

"I've been here only two months, you know, and I haven't done much," he said. His future in Germany seemed exciting and boundless. Eva smiled at his enthusiasm and spoke in German. "What kind of parties do you have in America?"

"Wir haben . . ." He shook his head and leaned on the stoop railing and they both laughed. "I'd better stick to English."

"You drink mostly cocktails in America, isn't that so?"

"That isn't the difference. It's that we're not so gay." And he thought: the girls are all very intellectual and sympathetic.

"Why are you not gay? There is a time for that."

"Oh, I had a lot of friends at the university," he said, "but I guess I'm glad to get away for a time,"

"Then you are glad to be in Germany."

"Certainly . . . yes." He hesitated, uncertain whether to shake her hand. He knew handshaking was the custom here and he did not want to break any customs.

"Can you meet me tomorrow?" she asked.

"Yes. I'm free every night."

"I will be in front of the Berlitz Language School on Kaiserstrasse. I showed it to you today. Remember? At seven o'clock . . . Good-by, Alan." She turned and went up the steps, leaving him alone on the sidewalk.

He saw her often in the next two weeks. It seemed he had known her a long time and their meetings were a certainty nothing could interrupt. His work was a perfunctory routine, done with a detached efficiency that left the eight hours of motor pool dispatching a distant blur when his back was turned on the gate guard and he headed for Kirchendorf and the Berlitz school where she would be waiting. He tried to find the best restaurant in town, finally choosing a tiny Italian eating place where the veal parmigiano was as good as he remembered it in New York.

On Sunday they rented bicycles and rode in the fine morning through villages of toy houses and manure smells, Eva shouting at him to be careful of the curious children. They passed hayfields, low-lying along the Rhine, where peasants worked in wooden shoes near an Army Engineer pontoon bridge. In the afternoon they stopped for rolls and wine in view of the hills along the Neckar and later they went back again over the flowing Autobahn into the city.

The evening was cooler as he walked with Eva to 22 Goethestrasse and stood outside saying good-by. They kissed now, but quickly, and she did not invite him inside. As he walked back to the kasern from the end of the street-car line, passing the noise and lights of the GI gasthauses that did not seem so ominous now, he was glad to be going home before midnight feeling like a schoolboy back from a movie date.

The following Saturday he climbed the stairs to the door of the Enlisted Men's Club, pushing through into the large, quiet room. At seven o'clock the colored ripples of the jukebox already lighted the empty dance floor as wait-resses hurried with beer from the kitchen, putting it in the cooler behind the bar for the anticipated rush of Saturday night customers. The week had been a series of surprise inspections and restricted passes and he had not been able to meet Eva. Tonight, if he could get out, he would have to go to her apartment, she could not be expecting him.

He sat at a table and ordered bourbon, letting his arms hang, trying to force relaxation through himself. The inspection had been miserable. The officers passed the blame along, enriched by threats, down the chain of com-mand to the enlisted men who handled the details. "Shit always tends downward," Brad had philosophized from his critical position as company clerk. No one could plead operational expediency. Well, he would go over the fence tonight if Brad could not get him that pass. The matter-of-fact decision surprised him. A new freedom from the previous weeks with Eva had nourished him with strange valor.

A noise of shuffling feet and voices sounded beyond the door and a group of colored soldiers came in talking together too loudly for the artificial dusk of the room. One of them spoke to Alan as they passed toward the bar.

"What say, Greene."

"Hi, Charlie."

Charlie Smith detached himself from his friends who were already de-manding beer. His OD's were immaculate.

"Hey man," he said, "didn't that jive-ass captain say some shit down there today?" He leaned on Alan's table in the confidential manner of shared distress.

"He sure did, Charlie," said Alan. "I didn't think we'd get out of that motor pool alive."

Charlie was pleased. "I ain't gonna see mah fraulein tonight," he con-fided. "Son-a-bitch got our passes pulled."

"There are ways and there are ways," said Alan, almost glad to share his determination with the homely little fellow.

"Man, you goin' over the fence?" His face split in a grin. "I couldn't hack that. They already got me on article fourteen. I'm staying right here and get destroyed."

"That sounds like the best thing to do all right," said Alan. And he thought: please don't invite me to the bar.

"Well . . . gotta get started, man," Charlie said, standing straight and dropping his hands to his pockets. "There's good booze tonight." He winked and moved away to the jukebox, crouching before it motionless for a moment until the "Select" light glowed in response to his nickel. He punched and watched fascinated while the record swung over and down onto the turntable. Earl Bostic's "Liebestraum" filled the room. He snapped his fingers and shuffled to the bar in time to the music.

"Well, hello, PFC Greene." The voice was at his ear, bringing him back sharply from the mesmerizing beat of the music. "I didn't expect to catch you slumming at the jungle club."

"It's the whiskey, Earl. Tax-free, you know." Alan swallowed the last of his bourbon.

"Won't you have a drink with me," said Earl, "before the place is over-run with Negroid and Caucasian types?" He was tall and effeminately handsome in the incongruous olive-drab uniform.

Alan caught the waitress's eye as she stalked by and he made a ∨ with his fingers. "Two beers," he said. He knew Earl did not like beer.

"I've got to leave soon, after I sample the authentic, rustic atmosphere," said Earl. He reviewed the room as if for the first time. "It's not much like those Greenwich Village parties, is it, Alan? The girls they bring up here are usually such pigs."

"I'm surprised I never met you in New York," said Alan. "We must have been to some of the some places together. NYU's and Columbians traveled in the same set."

Earl threw back his head and opened his mouth carefully to laugh. "And slept with many of the same girls," he said.

Alan watched the minutely groomed mustache and gleaming teeth. Rule number one to be learned at school: Good Grooming. The whiteness looked so striking against the skin tone. Earl would look especially congenial seated on the floor beneath a Picasso reproduction in a crowded apartment off Lower Broadway, talking earnestly about Walter White and Thurgood Marshall to a sympathetically nodding white girl on her fourth or fifth drink.

Earl ignored the waitress as she placed the beer. "Ah, the girls," he said, "the white ones that looked you over from a little cabal of highball drinkers before they came over and said they thought they recognized you from the university. I looked like *such* a wonderful dancer. We are always wonderful dancers, aren't we?" He laughed again, showing his teeth.

Alan tilted his beer glass, letting the foam remain on his upper lip.

"They were so beautifully liberal," said Earl, "and so easy. It was almost a shame to take advantage of them. They thought we were all hung like stallions."

"You showed 'em, huh Earl."

"It was our responsibility, Alan, to promote intercourse between the races." Earl giggled.

They are capped, thought Alan, his goddam teeth are capped.

"In a way it was a duty," said Earl. "I admit a pleasant one. Don't tell me you didn't play the sensitive liberal with the best of us."

"And after you had them once," said Alan, "they wore it like a proud badge and introduced you to all their friends by your first name as if you were a pet cocker spaniel."

Earl's intimate eyes above the fine mustache and slender nostrils mocked back across the table, accusing.

"You know, don't you," said Earl. He held out a pack of cigarettes. "You and I are a special kind of people."

Alan stood up. "Not you and I, Earl. I'm not hung like a stallion." He walked quickly between the tables that were starting to fill, to the stairs and down, out onto the street.

The night was moonless. He might have a chance with the fence if the pass was not in his locker. He went inside the barracks, bounding the stairs to his room, and found it slipped inside on the top shelf.

He had no trouble at the gate and he cut across the field toward the lights of Kirchendorf that glowed on the low clouds like the last traces of twilight. He walked rapidly past the toylike houses and barking dogs until the texture of the close country merged with larger shapes and beginning traffic into the city's outskirts. He saw the first gasthauses on Kaiserstrasse and the taxis discharging soldiers into the yellow rinse of light on the sidewalk. The Rendezvous Club's neon glinted behind the streaked window and he could hear the twanging guitar music rush through the momentarily opened door. He crossed the street and went in.

Inside he stood at the bar and ordered. Near him a private leaned on a scarred plank table talking to a young girl. Heavy rouge clogged the freshness in her cheeks and her head moved in tiny, forlorn spasms preceding stupor.

"Hey Giesla. Gome on, baby. Let's get out of here," said the soldier.

"I wanna dance, Herby," she said.

"Look, I told you we can't dance here. Let's go to the Hawaii Bar where they got nigger music."

"O.K.," said the girl, and she lurched to stand up, spilling beer on the table top where it spread out and dripped through the cracks to the floor. They stumbled to the door supporting each other.

Alan crushed puddles of foam with the thick bottom of his glass. The music and the smoke and the chatter flowed around him and he suddenly felt very conspicuous standing alone. He would go to Eva now, around and between the insidious, unanswerable challenge of the sprawled legs and crowding shoulders and, once outside, straight through the city to Eva.

On the sidewalk the drunken girl clung to a lamppost. The soldier tried to pull her away.

"Come on Giesla, we're going to your place." He jerked roughtly at her coat and she began to swear in German.

Alan tried to step around them and the girl threw herself on him, clinging damply, the whole length of her body tight against his. She smelled of vomit.

"Dance, wanna dance," she murmured.

"You're sick, you're just sick," Alan said, trying to get away, nearly falling with her.

"Hey, what the hell," said the soldier.

The girl raised her head, blinking, to look into Alan's face. She giggled. "Dance, big black man . . ."

Alan pushed her away and the soldier's lunging swing struck her high on the head. She went down slowly, whimpering, her legs spread out in front of her on the pavement like those of a stuffed doll. The soldier did not glance at the girl but came at Alan again, shouting curses that brought the sidewalk's loitering GI's to life. Their shadows flickered abruptly in the light from the Rendezvous Club before they disappeared into the closer darkness ringing the streetlight. Alan punched quickly and leaped the curb, hearing the soldier grunt on the sidewalk behind him.

"Watch out he ain't got a razor!"

"There he goes! There goes the nigger!"

Their voices faded as he dashed across the street and down the opposite walk toward the center of the city.

His heart was still thumping when he slammed the taxi door and stood outside 22 Goethestrasse. He waited a moment, searching the windows for light before going cautiously to the entrance and into the hall.

"Eva, Eva." His tapping was loud in the dark.

She opened the door and stood in a robe, her back to the reading lamp beside the rumpled bed. He could not see her clearly.

"Come in, Alan . . . Is something wrong?"

"Nothing. Nothing. I just came up."

The door clicked lightly as she closed it. From a basket in the corner the cocked ear drooped and the bright eye closed as the tiny dog prepared again to sleep.

Eva went to the bed, pushing back, gently, a faded lavender blanket, trailing it on the floor. He watched the soft, certain motions ripple the sheer of her robe.

"Komm. Kommst du bei mir," she said.

He sat beside her.

"We have seen the city, Alan."

She touched his arms and he leaned forward, putting his face on the smoothness above her breasts, his hand taut on the bed.

"Why did you wait so long, Liebling?" she said. "Oh, you are trembling."

"There was a fight tonight." He paused hopelessly. "It was stupid."

"It was a white soldier?"

He did not answer.

"I know, Alan, I know. In Germany too there are those swine. The woman who owns this building is one of them, always saying the dark babies will be killed when the Americans leave. I spit at her." She slid her hand along his back, kneading gently, caressing. "Ah, you are beautiful. What can she know about it?"

His lips spoke silently into her robe: please, please be still.

"In America there are not people who say what you must choose. Alan, could I be happy in America?"

He was slipping forward. The folds of cloth pressed against his lips and he could not speak.

J. F. POWERS

HE DON'T
PLANT
COTTON

". . . Baby grimaced in torment and did his best to look like ol' Uncle Tom out snatchin' cotton. . . ."

SPRING entered the black belt in ashes, dust, and drabness, without benefit of the saving green. The seasons were known only by the thermometer and the clothing of the people. There were only a few nights in the whole year when the air itself told you. Perhaps a night in April or May might escape the plague of smells, achieve a little of the enchantment, be the diminished echo of spring happening ardently in the suburbs, but it was all over in a night and the streets were filled with summer, as a hollow mouth with bad breath, and even the rain could not wash it away. And winter . . .

The beginning snow swirled in from the lake, dusting the streets with white. Baby squinted down the lonesome tracks. The wind twisted snow into his eyes, the flakes as sharp as sand, grinding, and his eyeballs were coated with cold tears. Baby worked his hands in his overcoat pockets to make heat. He saw a woman cross the street to catch the Big Red, which was coming now, but the woman refused stiffly to run for it. The wind went off hooting down the tracks ahead. Baby got on. The conductor held out one hand for the fare and yanked a cord twice with the other, prodding the red monster into motion.

Baby sat down inside. A cold breeze swept the floor, rattling old transfers and gum wrappers. Baby placed his feet uneasily on the heater to make the meager warmth funnel up his pants' legs. The dark flesh beneath the tuxedo was chilled to chalky gray at the joints. He listened to the wheels bump over the breaks in the track, and the warmth from the heater rose higher on his legs. He became warm and forgetful of the weather, except as scenery. The streets were paved evenly with snow twinkling soft and clean and white under the lights, and velvet red and green from the neon signs.

New York may be all right, he hummed to himself, but Beale Street's paved with gold. That's a lie, he thought; I been down on Beale. And Chicago, same way. All my life playing jobs in Chicago, and I still got to ride the Big Red. And that's no lie. Jobs were getting harder and harder to find. What they wanted was Mickey Mouse sound effects, singing strings, electric guitars, neon violins, even organs and accordions and harmonica teams. Hard to find a spot to play in, and when you did it was always a white place with drunken advertising men wanting to hear "a old song"—"My Wild Irish Rose" or "I Love You Truly." So you played it, of course, and plenty of schmaltz. And the college kids who wanted swing—any slick popular song. So you played that, too. And always you wanted to play the music you were born to, blue or fast, music that had no name. You managed somehow to play that, too, when there was a lull or the place was empty and you had to stay until 4 A.M. anyway.

Baby got off the streetcar and walked the same two blocks he saw every night except Tuesday. The wind had died down almost entirely and the snow whirled in big flakes end over end. Padding along, Baby told himself he liked winter better than summer. Then he came to the place, said, "How's it, Chief?" to the doorman, an Indian passing for Negro, went down three steps, and forgot all about winter and summer. It was always the same here. It was not so much a place of temperatures as a place of lights and shades and chromium, pastel mirrors, the smell of beer, rum, whisky, smoke —a stale blend of odors and shadows, darkness and music. It was a place of only one climate and that was it.

Baby's overcoat, hat, and scarf went into a closet and settled familiarly on hooks. His old tuxedo walked over to the traps. Its black hands rubbed together briskly, driving out the chill. One hand fumbled in the dark at the base of the big drum, and a second later a watery blue light winked on dully and flooded the drumhead, staring like a blind blue eye. Immediately the tuxedo sat down and worked its feet with a slight rasping noise into the floor. The fingers thumped testingly on the hide, tightened the snare. They knew, like the ears, when it was right. Gingerly, as always, the right foot sought the big drum's pedal. The tuxedo was not ready yet. It had to fidget and massage its seat around on the chair, stretch out its arms, and hug the whole outfit a fraction of an inch this way and that. Then the eyes glanced at the piano player, signaling ready. The drumsticks paused a moment tensely, slid into the beat, barely heard, accenting perfectly the shower of piano notes. Everything worked together for two choruses. Then the piano player tapered his solo gently, so that at a certain point Baby knew it was his. He bought the number to a lifeless close, run down. Too early in the evening.

"Dodo," Baby said to the piano player, "Libby come in yet?"

Dodo sent a black hand up, slow as smoke, toward the ceiling. "Upstairs," he said, letting the hand fall to the keyboard with a faint, far-off chord. It stirred there, gently worming music from the battered upright. Notes drew nearer, riding on ships and camels through a world of sand and water, till they came forthright from the piano, taking on patterns, as the other black hand came to life on the bass keys, dear to Dodo. Baby picked up his sticks, recognizing the number. He called it "Dodo's Blues," though he knew Dodo called it nothing. Every night about this time, when there was no crowd and Dodo hadn't yet put on the white coat he wore servicing the bar, they would play it. Baby half closed his eyes. With pleasure he watched Dodo through the clouds of rhythm he felt shimmering up like heat from his drums. Baby's eyes were open only enough to frame Dodo like a picture; everything else was out. It was a picture of many dimensions; music was only one of them.

Here was a man, midgety, hunchbacked, black, and proud—mostly all back and music. A little man who, when he was fixing to play, had to look around for a couple of three-inch telephone directories. Piling them on top of the piano bench, he sat down, with all their names and streets and numbers and exchanges under him. He had very little of thighs and stomach— mostly just back, which threw a round shadow on the wall. When he leaned farther away from the piano, so the light slanted through his hands, his shadow revealed him walking on his hands down the keyboard, dancing on the tips of fingery toes. Sometimes it seemed to Baby through half-closed eyes, when Dodo's body was bobbing on the wall and his hands were feet dancing on the keyboard, as though the dim light shaped him into a gigantic, happy spider. When he became a spider you could forget he was a man, hunchbacked, runtish, black; and he, too, could forget perhaps that he had to be careful and proud. Perhaps he could be happy always if his back and size and color and pride were not always standing in the way. The piano made him whole. The piano taught him to find himself and jump clean over the moon. When he played, his feet never touched the pedals.

People were beginning to fill the place. They finished off the number, Baby smiling his admiration, Dodo scrupulously expressionless.

"For a young man . . ." Baby said.

Dodo got down off the telephone directories and threw them under the piano at the bass end, beyond the blue glow of the big drum. He had seen Libby come down the steps from the dressing room—a red dress, a gardenia. Dodo went behind the bar and put on his white service coat. Libby sat down at the piano.

Helplessly attracted, several men came over from the bar and leaned on the piano. They stared, burdening Libby's body with calculations. Singly at first and then, gathering unity, together. Libby sang a popular song. The men went back to the bar to get their drinks, which they brought over and set on top of the upright. Libby sang the words about lost love, and the men licked their lips vacantly. At the end of the song they clapped fiercely. Libby ignored them with a smile.

"Say, that was just fine," one man said. "Where you from anyhow?"

With a little grin Libby acknowledged Baby. Baby, beaming his veteran admiration of a fine young woman, nodded.

"Where you from? Huh?"

"New Orleans."

"Well, you don't say!" the man blurted out joyfully. "We're from down South, too . . . Mississippi, matter of fact!"

Icily, Libby smiled her appreciation of this coincidence. She looked at Baby, who was also registering appropriately. Just think of that! Small world! And welcome to our city!

"Well, what do you know!" crowed the gentleman from Mississippi. "So you're from down South!" He was greatly pleased and already very drunk. He eyed his friends, four or five of them, distributing his discovery equally among them.

"You never know," he explained. Then he appeared to suffer a pang of doubt. He turned quickly to Libby again, as though to make sure she was still there. His eyes jellied blearily and in them an idea was born.

"I know," he said. "Sing . . . sing—sing 'Ol' Man River' for the boys. They all'd sure like that."

Without responding, Libby looked down at her hands, smiling. She measured chords between her thumbs and little fingers, working her amusement into the keys. Baby stared at the mottled hide of his snare drum, at the big one's rim worn down from playing "Dixieland." The gentleman from Mississippi got worried.

"Aw, sing it," he pleaded. So Libby sang a chorus. The gentlemen from Mississippi were overwhelmed. They loved the song, they loved the South, the dear old Southland. Land of cotton, cinnamon seed, and sandy bottom. Look away! Look away! They loved themselves. Look away! Look away! There was the tiniest touch of satire in Libby's voice, a slightly overripe fervor. Baby caught it and behind the bar Dodo caught it, but the gentlemen did not. Dodo had put down the martini glass he was polishing and look away! look away!—good.

At the bridge of the second chorus, Libby nodded "Take it!" to Baby. He stood up, staggering from the heat of the fields, clenching his black, toilworn fists. In profound anguish, he hollered, giving the white folks his all, really knocking himself out.

> "Tote that bar!
> Lift that bale!
> Git a little drunk—"

Baby grimaced in torment and did his best to look like ol' Uncle Tom out snatchin' cotton.

Behind the bar, unnoticed, Dodo's sad black face had turned beatific. "—And you land in jail!" Dodo could not see the other faces, the big white ones, but he could imagine them, the heads fixed and tilted. It was too dark in the place, and he could make out only blurrily the outlines of the necks. Ordinarily he was capable only of hating them. Now he had risen to great

unfamiliar heights and was actually enjoying them. Surprised at this capacity in himself, yet proud he could feel this way, he was confused. He
went further and started to pity them. But his memory stood up outraged
at his forgetfulness and said, Kill that pity dead. Then he remembered he
was really alone in the place. It was different with Libby and Baby, though
they were black, too. He did not understand why. Say their skin was thicker
—only that was not why. Probably this was not the first time they had jived
white folks to death and them none the wiser. Dodo was not like that; he
had to wait a long time for his kicks. From his heart no pity went out for
the white men. He kept it all to himself, where it was needed. But he had
to smile inside of him with Libby and Baby. Only more. Look at that fool
Baby! Jam up!

> "Bend your knees!
> Bow your head!
> And pick that cotton!
> Tiiillllll you're dead!"

Baby sat down with a thud, exhausted. The gentlemen from Mississippi
brayed their pleasure. My, it was good to see that black boy all sweatin' and
perspirin' that way. They clapped furiously, called for drinks, gobbled . . .

"And bring some for the darkies!"

Baby swallowed some of his drink. He looked at the beaten rim of the
big drum, then at the sticks. He took out his pocketknife and scraped the
rough, splintery places smooth. He glanced at Libby and ventured the kind
of smile he felt and knew she did. He finished his drink. The gentlemen from
Mississippi hung around the piano, getting drunker, shouting in one another's
faces. Nervously, Libby lighted a cigarette. A college boy tried to make conversation with her while his honey-haired girl assumed an attitude of genuine concern.

"Can you play 'Hot Lips'?" He was the real American Boy.

"Don't know it," Libby lied. She wished she didn't.

"Can you play 'Sugar Blues'?" Right back.

"Don't know it."

One of the Mississippi gentlemen, who had been hanging back, crowded
up to the piano, making his move. He drained his drink and pushed closer
to the piano so as to brush Libby's left hand with the front of his trousers.
Libby moved her hand, sounding a chord that Baby caught. The gentleman,
grinning lewdly, tried to follow her hand up the keyboard.

"That's all right," he snickered. "Play lots of bass, honey."

The first gentleman from Mississippi, drink in hand, stumbled over from
the bar. He told Libby to play that "Ol' Man River" song some more. Libby
hesitated. Then she lit into it, improvising all around it, and it was a pleasure
for Baby, but the first gentleman from Mississippi was not happy. He said
if that was the best she could do she had better try singing. Libby sang only
one chorus. The gentlemen from Mississippi, though they applauded, were
not gratified. There was an air of petulance among them. They remembered

another time they heard the song, but it was not clear now what had made it different and better. They saw Baby all right, but they did not remember that he was the one who had sung before, the good one that toted their bars, lifted their bales, and landed drunk in their jails. Something was wrong, but they saw no remedy. Each gentleman suspected the fault was personal, what with him drinking so heavy and all.

Dodo, behind the bar, had not enjoyed the song the last time, hating the coercion the white men worked on Libby and Baby, and feared his advantage was slipping away. In a minute he would be hating them to pieces again.

"Can you play 'Tiger Rag'?" The American Boy was back.

"No." Libby made a face and then managed to turn it into a smile for him. He held his drink up for the world to see on the night before the big game.

The honey-haired girl wrenched her face into a winning smile and hit the jack pot. "Can you play 'St. Louis Blues'?"

"How you want it?" Libby said. She put out her cigarette. "Blues, rhumba . . . what kind a way?"

"Oh, play it low down. The way *you people* play it." So Libby would understand, she executed a ponderous wink, narrowed her eyes, and made them glitter wantonly behind the lashes. "*You* know," she said.

Libby knew. She played "St. Louis," losing herself in it with Baby. She left the college boy and the honey-haired girl behind. She forgot she knew. She gazed at Baby with her eyes dreamy, unseeing, blind with the blue drum, her head nodding in that wonderful, graceful way. Baby saw his old tuxedo in the mirror, its body shimmying on the chair, and he was pleased. The drums, beating figures, rocked with a steady roll. They were playing "Little Rock getaway" now, the fine, young-woman music.

And Libby was pleased, watching Baby. And then, somehow, he vanished for her into the blue drum. The sticks still danced at an oblique angle on the snare, but there were no hands to them and Libby could not see Baby on the chair. She could only feel him somewhere in the blue glow. Abandoning herself, she lost herself in the piano. Now, still without seeing him, she could feel him with a clarity and warmth beyond vision. Miniature bell notes, mostly blue, blossomed ecstatically, perished *affettuoso*, weaving themselves down into the dark beauty of the lower keys, because it was closer to the drum, and multiplied. They came back to "St. Louis" again.

"Stop." The first gentleman from Mississippi touched Libby on the arm. "When I do that to you, that means 'Stop,'" he said. Libby chorded easily. "Some of the boys like to hear that 'ol' Man River' some more." He straightened up, turning to the other gentlemen, his smile assuring them it would not be long now.

"Kick off," Baby sighed.

But Libby broke into "St. Louis" again. Baby, with a little whoop, came clambering after, his sticks slicing into the drum rim, a staccato "Dixieland."

The first gentleman frowned, touching Libby's arm, "Remember what that means? Means 'Ol' Man River,' " he said calmly, as though correcting a slight error. "Toot sweet. Know what that means? That's French. Means right now." No harm done, however. Just that his friends here, a bunch of boys from down South, were dying to hear that song again—up to him to see that they got satisfaction—knew there would be no trouble about it.

"We'll play it for you later on," Libby said quickly. "We got some other requests besides yours. How many you got now, Baby?

Baby held up eight fingers, very prompt.

"Coming up," he said.

The first gentleman was undecided. "Well . . ." he drawled. Libby began a popular song. The first gentleman faced his friends. His eyes more or less met theirs and found no agreement. The boys looked kind of impatient, like a bunch of boys out for a little fun and not doing so well. He turned to Libby again.

"We just gotta have that 'Ol' Man River' some more. Boys all got their hearts set on it," he said. "Right away! Toot sweet! Toot—away!" There he'd gone and made a joke, and the boys all laughed and repeated it to each other. Libby played on, as though she had not heard. The first gentleman took hold of her arm. She gazed steadily up into his bleary eyes.

"Not now. Later."

"No, you don't. You gotta play it right now. For a bunch of boys from down South. They all got a hankerin' to hear that 'Ol' Man River' some more."

"So you best play it," another gentleman said, leaning down hard on the old upright piano. "On account of I'm gonna take and give ear. We kinda like how that old song sounds up North. Whatcha all need. The drummer will sing," he said, and looked at Baby. Baby looked back, unsmiling.

Libby chorded lightly, waiting for the gentlemen from Mississippi to get tired. They could not see how it was with her and Baby—never.

"You ain't gonna play?"

Baby's eyes strained hard in their sockets.

"We ain't comin'," Libby said.

Baby's eyes relaxed and he knew the worst part was over. They felt the same way about it. They had made up their minds. The rest was easy. Baby was even a little glad it had happened. A feeling was growing within him that he had wanted to do this for a long time—for years and years, in a hundred different places he had played.

Secretly majestic, Baby sat at his drums, the goal of countless uplifted eyes—beseeching him. For it seemed that hordes of white people were far below him, making their little commotions and noises, asking favors of him, like Lord, please bring the rain, or Lord, please take it away. Lord Baby. Waves of warm exhilaration washed into him, endearing him to himself. No, he smiled, I am sorry, no favors today. Yes, Lord, they all said, if that's the way it is, so be it.

But somebody objected. The manager's voice barked, far below, scarcely audible to Baby in his new eminence. ". . . honoring requests," he heard, and ". . . trouble with the local," and ". . . wanting to get a sweet-swing trio in this place a long time now." And the manager, strangely small, an excited, pale pygmy, explaining to the gentlemen from Mississippi, also small, how it was, "That's all I can do in the circumstances," and them saying, "Well, I guess so; well, I guess so all right; don't pay to pamper 'em, to give 'em an inch."

Baby noticed Libby had got up from the piano and put on her coat, the long dress hanging out at the bottom, red.

"I won't change," she said, and handed Baby the canvas cover for the snare drum.

"Huh?" Baby said foggily. He set about taking his traps apart. Dodo, not wearing his white service coat, came over to help.

"You don't have to," Baby said.

Chief, freezing outside in his long, fancy maroon coat, opened the door for them. "You all through, Baby?"

"Yeah, Chief. You told that right."

They walked down the street toward the car line. Baby, going first, plowed a path for Libby and Dodo in the snow. Window sills, parked cars, and trees were padded with it. The wind was dead and buried. Baby bore the big drum on his shoulder and felt the sticks pressing tight and upright in his vest pockets, two on each side. Libby had her purse and street clothes rolled up under her arm. Dodo carried the snare drum.

Softly as snow, Libby laughed, "That's all I can do in the circumstances," she said.

"I got your old circumstances," Baby said.

Then they were silent, tramping in the snow.

At the corner they waited in a store entrance for a southbound streetcar. Libby raised a foot now and then, shuddering with cold. Dead still, Dodo breathed down inside the collar of his overcoat, retarding his breath, frowning at the little smoke trickling out, as though it were the only thing left in the world to remind him he was alive. Baby talked of taking a cab and finally did go out into the street to hail one approaching. It slowed up, pulled over to the curb, hesitated . . . and lurched away, with Baby's hand reaching for the door. Baby watched the cab speed down the snowy street, following it for a few steps, speechless. There was nothing to do. Without looking, he saw Libby and Dodo shivering in the store entrance. They had seen the cab come and go. They had not moved an inch. They waited unfooled, as before, for the Big Red.

"What's wrong with you, Baby?" Libby called out. A tiny moment of silence, and she was laughing, gradually louder, mellow octaves of it, mounting, pluming . . .

Like her piano, it seemed to Baby—that fine, young-woman laughter.

"Why you laugh so much, woman?" he inquired plaintively from the street. Then he moved to join them, a few steps only, dallying at the curb to temper the abruptness of his retreat. Like her piano on "Little Rock"— that fine, young-woman laughter.

THE WATCHERS

"...She found a small acid gun in Sally's
purse and a knife in the pocket of her jacket.
'Just put them on the table,' Althea directed,
'and then sit down. Would you like some
coffee?'..."

FROM the moment Althea awoke that morning, she knew their building had been chosen. She knew it even before she saw the excitement in her husband's eyes as he handed her the official notice that had been put under their door.

"Well," he said, smiling at her while she read it, "what do you think of that?"

"I had a feeling, George," she said, "even before I opened my eyes, I had a feeling that this would happen today."

"We were due to be next," George said. "The setup here is about perfect for it."

"Will you be home early?" She watched him while he sipped his coffee.

"It won't start until late," he said. "It won't start until it gets dark. You know how these things are."

"Just the same," she said, "I couldn't bear it just sitting around and waiting for you. We have so much to do. We have to have dinner first and then change our clothes and find seats. We want to have good seats," she reminded him. "They won't reserve any for us, you know."

"Don't worry about it." He touched her cheek lightly with the back of his hand. "I'll be home in plenty of time."

"Do you have everything? I was never so scared in my life yesterday when I found your gun on the top of the dresser. I just couldn't believe my eyes. I wanted to run after you but I didn't know which route you had taken."

"I always carry a spare," he said. "You know that. I always keep a spare in my coat pocket. Why don't you trust me?"

"I know I'm being foolish," Althea said, kissing him goodbye. "Just be careful, that's all. I don't want you to be so sure of yourself that you'll get careless."

"You be careful," he said. "Do you have to go out today?"

She frowned. "I have to go marketing, and then I thought I'd go downtown and buy a new dress for tonight. All the women will be dressed up and I don't want to go looking like a frump."

"Watch out for the department stores," he reminded her. "They can be dangerous. Don't take any crowded elevators and check the dressing room before you try anything on."

She locked and double-locked the door after him, then fastened the chain before she had her own breakfast. Standing at the window while she drank her coffee, she thought how ridiculous it was the way they went through the same routine each morning as if the very fact that they had to take precautions was making them nervous. When they were first married two years ago, it would never have occurred to either of them that there was any reason for worry.

It must be because we're so much in love, she told herself, stacking the dishes in the washer. Love breeds its own vulnerability, its own fear.

When the signal flashed on the wall, Althea had just finished dressing. She watched it for a moment. It was their code, all right. Three lights in a row, the flickering pause, and then the slow, deliberate hold. She pressed the button that buzzed downstairs.

"Who is it?" she said, her mouth against the intercom.

"It's all right," said a woman's voice, clear and high and a bit too shrill. "I've already shown my identification to your doorman. I'm Sally Milford—Cary Milford's wife. My husband works in your husband's office."

"What do you want?" said Althea cautiously. "I'm much too busy to see anyone this morning. Besides, I'm on my way out." She bit her lip. George would be right if he scolded her for being careless. Why had she told this woman she was going out?

"I'll only take a moment of your time. It's important."

"Can't you tell me what it is over the intercom?"

"If I wanted to talk this way, I could have called you on the phone. I must see you. Please."

"All right," said Althea, reluctantly, knowing she was being foolish, "you can come up."

She checked her own gun even though she knew it was loaded and she palmed the small dagger—the one her mother had given her as a wedding present—the one with the jeweled handle.

"Things are so different now," her mother had said, sighing. She had lifted the dagger from the tissue paper and had studied it for a moment before she handed it to Althea. "In my day we could walk the streets without this sort of thing."

"That's not true," Althea reminded her. "You told me you used to wear stilt-like heels and you always carried a whistle in your purse."

"But that's not the same. It still wasn't like this," said her mother. "Did you know we weren't allowed to carry weapons?"

"You weren't?" said Althea, startled.

"That was before everyone realized that our laws were lagging behind our customs and public opinion. That was before the Citizen's Defense Act was passed."

"There is only one crime," Althea said firmly, "and that is to be a victim. Nothing makes sense otherwise."

"I suppose not." Her mother shook her head. "I guess I'm just being sentimental," she added wistfully. "Sometimes I miss the policemen we used to have. They would wear blue uniforms and they would drive around with sirens blaring and lights flashing. It seems a shame they became obsolete. Why I can even remember the time when we could take a walk in the park."

"In the park?" said Althea, incredulous. "You could actually do that?"

Now Althea bit her lip. There was no point in daydreaming. She stationed herself at the one-way peephole. The woman who now came within her range of vision was thin of face and well-dressed. She blinked her eyes nervously and hesitated before she knocked.

"Just a moment," said Althea. She unfastened the chain and the two locks, and then stepped back so that when the door opened she would be behind it. "Come in," she said.

"Where are you?"

"Right behind you," said Althea, her hand on her gun. "You're not very smart to walk right in like that, are you?"

"But I know who you are," said Sally Milford, her eyes wide with fright. "My husband and your husband are good friends."

"The first thing you have to learn," said Althea, "is not to trust anyone." She kicked the door shut. "Hold up your hands." She found a small acid gun in Sally's purse and a knife in the pocket of her jacket. "Just put them on the table," Althea directed, "and then sit down. Would you like some coffee?"

Sally shook her head, "Look," she said, her mouth trembling, "I wouldn't trouble you like this—I wouldn't have come at all if I didn't, in a way, know you. You see that, don't you?"

"No," said Althea firmly, "I don't see anything. Suppose you tell me what you want."

Sally clasped her hands on the edge of the table. "I have a brother-in-law who knows someone on the Board of Commissioners," she said, leaning forward in her eagerness, "and we heard that your apartment house has been chosen."

"These things are supposed to be a secret," Althea said sharply. "No one except the people involved is supposed to know. Don't you realize what can happen to you if they find out? And what can happen to me?"

"I'm sorry but I just couldn't help it. When I heard about it—all I could think was that I simply had to go. I have never been to a performance and, the way things look, I'll never have a chance."

"Where do you live?" Althea asked, putting the gun away.

"On the East Side. You know how safe it's getting to be over there. We haven't had an incident in months."

"That doesn't mean they won't choose your building eventually."

"Do you really think they will?"

"Why not?" said Althea.

"Then, in that case, why can't you make believe that we're visiting you or something? They do have special passes for visitors and then, when we're finally chosen, we could reciprocate. Cary and I could invite you and George. That way we could each see two performances."

"It wouldn't work," said Althea. "In the first place, we have the perfect setting for this sort of thing. That's why we picked this particular apartment building. We could have had a much better place to live but both George and I agreed that our best chance was being here. We had to wait two years for this day, and if they ever suspect that this was a put-up thing, you know what would happen to us."

"I suppose I was foolish to even hope." Sally stood up. "I thought it would work out."

"It won't," said Althea, feeling a sudden pity for her. "Believe me, Sally, it won't. I happen to know that Mrs. Tremont, who lives on the third floor, has her sister-in-law staying with her; that, of course, makes it possible for her sister-in-law to go tonight, but if she had just arrived today someone would be sure to report it and Mrs. Tremont would get into trouble."

"You said you were going out," said Sally. "Do you want a ride with me?"

"I'm going downtown," said Althea. "I thought I'd buy a new dress for tonight."

"I haven't been shopping in ages," said Sally. "Cary won't let me go without him and he's been much too busy on Saturdays. We could shop together and maybe have lunch."

"Just remember one thing," Althea warned as she reached for her coat and hat. "No matter what you say, I won't change my mind. You can spend the whole day with me if you like but I still won't change my mind."

"I know you're right," said Sally as they pressed the button for the elevator. "It's just that I'm glad to have some company on the subway."

"Are you still taking the subway?" Althea stared at her, amazed. "George insists that I take the bus. Not taxis—they're not too reliable anymore but a bus is still fine."

"It takes too long," said Sally. "The subway is much quicker. I have my own system. I never wait on a platform if I'm alone and I usually ride in the first car where the motorman is and, just in case anyone is following me, I change at every other stop."

"Now," said Althea, watching as the elevator stopped at their floor, "run!"

They pounded through the corridor and down one flight of steps. Then they rang for the elevator again. When it arrived, it was empty and they rode it the rest of the way down.

It turned out to be, Althea told George later, a rather pleasant day. With the two of them together, the shopping proved much easier. Sally stood watch while Althea tried on dresses and Althea stood guard while Sally shopped. When they finally parted, it was after four.

Althea took a bus uptown again and got off three blocks before her destination. She glanced behind to make sure she wasn't being followed; then she bought a steak at the meat market. Steak would be the quickest thing to cook for dinner and she didn't want to load her arms with too many packages. It was difficult enough carrying the dress, although she had insisted that the clerk put it in a shopping bag instead of a box. With a shopping bag she would feel less clumsy and have one hand free.

The doorman beamed at her when she entered the lobby.

"This is a great day for us," he said.

Althea nodded. "I bought a new dress," she told him happily, "a black sheath."

"I'll ride the elevator with you if you like," he offered generously. "Most of the tenants are home by now."

"You're not supposed to leave your post," Althea reminded him. "Anyone could come in while you were away. You know what happened to the last doorman we had?"

"You're right," he admitted. "For a moment I forgot."

"By the way," she whispered, "do you know who will be giving the performance?"

He shook his head. "No one knows," he said. "I've been asking but no one knows for sure. I think it's a young one. They usually are."

"You'd think those kids could learn," said Althea, ringing for the elevator. "My parents were pretty strict with me—I can tell you that."

"That's the best way," the doorman said. "You have to be firm with them. I always say that from the time they can walk, they can be taught. Now, you take that kid of Mrs. Hammond. You know the Hammonds on the fifth floor? He got his first slash today and was sent home from school in disgrace."

"Oh, no," said Althea, in horror. "He's only eleven. He's only allowed two more mistakes."

"The way Mrs. Hammond spanked him, he'll learn," the doorman said. "That'll never happen to him again, I can tell you that."

"Who was the other boy?"

"It was a girl," said the doorman. "A pretty little thing, I understand. Well, she'll get her first gold star for that."

"I got a gold star when I was twelve," said Althea, stepping into the elevator.

She rode it to the fourth floor and got out. She took the stairs the rest of the way, then stood before her own front door for a moment, listening. When she was positive it was safe, she inserted her key in the lock.

At precisely six o'clock George came home and, by seven thirty, they had finished dinner and were dressed.

"I'd like to go now," said Althea, impatiently.

"It won't get dark until eight," George said. "You know how it is this time of year. Even then, we'll have to wait a while."

"I can see the stands from here," said Althea, craning her neck as she peered out of the window. "People are beginning to arrive now. Please, darling, let's go."

"You're like a child," he said, hugging her. "Just an anxious little kid."

"I can't help it," she said. "I'm excited. Aren't you thrilled, George?"

"Come on," he said, indulgently. He looked at her, chic and lovely in her new black sheath. "No pockets," he said, shaking his head. "What made you buy a dress without any pockets? I didn't know they made them that way anymore."

"I'll only wear it when I'm with you," she said. "Besides, I have a knife in my purse."

"Just see that you keep it handy." He held the door for her. "I'm glad you used your head this morning."

"For a moment I was tempted," Althea confessed. "Sally seems like a sweet person and it might be fun if we could go there sometimes, but then I realized we'd be taking a chance."

"It doesn't pay to take chances," said George. "Otherwise you can end up giving the performance instead of watching it."

"The doorman told me it was a young one. Probably a girl."

"It usually is," said George.

"Do you know what she did?" Althea asked as they walked through the back of the lobby and out into the courtyard. "No one seems to know what she did."

"Probably something stupid," said George, looking around and waving to their neighbors. "You know, honey, you were right. The stands are filling up."

The stands had been placed next to their building. They were permanent, sturdily built of brick and stone, and erected when the building itself had been new. Optimistically every building had its stands ready for the day when it would be chosen, and Althea looked around proudly as she and George found seats in the second row.

Mr. and Mrs. Hammond were there and seated between them was their son, Timmy. Timmy's right arm was bandaged and he huddled close to his mother.

"I heard about it," said Althea, with sympathy. "I'm sure Timmy will never let it happen again."

"Because she was pretty. Because it was a girl," said Mrs. Hammond bitterly. "She called to him and he ran right over, leaving his knife in his pocket as if a knife ever did anybody any good in a pocket. Just because it was a little girl, he trusted her. But he's learned his lesson, haven't you, Timmy?" she said, slapping him across the face.

"No more," Timmy wept, putting his bandaged arm across his eyes. "Please, Mommy, don't hit me anymore."

He'll never amount to anything, Althea thought, staring at him in dismay. Only three chances and he's used up one already. He's too soft. When I have a child—

She thought about it for a moment, longing for a child but the apartment they were in was too small and they hadn't wanted to move until they had a chance at a performance. Maybe now—maybe now that they were finally spectators—perhaps now that the longed-for, dreamed-about moment had finally arrived, they could move to a larger place and she would have a child.

"You have to train them from the beginning," she whispered to George.

"Sure," he said, knowing what she meant. "It won't happen to us."

"It won't happen to us," she agreed, seeing the way George, even now, even at this moment of pleasure and relaxation, kept his hand in his pocket; George's hand curled over the bulge of his gun.

Althea leaned back. She had known, of course, what the stage setting would be but, just the same, sitting there, part of the expectant, eager audience, she had to admire its reality.

It represented a street scene. It could have been Althea's own street with its middle-class, red-brick buildings, the old-fashioned canopies extending from the wide entrances to the edge of the curb. Behind the lighted windows of the buildings, Althea could see the people, all the families together, having dinner, watching television, reading, talking, laughing—all the people of the city settling down for the night.

In the center of the stage was a street lamp, still unlit although it was twilight now; on the far right, there was à fire hydrant. The first floor of the center building was occupied by a shop. The sign said, "ANTIQUES," and Althea could see the lovely things in the window—the paintings in the carved, ornate frames, the delicate crystal goblets, a curved brass bowl. Suddenly the street light went on, dominating the center of the stage with its soft, gentle glow.

The curtain is rising, thought Althea, taking a deep breath. She always loved that moment in the theater, that magic moment when all the murmuring and the movement and the whispering stopped, the hush and wonder when the curtain rose and the stage lay there before them, the play ready to begin.

Someone somewhere in the back coughed and Althea drew a deep, sighing gasp of impatience.

The stage became alive. From the center building a man emerged, a nondescript man walking his dog at night. The dog tugged and the man whistled softly between his teeth as the two of them walked down the street. The stage became empty again and Althea clasped her hands in her lap, amazed to discover that they were shaking.

At the far right two shadows blurred, moved, took form. Now a girl and a boy strolled down the street. His arm was flung around her shoulders and, from the way she smiled at him, Althea knew they were in love. They moved slowly across the stage. They stopped before the antique shop and the girl pointed to the brass bowl and the boy nodded and gestured expansively, showing her there was nothing in the world he wouldn't get for her. They disappeared on the far left and the stage was empty again.

Althea unclasped her hands and, because her palms were wet, she rubbed them furtively together. Beside her she could hear the sound of George's breathing, slow, heavy, as if each breath were an effort.

Onstage, in the lighted backdrop, in the center building, some of the windows began to darken as if the occupants were retiring for the night.

It's getting late, thought Althea, watching. The lights are dimming all over the city. People are yawning and stretching and getting into bed and even the sounds of the distant traffic seem muted as if someone had muffled all the rolling wheels.

A shadow, part of the shadow of the building, almost part of the square shape of the center building, took on form, and Althea saw that it was a man, a man who had been there all the time, hiding there without her being conscious of his presence.

From the far right she could hear the clicking of high heels on the pavement. Someone else, she thought, will walk down this street this night.

There was a rustle and a stir in the stands.

"Please, Mommy," Timmy whispered. "I don't want to stay here."

"Oh, you'll stay all right," said Mrs. Hammond grimly. "You just open your eyes wide. You watch everything, Timmy Hammond, if you know what's good for you."

"Be quiet down there," someone hissed. "Do you want to spoil everything?"

Althea gripped George's arm.

The footsteps grew louder and a girl came into view, entering downstage from the right. The shadow that was the man moved, and then became very still, waiting.

The girl moved across the stage. She paused under the street light. She touched the lamppost as if the feel of it under her fingers gave her some sort of reassurance. She hesitated, reluctant to leave the light.

Althea could see her clearly now. She was very young. She could be no more than nineteen—perhaps twenty. She wore a red suit and a little red beret with a feather stuck jauntily in it and her handbag was tucked under her arm. Her hair was blond and it tumbled loose over her shoulders.

Althea watched absorbed as the second figure moved again, the man crouching and then straightening as he ran toward the light, toward the girl in the red suit. At the clear view of his black-jacketed, black-clad figure, there was a sudden roar of applause. Althea clapped until her hands ached.

Out of the dark, into the light, he moved. The girl had her back toward him, not seeing him as the watchers saw him—sinuous, beautiful in his grace, tall, broad of shoulder, his hair allowed to grow long in back and his black cap set on the back of his head. The knife in his hand caught the light and sparkled.

He ran and then stopped. Deliberately, he stalked her. Professional that he was, he began to move slowly, coming down light on the balls of his feet.

The girl whirled around and, at the sight of him, she made a little whimpering sound in her throat. Her back now to the audience, she darted to the left and, as if they were part of a rigid dance pattern, the man stepped after her. She turned and ran to the right, her heels clicking frantically but he was there before her.

"Please," said the girl in the red suit. She darted back to the lamppost, back where the light was the brightest, where she could be seen most clearly. She turned and faced the backdrop, faced the buildings, the windows where the people were. Her right hand still clutched her purse, her left was now at her throat.

"Oh, please." Her voice rose to a keening wail of terror and anguish.

"Please," she screamed, her voice begging, her body begging. Then blindly she turned again and ran.

This cry in the night had awakened the sleepers. It had roused the dreamers. The darkened windows in the backdrop were illuminated again. Figures moved; there were silhouettes framed in the windows. The sleepers were awake. The dreamers had stopped dreaming and the city was alert and watching.

"Help me."

The city held its breath and listened.

"Please, help me."

But, Althea saw, she couldn't run far enough. She couldn't run fast enough. The man had her pinned against the wall now, pinned against the lighted, listening backdrop of the building and her handbag fell to the ground.

"I beg you." She was almost hidden by the man's bulk as he bent over her. "Won't someone help me?"

The man in the black jacket raised his arm and the knife flashed. The girl screamed in agony, her cheek now as crimson as her suit. Dodging under his arm, she ran again, the slowing rhythm of her clicking heels the only sound to be heard.

The man watched her for a moment. The quiet, lighted windows watched and the filled stands watched. The man stood very still as if he were resting and then, gracefully, quickly, easily, he caught her again.

That does it, thought Althea. her heart pounding; that does it.

The knife gleamed and Althea held her breath. The arm lifted. The black-draped arm lifted and fell, lifted and fell. The red suit crumpled, falling as if it were empty, the red suit only a splotch now on the pavement. Then the man moved toward the hushed, absorbed watchers.

And there he stood, bowing and smiling, the knife dripping red at his side. Over and over again he took his bow while they all gave him the ultimate, the supreme tribute of their silence.

MAX SHULMAN

LOVE IS
A FALLACY

*"... It is after all, easier to make a beautiful
dumb girl smart than to make an ugly smart
girl beautiful...."*

CHARLES Lamb, as merry and enterprising a fellow as you will meet in a
month of Sundays, unfettered the informal essay with his memorable *Old
China* and *Dream Children*. There follows an informal essay that ventures
even beyond Lamb's frontier. Indeed, "informal" may not be quite the right
word to describe this essay; "limp" or "flaccid" or possibly "spongy" are perhaps more appropriate.

Vague though its category, it is without doubt an essay. It develops an
argument; it cites instances; it reaches a conclusion. Could Carlyle do more?
Could Ruskin?

Read, then, the following essay which undertakes to demonstrate that
logic, far from being a dry, pedantic discipline, is a living, breathing thing,
full of beauty, passion, and trauma.

—AUTHOR'S NOTE

Cool was I and logical. Keen, calculating, perspicacious, acute and astute
—I was all of these. My brain was as powerful as a dynamo, as precise as a
chemist's scales, as penetrating as a scalpel. And—think of it!—I was only
eighteen.

It is not often that one so young has such a giant intellect. Take, for example, Petey Burch, my roommate at the University of Minnesota. Same
age, same background, but dumb as an ox. A nice enough fellow, you understand, but nothing upstairs. Emotional type. Unstable. Impressionable.
Worst of all, a faddist. Fads, I submit, are the very negation of reason. To be
swept up in every new craze that comes along, to surrender yourself to idiocy
just because everybody else is doing it—this, to me, is the acme of mindless-
ness. Not, however, to Petey.

One afternoon I found Petey lying on his bed with an expression of such distress on his face that I immediately diagnosed appendicitis. "Don't move," I said. "Don't take a laxative. I'll get a doctor."

"Raccoon," he mumbled thickly.

"Raccoon?" I said, pausing in my flight.

"I want a raccoon coat," he wailed.

I perceived that his trouble was not physical, but mental. "Why do you want a raccoon coat?"

"I should have known it," he cried, pounding his temples. "I should have known they'd come back when the Charleston came back. Like a fool I spent all my money for textbooks, and now I can't get a raccoon coat."

"Can you mean," I said incredulously, "that people are actually wearing raccoon coats again?"

"All the Big Men on Campus are wearing them. Where've you been?"

"In the library," I said, naming a place not frequented by Big Men on Campus.

He leaped from the bed and paced the room. "I've got to have a raccoon coat," he said passionately. "I've got to!"

"Petey, why? Look at it rationally. Raccoon coats are unsanitary. They shed. They smell bad. They weigh too much. They're unsightly. They—"

"You don't understand," he interrupted impatiently. "It's the thing to do. Don't you want to be in the swim?"

"No," I said truthfully.

"Well, I do," he declared. "I'd give anything for a raccoon coat. Anything!"

My brain, that precision instrument, slipped into high gear. "Anything?" I asked, looking at him narrowly.

"Anything," he affirmed in ringing tones.

I stroked my chin thoughtfully. It so happened that I knew where to get my hands on a raccoon coat. My father had had one in his undergraduate days; it lay now in a trunk in the attic back home. It also happened that Petey had something I wanted. He didn't *have* it exactly, but at least he had first rights on it. I refer to his girl, Polly Espy.

I had long coveted Polly Espy. Let me emphasize that my desire for this young woman was not emotional in nature. She was, to be sure, a girl who excited the emotions, but I was not one to let my heart rule my head. I wanted Polly for a shrewdly calculated, entirely cerebral reason.

I was a freshman in law school. In a few years I would be out in practice. I was well aware of the importance of the right kind of wife in furthering a lawyer's career. The successful lawyers I had observed were, almost without exception, married to beautiful, gracious, intelligent women. With one omission, Polly fitted these specifications perfectly.

Beautiful she was. She was not yet of pin-up proportions, but I felt sure that time would supply the lack. She already had the makings.

Gracious she was. By gracious I mean full of graces. She had an erectness of carriage, an ease of bearing, a poise that clearly indicated the best of breeding. At table her manners were exquisite. I had seen her at the Kozy Kampus Korner eating the specialty of the house—a sandwich that con-

tained scraps of pot roast, gravy, chopped nuts, and a dipper of sauerkraut—
without even getting her fingers moist.

Intelligent she was not. In fact, she veered in the opposite direction. But I
believed that under my guidance she would smarten up. At any rate, it was
worth a try. It is, after all, easier to make a beautiful dumb girl smart than to
make an ugly smart girl beautiful.

"Petey," I said, "are you in love with Polly Espy?"

"I think she's a keen kid," he replied, "but I don't know if you'd call it
love. Why?"

"Do you," I asked, "have any kind of formal arrangement with her? I
mean are you going steady or anything like that?"

"No. We see each other quite a bit, but we both have other dates. Why?"

"Is there," I asked, "any other man for whom she has a particular fond-
ness?"

"Not that I know of. Why?"

I nodded with satisfaction. "In other words, if you were out of the picture,
the field would be open. Is that right?"

"I guess so. What are you getting at?"

"Nothing, nothing," I said innocently, and took my suitcase out of the
closet.

"Where are you going?" asked Petey.

"Home for the weekend." I threw a few things into the bag.

"Listen," he said, clutching my arm eagerly, "while you're home, you
couldn't get some money from your old man, could you, and lend it to me so
I can buy a raccoon coat?"

"I may do better than that," I said with a mysterious wink and closed
my bag and left.

"Look," I said to Petey when I got back Monday morning. I threw open the
suitcase and revealed the huge, hairy, gamy object that my father had worn
in his Stutz Bearcat in 1925.

"Holy Toledo!" said Petey reverently. He plunged his hands into the raccoon coat and then his face. "Holy Toledo!" he repeated fifteen or twenty
times.

"Would you like it?" I asked.

"Oh yes!" he cried, clutching the greasy pelt to him. Then a canny look
came into his eyes. "What do you want for it?"

"Your girl," I said, mincing no words.

"Polly?" he said in a horrified whisper. "You want Polly?"

"That's right."

He flung the coat from him. "Never," he said stoutly.

I shrugged. "Okay. If you don't want to be in the swim, I guess it's your
business."

I sat down in a chair and pretended to read a book, but out of the corner of
my eye I kept watching Petey. He was a torn man. First he looked at the
coat with the expression of a waif at a bakery window. Then he turned away
and set his jaw resolutely. Then he looked back at the coat, with even more

longing in his face. Then he turned away, but with not so much resolution this time. Back and forth his head swiveled, desire waxing, resolution waning. Finally he didn't turn away at all; he just stood and stared with mad lust at the coat.

"It isn't as though I was in love with Polly," he said thickly. "Or going steady or anything like that."

"That's right," I murmured.

"What's Polly to me, or me to Polly?"

"Not a thing," said I.

"It's just been a casual kick—just a few laughs, that's all."

"Try on the coat," said I.

He complied. The coat bunched high over his ears and dropped all the way down to his shoe tops. He looked like a mound of dead raccoons. "Fits fine, he said happily.

I rose from my chair. "Is it a deal?" I asked, extending my hand.

He swallowed. "It's a deal," he said and shook my hand.

I had my first date with Polly the following evening. This was in the nature of a survey; I wanted to find out just how much work I had to do to get her mind up to the standard I required. I took her first to dinner. "Gee, that was a delish dinner," she said as we left the restaurant. Then I took her to a movie. "Gee, that was a marvy movie," she said as we left the theater. And then I took her home. "Gee, I had a sensaysh time," she said as she bade me good night.

I went back to my room with a heavy heart. I had gravely underestimated the size of my task. This girl's lack of information was terrifying. Nor would it be enough merely to supply her with information. First she had to be taught to *think*. This loomed as a project of no small dimensions, and at first I was tempted to give her back to Petey. But then I got to thinking about her abundant physical charms and about the way she entered a room and the way she handled a knife and fork, and I decided to make an effort.

I went about it, as in all things, systematically. I gave her a course in logic. It happened that I, as a law student, was taking a course in logic myself, so I had all the facts at my finger tips. "Polly," I said to her when I picked her up on our next date, "tonight we are going over to the Knoll and talk."

"Oo, terrif," she replied. One thing I will say for this girl: you would go far to find another so agreeable.

We went to the Knoll, the campus trysting place, and we sat down under an old oak, and she looked at me expectantly. "What are we going to talk about?" she asked.

"Logic."

She thought this over for a minute and decided she liked it. "Magnif," she said.

"Logic," I said clearing my throat, "is the science of thinking. Before we can think correctly, we must first learn to recognize the common fallacies of logic. These we will take up tonight."

"Wow-dow!" she cried, clapping her hands delightedly.

I winced, but went bravely on. "First let us examine the fallacy called Dicto Simpliciter."

"By all means," she urged, batting her lashes eagerly.

"Dicto Simpliciter means an argument based on an unqualified generalization. For example: Exercise is good. Therefore everybody should exercise."

"I agree," said Polly earnestly. "I mean exercise is wonderful. I mean it builds the body and everything."

"Polly," I said gently, "the argument is a fallacy. *Exercise is good* is an unqualified generalization. For instance, if you have heart disease, exercise is bad, not good. Many people are ordered by their doctors *not* to exercise. You must *qualify* the generalization. You must say exercise is *usually* good, or exercise is good *for most people*. Otherwise you have committed a Dicto Simpliciter. Do you see?"

"No," she confessed. "But this is marvy. Do more! Do more!"

"It will be better if you stop tugging at my sleeve," I told her, and when she desisted, I continued. "Next we take up a fallacy called Hasty Generalization. Listen carefully: You can't speak French. I can't speak French. Petey Burch can't speak French. I must therefore conclude that nobody at the University of Minnesota can speak French."

"Really?" said Polly, amazed. *"Nobody?"*

I hid my exasperation. "Polly, it's a fallacy. The generalization is reached too hastily. There are too few instances to support such a conclusion."

"Know any more fallacies?" she asked breathlessly. "This is more fun than dancing even."

I fought off a wave of despair. I was getting nowhere with this girl, absolutely nowhere. Still, I am nothing if not persistent. I continued. "Next comes Post Hoc. Listen to this: Let's not take Bill on our picnic. Every time we take him out with us, it rains."

"I know somebody just like that," she exclaimed. "A girl back home— Eula Becker, her name is. It never fails. Every single time we take her on a picnic—"

"Polly," I said sharply, "it's a fallacy. Eula Becker doesn't *cause* the rain. She has no connection with the rain. You are guilty of Post Hoc if you blame Eula Becker."

"I'll never do it again," she promised contritely. "Are you mad at me?"

I sighed deeply. "No, Polly, I'm not mad."

"Then tell me some more fallacies."

"All right. Let's try Contradictory Premises."

"Yes, let's," she chirped, blinking her eyes happily.

I frowned, but plunged ahead. "Here's an example of Contradictory Premises: If God can do anything, can He make a stone so heavy that He won't be able to lift it?"

"Of course," she replied promptly.

"But if He can do anything, He can lift the stone," I pointed out.

"Yeah," she said thoughtfully. "Well, then I guess He can't make the stone."

"But he can do anything," I reminded her.

She scratched her pretty, empty head. "I'm all confused," she admitted.

"Of course you are. Because when the premises of an argument contradict each other, there can be no argument. If there is an irresistible force, there can be no immovable object. If there is an immovable object, there can be no irresistible force. Get it?"

"Tell me some more of this keen stuff," she said eagerly.

I consulted my watch. "I think we'd better call it a night. I'll take you home now, and you go over all the things you've learned. We'll have another session tomorrow night."

I deposited her at the girls' dormitory, where she assured me that she had had a perfectly terrif evening, and I went glumly home to my room. Petey lay snoring in his bed, the raccoon coat huddled like a great hairy beast at his feet. For a moment I considered waking him and telling him that he could have his girl back. It seemed clear that my project was doomed to failure. The girl simply had a logic-proof head.

But then I reconsidered. I had wasted one evening; I might as well waste another. Who knew? Maybe somewhere in the extinct crater of her mind, a few embers still smoldered. Maybe somehow I could fan them into flame. Admittedly it was not a prospect fraught with hope, but I decided to give it one more try.

Seated under the oak the next evening I said, "Our first fallacy tonight is called Ad Misericordiam."

She quivered with delight.

"Listen closely," I said. "A man applies for a job. When the boss asks him what his qualifications are, he replies that he has a wife and six children at home, the wife is a helpless cripple, the children have nothing to eat, no clothes to wear, no shoes on their feet, there are no beds in the house, no coal in the cellar, and winter is coming."

A tear rolled down each of Polly's pink cheeks. "Oh, this is awful, awful," she sobbed.

"Yes, it's awful," I agreed, "but it's no argument. The man never answered the boss's question about his qualifications. Instead he appealed to the boss's sympathy. He committed the fallacy of Ad Misericordiam. Do you understand?"

"Have you got a handkerchief?" she blubbered.

I handed her a handkerchief and tried to keep from screaming while she wiped her eyes. "Next," I said in a carefully controlled tone, "we will discuss False Analogy. Here is an example: Students should be allowed to look at their textbooks during examinations. After all, surgeons have X-rays to guide them during an operation, lawyers have briefs to guide them during a trial, carpenters have blueprints to guide them when they are building a house. Why, then, shouldn't students be allowed to look at their textbooks during an examination?"

"There now," she said enthusiastically, "is the most marvy idea I've heard in years."

"Polly," I said testily, "the argument is all wrong. Doctors, lawyers, and carpenters aren't taking a test to see how much they have learned, but students are. The situations are altogether different, and you can't make an analogy between them."

"I still think it's a good idea," said Polly.

"Nuts," I muttered. Doggedly I pressed on. "Next we'll try Hypothesis Contrary to Fact."

"Sounds yummy," was Polly's reaction.

"Listen: If Madame Curie had not happened to leave a photographic plate in a drawer with a chunk of pitchblende, the world today would not know about radium."

"True, true," said Polly, nodding her head. "Did you see the movie? Oh, it just knocked me out. That Walter Pidgeon is so dreamy. I mean he fractures me."

"If you can forget Mr. Pidgeon for a moment," I said coldly, "I would like to point out that the statement is a fallacy. Maybe Madame Curie would have discovered radium at some later date. Maybe somebody else would have discovered it. Maybe any number of things would have happened. You can't start with a hypothesis that is not true and then draw any supportable conclusions from it."

"They ought to put Walter Pidgeon in more pictures," said Polly. "I hardly ever see him any more."

One more chance, I decided. But just one more. There is a limit to what flesh and blood can bear. "The next fallacy is called Poisoning the Well."

"How cute!" she gurgled.

"Two men are having a debate. The first one gets up and says, 'My opponent is a notorious liar. You can't believe a word that he is going to say.' . . . Now, Polly, think. Think hard. What's wrong?"

I watched her closely as she knit her creamy brow in concentration. Suddenly a glimmer of intelligence—the first I had seen—came into her eyes. "It's not fair," she said with indignation. "It's not a bit fair. What chance has the second man got if the first man calls him a liar before he even begins talking?"

"Right!" I cried exultantly. "One hundred percent right. It's not fair. The first man has *poisoned the well* before anybody could drink from it. He has hamstrung his opponent before he could even start. . . . Polly, I'm proud of you."

"Pshaw," she murmured, blushing with pleasure.

"You see, my dear, these things aren't so hard. All you have to do is concentrate. Think—examine—evaluate. Come now, let's review everything we have learned."

"Fire away," she said with an airy wave of her hand.

Heartened by the knowledge that Polly was not altogether a cretin, I began a long, patient review of all I had told her. Over and over and over again I cited instances, pointed out flaws, kept hammering away without let up. It was like digging a tunnel. At first everything was work, sweat, and darkness. I had no idea when I would reach the light, or even *if* I would. But I persisted. I pounded and clawed and scraped, and finally I was rewarded. I saw a chink of light. And then the chink got bigger and the sun came pouring in and all was bright.

Five grueling nights this took, but it was worth it. I had made a logician out of Polly; I had taught her to think. My job was done. She was worthy of me at last. She was a fit wife for me, a proper hostess for my many mansions, a suitable mother for my well-heeled children.

It must not be thought that I was without love for this girl. Quite the contrary. Just as Pygmalion loved the perfect woman he had fashioned, so I loved mine. I determined to acquaint her with my feelings at our very next meeting. The time had come to change our relationship from academic to romantic.

"Polly," I said when next we sat beneath our oak, "tonight we will not discuss fallacies."

"Aw, gee," she said, disappointed.

"My dear," I said, favoring her with a smile, "we have now spent five evenings together. We have gotten along splendidly. It is clear that we are well matched."

"Hasty Generalization," said Polly brightly.

"I beg your pardon," said I.

"Hasty Generalization," she repeated. "How can you say that we are well matched on the basis of only five dates?"

I chuckled with amusement. The dear child had learned her lessons well.

"My dear," I said, patting her hand in a tolerant manner, "five dates is plenty. After all, you don't have to eat a whole cake to know that it's good."

"False Analogy," said Polly promptly. "I'm not a cake. I'm a girl."

I chuckled with somewhat less amusement. The dear child had learned her lessons perhaps too well. I decided to change tactics. Obviously the best approach was a simple, strong, direct declaration of love. I paused for a moment while my massive brain chose the proper words. Then I began:

"Polly, I love you. You are the whole world to me, and the moon and the stars and the constellations of outer space. Please, my darling, say that you will go steady with me, for if you will not, life will be meaningless. I will languish. I will refuse my meals. I will wander the face of the earth, a shambling, hallow-eyed hulk."

There, I thought, folding my arms, that ought to do it.

"Ad Misericordiam," said Polly.

I ground my teeth. I was not Pygmalion; I was Frankenstein, and my monster had me by the throat. Frantically I fought back the tide of panic surging through me. At all costs I had to keep cool.

"Well, Polly," I said, forcing a smile, "you certainly have learned your fallacies."

"You're darn right," she said with a vigorous nod.

"And who taught them to you, Polly?"

"You did."

"That's right. So you do owe me something, don't you, my dear? If I hadn't come along you never would have learned about fallacies."

"Hypothesis Contrary to Fact," she said instantly.

I dashed perspiration from my brow. "Polly," I croaked, "you mustn't take all these things so literally. I mean this is just classroom stuff. You know that the things you learn in school don't have anything to do with life."

"Dicto Simpliciter," she said, wagging her finger at me playfully.

That did it. I leaped to my feet, bellowing like a bull. "Will you or will you not go steady with me?"

"I will not," she replied.

"Why not?" I demanded.

"Because this afternoon I promised Petey Burch that I would go steady with him."

I reeled back, overcome with the infamy of it. After he promised, after he made a deal, after he shook my hand! "The rat!" I shrieked, kicking up great chunks of turf. "You can't go with him, Polly. He's a liar. He's a cheat. He's a rat."

"Poisoning the Well," said Polly, "and stop shouting. I think shouting must be a fallacy too."

With an immense effort of will, I modulated my voice. "All right," I said. "You're a logician. Let's look at this thing logically. How could you choose Petey Burch over me? Look at me—a brilliant student, a tremendous intellectual, a man with an assured future. Look at Petey—a knothead, a jitterbug, a guy who'll never know where his next meal is coming from. Can you give me one logical reason why you should go steady with Petey Burch?"

"I certainly can," declared Polly. "He's got a raccoon coat."

POEMS

Poetry includes a wide range of form and expression. It is much easier to recognize a poem than to define one, but a limited definition is possible if we examine the language of poetry closely.

The natural language of children is poetry. The child exclaims, "Daddy, look! A piece of rain!" when he sees a puddle. He is speaking poetry, for, to the child, the statement is literal and quite accurate: a puddle *is* a "piece of rain" if we think about it a little. And the child's remark is also *original:* a puddle has never been named in quite that way before. Originality is in the very nature of poetry. Why does the child say it in that way? He really saw the puddle, closely, and with his own eyes. This means that the experience was his own and no other's. And because he probably did not know the word "puddle," he naturally used words from his own vocabulary. These words were accurate in describing both the existence of the puddle and his sensous perception of it. The mature poet does the same thing: though he has many words to choose from, he finds those words which seem true to his experience and more original.

But someone is thinking, "I don't understand poetry; I'm not used to expressions like a 'piece of rain.' " We all know that a puddle is called a puddle and it means a small, shallow pool of water. Yet the child's words for a puddle do something surprising and magical: they cause us to think again of what we mean when we use the words. We see the puddle in a new way, or perhaps for the first time; perhaps we fall under the spell of the words, which seem to give us the observer's experience in a unique way.

Communicating experience is the most important thing poetry does, though we cannot say that this is the "use of poetry." Through the communication of the poet's experience, the reader learns to see and feel for himself what the poet saw and felt, what sensory experience made him create the poem.

Our everyday speech in prose, of course, is filled with expressions which are not meant to be taken literally as "facts." We say "eye of a needle," "son of a gun," electrical "current," "She's a swinger!" and other such "illogical" things; we use these expressions because the metaphors, or "poetic" comparisons they make are true to our experience and feelings about these things. A poem, however, makes frequent use of the *concrete* words about things to be seen and touched.

The *sound* of language adds another dimension. Anger, for example, has its own recognizable rhythms and sound patterns. Notice the way you would say, "I won't, I won't, I won't!" Each repetition adds a layer of emphasis so that the sound is part of the poetic meaning. The relationship of sound and sense is carefully controlled by the poet, keeping the language in the right key and expressing the rhythm that best fits the sense and meaning.

Robert Burns' line, "My love is like a red, red rose," if read as literal fact, certainly does not compliment his sweetheart. If the unfortunate girl were really so "red," she would have a very serious skin condition and should probably see her doctor. But if we read the line in the same sense that we listen to the child exclaim about the puddle, then the meaning is something different. The poet is saying that his love has those qualities which we value in a rose: softness, sweetness, freshness. She has smooth skin, beauty, and symmetry; perhaps she is pleasantly perfumed. And the repetition of "red" gives the word special significance. A "white, white" rose would certainly be another woman. When we think of the color red, the associations are love, warmth, even passion, whereas white suggests more spiritual, less passionate, less sensual qualities. The fact that a rose has thorns contributes another intriguing dimension to the comparison. If the language of poetry seems difficult, or different, it is often because in our everyday world we limit our thoughts and feelings to the abstract, vague, and unemotional meanings of words, and do not free our minds to pick up the rich echoes of feeling and meaning that words so often bring to mind.

Reading and enjoying poetry does not call for learning elaborate techniques for analyzing meaning. A response to the adult experiences communicated by the skilled poet does require a lively alertness to some serious and often sophisticated uses of language. Nevertheless, in communicating his experience, the poet tries to go back to the roots of a simple, basic language—the language of seeing and feeling clearly, personally, and originally. One might say that poetry tries to use words that go beyond the words themselves into the very heart of the experience. As Robert Frost said, "Poetry is what is left when the words are taken away."

THE BAT
IN THE
MONASTERY

*From the statements of this poem we vividly
see the personality of the narrating "I,"
torn as anyone might be between partici-
pating in a grisly event and seeing it with
the wisdom of an observer.*

WE KILLED a bat last night
in our recreation room. Five priests
dropped their masks and newspapers, grasped
each a weapon—broom barrel magazine whatever—
and lunged and flailed the black intruder.
(Poor Luther, I thought.) He soared, swooped,
swept the room with vine wings, fluttering
a hum of terror while priests laughed and ducked
and tried to capture him. He settled
finally from exhaustion and despair,
waited on the wall behind the heavy drape.

Big Ned killed him.
With a broom he whaled the hell out of that bat
that never hurt a soul. Cheers were deafening.
A tiny thing, a dirty mouse with wings
crumpled now and scudded to the gutter
like an autumn leaf. Farewell, bat.

The party ended. We picked our way
back to our cells, isolate again, estranged.

Well, anyhow, we got that intruder.

AUTO WRECK

Here is a fine example of the poet using
word and sound with the sureness and depth
of vision with which an artist uses stroke
and color.

ITS quick soft silver bell beating, beating,
And down the dark one ruby flare
Pulsing out red light like an artery,
The ambulance at top speed floating down
Past beacons and illuminated clocks
Wings in a heavy curve, dips down,
And brakes speed, entering the crowd.
The doors leap open, emptying light;
Stretchers are laid out, the mangled lifted
And stowed into the little hospital.
Then the bell, breaking the hush, tolls once,
And the ambulance with its terrible cargo
Rocking, slightly rocking, moves away,
As the doors, an afterthought, are closed.

We are deranged, walking among the cops
Who sweep glass and are large and composed.
One is still making notes under the light.
One with a bucket douches ponds of blood
Into the street and gutter.
One hangs lanterns on the wrecks that cling,
Empty husks of locusts, to iron poles.

Our throats were tight as tourniquets,
Our feet were bound with splints, but now,
Like convalescents intimate and gauche,
We speak through sickly smiles and warn
With the stubborn saw of common sense,
The grim joke and the banal resolution.
The traffic moves around with care,
But we remain, touching a wound
That opens to our richest horror.
Already old, the question Who shall die?

Becomes unspoken Who is innocent?
For death in war is done by hands;
Suicide has cause and stillbirth, logic;
And cancer, simple as a flower, blooms.
But this invites the occult mind,
Cancels our physics with a sneer,
And spatters all we knew of denouement
Across the expedient and wicked stones.

MAY SWENSON

SOUTHBOUND
ON THE
FREEWAY

*The same device which Paul Tabori used in
his satiric Martian piece is used by the poet
to give the reader a fresh look at something
within his daily experience.*

A TOURIST came in from Orbitville,
parked in the air, and said:

The creatures of this star
are made of metal and glass.

Through the transparent parts
you can see their guts.

Their feet are round and roll
on diagrams—or long

measuring tapes—dark
with white lines.

They have four eyes.
The two in the back are red.

Sometimes you can see a 5-eyed
one, with a red eye turning

on the top of his head.
He must be special—

the others respect him,
and go slow,

when he passes, winding
among them from behind.

They all hiss as they glide,
like inches, down the marked

tapes. Those soft shapes,
shadowy inside

the hard bodies—are they
their guts or their brains?

HENRY REED

NAMING OF PARTS

*In this poem by Henry Reed, the voice of
the poet is mingled with that of the instructor. Yet, the voice of the poet quite effectively
remains alone.*

TODAY we have naming of parts. Yesterday,
We had daily cleaning. And tomorrow morning,
We shall have what to do after firing. But today,
Today we have naming of parts. Japonica
Glistens like coral in all of the neighbouring gardens,
   And today we have naming of parts.

This is the lower sling swivel. And this
Is the upper sling swivel, whose use you will see,
When you are given your slings. And this is the piling swivel
Which in your case you have not got. The branches

Hold in the gardens their silent, eloquent gestures,
    Which in our case we have not got.

This is the safety-catch, which is always released
With an easy flick of the thumb. And please do not let me
See anyone using his finger. You can do it quite easy
If you have any strength in your thumb. The blossoms
Are fragile and motionless, never letting anyone see
    Any of them using their finger.

And this you can see is the bolt. The purpose of this
Is to open the breech, as you see. We can slide it
Rapidly backwards and forwards: we call this
Easing the spring. And rapidly backwards and forwards
The early bees are assaulting and fumbling the flowers:
    They call it easing the Spring.

They call it easing the Spring: it is perfectly easy
If you have any strength in your thumb: like the bolt,
And the breech, and the cocking-piece, and the point of balance,
Which in our case we have not got; and the almond-blossom
Silent in all of the gardens and the bees going backwards and forwards,
    For today we have naming of parts.

ROBERT GRAVES

THE TRAVELERS
CURSE
AFTER MISDIRECTION

*This poem is an interesting study in lan-
guage because of Graves' total reliance on
variations of the angry invective for the
meaning and effect of his poem.*

MAY they wander stage by stage
Of the same vain pilgrimage,
Stumbling on, age after age,

Night and day, mile after mile,
At each and every step, a stile;
At each and every stile, withal,
May they catch their feet and fall;
At each and every fall they take,
May a bone within them break;
And may the bones that break within
Not be, for variation's sake,
Now rib, now thigh, now arm, now shin,
But always, without fail, THE NECK.

KENNETH   REXROTH

A BESTIARY

_Central to these verses by Kenneth Rexroth
is the subtle technique of juxtaposing statements to imply a moral or an idea for the
reader's consideration._

Deer

DEER are gentle and graceful
And they have beautiful eyes.
They hurt no one but themselves,
The males, and only for love.
Men have invented several
Thousand ways of killing them.

Herring

The herring is prolific.
There are plenty of herrings.
Some herrings are eaten raw.
Many are dried and pickled.
But most are used for manure.
See if you can apply this
To your history lessons.

LION

The lion is called the king
Of beasts. Nowadays there are
Almost as many lions
In cages as out of them.
If offered a crown, refuse.

YOU

Let Y stand for you who says,
"Very clever, but surely
These were not written for you
Children?" Let Y stand for yes.

W. H. AUDEN

THE
UNKNOWN
CITIZEN

*Irony, which is the essence of satire, is ex-
emplified by the obvious conflict of attitudes
toward the "unknown citizen," between the
narrator and the poet in the background.*

(To JS/07/M/378 This Marble Monument Is Erected by the State)

HE WAS found by the Bureau of Statistics to be
One against whom there was no official complaint,
And all the reports on his conduct agree
That, in the modern sense of an old-fashioned word, he was a saint,
For in everything he did he served the Greater Community.
Except for the War till the day he retired
He worked in a factory and never got fired,
But satisfied his employers, Fudge Motors Inc.
Yet he wasn't a scab or odd in his views,
For his Union reports that he paid his dues,

(Our report on his Union shows it was sound)
And our Social Psychology workers found
That he was popular with his mates and liked a drink.
The Press are convinced that he bought a paper every day
And that his reactions to advertisements were normal in every way.
Policies taken out in his name prove that he was fully insured,
And his Health-card shows he was once in hospital but left it cured.
Both Producers Research and High-Grade Living declare
He was fully sensible to the advantages of the Installment Plan
And had everything necessary to the Modern Man,
A phonograph, a radio, a car and a frigidaire.
Our researchers into Public Opinion are content
That he held the proper opinions for the time of year;
When there was peace, he was for peace; when there was war, he went.
He was married and added five children to the population,
Which our Eugenist says was the right number for a parent of his
    generation,
And our teachers report that he never interfered with their education.
Was he free? Was he happy? The question is absurd:
Had anything been wrong, we should certainly have heard.

KENNETH FEARING

DIRGE

*The jarring rhythm, best conveyed when
read aloud, and the intended irony of the
title, combine to give the poem its satiric
meaning.*

1-2-3 WAS the number he played but today the number came 3-2-1;
    bought his Carbide at 30 and it went to 29; had the favorite at Bowie
    but the track was slow—

O, executive type, would you like to drive a floating power, knee-action, silk-upholstered six? Wed a Hollywood star? Shoot the course in 58? Draw to the ace, king, jack?
O, fellow with a will who won't take no, watch out for three cigarettes on the same, single match; O democratic voter born in August under Mars, beware of liquidated rails—

Dénouement to dénouement, he took a personal pride in the certain, certain way he lived his own, private life,
but nevertheless, they shut off his gas; nevertheless, the bank foreclosed; nevertheless, the landlord called; nevertheless, the radio broke,

And twelve o'clock arrived just once too often,
just the same he wore one grey tweed suit, bought one straw hat, drank one straight Scotch, walked one short step, took one long look, drew one deep breath,
just one too many,

And wow he died as wow he lived,
going whop to the office and blooie home to sleep and biff got married and bam had children and oof got fired,
zowie did he live and zowie did he die,

With who the hell are you at the corner of his casket, and where the hell we going on the right hand silver knob, and who the hell cares walking second from the end with an American Beauty wreath from why the hell not.

Very much missed by the circulation staff of the New York Evening Post; deeply, deeply mourned by the B.M.T.,

Wham, Mr. Roosevelt; pow, Sears Roebuck; awk, big dipper; bop, summer rain;
bong, Mr., bong, Mr., bong, Mr., bong.

E.E. CUMMINGS

MY SWEET
OLD ETCETERA

*E.E. Cummings is fond of using the tech-
nique of deliberately misusing English
syntax and punctuation to insure that his
poems will be read carefully.*

my sweet old etcetera
aunt lucy during the recent

war could and what
is more did tell you just
what everybody was fighting

for,
my sister

isabel created hundreds
(and
hundreds) of socks not to
mention shirts fleaproof earwarmers

etcetera wristers etcetera, my
mother hoped that

i would die etcetera
bravely of course my father used
to become hoarse talking about how it was
a privilege and if only he
could meanwhile my

self etcetera lay quietly
in the deep mud et

cetera
(dreaming,
et
   cetera, of
Your smile
eyes knees and of your Etcetera)

E.E. CUMMINGS

WHEN MY LOVE
COMES TO SEE
ME IT'S

*This poem, celebrating love, sex, youth, and
innocence, contains Cummings' delight-
fully unsettling mixture of slang, clichés,
and unique word combinations.*

when my love comes to see me it's
just a little like music, a
little more like curving colour (say
orange)
        against silence, or darkness . . . .

the coming of my love emits
a wonderful smell in my mind,

you should see when i turn to find
her how my least heart-beat becomes less.
And then all her beauty is a vise

whose stilling lips murder suddenly me,

but of my corpse the tool her smile makes something
suddenly luminous and precise

—and then we are I and She . . . .

what is that the hurdy-gurdy's playing

EDNA ST. VINCENT MILLAY

LOVE
IS NOT
ALL

*The poem's speaker here rejects stuffy
sentimentality in the neatly built stages
of a formal Shakespearean sonnet.*

LOVE is not all: it is not meat nor drink
Nor slumber nor a roof against the rain;
Nor yet a floating spar to men that sink
And rise and sink and rise and sink again;
Love can not fill the thickened lung with breath,
Nor clean the blood, nor set the fractured bone;
Yet many a man is making friends with death
Even as I speak, for lack of love alone.
It well may be that in a difficult hour,
Pinned down by pain and moaning for release,
Or nagged by want past resolution's power,
I might be driven to sell your love for peace,
Or trade the memory of this night for food.
It well may be. I do not think I would.

WILLIAM CARLOS WILLIAMS

THE DANCE

*The "Kermess," painted by Pieter Breughel,
depicts a lumbering circle dance of well-fed
peasants celebrating a feast day.*

IN BREUGHEL's great picture, The Kermess,
the dancers go round, they go round and
around, the squeal and the blare and the

tweedle of bagpipes, a bugle and fiddles
tipping their bellies (round as the thick-
sided glasses whose wash they impound)
their hips and their bellies off balance
to turn them. Kicking and rolling about
the Fair Grounds, swinging their butts, those
shanks must be sound to bear up under such
rollicking measures, prance as they dance
in Breughel's great picture, The Kermess.

WILLIAM CARLOS WILLIAMS

THE BULL

*Subject of many ancient myths and often
depicted in ancient art, the bull is the conflicting symbol of masculinity and divinity
in this poem by William Carlos Williams.*

IT IS in captivity—
ringed, haltered, chained
to a drag
the bull is godlike

Unlike the cows
he lives alone, nozzles
the sweet grass gingerly
to pass the time away

He kneels, lies down
and stretching out
a foreleg licks himself
about the hoof

then stays
with half-closed eyes,
Olympian commentary on
the bright passage of days.

—The round sun
smooths his lacquer
through
the glossy pinetrees

his substance hard
as ivory or glass—
through which the wind
yet plays—
                milkless

he nods
the hair between his horns
and eyes matted
with hyacinthine curls.

JOHN HEATH–STUBBS

THE
LADY'S
COMPLAINT

*The measured buildup of melodrama gives
an interesting mixed effect of pathos combined with satiric amusement.*

I SPEAK of that lady I heard last night,
  Maudlin over her gin and water,
In a sloppy bar with a fulvous light
  And an air that was smeared with smoke and laughter:
  How youth decamps and cold age comes after,
In fifty years she had found it true—
  She sighed for the damage that time had brought her:
"Oh, after death there's a judgement due.

"What once was as sleek as a seal's pelt,
  My shapeless body has fallen from grace;
My soul and my shoes are worn down to the welt,
  And no cosmetic can mask my face,
  As under talcum and oxide you trace

How the bones stick out, and the ghost peeps through—
   A wanderer, I, in Wraith-bone Place,
And after death there's a judgement due.

"My roundabout horses have cantered away,
   The gilded and garrulous seasons are flown;
What echo is left of the rag-time bray
   Of the tenor sax and the susaphone?
   But I was frightened to sleep alone
(As now I must do, as now I must do)
   And a chittering bat-voice pipes 'Atone,
For after death there's a judgement due.'

"Green apples I bit when I was green,
   My teeth are on edge at the maggotty core;
Life is inclement, obscure, obscene;
   Nothing's amusing—not any more;
   But love's abrasions have left me sore—
To hairy Harry and half-mast Hugh
   I gave the love I was starving for,
And after death there's a judgement due.

"Potentate, swirling in stark cold air
   The corn from the husks—I offer to you
My terror-struck and incredulous prayer,
   For after death there's a judgement due."

LANGSTON HUGHES

DREAM VARIATION

*This lyric poem by Langston Hughes is an
excellent example of that elusive quality in
poetry which can express an overpowering
outburst of emotion.*

To FLING my arms wide
In some place of the sun,
To whirl and to dance

Till the white day is done.
Then rest at cool evening
Beneath a tall tree
While night comes on gently,
   Dark like me,—
That is my dream!

To fling my arms wide
In the face of the sun,
Dance! whirl! whirl!
Till the quick day is done.
Rest at pale evening . . .
A tall, slim tree . . .
Night coming tenderly
   Black like me.

GREGORY CORSO

GIANT TURTLE

*Through the rhythm and repetition of words,
the poet breathes life into his subject.*

You rise from the sea an agony of sea
Night in the moonlight you slow the shore
Behind you webbed-tracks mark your ordeal
An hour   in an hour you cease your slow
Hind legs now digging   digging the sand the damp the sand
The moon brightens   the sea calms
Your mouth pumping   your eyes thickly tearing
You create a tremendous hole   you fall flat
Exhaust   sigh   strain
Eggs eggs eggs eggs eggs eggs eggs eggs eggs
Eggs   eggs   eggs   eggs   egg   egg   egg
Heave   exhaust   sigh   flat
Your wet womb speckled with sand   you turn slow
Slow you cover the hole the eggs slow   slow
You cease your slow
Dawn
And you plop in the sea like a big rock

HURT HAWKS

*Here, as in many of his other poems, Jeffers
contrasts the noble beauty of nature with
the pathos of man.*

THE broken pillar of the wing jags from the clotted
    shoulder,
The wing trails like a banner in defeat,
No more to use the sky forever but live with famine
And pain a few days: cat nor coyote
Will shorten the week of waiting for death, there is game
    without talons.
He stands under the oak-bush and waits
The lame feet of salvation; at night he remembers freedom
And flies in a dream, the dawns ruin it.
He is strong and pain is worse to the strong, incapacity is
    worse.
The curs of the day come and torment him
At distance, no one but death the redeemer will humble
    that head,
The intrepid readiness, the terrible eyes.
The wild God of the world is sometimes merciful to those
That ask mercy, not often to the arrogant.
You do not know him, you communal people, or you have
    forgotten him;
Intemperate and savage, the hawk remembers him;
Beautiful and wild, the hawks, and men that are dying,
    remember him.

I'd sooner, except the penalties, kill a man than a hawk;
    but the great redtail
Had nothing left but unable misery
From the bone too shattered for mending, the wing that
    trailed under his talons when he moved.
We had fed him six weeks, I gave him freedom,
He wandered over the foreland hill and returned in the
    evening, asking for death,
Not like a beggar, still eyed with the old

Implacable arrogance. I gave him the lead gift in the
     twilight. What fell was relaxed,
Owl-downy, soft feminine feathers; but what
Soared: the fierce rush: the night-herons by the flooded
     river cried fear at its rising
Before it was quite unsheathed from reality.

ERIC BARKER

DESERTED

*The kind of poetry which Wordsworth called
"an emotion recollected in tranquility" is
exemplified in Barker's description of his
feelings on coming upon a deserted house.*

EVERYTHING in the house was like the kitchen door
the wind blew half-way open, waiting
for wind to blow it shut again.
Everything in the house was like that:
half-open or shut; falling asleep
or sleeping; everything in the garden
either dying or dead. But when the wind sprang up,
that hollow shell was full of sound
as a conch is of the sea;
the rotting curtains and the dusty webs
swaying in the same wave
as the dead flowers in the garden.

I came upon it first on such a day
and stopped to look in through a broken window,
and the wind rushed in behind me,
scouring it like a bell,
and poured out through the other side
flattening the wild oats in the opposite field
with its broad and whistling scythe.

And I went on, not caring for that sound,
though I love the wind as well as any man
close-lived to woods and fields,
and often lie awake at night
simply to listen when it walks the roof
or lets me know it's in the chimney,
or stroking the backs of the nearby sleeping birds.
But that wind had a different sound.
I cannot tell you how it filled the house
unless you've wondered how Niobe mourned.
It made me think of those who lived there once,
who must have chosen such a cloud-loved hill
for what to them was seeming permanence.
And what ill circumstance had tripped them up,
and set against the walls those smouldering fires
that eat a house to death with shameless wounds.

ELIZABETH BISHOP

THE FISH

The fish emerges from this poem with de-
finitive characteristics which the author
achieves through precise description, meta-
phor, and simile.

I CAUGHT a tremendous fish
and held him beside the boat
half out of water, with my hook
fast in a corner of his mouth.
He didn't fight.
He hadn't fought at all.
He hung a grunting weight,
battered and venerable
and homely. Here and there
his brown skin hung in strips
like ancient wall-paper,
and its pattern of darker brown

was like wall-paper:
shapes like full-blown roses
stained and lost through age.
He was speckled with barnacles,
fine rosettes of lime,
and infested
with tiny white sea-lice,
and underneath two or three
rags of green weed hung down.
While his gills were breathing in
the terrible oxygen
—the frightening gills,
fresh and crisp with blood,
that can cut so badly—
I thought of the coarse white flesh
packed in like feathers,
the big bones and the little bones,
the dramatic reds and blacks
of his shiny entrails,
and the pink swim-bladder
like a big peony.
I looked into his eyes
which were far larger than mine
but shallower, and yellowed,
the irises backed and packed
with tarnished tinfoil
seen through the lenses
of old scratched isinglass.
They shifted a little, but not
to return my stare.
—It was more like the tipping
of an object toward the light.
I admired his sullen face,
the mechanism of his jaw,
and then I saw
that from his lower lip
—if you could call it a lip—
grim, wet, and weapon-like,
hung five old pieces of fish-line,
or four and a wire leader
with the swivel still attached,
with all their five big hooks
grown firmly in his mouth.
A green line, frayed at the end
where he broke it, two heavier lines,
and a fine black thread

still crimped from the strain and snap
when it broke and he got away.
Like medals with their ribbons
frayed and wavering,
a five-haired beard of wisdom
trailing from his aching jaw.
I stared and stared
and victory filled up
the little rented boat,
from the pool of bilge
where oil had spread a rainbow
around the rusted engine
to the bailer rusted orange,
the sun-cracked thwarts,
the oarlocks on their strings,
the gunnels—until everything
was rainbow, rainbow, rainbow!
And I let the fish go.

KENNETH PATCHEN

THE FOX

*The structure and organization of its mea-
sured stanzas are greatly responsible for
the poem's impact.*

BECAUSE the snow is deep
Without spot that white falling through white air

Because she limps a little—bleeds
Where they shot her

Because hunters have guns
And dogs have hangmen's legs

Because I'd like to take her in my arms
And tend her wound

Because she can't afford to die
Killing the young in her belly

I don't know what to say of a soldier's dying
Because there are no proportions in death.

THEODORE ROETHKE

ELEGY
FOR
JANE

*Through an almost mystical identification
with the things of nature, the poet is able
to express deep tenderness.*

I REMEMBER the neckcurls, limp and damp as tendrils;
And her quick look, a sidelong pickerel smile;
And how, once startled into talk, the light syllables leaped for her,
And she balanced in the delight of her thought,
A wren, happy, tail into the wind,
Her song trembling the twigs and small branches.
The shade sang with her;
The leaves, their whispers turned to kissing;
And the mould sang in the bleached valleys under the rose.

Oh, when she was sad, she cast herself down into such a pure depth,
Even a father could not find her:
Scraping her cheek against straw;
Stirring the clearest water.

My sparrow, you are not here,
Waiting like a fern, making a spiney shadow.
The sides of wet stones cannot console me,
Nor the moss, wound with the last light.

If only I could nudge you from this sleep,
My maimed darling, my skittery pigeon.

Over this damp grave I speak the words of my love:
I, with no rights in this matter,
Neither father nor lover.

MARY PHILLIPS

DIALOGUE
FROM A BRIDE'S
PRIMER

*The three short poems which follow are
examples of student writing and show the
range of mood and style which students can
achieve—and enjoy.*

COME walk with me. We'll never see
A brighter springtime dawn.
  You go along, my darling;
  I'll put the kettle on.

The hills are wild with poppies;
They came up, overnight.
  But I must make the noon meal,
  And set the nursery right.

The trees have turned; the sunset
Paints them deeper gold.
  I know. I saw them yesterday.
  The year is growing old.

It's snowing hard. We're in for
Bitter days ahead.
  It's pretty, though, white frosting.
  Won't you come on up to bed?

  Come walk with me. We'll never see
  A sweeter springtime moon.
You take the boys. I'm pressed for time.
(I'm meeting someone, soon.)

MICHAELE SHERRY

FRIENDS

The
noisy chip-shouldered boys bunched through
           on shouting feet
           old mr. ackerman's garden
Cursing violently
their youth
           he wrinkled a fist
           and banged back into his sarcophagus
So they celebrated
his funeral
           with garbagecan lids
           and no one else knew the old man
           well enough
           to steal his doormat

STEPHAN TAUGHER

CITY PEOPLE

When I walk down
Stampeded
Streets in San Francisco
With crowds
Of people all in the smart
Styles
And knowing where they are
Going
I always feel like I am one of them
Steers
In a big stockyard especially
At intersections
When the little green sign says
WALK
In other words
GO
And they all really do
Go
In the city.

ACKNOWLEDGMENTS
FOR POETRY

EXERCISES

TECHNIQUES OF READING

Reading for college courses does not necessarily demand extraordinary skills. The main hurdles are learning to read with interest, developing a reasonable concern for the subject, and learning to read rapidly enough to complete assignments and read for enjoyment without devoting a disproportionate amount of study time to it. Perhaps the key word is *concentration;* a student must somehow develop a way of avoiding distraction, ignoring noise and even the pleasanter sounds of the dormitory or Student Union. Sometimes he must shut off hunger and loneliness pangs in favor of a devoted interest in the subject matter he is reading.

Every student must learn to solve these problems, each in his own way, but an awareness of some of the difficulties may make the task easier.

Visual Problems

Unless you happen to have comparatively serious visual difficulties, chances are that you have not had regular eye examinations. The student who discovers that he should wear glasses when he is seven years old often becomes a rapid, efficient reader, one who is far ahead of his classmates. But those who presumably have "normal vision" sometimes have minor handicaps that go unnoticed until the unusually heavy reading load of college studies brings them forcibly to attention. Then, even a minor visual maladjustment is apt to be a major stumbling block to rapid reading and accurate comprehension. The obvious remedy is to arrange for a thorough examination by a qualified eye specialist before embarking on a taxing study schedule.

Reading Habits

The student who has made a hobby of spare-time reading is usually able to develop adequate skills with no special instruction nor even much conscious effort on his part. He has already acquired a broad range of interests; he has adjusted his use of leisure time and already has great powers of concentration. The competition for his time, however, becomes increasingly demanding during the high school years. Reading often has to take second place to club functions, social affairs, community service, and sports—to name only a few of the student's usual activities. Television also robs a student of reading time, particularly during the evening and weekend hours when the programs are designed to be of most interest to him.

Yet college requires a prompt and permanent shift in the direction of more reading—reading, indeed, of much more demanding material. The student quickly discovers that only a fraction of what he is expected to know on examinations comes from those gems of wisdom offered by his instructors. In some cases, college instructors spend most or all of the class time on discussion sessions which provide little or no information suitable for examinations. In some colleges—not yours, of course—you may hear of an instructor who harbors the quaint attitude that no other course the student is taking is very important; all study time, therefore, should be devoted to the one course he is teaching. In other colleges—nowhere nearby— you may even hear of an instructor who demands almost total recall of what seems to his students to be a batch of petty, inconsequential details. If a student reads only with passive interest—or no interest at all—he is usually in serious difficulty in one or more of his courses from the beginning.

The only hope of success in meeting this changed situation is to develop new techniques of study. Among them should be a continuous program of self-evaluation to insure that some progress is made in every course every week. Briefly, some of these areas lend themselves easily to self-evaluation:

(1) *Regular vocabulary drill.* Keep a list of the unfamiliar words as you encounter them, and spend a few minutes each day checking them in your dictionary. It is not helpful to try to look them up when you first encounter them, as the dictionary is apt to interrupt the logic of what you are reading. Besides, they can usually be understood reasonably well in the context. But *mastery* of the words—familiarity adequate to use a word in one's own writing—is gained only by systematic study. The jargon or argot terms in the various academic areas will become familiar very quickly; the more abstruse words in the general vocabulary of sophisticated writers takes a little longer.

(2) *Scanning for meaning.* Much of what one reads in college does not require close analysis. The voluminous background readings for many courses can be managed by the technique of scanning, or looking for specific answers.

Students will learn fairly quickly to locate topic sentences in key positions in each series of paragraphs. If the topic sentence is not at the beginning or end of a paragraph, it may be located in a position that points backward or forward in the reading unit, either through a preceding paragraph or later summary one, or following an opening sentence that connects it to the context of the entire reading unit.

Summarizing statements, too, are found in key locations before or after a series of supporting detail that may profitably be skipped in a skimming operation. If you learn to recognize quickly the structure of an argument, picking out the inductive, deductive, or comparative pattern, you can temporarily skip much of the supporting detail which leads up to, or follows after, the summary generalizing statement of the argument. (Once you have located the arguments that interest you, of course, you owe it to yourself and your fellow readers to test the evidence or the proof carefully to see how reliable you think the argument is.)

These techniques of skimming and rapidly identifying the elements of your reading are invaluable in combing through material for research papers. With efficient skimming you can note for yourself a great range of information which may seem immediately useful to the purpose in front of you. If you develop the habit of writing your own quick summary notes of the main arguments spotted in a reading passage, you can get a double benefit from the material. First, you can be sure that you have not misunderstood or passed over important information, and, second, you can give yourself a convenient reference guide to what you have scanned, in case you need a better look at it later. Often a slightly changed view of your topic of interest may send you back to material you have already "covered" to get a new perspective on what you were writing about.

While you are skimming, however, you will probably do best to concentrate on your purpose of picking out the main shape of your reading and not take time for close study unless the material is immediately important to your topic. For the reading you will do in this book, skimming may be most useful when a writing or discussion assignment asks you to search backward or forward for material elsewhere in the book that will add something to your views on the current reading project.

(3) *Organizing notes.* At some point, every student decides that his best friend is his typewriter. Even the least skillful typist becomes more proficient when faced with term papers, weekly themes, and reports. The typewriter can also be a great aid in organizing your classroom lecture notes. In fact, whether or not you own or use a typewriter, you can increase your understanding of a lecture or of a reading selection by making a set of outline notes that shows at a glance what its main points were. With outline notes in neat order, you can spot quickly any slips or understanding caused by momentary straying of attention, and give yourself a chance to check matters of information, confusion of terms, gaps in the argument, and, of course, relevance to the assignment or examination topic. A complete set of typed notes has made more than one student outrageously popular during the cram sessions before final examinations.

(4) *Review of assignments*. Instructors faithfully believe that students read assignments regularly and on time. Most students do, of course. Yet piecemeal reading prompted by the necessity to hack up a three-hour study session into segments that will fit four or five different courses is neither efficient nor effective. The student who makes up some kind of chart, keeps an assignment notebook, or merely pins up slips of paper on the closet door, is in control of what he is expected to do, though he may not do it by the clock. Experiment with using a whole afternoon and evening to get ahead of one course for a week or more. If your instructor in one course insists upon giving you a new assignment every day, perhaps another instructor will give you all the assignments in advance for the term. Your task is to reconcile the time you have with what you must do, and a constant check of the assignments is essential. When your instructor mentions on the first day of class that he is going to ask you to read *Gulliver's Travels* sometime during the term, be prepared. Don't wait for the inevitable Friday when he mentions that he expects to talk about Gulliver in class on Monday.

Efficient Reading

The controversy over rapid reading has generated more heat than light in recent years. Many academicians are actively opposed to the so-called speed reading courses, on the ground that the student misses too much when he reads so fast. The proponents of the various speed reading systems, however, have an impressive record of increasing both speed and comprehension. The real objective of rapid reading is efficiency, of course. A nutshell version of the case for rapid reading may be of help to the student whose skills have not been recently tested.

Speed of reading always varies somewhat with the difficulty of the material to be read. If the student can read only 250 words per minute on the average, he is handicapped for college work. A speed of 300–350 words per minute is average for most college freshmen, though the increasing number of speed courses now given in high schools will probably increase this average soon. Developing an average speed of 400–500 words per minute should be the minimum goal, as this range is efficient for almost all kinds of academic reading, with the possible exception of those areas of science that depend upon mathematical formulas. Attaining a speed in the range of from 500–1000 words per minute or more is easily managed with proper training and conscientious practice; but the student should decide what is best for himself when he has found out what he can do.

No special technique for learning to read faster is absolutely necessary, but some help with timing and some encouragement from someone else makes the project more enjoyable. First of all, force yourself to read faster, always moving forward, never backward in the line or up the page. Begin with easy, familiar material, then try the harder pieces when you have convinced yourself that you are not "studying" or "worrying" your way down the page.

Measuring your actual speed can be done either by using one of the many workbooks available containing passages for which the number of words and a set of questions are already provided, or you can measure your own material. Count the number of words in a column inch of the printed page, then multiply that figure by the total number of column inches in the whole article. This will give you an approximation of your rate of speed. Divide the number of words in the article by the number of minutes you needed to read it.

When you have discovered your own rate, examine the mechanical impediments to rapid reading. Can you concentrate for ten minutes, for half an hour or an hour without stopping? Can you write down a summary of what you have read after you finish a whole essay or story? Do you find yourself looking at every word, or can you see a half-line or a whole line with one fixation of the eyes? These are the key questions. The efficient reader needs only to be aware of the mechanical process of reading to overcome whatever might slow his progress. The final problem, comprehension, requires a set of questions for practice, but your grades on examinations will also be a measure of the effectiveness of your efforts to read more efficiently.

The student who is honest with himself keeps measuring his progress from week to week. Self-satisfaction is no substitute for self-evaluation. If your progress is slow and discouraging at first, keep trying. Skill in reading, like skill on the guitar, skill on the waves or the ice, or even skill in eating with chopsticks requires practice.

A PERSIAN COURTSHIP · ANNE SINCLAIR MEHDEVI
page 6

In this essay, an American bride tells a delightful story of modern Persia, her husband's homeland, and gives us an intimate view of a world of changing customs.

PROBLEMS

1. What aspects of the change from the social pattern of the old Persia to that of the modern world affect young Persian women?

2. What are the differences between Sari's situation and that of an educated American girl of the same age?

3. What are some of the commonly accepted meeting places for young people in America that are unavailable in Persia for young women of Sari's class?

4. What are the differences between Sari's world and that of the chauffeur, Later-On, and his bride?

5. Mrs. Mehdevi suggests that Sari's marriage will be a happy one. What details in the story support this impression?

COMPREHENSION QUIZ

Mark T or F for true or false.

_____ 1. Until forty years ago, the people of Iran had only a first name.
_____ 2. Girls from the educated classes in Iran have fewer chances than American girls to meet eligible young men.
_____ 3. Persian girls are not allowed to cook because their religion forbids them from handling food.
_____ 4. Marriages arranged by parents are now outlawed in Iran.
_____ 5. Polygamy has been illegal in Iran since the close of World War II.
_____ 6. Old-fashioned weddings in Iran are solemn and serious affairs.
_____ 7. A Persian girl never sees her husband until the day of the wedding.
_____ 8. The Persian wedding ceremony is over when the bride and groom drink from the same cup.
_____ 9. Persian men do not believe in kissing their fiancées.
_____10. Persian women are displeased when Persian men marry foreign women.

VOCABULARY

Write a brief definition of the meaning of the following words as applicable in the context of the essay. Check your definitions with the dictionary to be sure they are precise, and make a list of any other words which are unfamiliar to you for further study.

mentor	deride
arbiter	tulle
houris	unchaste
opalescent	minions
perfidious	recourse
illusory	obliterate
acolyte	rotund
immaculate	mercurial
affronted	balustrade
ogling	incandescent

CHARACTERIZATION

After you have read the story, test your memory of the characters. Write a sentence or phrase on each indicating who they are or what they do in the story.

Mitrah

Sari

Shemshad

Later-On

Shayla and Layla

Mohamed

Golam Ali

FOR WRITING

1. Mrs. Mehdevi's account of the old-fashioned Persian wedding captures the color and movement vividly. Write a sketch of a wedding you have attended; try to make your reader see and feel the scene.
2. Write an essay comparing the social world Sari lives in to that of a girl of similar background in America.

A SMALL BURIED TREASURE · JOHN FISCHER
page 15

COMPREHENSION QUIZ

Mark T or F for true or false.

_____ 1. The author and Aleko were traveling in a Cadillac in northern Greece.

_____ 2. Aleko suggested that the author should purchase a gold bracelet made in the eighth century.

_____ 3. Aleko drove the author to Moustheni to inspect a recently-opened tumulus.

_____ 4. Some of the people of Moustheni tried to keep the travelers from finding the site of the grave.

_____ 5. After Aleko and his friends were arrested for grave robbing twenty years earlier, he had left the village in handcuffs.

_____ 6. Aleko and his friends became grave robbers because they were bored and hungry.

_____ 7. The boys' findings, although small, had enabled them to pay for their education.

_____ 8. When the boys first found the necklace belonging to Diana, they sent it to one of the boys' uncles to be appraised.

_____ 9. Aleko insisted on paying for everything because he wanted to impress his friends in the village.

_____10. The treasure which the boys found was eventually placed in a museum.

VOCABULARY

Define the following words as they appear in the context of the story:

obliquely	drachma
cherished	cobbled
mandatory	hovel
diffidently	spectral
tumuli	homage
bellicose	archaic

The following words are used partly as allusions and partly as names of actual places important to the story. Put "X" beside the allusions, then be sure you can identify all the names.

The Prodigal Son

Hercules

Thermopylae

Aegean Sea

Dorians

St. Demetrios

Alcibiades

Achaeans

PROBLEMS

The events in Mr. Fischer's narrative are arranged to create suspense, with certain lines used as transitions between the parts of the story.

1. Which line indicates that Aleko will talk about treasures in the old graves?

2. Which line creates suspense as the author and Aleko enter Moustheni?

3. Which line signals the return to Aleko's story, following the visit to Moustheni?

4. Which line suspends Aleko's narrative just before the surprise ending?

FOR WRITING

1. Locate an article in *Horizon, National Geographic,* or a similar source which tells about the discovery of an important archeological find or an art treasure. Rewrite the story of the discovery in your own words, saving the most interesting aspect for the last paragraph or, if possible, the last line. Acknowledge your source in a footnote.
2. Write a brief character sketch of Aleko, keeping in mind the details Mr. Fischer includes to help the reader see him clearly. Consider such lines as these before you write:
   a. "It would be good for them to see me traveling in my own car and with an American friend."
   b. "Aleko insisted on paying for everything."
   c. "All the way back to the main road Aleko grinned in silent satisfaction."
   d. ". . . the very image of the man of affairs who has to be off to the pressing business of the outside world."

LEGEND ALOFT · JOHN FISCHER
page 20

This short sketch concerns an "encounter with fear" and a choice between conspicuous heroism and self-preservation. The three strangers were finally saved from the terrible choice when the engines "roared back to life," but the story might have ended in a fatal crash with no one left to write about it.

FOR WRITING

Write a brief sketch of an "encounter with fear" or an account of an event that involved a choice similar to the one in Mr. Fischer's "legend." You may base it either on your own experience or the experience of others. Make the details as succinct and striking as possible so as to achieve the maximum effect from the incident itself.

FAREWELL, MY LOVELY! · LEE STROUT WHITE
page 22

This essay, now more than twenty years old, has been a perennial favorite. When this tribute to the "tin Lizzie" first appeared, a few of them were still on the roads, especially in small, isolated towns where people kept a piece of machinery running almost indefinitely. We have difficulty envisioning this ancient automobile today, although many of them appear at antique motor shows and in museums devoted to early cars. From the authors' description, however, we can still get a vivid idea of the looks and "personality" of the Model T Ford.

PROBLEMS

1. When was the last Model T built?

2. Where could the Model T owner find gadgets to embellish his car?

3. The authors use a number of descriptive terms to identify and distinguish the Model T. List them in the order in which they occur in the essay:

4. What term is used to describe the transmission?

What does the word mean in this context?

5. What was the most remarkable quality in the performance of the car?

How did it compare with other cars of the same time in this respect?

6. What was the height of the Model T?

7. Where was the gas tank located?

8. List some of the modern conveniences mentioned by the authors that were lacking in the old Model T:

9. What were some of the mechanical problems the owner was likely to face?

10. What did the driver have to do to start the car?

Why was this process dangerous?

11. What was the function of the timer?

12. Why did the "Number One Bearing" frequently burn out?

FOR FURTHER CONSIDERATION

1. One of the interesting aspects of this account is the way in which the authors present all the shortcomings of the Model T but, at the same time, they manage to indicate how much they loved it. Locate the passages which reveal this attitude, then decide what kind of men were Model T owners. The short piece at the end of the essay will help to illuminate this question.

2. Consider the remarkable differences between the Model T and modern cars. Try to determine the ways in which this very popular car was unique in its own time—and in ours—and which mechanical features were abandoned by the manufacturers when later automobiles were designed.

FOR WRITING

Write a short, explicit essay on one of the following topics:

1. How to Start a Model T Ford.

2. The Owner of the Model T: A Man Enthroned.

3. The Planetary Transmission.

4. Unique Mechanical Aspects of the Model T Ford.

FROM THE SUBWAY TO THE SYNAGOGUE · ALFRED KAZIN
page 27

This excerpt from Mr. Kazin's account of his early schooling is severely honest. As he passes his old school, recalling his fear of it, he remembers in precise detail how he felt in the hostile world of the Brownsville neighborhood.

PROBLEMS

1. What did the boy believe to be the chief reason one went to school?

2. What lines give us his impressions of:

a. his school

b. his teachers

c. the principal

d. his parents

3. Why was "character" a "bitter thing" to the boy?

4. What complex set of values caused the boy and his family to be "ashamed"?

5. Why was stammering such a severe handicap to the boy?

6. Explain the circumstances which led to the boy's despair on the steps of the drug store.

VOCABULARY

With the help of your dictionary, define these words as they are used in the context of the essay.

pretentious

implacably

abysmal

obsequiously

demonstrative

refractory

tacitly

ordeal

quailing

stupefaction

STYLE

Mr. Kazin achieves *unity* in this essay partly by the repetition of key ideas. For example, we can trace the repetition of the "unending series of tests" and the way in which they were supposed to represent success or failure in the "record book." The unity of the sketch, of course, depends upon the single subject—the device of reminiscence about a short period in his life in which several related scenes are recalled.

Coherence is the quality shown by the transitions between paragraphs, as in the analogy between God Himself and the respect owed to teachers at the end of the second and the beginning of the third paragraphs.

A third aspect of style, *emphasis,* is shown in the repetition of descriptive details and vivid comparisons. The last two paragraphs are especially effective in the use of metaphor and vivid imagery.

Study the essay and mark the passages which you think exemplify these aspects of style.

FOR WRITING

1. Write a short analysis of Mr. Kazin's education at the Brownsville school. If you have attended what was considered a "tough school," use your own experience for comparison. Try to decide—and explain—whether or not the pain of constant testing made the student a "success."

2. What scene or object reminds you of your own school days? Write a sketch in which you recall a symbol of your life in school and show how it objectifies your feelings about it.

REMINISCENCES OF CHILDHOOD · DYLAN THOMAS
page 33

Thomas' prose, like his poetry, is full of visual imagery and echoes of sensuous sound. This piece recreates in luxurious detail the directness and wonder of the child's world.

PROBLEMS

1. Which war does Thomas refer to as the "Great War"?

2. What does "watched the Punch and Judy" mean?

3. Look at a map of Wales, then list some of the "wild names like peals of bells in the darkness."

4. Why could a boy belong to only one "secret society"?

5. Which task did Thomas choose as his initiation to the secret society? Why?

6. What were some of the wonders the boys found in their little park? (Try to distinguish between the real and imaginary ones.)

7. What does Thomas tell us about the subject of the poem, "The Hunchback in the Park"?

8. Who was the "whiskered snake in the grass one must keep off of"?

STYLE

Thomas' language often communicates more in a figurative than in a literal sense. Here are two examples:

1. "... ships steaming away into wonder and India ..."
2. "... half-people who rode on nightmares ..."

Find five other examples like those above:

1.

2.

3.

4.

5.

FOR FURTHER CONSIDERATION

1. The phrase "... the crowds in the streets with leeks in their hats ..." refers to an ancient Welsh custom. Look up *leeks* in the dictionary and try to discover what the allusion means.

2. The fantasy of flying in one's dreams was shared by the Russian surrealist, Marc Chagall. To help visualize the scene at the end of Thomas' sketch, browse among the art books in your library to find a reproduction of some of Chagall's fantasies on canvas.

FOR WRITING

1. Write a brief reminiscence of childhood, using as your first sentence Thomas' "The memories of childhood have no order" and as your last sentence, "The memories of childhood have no order, and no end."

2. A similar piece by Dylan Thomas, "A Child's Christmas in Wales," was recorded before the poet died. Listen to it in your school library (or in a record shop), preferably with a copy of the story to help you see and hear at the same time. Write a report on the story, showing how the sound helps to convey the ideas more completely to the reader's imagination.

3. Compare the purposes of Thomas' "Reminiscences of Childhood" to those in Kazin's account of his Brownsville schooldays. You will not be able to compare specific scenes, but the philosophical intention of the two pieces can be managed in a short theme.

A TIME OF JUVENILES · ERIC HOFFER
page 37

This essay is more formal than many of the others in this book: it proposes a thesis and supports it through evidence and argument. Thus, the order of the ideas and the quality of the reasoning are most important to the meaning.

COMPREHENSION QUIZ

Mark T or F for true or false.

_____ 1. Historically, only adolescents have demonstrated juvenile mentality.

_____ 2. Whole societies, as well as individuals, can act like juveniles.

_____ 3. The author agrees with Koestler that revolutionaries are men who have failed to grow up.

_____ 4. One theory is that the historical situation produces childish behavior in different types of people in all ages.

_____ 5. In comparison with any other hundred-year period in history, the world has not changed very drastically in the last century.

_____ 6. One example of how societies face change is the primitive ritual of rebirth.

_____ 7. The author says that Moses invented the idea of "the chosen people" in order to prepare the Hebrews for their new life.

_____ 8. The Industrial Revolution was not as profound a change as the freeing of the slaves.

_____ 9. Much of the primitive behavior in society can be blamed on machines.

_____10. Hoffer states that embracing mass movements such as Birchism and Communism are juvenile behavior.

_____11. "Plasticity" is the ability of a society to make great changes and maintain its homogeneity.

_____12. The author offers automation as a solution to the problems of the "time of juveniles."

VOCABULARY

credulity

plausible

aberration

apocalyptic

denouement

paradox

indictment

puerility

FOR WRITING

1. Several famous political leaders of the twentieth century would not fit Hoffer's category of "juveniles," perhaps because they were not "revolutionaries." Study the career of one of them and write a theme using him as an example of the *mature* leader. Keep Hoffer's essay in mind in making your choice of subject.

2. Read Shakespeare's three plays, *Henry IV*, Parts I and II, and *Henry V*, then write an analysis of the young Hotspur's career.

Like Thomas' "Reminiscences of Childhood," this essay is an informal, personal recollection which makes its point indirectly. The personal essay depends heavily upon description, tone, and mood for its effect. Thus, White's details help us to see and feel with him, to experience the remembered world of a summer at the lake.

PROBLEMS

1. Early in the essay, White says, "I could tell that it was going to be pretty much the same as it had been before." "Pretty much," however, suggests that it was not exactly the same. What is the first sentence that suggests that it was not quite the same and that the years had brought some change?

2. What does the repeated phrase, ". . . there had been no years," mean in the context of the essay?

3. List the things that had changed since White's childhood at the lake. If they represent improvements (or changes of which White approved), mark them with "X."

4. Though there is no plot in an essay, the order of the details is very important. Why do you think White left the description of the thunderstorm until last?

5. What effect does the last sentence have in reinforcing the *theme* of the essay?

FOR WRITING

Describe a favorite vacation spot visited by your family when you were a child. Try to recreate your experiences so as to make your reader see and feel the place. Include details about the games, the natural beauty (or lack of it), the people who went there, and what you did by yourself. Take time to revise the paper carefully to make the descriptions as precise and vivid as possible.

INJELITITIS OR PALSIED PARALYSIS · C. NORTHCOTE PARKINSON
page 49

PROBLEMS

1. Why does Parkinson prefer the diagnostic method of the British medical specialists?

2. How are the main stages of the disease, Injelititis, recognized?

3. What is the significance of the word "judgment" in the context of the essay?

4. What situation can cause the rare example of a "natural cure" for Injelititis?

5. Why do executives prefer a low standard of competence in an organization?

6. What analogy does Parkinson use to define the *smugness* of the injelitant organization?

7. What is the chief characteristic of the tertiary stage of the disease?

8. What are the two main principles which should govern the treatment of the disease?

   a.

   b.

9. What are the names of the "drugs" Parkinson suggests as possible remedies in the primary stages of the disease?

10. What is Parkinson's recommendation when the tertiary stage has been reached?

FOR FURTHER CONSIDERATION

Professor Parkinson employs an ancient device for naming individuals and organizations descriptively. Consider the metaphorical effect of "Mr. Cypher," "Toprank," "Lowgrade," and "Much-Striving" in the context of the essay. These descriptive names have been used to advantage in literature, especially in the drama of Ben Jonson and his admirers, the Restoration dramatists of the late seventeenth century. The device is as old as Aesop, however, making further description of a type character quite superfluous.

LANGUAGE

Professor Parkinson occasionally uses expressions which are not immediately familiar to Americans. What would be the American usage for the following words in italics?

1. The *operatives* assigned to the task . . .

2. . . . an *estate agent* . . .

3. . . . the *vendor* . . .

4. . . . when the germ of the disease is *on holiday* . . .

5. . . . the directives *issuing from* a second-rate chief . . .

6. . . . the whitewash is *flaking off* the ceiling . . .

7. . . . The cloakroom *tap* cannot be turned off . . .

8. . . . repetition of the treatment would *set up a fresh* irritation . . .

9. It can be *founded afresh* . . .

10. This drug is an *immediate stimulus* . . .

FOR WRITING

Professor Parkinson's essay is one of several he has written on problems of administration, organization, and the economics of the business world. Some are included in the volume from which this essay is reprinted, *Parkinson's Law and Other Studies in Administration,* and others are in later volumes. Look up one or more of his books in your college library and write a brief analysis of one of the essays. Organize your analysis to include a discussion of his *aims* and *methods.* Decide what the *target* is, and show how he illustrates and illuminates the subject with analogies, metaphorical language, caricature, and other devices.

STREET ELBOW · RIXFORD KNIGHT
page 55

Trying to discover the origins of common names for objects, people, and places can provide scholars with much information about language and society. In this anecdote, Knight has pointed out a semantic problem while drawing a delightful sketch of the baffled plumber.

COMPREHENSION QUIZ

Read the essay rapidly once, then answer the questions without looking back at the text.

_____ 1. The plumber was making repairs on the pipes in the street.

_____ 2. The *regular* elbow has two female ends.

_____ 3. The author was arguing with the plumber to find out how much he knew about the plumbing business.

_____ 4. The author suggested that the word *hermaphrodite* might give a more accurate description of the street elbow.

_____ 5. The plumber's father had been a plumber for more than thirty-five years.

_____ 6. The plumber's father had invented the term *street elbow*.

_____ 7. The ancient Aryans probably had neither streets nor plumbing.

_____ 8. The plumber knew a man named Street who used to be in the plumbing business.

_____ 9. The author's encyclopedia correctly described the street elbow.

_____10. The plumber was finally convinced that the street elbow should have two male ends.

FOR WRITING

All trades and professions have special terminology to describe tools, materials, functions, or methods. Write an essay on some of the special terms used in a trade or hobby with which you are familiar, such as electronics, hot-rodding, or surfing, or the argot of one of the professions. Try to show how the terms describe, identify, or explain. Examine them for accuracy and appropriateness. Remember that many such expressions are metaphorical. Choose a limited number of terms related to a single area and explore them fully.

COME ACROSS WITH THE FACTS · JAMES THURBER
page 59

Thurber is aiming at two targets in this short satire; in fact, he seems to be using one as reinforcement for the other. While he tells "Mrs. Quibble" about his distressing correspondence with school children, she provides a demonstration—unwittingly— of the ineffectiveness of her own education.

PROBLEMS

1. Is Thurber unfair in his revelation of Mrs. Quibble? Explain.

2. Is Thurber unfair to the children who write to him? Why?

3. How does the setting of the sketch add to the humor of it?

4. In what way does Mrs. Quibble's dialogue demonstrate the central point of the satire?

5. List one or more term paper assignments similar to those reported to Thurber by the children. (If you were never given such an assignment, invent some.)

6. List the examples of Mrs. Quibble's faulty English and provide the acceptable term beside it:

a.   e.

b.   f.

c.   g.

d.

FOR WRITING

Discuss one of the following statements in a short theme:
1. Thurber is criticizing a basic flaw in our system of educating students.
2. Thurber's aim in this satire is to draw a caricature of a modern Mrs. Malaprop.

HALF–LIFE BEGINS AT 30 · "A. B. C."
page 61

The chief methods of satire used in this short essay are (1) a far-fetched analogy between hot atoms and human brains; (2) an apparently straightforward description of a series of events which might be written at the end of the century; (3) exaggeration and generalization based on actual events of our own time. The author's target is the "crusade for new know-how," as he inelegantly calls it. He suggests that the scramble for repeated doses of professional education will result in absurdities and perhaps an actual shortage of useful knowledge.

FOR DISCUSSION

1. In the context of the essay, what does the author mean in the statement that ". . . an old doctor who let his patients eat, drink, and smoke as usual was often saluted as a sage."

2. Discover the nearest "plastic palace full of specialists and computers" (called "complexes") and find out what kind of research is being done there. You may have one or more of them on your own campus.

3. What kind of information can be dumped into a computer and left there, "like so much surplus wheat"? (Later in the article, the author mentions the data used by the census bureau.) Can you justify such storage of information?

4. Compare the uses of computers suggested in this article with the limitations discussed in Lucy Eisenberg's article, "What Computers Can't Do" (page 74).

FOR WRITING

1. Explore the problem of professional education as a way to avoid "status slippage" in the case of a newspaper reporter, an architect, and a politician.
2. Look up the catalog of graduate courses offered by the nearest large university and study it as you would if you were an experienced professional looking for more education in your field. Write an outline of the courses or specialized program you could take and analyze how this additional education would help you to get a better job or a higher position.

The main device of this satire is the presentation of an observer who is completely unfamiliar with the subject and the giving to him of an occasion to comment objectively and dispassionately on it. The same device is used, for example, in May Swenson's poem, "Southbound on the Freeway," (page 316) and in several more famous satires of an earlier time. The "Martians" appear in literature frequently, of course, and have become a kind of convention for the detached, objective observer.

PROBLEMS

1. What basic differences between the hypothetical Martians and Earthmen are implied in this satire?

2. What is XU's understanding of the meaning of "sin"?

3. What does XU say is the definition of "happiness"?

4. Which human characteristic meets with XU's approval?

5. Which of the foibles XU deals with do you think could be corrected in a more sensible (or ideal) society?

FOR WRITING

Several major satires have employed the detached observer technique to point out the follies in the world at the time the books were written. Among them are Sir Thomas More's *Utopia*, Jonathan Swift's *Gulliver's Travels*, Voltaire's *Candide*, and Samuel Butler's *Erewhon*. Read one of these famous classics and write an essay on the technique employed to point out man's folly.

DEAR MUMMY · MARYA MANNES
page 68

The epistolary style of this satire reveals a set of social attitudes which the author places in a very harsh light. The keynote of the piece is irresponsibility. The older generation (the grandparents) assumes that the "honest values" still apply to life in Crestview—Miss Mannes' name for expensive suburbia—yet the grandparents are floating about on a yacht called "Fool's Paradise." The middle generation is represented by a doting mother and a semi-detached father whose business practices are questionable. The subject of the correspondence is a boy named Doug; his behavior shocks his grandparents, but his parents believe that he can do no wrong. The essential morality is revealed ironically.

PROBLEMS

1. Identify each of the following and write a sentence of characterization to show the "type":

   a. Addie (Mrs. Howard Andrews)

   b. Mummy (Mrs. Curtis Munson)

   c. Ginny Maitland

   d. Franny Westover

   e. Howard Andrews

   f. Curtis Munson

   g. Doug Andrews

2. How does Mrs. Andrews defend her son's education and attitudes?

3. What is Howard Andrews' explanation for his son's alleged irresponsibility at the Westover party?

4. How did Doug's parents reward him for "getting into Yale"?

FOR WRITING

1. Evaluate the attitudes of Mr. and Mrs. Andrews toward their son and his friends. Try to put the blame for Doug's problems where it belongs, but think carefully about the ultimate responsibility of a young man for his own behavior.
2. In the last letter, Addie writes that ". . . the generations don't always mix." Then she adds, "Young people are more realistic, don't you think?" Discuss this opinion in the light of the events in the story.

THE MAN WHO WAS PUT IN A CAGE · ROLLO MAY
page 72

Rollo May's short satire is cast in what resembles the form of a fable. The three characters are not given names, but their functions express how they reflect the theme: freedom in relation to happiness, personality, dignity, and sanity.

PROBLEMS

1. Fables usually have animal characters with typical "natures," such as fox, pig, vulture, or dog. Sometimes human types are used, such as fisherman, baker, thief, or emperor. What functions do the three figures in this modern satire seem to possess, as revealed by the names they are given?

   a. The King

   b. The Average Man

   c. The Psychologist

2. What gradual changes took place in the man in the cage?

3. Would the outcome of the fable be different if the man had chosen to take part in the experiment voluntarily? Explain.

4. Why do you think the author ended the story with the psychologist?

FOR WRITING

1. Write a short narrative to illuminate one of the following pairs of abstractions:
      tolerance and friendship
      fear and bigotry
      knowledge and creativity
2. There is an obvious lesson in May's satire, if his premises are correct. We still put men in cages when we jail them for crime. Does confinement destroy a man as thoroughly as the "average man" in the cage? Discuss the validity of the satire, keeping in mind that the experiment was done on a man who was unjustly imprisoned.

WHAT COMPUTERS CAN'T DO · LUCY EISENBERG
page 74

Mrs. Eisenberg says, "A computer is a calculating machine." But the complex machinery we now familiarly call a computer has started another technical revolution, affecting many more aspects of life than mere calculation. In this article, the author explores the present limits of the computer in the area of "thinking."

PROBLEMS

Explain or define the following terms from the information given in the article. Use your dictionary if necessary, but make your definitions fit the present context.

1. pattern recognition

2. the basic components of the computer:

   a. the executive

   b. the memory

   c. the control

3. cognition

4. categorization

5. cybernetics

6. an innate idea

7. electrode

8. stimulus

9. simulate

10. computer program

11. intelligence

COMPREHENSION QUIZ

Mark T or F for true or false.

_____ 1. The creator of Pandemonium has a spare-time hobby of model shipbuilding.
_____ 2. Computers cannot do evaluation of equations.
_____ 3. IBM has programmed a computer to play checkers.
_____ 4. Computers can handle words well enough to carry on a simple conversation.
_____ 5. Programmers have generally overlooked pattern recognition in their efforts to design intelligent machines.
_____ 6. Biologists have discovered the rules the human brain uses to recognize patterns.
_____ 7. What is known today about the biology of pattern recognition is based on the work of a psychiatrist, Warren McCulloch.
_____ 8. The first experiments in studying pattern recognition were done with frogs.
_____ 9. Pandemonium could easily read cursive writing.
_____10. Mr. Samuel's checker-playing machine can regularly defeat the man who programmed it.

VOCABULARY QUIZ

Put the number of the best synonym from the right-hand column in the space to the left of the word it matches. Each set is self-contained, but there are two extra choices that will not match.

_____amenable
_____formidable
_____ambiguous
_____rabid
_____inimitable
_____pandemonium

1. wild disorder
2. not clear
3. intelligence
4. causing dread or fear
5. violent; raging
6. hubris
7. responsible
8. matchless

_____pessimism
_____cursive
_____mediocre
_____discrete
_____integral
_____idiomatic

1. essential
2. scrambled
3. to expect the worst
4. usual characteristic of a language
5. writing with letters joined
6. recognizably separate parts
7. functional
8. ordinary

FOR WRITING

1. One of the best ways to discover the uses of computers is to visit an installation where they are in use. Your instructor will help you arrange a visit to one that is on or near your campus. Find out what kinds of machines are used and what kinds of problems are solved with them, then write a report on your findings.

2. After reading the essay carefully, ask one of your mathematics or psychology instructors about the feasibility of the computers' "thinking." Test some of Mrs. Eisenberg's statements, then write a discussion of what you discover.

BERTRAND RUSSELL ON THE SINFUL AMERICANS · JOHN FISCHER
page 82

John Fischer contends in this series of letters that Professor Russell misunderstands American policy on war and weapons, and that his published criticism is based upon out-of-date information or misinformation. Neither writer represents the official view of his country, but each reflects a substantial segment of public opinion in both countries. Not all British people share Professor Russell's opinion, and many Americans would not agree with Mr. Fischer. The questions raised, however, are serious ones; no citizen of today's world can avoid them.

PROBLEMS

These problems should be worked out on scratch paper to enable you to come to some conclusions about the basic premises of the argument between the two correspondents.

1. Make a summary list of the points of argument advanced by Professor Russell in his letter of March 4, 1963. If you think Mr. Fischer successfully refuted any or all of them, put a check mark beside those items.
2. Make a summary list of Mr. Fischer's contentions in his letters of March 21 and April 3. If you think he provided adequate support for the items in his argument, put a check mark beside those items.
3. Match the two lists to see whether all phases of the argument are covered. Write a short summary of what the argument was all about. (An argument of this kind is never "won," of course. Neither author conceded that the other had convinced him, though Mr. Fischer acknowledged his agreement with certain premises advanced by Professor Russell.)

VOCABULARY QUIZ

Put the number of the best synonym from the right-hand column in the space to the left of the word it matches. Each set is self-contained, but there are two extra choices that will not match.

_____acquiesce	1. pertaining to the art of using words effectively
_____extirpate	2. to destroy completely
_____genocide	3. statistical
_____unequivocal	4. systematic killing of a whole nation
_____rhetorical	5. to consent without protest
	6. a contention
	7. straightforward; clear

_____echelon	1. incapable of error
_____abominable	2. compliant
_____fanatic	3. unreasonably enthusiastic
_____infallibility	4. a step-like formation of units
_____exploit (v.)	5. stumbling
	6. disgusting; vile
	7. to use unfairly for profit

Walter Lippmann's writings in the mid-twentieth century have included several books and a syndicated column that has influenced the thought of millions of Americans. Here he speaks optimistically of our political future and proposes that the Western economic community be considered our best security against the threat of nuclear war.

PROBLEMS

1. Before the nuclear age began, what were the *purposes* of war?

2. What would be the *effects* of a full nuclear war?

3. What would be the political effect on the American republic after a nuclear war?

4. What does Lippmann say might cause a nation to "press the button for a nuclear war"?

5. What are the various aspects of the "competition between two societies"—the Western world and communism?

    a.   c.   e.

    b.   d.

6. What has been the purpose of the "progressive movement" which began during the administration of Theodore Roosevelt?

7. What are the characteristics of the civilized and enlightened men in our age?

    a.   b.   c.

FOR WRITING

In view of the political and international developments in the world since Mr. Lippmann's article was written (1962), write a discussion of the current validity of one of the following statements:

1. "For while nuclear weapons have made war, the old arbiter of human affairs, an impossible action for a rational statesman to contemplate, we do not have any other reliable way of dealing with issues that used to be resolved by war."

2. "As long as there exists a balance of power and of terror, neither side can impose its doctrine and its ideology upon the other."

THE PATIENT'S RIGHT TO DIE · JOSEPH FLETCHER
page 95

Joseph Fletcher deals with a problem which most of us will confront at some time in our lives, either as members of a family which must decide about death or as potential patients. Along with the many benefits which medicine has given us, there are some problems requiring moral judgments; specifically, they concern the questions of prolonging life and prolonging death. Whatever our individual views may be, it is this kind of serious questioning which has altered the doctrine and caused reappraisal among theologians as well as among laymen and doctors.

PROBLEMS

Most of these questions involve opinions rather than verifiable facts, but they will require you to come to grips with Professor Fletcher's ideas, whether you agree with them or not. Write down the evidence or the reasons for your views wherever possible.

1. What is the main issue in this essay?

2. Do you agree with the statement, "In certain cases it is indecent to go on living," as Nietzsche observed?

3. How does the term "human dignity" apply to the problem discussed in this essay?

4. Is it more important for a doctor to prolong life or to alleviate suffering?

5. Should the ultimate decision as to when a person may die be left entirely to doctors?

6. What is the difference between direct and indirect euthanasia?

7. Should the distinction between civil law and medical morality be a matter for the courts to decide?

VOCABULARY

Make your own list of medical terms used in the article and check them with the dictionary if the meaning is unclear from the context. Write a brief definition of the following words as used in the essay.

ultimate

irrational

phobic

adversary

waning

ministrations

contrivances

irreparable

protracted

idolatrous

minimal

specious

FOR WRITING

1. When the author says, "Natural or physical determinism must give way to the morality of love," he is stating his position on indirect euthanasia. What do you think his "morality of love" includes? Write a definition of this concept.
2. "Birth control, artificial insemination, sterilization, and abortion are all medically discovered ways of fulfilling and protecting human values and hopes in spite of nature's failures or foolishnesses. Death control, like birth control, is a matter of human dignity."

Choose one of the four medical techniques listed at the beginning of the quotation as a subject for an essay. You need not take a position *for or against* the questions implied until your study of the problem leads you to a firm position. In this way, you can keep an open mind and be more judicious in presenting the evidence. Examine the legal aspects if you can find authoritative evidence about them, or confine your discussion to the moral or philosophical aspects. All of these techniques are *legal* in some parts of the world, though taboo and custom vary greatly.

VIOLENCE IN THE CITY STREETS · JANE JACOBS
page 103

According to Jane Jacobs, the marvelous redevelopment now under way in American cities is creating problems which deny the city dweller one of his first rights—safety in the streets. A city dweller herself, Mrs. Jacobs challenges some of the basic concepts of city planning.

PROBLEMS

1. Who keeps the city's streets safe?

2. What are the qualities of a city street that make it safe?

    a.

    b.

    c.

3. What conclusions does the author draw about safety from the following examples? Indicate whether the areas are safe or unsafe and why.

Los Angeles

North End, Boston

Roxbury

Hyde Park-Kenwood, Chicago

Upper Broadway, New York

"Blenheim Houses"

4. How do people living in rich neighborhoods provide for safety?

5. What advantages to public safety are provided by stores, bars, and restaurants?

    a.

    b.

    c.

    d.

6. How are city planners making the streets unsafe?

FOR FURTHER CONSIDERATION

Most of the city planning today is done by professional architects who have long-range aesthetic considerations in mind rather than the safety aspects which Mrs. Jacobs is concerned about. Many of the "blighted" areas being replaced in our older cities are unsafe from the hygienic point of view, or they are crowded, dirty, and impossible to renovate. Look among the books on architecture and city planning in your library to find some philosophical tenets which guide the urban renewal experts. Then try to reconcile Mrs. Jacobs' warnings with the views of the experts. Is it possible to plan modern, clean, beautiful cities and safeguard the streets merely by the arrangement of buildings, parks, and shopping centers?

Additional support for Mrs. Jacobs' thesis is in the article by Martin Gansberg, "38 Who Saw Murder Didn't Call the Police," (page 177) and the story by Florence Engel Randall, "The Watchers" (page 292).

VOCABULARY

Define these words as they are used in the context of the essay.

intricate	cajoling
superannuated	extraneous
demarcation	beleaguered
sanctions	opprobrious
proponents	sequestered
ludicrous	amenity

FOR WRITING

1. The author writes of the need for distinction between public and private spaces, but she does not explain in detail why such a demarcation is needed. Discuss this question, using examples to support your views.
2. Sometimes people have had very happy lives in what most modern parents would consider undesirable neighborhoods. Bill Cosby and Sam Levinson, for example, have created warmly humorous characterizations from their childhood backgrounds. Describe such a neighborhood, either based on your own experience or upon the published (or recorded) material of someone who has lived in a lively, honest section of a large city.

LOVE OR MARRIAGE? · ERNEST VAN DEN HAAG
page 113

Mr. Van den Haag attacks the popular concept of love and marriage as indispensable to each other and argues that our insistence upon this premise is related to divorce.

PROBLEMS

Answer these questions from the context of the essay, noting any with which you do not agree.

1. What is the author's definition of:

a. love

b. affection

2. What is the importance of sex gratification to marriage?

3. If "certainty of one's love eliminates the longing," what happens to love when people marry?

4. What is the importance of the "child's image of the perfect parent"?

5. Who was the earliest writer on the subject of love mentioned in the essay?

6. One of the arguments can be put in a syllogistic form:

> A good marriage is lasting.
> A marriage based on love cannot last.
> Therefore, a marriage based on love is not a good marriage.

Does the author's essay support this argument or not? Write the evidence for your opinion by paraphrasing the appropriate passages.

FOR FURTHER CONSIDERATION

1. Read Anne Sinclair Mehdevi's account of "A Persian Courtship" (page 6) and consider the customs there in the light of Van den Haag's discussion of marriage and love. The "arranged marriage" is still prevalent in many parts of the world. Why does the young Persian girl, Sari, prefer the Western idea of love?

2. At random, look through any women's magazines available to you, and note any articles which would support the following statement: "This is the promise of marriage. Movies, songs, TV; romance magazines, all intensify the belief that love alone makes life worthwhile, is perpetual, conquers the world's evils, and is fulfilled and certified by marriage."

3. Consider the author's statement that "... the young have a disproportionate share of divorces." Locate whatever statistics are available about the age of those who sue for divorce in your locality. An interesting way to go about it is to examine the "vital statistics" column of your local newspaper for several days, and tabulate the marriages and divorces according to the ages published.

FOR WRITING

Choose one of the following premises from the article and write an essay in which you either defend or attack it:

1. Hollywood's "romances are shoddy clichés."

2. "In an enduring relationship, physical gratification is an effect and not a cause."

3. "If the relationship is stabilized, love is replaced by other emotions."

4. "Love as we know it is a Christian legacy."

5. "The yearning for love, attended by anxiety to prove oneself well-adjusted and normal, turns into eagerness to get married."

THE NEW AMERICAN FEMALE · MARION K. SANDERS
page 120

In this article, Mrs. Sanders examines some of the current issues associated with what she calls "the Woman problem" and finds that many writers and statisticians have distorted both the problem and the solution. The focus of much of the concern is on "the Educated Woman, also known as the Trapped Housewife."

LANGUAGE

Along with many clichés, which are consciously used for stylistic effect, Mrs. Sanders employs a number of allusions, metaphorical expressions, puns and startling phrases. All of them can be translated, so to speak, from the context of the article—with perhaps a little help from a dictionary. Write the best plain-language explanation beside each item.

1. demi-feminism

2. little-girl bangs

3. corn-fed Queen Victoria

4. a latter-day Great Whig Hostess

5. salons filled with fashionable wits and dandies

6. "male curmudgeonism"

7. gathering of female eminences

8. a rabble of TV cameramen

9. "liberality of sentiment"

10. simultaneously and seriatim

11. Feminology

12. the basic gambits

13. Salvation Through Job gospel

14. Suffragists of yore

15. the Friedan Syndrome

16. spinster mercenaries

FOR WRITING

Mrs. Sanders minimizes "the Woman problem" in her article, while she acknowledges that many other writers—especially the Feminologists—have other views. Define one phase of the argument, such as "educated women are usually unhappy housewives," or "the talents of professional women are wasted when they give up careers for families," and write an argument for the other side. You might look up some of the writers mentioned in the article to find support for your view. Remember that you can write a good argument without agreeing with it if you are logical and consistent.

THE SOPHISTICATED MAN · MARYA MANNES
page 129

Marya Mannes draws a portrait of the sophisticated man she prefers, based on her own taste and standards. The essay, however, is highly provocative; though we may agree with her premise that there *are* some standards by which we can judge sophistication, we end with only *one* kind of man—the one Miss Mannes portrays here.

PROBLEMS

1. Briefly summarize the characteristics of the sophisticated man as given in the essay. You may prefer other categories than these:

  a. dress:

  b. experience:

  c. taste and manners:

  d. interests:

2. Why does Miss Mannes prefer the man who has had experience with "many women"?

3. What are the characteristics of the man whose "heart may be gold, but his company is leaden"?

4. What rule should the sophisticated man follow in choosing gifts for a woman?

FOR WRITING

1. Defend the "ordinary husband" by writing a sketch of his character. He is mentioned in the essay, but none of his better qualities are introduced.
2. A basic tenet of morality—long respected though increasingly ignored—is virginity. Miss Mannes apparently advocates "experience" but objects to promiscuity, at least for her sophisticated man. Write a discussion of this problem, either from the point of view of the man or of a woman. Be careful to state your position unequivocally.
3. Miss Mannes rejects the "glad-handing Shriner" and the "bearded Zen seeker and café poet," because ". . . they both abide by the conventions of their groups, their horizons equally limited." Examine this premise carefully, then write a more extended argument *for or against* conformity or the "conventions of the group."

LOVE, DEATH, SACRIFICE, AND SO FORTH · WILLIAM SAROYAN
page 135

The American public has always been interested in the extraordinary problems of ordinary people. In fact, the very ordinary nature of most of our lives makes us want something extraordinary to happen, which encourages the film makers to create the unusual over and over again. As a result, we are not satisfied unless the situations are magnified, the characters exaggerated, the events piled on. We want to experience strong feelings, so we demand intensely emotional drama, even when it is not believable. What is called melodrama in the theater, soap opera on television or radio, we have dubbed "typical Hollywood" drama.

In the hypothetical film about Tom Garner, Mr. Saroyan finds the subject for his satire of Hollywood drama. He gives his version of a suicide on the screen and contrasts it to a real suicide. The target is not only Hollywood's unbelievable films but also the public, those who accept the impossible plot and fake characters.

PROBLEMS

1. Locate the passages in which Saroyan describes—and judges—the characters, as in this sentence about Tommy: "Tom's son is an irresponsible but serious and well-dressed young man."

    a. Tom:

    b. Sally:

    c. Tom's second wife:

2. The film does not observe any rules for unity of time, place, or action, but rather skips from one vignette to another. List two other scenes such as the one shown in these lines: "Tom saw that it would mean a lot to Sally if he became ambitious. Sitting at the supper table he said that he would."

    a.

    b.

3. Saroyan echoes the trite language of the film dialogue when it serves his purpose, and adds homely judgments in such clichés as this: "We know he'll be man enough to do it." Find three more examples like this one.

    a.

    b.

    c.

4. The reactions of the audience are revealed at strategic moments as Saroyan re-creates the action on the screen. For example, "The atmosphere of the theater is becoming electrical with the apprehension of middle-aged ladies who have spent the better part of their lives in the movies, loving, dying, sacrificing themselves to noble ideas . . ." Locate two more instances in which Saroyan ridicules the audience's reactions.

a.

b.

5. How is the real suicide different from the Hollywood version?

FOR FURTHER CONSIDERATION

1. This essay originally appeared in 1934, less than five years after the beginning of the "talking" films. The dramatic tradition of the silent movies had been very uneven in quality, but the dimension of sound was not entirely an aesthetic improvement, either. Locate a history of the films in your college library and try to discover what the state of the art really was in 1934. Was it really as bad as Saroyan indicates? Some critics think the true nadir came later, but the popularity of the films during the decade of the 1930s far exceeded that of all other art forms.

2. Much of the humor of this essay is the result of Saroyan's glib treatment of what the movie-going public was taking seriously. At times he is merely offhand: "Nature did it. You know how nature is and all that." Often he mocks the pretentiousness of Hollywood by placing the colloquial remark after the dignified statement: "The dignity of life is preserved. Everything is hotsy-totsy." Study the other instances of the author's flippant language as a technique of satire.

FOR WRITING

1. Choose a popular television serial and follow it for a week, then write a synopsis of the plot—or try to tell what happened, at least. Use the names of the characters to make your discussion specific.
2. Write a brief description of the characters in what you would call a typical Hollywood movie. Some of the older ones appear on television; the later ones, however, may show a different kind of character presentation.
3. Write a brief essay justifying either TV "soap opera" or the typical Hollywood movie on the grounds that it is American folklore.

GITARS, FOLK SONGS, AND HALLS OF IVY · ARNOLD SHAW
page 139

Mr. Shaw's article offers an insight into one aspect of popular culture represented by the latest "folk-song revival" and compares it to some of the other popular "movements" in our century. Some readers may disagree with his emphasis, but the materials are here for a more thorough study of music and society in our time.

PROBLEMS

1. What were the "three major folk-song revivals" since World War I?

    a.

    b.

    c.

2. Summarize what Mr. Shaw tells us about the career of "Leadbelly."

3. How does Mr. Shaw define rock 'n' roll?

4. What three concepts are emphasized in the traditional definition of folk music?

    a.

    b.

    c.

5. What are some of the various contemporary "schools" of folk singers as Mr. Shaw describes them?

FOR WRITING

1. Write a rebuttal of one or the other of the following quotations:
    a. "But obviously, the teen-agers and pre-teen-agers who are 'sent' by The Beatles do not constitute the audience of folk [music]."
    b. "The youth of today, torn by the insecurity and general immorality of the times, have turned to the stability and the simplicity implicit in traditional songs." (Quoted from Oscar Brand)
2. Mr. Shaw's review of the "folk frenzy" appeared in 1964. Like most accounts of popular culture, it can be modified by adding the perspective of time. Bring the essay up to date by considering the current folk scene, the new singers, and the new kinds of music.

THE WELL OF ENGLISH, NOW DEFILED · WILLARD THORP
page 153

This essay—a favorite among teachers, for obvious reasons—analyzes the student's difficulties in learning to write. Professor Thorp isolates a number of "defilers" which make modern prose vague and ineffective.

PROBLEMS

1. Give a summary definition of "No-English."

2. What are the major sources of "defilement" in English prose in the order Professor Thorp presents them?

    a.

    b.

    c.

    d.

    e.

    f.

3. What are the characteristics of the language which Sandy must master in order to be an effective writer?

4. Who are the *exemplary* prose writers mentioned throughout the essay?

    a.

    b.

    c.

    d.

FOR WRITING

1. Gather some choice specimens from current magazines of one type of "defilers"— "hot-rod style" or advertising style, for example. Analyze them for their precision, meaning, and effect. Be careful to distinguish good metaphors from careless, vague, inaccurate terms.
2. If you can do so without offending your instructors, pick a passage at random from one of your current textbooks and analyze it for clarity in the light of Professor Thorp's analysis of academic prose.

THE AMBUSH · CAPTAIN JAMES MORRIS
page 161

With directions to "find the Viet Cong and kill them," Captain Morris set off on his mission. His story is a straightforward account of the actual ambush, but it is also a revealing study of a soldier's reactions to a new and (to most Americans) unusual kind of warfare.

PROBLEMS

1. Briefly describe the narrator's companion, Cowboy. How do his actions make the author's choice of the word "warrior" better than "soldier"?

2. What details create a sense of time and place in the narrative?

3. What details does the essay include which give us clues to the "social amenities" of the villagers?

4. The following lines are taken sequentially from the narrative. Locate each of them in the context, then note what kind of information it gives us about the narrator's reactions and feelings.

a. "That sort of thing never happened to John Wayne."

b. "I thought that was jolly."

c. "I started to shake uncontrollably. I was not cold and I was not afraid."

d. "I wanted nothing to live out there."

e. "Nothing to do but shrug it off."

f. "I wanted to take the stiffs back with the rest of the gear."

g. "We stopped for a beer in Cheo Reo and still made it to camp by noon."

VOCABULARY

Use your dictionary as far as it is helpful with these words, then write your own definitions based on the context for the rest. If possible, indicate the origins of the slang terms.

resilient

guttural

luminous

elation

astringent

yards

flake out

skittered

stitched

flicks

Grease Gun

hunkered

poncho

twitchy

FOR WRITING

1. Discuss whether you would rather have Cowboy or Captain Morris in command of a squad for an ambush. Give details from the narrative to support your view.
2. Write an analysis of the style of the author, considering the kind of sentences he uses, the slang terms, the side observations and judgments, and the tone—the way he expresses his attitude toward the venture and the people he describes.
3. Write an account of a brief war engagement, either from your own experience or a newspaper account. Try to show the way you—as narrator—feel about it.

A BRAVE SELF FAR AT SEA · LOUDON WAINWRIGHT
page 167

These short pieces by Loudon Wainwright appeared in the editorial pages of *Life* during the weeks immediately following the events they describe. Mr. Wainwright follows the usual plan for an editorial: (1) giving a statement of the event or subject to be discussed; (2) clarifying the subject through an explanation of the points concerned; and (3) expressing an opinion on the subject. The author makes his opinion more significant to us by his careful management of the details.

FOR WRITING

Robert Manry's exploit prompted Mr. Wainwright to say, ". . . by extending himself in such a bold and extravagant way, he somehow dignifies each individual and braces all of us." Write a brief account of the exploit of someone else who has done a similar, self-designed feat. You can base it upon personal experience or upon a published news account, if you prefer.

HOT PURSUIT OF TURNPIKE FLYERS · LOUDON WAINWRIGHT
page 169

COMPREHENSION QUIZ

Mark T or F for true or false.

_____ 1. The author was not usually afraid to drive in holiday traffic.

_____ 2. The author decided to spend his Labor Day weekend doing research for the National Safety Council.

_____ 3. The state trooper whom Mr. Wainwright rode with was interested in radar speed enforcement and new to the Connecticut State Troopers.

_____ 4. Connecticut maintains a hidden radar station ten yards off the turnpike near Westport.

_____ 5. During most of the day, the author saw little evidence of speeding on the turnpike.

_____ 6. The car which Trooper Waite and the author followed was driven by a teenager.

_____ 7. At one point, Waite and the author were traveling at a speed of 120 miles per hour.

_____ 8. The driver of the speeding car defended himself by saying he was on an emergency errand.

_____ 9. State Trooper Hughes, with whom the author had a trip earlier, was involved in a crash in which the driver and two teenage girls were killed.

_____10. Fewer than fifty accidents took place on Connecticut's roads as a result of the Holiday Safety Program.

THE FIERY PANGS OF CONSCIENCE · LOUDON WAINWRIGHT
page 172

COMPREHENSION QUIZ

Answer the questions according to the views expressed by the author, T for true or
F for false.

_____ 1. Morrison committed suicide as a protest against naming Robert McNamara
as Defense Secretary.

_____ 2. Those who protest our country's military involvement in Vietnam are
usually Communist dupes.

_____ 3. The author supports our involvement in Vietnam until there is a reasonable
settlement.

_____ 4. The people who heckled the New York marchers tended to be more violent
than the protesting marchers.

_____ 5. For people like the hecklers, war is a splendid time for forgetting conscience.

_____ 6. The need for united effort in winning a war often causes thoughtful people
to condone or overlook inhumanity to others.

_____ 7. In an undeclared war, it is easier to overlook one's conscience and to accept
the outrages against innocent persons.

_____ 8. Those who wage war in Vietnam can do so because their army training has
relieved them of an individual conscience.

_____ 9. The author deplores the offenses which the United States commits against
humanity while trying to achieve a humane objective.

_____10. Norman Morrison's death destroyed his conscience as well as his body.

WHO KILLED BENNY PARET? · NORMAN COUSINS
page 175

COMPREHENSION QUIZ

Mark T or F for true or false.

_____ 1. Mr. Cousins first met Mike Jacobs at a meeting of the New York State Boxing Commission.
_____ 2. Mr. Jacobs said that killers are needed in the ring to draw a crowd.
_____ 3. Benny Paret was killed in the third round of a ten-round fight.
_____ 4. Millions of people watched the killing on television.
_____ 5. Governor Rockefeller appointed three committees to investigate the death of Paret.
_____ 6. The New York State Boxing Commission refused to allow the probe on the grounds that such an investigation would hurt boxing.
_____ 7. Mr. Paret's manager lost his manager's license as a direct result of the probe.
_____ 8. The investigations proved that fight managers deliberately encourage mauling and other illegal procedures in the ring.
_____ 9. Mr. Cousins believes that the public can be trained to appreciate boxing skills as well as "pole-axe" knockouts.
_____10. Mr. Cousins believes that the responsibility for Paret's death lies with the public which considers boxing entertainment.

STYLE

This editorial is a model of the short essay in several respects:
(1) The reader's interest is immediately engaged, not only by the arresting title but by the anecdotal introductory paragraph.
(2) Mr. Cousins uses authority to support opinion. Mr. Jacobs is quoted directly as an authority on professional boxing.
(3) The logical and orderly arrangement of the paragraphs provides direction to the reader and the topic sentences are linked for coherence.
(4) The tone of the piece is consistent with the subject. Mr. Cousins leaves us in no doubt as to his *position*, reiterated throughout the last two paragraphs.

FOR WRITING

Several so-called sports are illegal in America today and others have been outlawed in the past on grounds of excessive cruelty. Perhaps the butchery of the Roman gladiators is the oldest example, followed in later ages by bear-baiting, cock-fighting—still practiced in many countries—and bull-fighting, still the most important entertainment in Spain. Examine the popularity of one of these sports in an essay.

38 WHO SAW MURDER DIDN'T CALL THE POLICE · MARTIN GANSBERG
page 177

In any form, this story would be shocking, simply because it happened. Yet the author gives the story away in the first sentence. It is a news account written two weeks after the killing, published in *The New York Times* on March 27, 1964, when most of the facts were first available for a complete account of the crime.

COMPREHENSION QUIZ

Mark T or F for true or false.

_____ 1. The murder took place in Kew Gardens, a park on Long Island.
_____ 2. The woman was followed from the parking lot of the railroad by the murderer.
_____ 3. When Miss Genovese called for help the first time, someone frightened her assailant away by shouting, "Let that girl alone!"
_____ 4. When the lights of the apartment went out, the killer returned and stabbed Miss Genovese again.
_____ 5. The injured woman crawled to her apartment door, but the killer returned and stabbed her a third time.
_____ 6. More than an hour passed before a passer-by discovered the body and called the police.
_____ 7. The man who finally called the police had been afraid to call because he had a previous police record.
_____ 8. The murderer, a married man, confessed to two other slayings.
_____ 9. Some of the people in the neighborhood said they had not called because the woman was known to have a bad reputation.
_____10. Following the murder, most of the thirty-eight who saw the crime moved away from the neighborhood.

THE WORLDWIDE PLAGUE OF CITY RIOTS · ANONYMOUS
page 181

This editorial appeared after the summer riots in Watts, a suburb of Los Angeles, and was written by a staff contributor to the London newspaper, *The Economist*. Although the account concerned violence in 1965, it was a prediction of more to come, and the reasons for racial tension and violence were based on an awareness of the global tensions.

FOR WRITING

Discuss one of the following quotations, using the essay as additional evidence:
1. "It was an insurrection of anarchy, an outburst against any kind of system by the people left at the bottom."
2. "The whites are certainly going to be in the middle of a rolling race row for years to come, if only because for the last couple of centuries they have been in a position to be beastly to everybody else, and everybody else is now in a mood to get his own back."

WHAT ARE AMERICANS LIKE TODAY? · JOHN STEINBECK
page 185

In these two passages, one of America's most famous writers turns his attention to the race problem and its effects. His observations are based on his long and sincere attempt to see his world and report it faithfully.

FOR STUDY

1. Consider the ways Mr. Steinbeck supports these observations:

   a. the difference between Americans and an American

   b. his uncertainty about what the American image is

   c. the superiority of the Cooper family

   d. his basic unfitness to take sides in the racial conflict

   e. his knowledge that he would not be wanted in the South

2. Examine the effective use of figurative expressions in these examples:

   a. semantic deadfall

   b. being a limb of the nation its pain spreads out to all America

   c. gelatin plate of babyness

   d. the curtain of fear and anger

   e. the blight can disappear

FOR WRITING

Write an account of an incident in which you became aware of unreasoning prejudice in one of your friends or acquaintances. Recall (or invent) the situation in which the prejudice was expressed in sufficient detail so that the reader can understand what your reaction was without directly *stating* that reaction.

THE CHEERLEADERS · JOHN STEINBECK
page 188

In this scene, Mr. Steinbeck describes a vicious crowd of people whom he felt that he was compelled to observe. His determination to see the spectacle is clearly indicated in the way he narrates the preliminary events: the long drive to New Orleans, his encounters along the way, his elaborate preparations for seeing the "show." The final scene at the school takes up the lesser part of his narrative; the preliminary account established the author's point of view.

FOR STUDY

1. To what does Steinbeck compare the whole scene involving the cheerleaders?

2. Locate at least four expressions which develop this comparison.

3. How many incidents does he record in which people casually mistake Charley for a "nigger"?

4. Note the descriptions of the "cheerleaders" and the way the crowd reacts to them. Why does he introduce them at the beginning as "a group of stout middle-aged women who, by some curious definition of the word 'mother'. . ." and later notes that one does not wear a wedding ring?

5. Why does the author regret that the "show" was broadcast to the world?

FOR FURTHER CONSIDERATION

1. Compare the fight fans described by Mr. Jacobs in the editorial, "Who Killed Benny Paret?" by Norman Cousins (page 175) to the crowd in front of the New Orleans school.

2. Do you see any resemblances—ironic or otherwise—in the audience described in Florence Engel Randall's story, "The Watchers" (page 292) to the crowd waiting for the "cheerleaders"?

FOR WRITING

The desegregation of schools in the South, and in some cities elsewhere, has been a painful and bitter battle for many years. Find a recent article or book on this subject and write your own account of it in the form of an editorial.

ON ILLUSIONS ABOUT AMERICA · ERIC SEVAREID
page 194

These five excerpts from *This Is Eric Sevareid* illustrate the method of an experienced news analyst in dealing with current issues. Since they were originally occasional pieces—brief editorial comments on the news of the day—Mr. Sevareid does not include the corroborative evidence that would be essential if he were writing a more formal essay.

COMPREHENSION QUIZ

Mark T or F for true or false.

_____ 1. The United States is now approaching its teens.
_____ 2. Many nations which we have helped are not particularly grateful to us.
_____ 3. China has not lost its essential self-confidence.
_____ 4. Loss of American self-confidence could lead to loss of direction.
_____ 5. The "Point Four" paragraph was written into Mr. Truman's inaugural speech by his advisors.
_____ 6. Americans are not as materialistic as the French or black Africans.
_____ 7. Americans are more class conscious than well-to-do Latin Americans.
_____ 8. America's fantastic variety of manners, ambitions, and desires is the reason for our numerous laws and regulations.
_____ 9. The best academic centers for studying Russia are located in the United States.
_____10. We must learn patience to gain the respect of our allies.

VOCABULARY

Use your dictionary for unfamiliar terms and write your own definitions for those you know.

cynicism

chagrinned

illusions

riven

profusion

ecclesiastical

eminence

impotent

ON PROGRESS · ERIC SEVAREID
page 196

In this excerpt, Mr. Sevareid presents a series of comparisons to support his comment on the results of progress as seen in the huge urban center. Much of the strength of this brief essay lies in the evidence used to support the comparisons.

PROBLEMS

1. To what does Mr. Sevareid compare each of the following:

   a. progress:

   b. skyscrapers:

   c. city streets:

   d. buses and subway cars:

   e. Americans

   f. cities

2. What inconveniences do New Yorkers share with the inhabitants of cathedral cities in medieval Europe?

   a.

   b.

   c.

   d.

   e.

3. How are ordinary Americans and Russians alike?

   a.

   b.

   c.

FOR FURTHER CONSIDERATION

The allusion to Parkinson's Law refers to the lead essay in the book by C. Northcote Parkinson entitled, *Parkinson's Law and Other Studies in Administration*. Briefly stated, the "law" is that work expands so as to fill up the time available in which to do the work. Another essay from this collection appears (page 49) above, "Injelititis or Palsied Paralysis."

FOR WRITING

Observe a construction site for a large building in progress and consider Mr. Sevareid's objections to it. How long has the building been under construction? What older buildings were torn down to make way for it? Will the final result be a beautiful structure? How many people will it serve and for how many hours a day? Write an essay on the "progress" of this project.

ON GOING TO THE MOON · ERIC SEVAREID
page 198

A whole new branch of reporting has been developed, requiring competent writers with a background of scientific knowledge, and demanding intelligent and responsible readers as well. The excitement attending the flights of the astronauts and the other ventures in space often hinders calm, rational judgment of the "race for space." Mr. Sevareid's remarks here help to temper the enthusiasm and put the alternatives in better perspective.

PROBLEMS

1. Does Mr. Sevareid believe we really will "go to the Moon"? Why?

2. What are the considerations now being pondered by the worriers—the practical men?

    a.
    b.
    c.
    d.

3. What analogy does he use to illustrate the impending "transfiguration" of our world?

4. What does he say will be the ultimate effect of space exploration?

LANGUAGE

Write a brief explanation of these expressions from the article:

unquenchable spirit

contemptuously assailed

pinch-penny mossbacks

fathomless world of human endeavor

What is a vision to some is a specter to others

profound transfiguration

cataclysmic honor

ON THE NEGRO PASSION · ERIC SEVAREID
page 201

PROBLEMS

1. Give the most succinct definition you can of what Mr. Sevareid calls "the Negro Passion."

2. Why will the Negro leaders win?

3. How will the struggle "dominate American politics"?

4. What lesson must we learn from "past rebellions against oppression"?

VOCABULARY

surcease	dearth
inchoate	frenetic
prism	ennobles
rhapsodize	anomalies

ON BIRTH CONTROL · ERIC SEVAREID
page 203

In this article, Mr. Sevareid voices the fears of leaders in most of the countries in the world. With a steadily rising birth rate, accelerating in those countries that can least afford it, the planet Earth is filling up at an alarming rate and being systematically depleted of its resources. The major problem in the world today is the relationship of population to the supply of food.

FOR WRITING

Discuss one of these aspects in an essay of opinion:

1. "Such a traveler has a choice of obsessions these days. He may return with a burning urge that America plunge into these places and these miseries with all its energy, money and talent; he may feel the opposite urge that we get out completely and leave the mass tragedies to God and nature . . ."
2. "For India and Pakistan, for parts of Latin America, North Africa and the mid-East, there is, so I have come to believe, no chance of the stable economic growth and progress in enlightenment that our foreign-aid programs are designed to help achieve, without direct recourse to birth-control practices on a massive scale."

HOOK · WALTER VAN TILBURG CLARK
page 207

Clark's story, though its central character is not human, demonstrates one of the major values of short fiction. It helps us to see and feel the natural world, its triumphs and defeats, and it shows the resourcefulness of a magnificent creature struck down tragically and unfairly. The hawk's nature, as we see it in this story, is consistent and, within the pattern of fulfilling his nature, Hook meets every challenge. When he is shot down, his nature is altered and he is forced to live in a way that is dishonorable for a hawk. Yet he struggles to survive and surmount the disastrous damage to his wing, his lost eye, and his gradual starvation.

PROBLEMS

1. Write a caption or title which describes or summarizes the action in each of the five parts of the story:

I.

II.

III.

IV.

V.

2. What are the "three hungers" in a hawk's life?

3. Write a short description of Hook's appearance and "character" when he is at the height of his power.

4. How does Clark describe the natural wilderness where Hook lived? Note the features of the landscape that might identify the region.

5. Why does Hook despise the gulls?

6. Does the author imply that the Japanese farmer was justified in shooting Hook? Explain your answer.

7. How do hawks train their fledglings for survival?

8. Does the author admire or condemn the hunting instinct and the appetite for battle in the hawk? What lines provide support for your answer?

9. What incident or situation led to Hook's final battle?

FOR FURTHER CONSIDERATION

The imagery in this story provides a vivid sensory impression to the reader. Locate the following passages in their context and think about the way in which the meaning and feeling are expressed.

the surf flowered white

like a small and feathered dervish

one after another coasted his beat

he ate . . . well enough, in a vulture's way

he would have been like a handful of air

the thickets full of song and chatter

content with his shard of life

ripped . . . by the whetted horn

the fringe of the grass fires

weaponless gulls

night chants of the little frogs

his shot-aching breast

FOR WRITING

1. Write a sketch about a wild creature you have observed, using precise imagery and careful description to make your reader see and feel what you experienced when you saw it.

2. The *National Geographic, Nature Magazine,* and several other publications regularly offer feature articles on wild animals. Browse through whatever sources are available to you and then write an essay describing an exotic animal that is unfamiliar in our country. Be sure to acknowledge your sources properly.

THE BOARDING HOUSE · JAMES JOYCE
page 221

Joyce's *Dubliners* appeared in 1914, containing a number of short stories now regarded as modern masterpieces. One of his main achievements was to show a moment of illumination or realization in which the main character in the story is led to a consciousness of his own predicament, a realization of success or failure. In "The Boarding House," Bob Doran realizes how he has been duped and how his own weakness has betrayed him. In addition, we have a portrait of a woman with "an iron whim," and of her apparently compliant daughter who seems to know exactly how to manage her own future. Here is an insight into Dublin a half-century ago, a staid, conventional, but still realistic social milieu.

COMPREHENSION QUIZ

Mark T or F for true or false.

_____ 1. The woman in the story who is nicknamed "The Madam" was the daughter of a plumber.

_____ 2. Her husband took to drink after his father-in-law died.

_____ 3. Both women fully understood that the seduction of the boarder was to provide the daughter with a husband who could provide well for her.

_____ 4. The madam's son, Jack, had threatened to do violence to anyone who did not respect his sister's "honor."

_____ 5. Most of the lodgers were willing to flirt harmlessly with Polly.

_____ 6. The setting of the story was in London about 1900.

_____ 7. Polly didn't want to marry Mr. Doran because she was ashamed of herself.

_____ 8. When Mr. Doran confessed to the priest, he got little satisfaction.

_____ 9. Mr. Mooney repeatedly tried to interfere in Mrs. Mooney's business because he thought she had robbed him.

_____10. Mrs. Mooney left Mr. Doran no alternative but to face her and confess the truth.

PROBLEMS

1. How does the author describe Mrs. Mooney?

2. What incidents caused Mrs. Mooney to separate from her husband?

3. What kind of people lived in Mrs. Mooney's boarding house?

4. How is Polly introduced to the reader?

5. What are Mrs. Mooney's plans for her daughter's future?

6. What is the function of Jack Mooney as a character in the story?

7. What incident began Mr. Doran's downfall?

8. Why did Mr. Doran fear exposure of his affair with Polly?

9. What is your impression of Polly's reaction when she tells Bob that her mother wants to see him?

FOR FURTHER CONSIDERATION

1. Locate the allusions in the story to (1) the religious life of the characters and (2) the commercial life in Dublin. How do these factors contribute to the meaning of the story?

2. What changes in social customs have occurred since this story was written? Joyce does not hint that Polly is about to become a mother. He simply indicates that the "affair" was enough to make her a "ruined" woman and that her behavior (or Bob's) required "reparation." How would a young man in Mr. Doran's predicament behave today?

FOR WRITING

1. Write a short character sketch of Mrs. Mooney. Consider her apparent beliefs, her way of managing her affairs, and her role in the story.

2. Read one or more of the other stories in Joyce's *Dubliners* and write an analysis of it or a comparison with "The Boarding House." You may notice some resemblances between the other central figures and Bob Doran which will be useful in organizing your paper.

THE CATBIRD SEAT · JAMES THURBER
page 226

One of Mr. Thurber's techniques is to establish an unusual or ridiculous situation, then let the characters work it out in a way that reveals their own aberrations. Mr. Martin, a "Milquetoast" type, is really the victor over a noisy woman who offends him, yet the reader is aware, through irony, that Mrs. Barrows may be right in her determination to remodel the antiquated business procedures of the F. & S. Company.

COMPREHENSION QUIZ

Mark T or F for true or false.

_____ 1. One of Mr. Martin's assistants suggested that Mrs. Barrows might be a Dodger fan.

_____ 2. The events of the story refer to a period of about three years.

_____ 3. One of Mrs. Barrows' expressions, "sitting in the catbird seat," meant "going on a rampage."

_____ 4. The author characterizes Mr. Martin as a bachelor who concealed his secret vices of drinking and smoking to fool his employer.

_____ 5. Mrs. Barrows decided to examine Mr. Martin's business methods because she suspected him of dishonesty.

_____ 6. Mr. Martin ran a department of ten people, including himself.

_____ 7. Mr. Fitweiler had engaged Mrs. Barrows as a "special assistant" after meeting her at a party.

_____ 8. Mrs. Barrows was ordinarily a quiet, modest woman who never raised her voice in the presence of the other employees.

_____ 9. Mr. Martin abandoned his original plan to "rub out" Mrs. Barrows when an alternative scheme occurred to him—one that involved less risk.

_____10. At the end of the story, Mr. Fitweiler apparently feels that Mr. Martin has been an innocent victim of Mrs. Barrows' aberration.

PROBLEMS

1. Why does Mr. Martin decide to "rub out" Mrs. Barrows?

2. From the evidence given in the story, how would one describe the F. & S. Co. before Mrs. Barrows came?

3. What kind of impression does Mrs. Barrows make on the older employees?

4. What lines show how Thurber wants us to envision Mrs. Barrows?

5. What immediate changes were made in F. & S. Co. after Mrs. Barrows came?

6. Does Thurber want the reader to consider Mr. Martin a "hero"? Why?

7. What was the original scheme conceived by Mr. Martin to "rub out" Mrs. Barrows?

8. At what point in the story does Mr. Martin change his plan?

9. What factors did Mr. Martin consider that persuaded him to change his plan?

10. Why doesn't Mr. Fitweiler realize that Mr. Martin has plotted successfully against Mrs. Barrows?

FOR WRITING

1. In what circumstances would Mr. Martin rather than Mrs. Barrows be considered the "butt of the joke"? Describe an alternate plot which would show a reversal of the situation given in this story.
2. "Injelititis, or Palsied Paralysis," by C. Northcote Parkinson (page 49) describes the processes that lead to morbidity in private business. Compare the situation of the F. & S. Co. to the analysis in Parkinson's essay.

HOW MR. HOGAN ROBBED A BANK · JOHN STEINBECK
page 269

COMPREHENSION QUIZ

Mark T or F for true or false:

_____ 1. Mr. Hogan did not plan his robbery in advance because he didn't want any complications.

_____ 2. Mr. Hogan worked in a drugstore owned by Mr. Fetucci.

_____ 3. When his daughter Joan was born, Mr. Hogan had been working for Mr. Fetucci for about three years.

_____ 4. Thursday was the best day for a robbery, because it was payday at the American Can Company.

_____ 5. The Hogan family received a surprising bequest from Uncle Larry.

_____ 6. One of the family pastimes was going to the movies.

_____ 7. The time required for preparation and execution of the robbery was only 17½ minutes.

_____ 8. The gun used in the robbery was a frightening black Colt revolver.

_____ 9. Mr. Hogan's battle with the alley cat in the storeroom delayed the robbery for three minutes.

_____10. Mr. Hogan regretted that he had robbed the bank for a mere twelve hundred dollars.

PROBLEMS

1. From the account given in the story, draw a simple diagram of the street plan around the store and the bank, labelling the buildings, Main Street, Spooner Street, and the alley. Draw a dotted line to show Mr. Hogan's route to the bank.

2. Suppose that you are the unfortunate bank teller, Will Cup, asked to make a written statement explaining the robbery. Write down what you saw and what you did. Add any pertinent observations that might help the investigators.

3. What circumstances helped Mr. Hogan choose the Saturday before Labor Day, 1955, at 9:04½ A.M. as the time for the bank robbery?

4. What were the two hiding places Mr. Hogan used for the stolen cash? Why would they be good places for his purpose?

STYLE AND TONE

The tone of this story is closely controlled by the meticulous details. Some are relevant to the plot but many of them provide information that is useful only for background ideas. Examine the following details and indicate after each one what kind of information is provided in terms of plot, character, or general background.

a. "Mrs. Hogan drank her tea slowly, scalding hot, and read her fortune in the tea leaves."

b. "John knows the ropes. Been with me—how long you been with me, John?"

c. "That was the year John and Joan had the mumps and Mrs. Hogan got her teeth pulled and was fitted for a denture."

d. "The children were excited because the 'I Love America' Essay Contest was due to be concluded and the winners announced . . ."

e. "Ruth and I are going to Altar Guild this afternoon. It's at Mrs. Alfred Drake's. You know, they just came to town. I can't wait to see their furniture."

f. "Mr. Hogan slipped his toe under the trigger of the floor alarm . . ."

g. "He heard all about it and offered his opinion when it was asked for. He said he didn't think the fellow could get away—where could he get to?"

FOR WRITING

The reader of Steinbeck's story is immediately faced with the question, "How did Mr. Hogan get away with the robbery?" Our customary ideas of justice seem to be almost irrelevant here, for the author does not offer us any clues to an implied moral judgment. Discuss this question, including an analysis of the tone and characterization of the story as evidence.

A MAN ALONE · LEE TRAUX
page 275

PROBLEMS

1. What does the story tell us about Alan Greene?

   a. his education

   b. his manners

   c. his taste

   d. what his job is in the Army

   e. his attitude toward the other GI's

2. At what point in the story is the reader made aware that Alan's skin marks him as "a man alone"?

3. Why did the two soldiers on the ancient green trolley sit "watching them covertly" when Alan and Eva were together?

4. What is Alan's opinion of cap-toothed Earl? Which lines in the story reveal it best?

5. What is the nature of the friendship between Alan and his bunkmate, Brad?

6. The incident in front of the Rendezvous Club near the end of the story reveals several different attitudes. Briefly state what the incident tells us about the attitudes of the following people:

   a. the drunken girl

b. her soldier friend

c. the loitering GI's

7. In several passages, the author indicates that there are certain places and kinds of situations that Alan avoids or seems afraid of. What are those places and situations? Explain why he avoids them.

LANGUAGE

Locate the following phrases in the context of the story and write down what each of them describes:

olive-drab cocoons

a toy erector set above the trees

the gauntlet benches

a little cabal of highball drinkers

the yellow rinse of light on the sidewalk

FOR WRITING

1. In the conversation between Eva and Alan while they are standing before the old Gestapo headquarters, Alan says that he really doesn't know anything about war. The setting of the story tells us why: he is a soldier stationed in Germany long after the war has ended. But his statement seems strange, nevertheless. Write a discussion of the role of the peacetime soldier who has never really experienced war.
2. Although Eva is described very briefly at the beginning of the story, the author does not tell us very much about her. Much of what is implied comes to us through Alan and through an implied analogy to other women Alan has known. Study what Eva does and says in the story, then write an analysis to show what she wants and what she is like.

HE DON'T PLANT COTTON · J. F. POWERS
page 284

PROBLEMS

1. How does the author make Baby the central figure in the story?

2. When Baby thinks of Libby, his appreciation takes the form of a repeated compliment. What is it?

3. Explain this sentence in the context of the story: "Probably this was not the first time they had jived white folks to death and them not the wiser."

4. How is Dodo different—as a character in the story—from Libby and Baby?

5. Does the author want us to think that these characters are especially good musicians? If they were either very good or very bad, would the meaning of the story be different?

6. Why does the band feel as they do about the song, "Old Man River"?

7. Although the events in the story suggest that a major theme is the prejudice of the "gentlemen from Mississippi," can you detect another—perhaps more important —theme? Explain.

8. At the end of the story when Baby tries to hail a cab, why does Libby laugh at him as Libby and Dodo wait "unfooled"?

FOR WRITING

1. Write a short description of the "gentlemen from Mississippi."

2. Explain how music is a bond between the main characters in the story. Look up the word "blues" in a standard musical reference source and determine how it is applicable in this story, then examine the passages for evidence for your theme.

3. Look up one or more of the essays by James Baldwin, author of *The Fire Next Time*. Like Powers, Baldwin makes a strong point of the inability of white people to get beyond the black *face* of the Negro to see the *man*. Write a discussion of this idea, using whatever evidence you find and include the premises implied in Powers' story for support.

THE WATCHERS · FLORENCE ENGEL RANDALL
page 292

The essay by Jane Jacobs, "Violence on the City Streets" and the news account by Martin Gansberg, "38 Who Saw Murder Didn't Call the Police" are related to Mrs. Randall's story, "The Watchers," in that all three pieces concern murderous depravity and the terror it induces. The story, however, impresses us in quite a different way than the other pieces do. It is a satire—an art form designed to correct social abuses —and requires active participation by the reader to supply another dimension to the ideas. Once the reader has *experienced* the satire, it becomes a part of his own thought because he has contributed to it himself.

Satire is not necessarily pleasant or amusing, because the aim of satire is to expose unpleasant aspects of life. Many people prefer to ignore or cover up the less pleasant views of human existence, but the satirist, a sensitive, brave person, loves humanity enough to try to make it better.

FOR STUDY

Locate the following ironic statements in the story:

1. "Love breeds its own vulnerability, its own fear."

2. "There is only one crime, and that is to be a victim. Nothing makes sense otherwise."

3. "It doesn't pay to take chances. Otherwise you can end up giving the performance instead of watching it."

4. "... They all gave him the ultimate, the supreme tribute of their silence."

Locate some other statements which are intended as irony and list them for class discussion.

FOR WRITING

1. An implied code of behavior appears in this story, induced, of course, by the "social conditions" of the time. Write a straightforward explanation of this code based on the incidents in the story.

2. Several major satires have employed the "timeless future" as a setting, while others use specific hypothetical dates, such as in Orwell's *1984*. Shirley Jackson's famous story, "The Lottery," employs a time setting which may be in the past, but it does not seem to reveal any historical date or place. This device is an aspect of fantasy; that is, a hypothetical world is created in which *only the story's own values apply*. Thus the writer frees himself from the values applicable to either a historical or recognizably contemporary setting. With the help of your instructor, locate a short satire similar to these and write an analysis of the fantasy device or the way in which the values of the story are detached from either history or current values.

LOVE IS A FALLACY · MAX SHULMAN
page 301

The author's note suggests that he was writing an argument in the informal essay tradition. He also succeeded in writing a delightful piece of short fiction: it has characters, it has a plot, and it has a message—for someone.

PROBLEMS

1. List the definitions of the fallacies as given in the story:

dicto simpliciter

hasty generalization

post hoc

contradictory premises

ad misericordiam

false analogy

hypothesis contrary to fact

poisoning the well

2. Polly replies to her suitor by identifying six fallacies in his arguments. List each fallacy then give the sentence (in summary, if you wish) to which she applied it:

a.

b.

c.

d.

e.

f.

3. How does the narrator describe Petey Burch?

4. How does he describe Polly Espy before she appears in person?

5. What was the narrator's "shrewdly calculated reason" for wanting Polly Espy to "go steady"?

6. From your own experience, what do you think Polly would do if she had discovered the raccoon coat "deal"?

VOCABULARY

fraught	logic
pelt	desist
cerebral	pitchblende
scalpel	hamstrung
waif	contrite

FOR WRITING

1. Write an argument in favor of the latest campus fad, showing how it contributes to "student life." In past years (after raccoon coats), goldfish-swallowing, bed-pushing, telephone-booth-stuffing, and panty raids, for example, have been favorite campus games. Be careful to avoid the fallacies!
2. Write an analysis of the *logic* in one of the following statements:
   a. "My desire for this young woman was not emotional in nature. She was, to be sure, a girl who excited the emotions, but I was not one to let my heart rule my head."
   b. "Just as Pygmalion loved the perfect woman he had fashioned, so I loved mine."
   c. "It is, after all, easier to make a beautiful dumb girl smart than to make an ugly smart girl beautiful."

A BAT IN THE MONASTERY · JOHN L'HEUREUX
page 313

PROBLEMS

1. What lines tell us about the "setting" of the poem?

2. What is implied by the parenthetic comment: "Poor Luther, I thought."

3. What does the following passage tell us about the speaker's attitude toward his subject?

> Big Ned killed him.
> With a broom he whaled the hell out of that bat
> that never hurt a soul . . .

4. What do these lines tell us about the "characters" in the poem?

> . . . We picked our way
> back to our cells, isolate again, estranged.

5. Twice in the poem, the bat is called an "intruder." How does this term apply to the meaning of the poem?

6. What was the priests' "recreation"?

VOCABULARY

flailed	despair
swooped	scudded
whaled	isolate
crumpled	estranged

FOR WRITING

Write a short discussion of bats, indicating how people usually respond to them. What associations do they have in our minds? From this consideration, explore the possibility that the bat implies something more than a "tiny thing, a dirty mouse with wings."

This poem describes the kind of daily tragedy which threatens everyone who drives automobiles. Besides providing a stark description of the scene, the poem also suggests the morbid fascination people feel when they encounter a terrible accident.

PROBLEMS

1. What are the "grim joke and the banal resolution"?

2. Which *senses* are appealed to in the first two stanzas?

3. Is the word *deranged* to be taken literally? What is its meaning here?

4. Which words or phrases in the third stanza show what the narrator feels about the victim (or victims)?

5. Why does accidental death horrify the narrator more than death by drowning or in war?

6. If the narrator were the other party involved in the accident, would the meaning of the poem be any different?

7. Read question 5 again, then attempt a paraphrase of the meaning of the last stanza.

SOUTHBOUND ON THE FREEWAY · MAY SWENSON
page 316

PROBLEMS

1. Name the actual objects described by the "tourist" from "Orbitville":

the creatures . . . made of metal and glass

their feet are round and roll . . .

on . . . long measuring tapes

The two in the back are red

. . . a 5-eyed one . . .

2. What is the answer: are the "soft shapes" inside "the hard bodies" really "their guts or their brains"?

FOR FURTHER CONSIDERATION

The technique of the "detached observer" is shown also in Paul Tabori's short satire, "The Martian Memo" (page 64). Here the "tourist" from "Orbitville" is not specifically identified, but his observations on the "creatures of this star" are similar. Do our freeways make a *logical* picture as we inch along on them, or is there really more exercise of "guts"? Consider also the essay by Loudon Wainwright, "Hot Pursuit of Turnpike Flyers" (page 169).

There are really two "speakers" in this poem, but one of them (the poet) is not really speaking aloud. His ideas come to us as a soliloquy. The other speaker is actually heard by the poet, so we "hear" what he has to say, but it is all mixed up with the soliloquy. Try to separate the two voices by the *tone* of what is said.

PROBLEMS

1. What is the "other speaker" doing in the poem?

2. What is the poet doing?

3. What does the repetition of "Which in our case we have not got" emphasize?

4. What are the "parts" and what are they used for?

5. What *images* are in the mind of the poet (other than the "parts")?

6. What is the poet's attitude toward the lesson in "naming of parts"?

THE TRAVELER'S CURSE AFTER MISDIRECTION · ROBERT GRAVES
page 318

Poems can be written for almost any reason, prompted by any emotion. This poem is obviously written out of anger, but it is anger controlled and shaped for a purpose. Note that the caption includes the parenthetical phrase, "from the Welsh."

PROBLEMS

1. What is the narrator angry about?

2. Would you be able to answer the first question if the poem had no title? Explain.

3. What is the connotation of *pilgrimage* in this context?

4. Does the speaker have a "method in his madness"? Explain.

5. Does the last line of the poem suggest a thoroughly evil intention or is it merely whimsical?

FOR FURTHER CONSIDERATION

One of the oldest literary devices is invective, the cursing or imprecation of evil against an enemy, an adversary, or to merely vent anger. In medieval times, invective was forbidden, probably because people believed in the continual malevolent presence of demons and lesser creatures who would seize the opportunity to place the soul of the blasphemer in jeopardy. Nevertheless, a rich tradition of invective has survived, appearing in literature from the earliest ages, from Aesop and Homer on. There are no rules for it, but Graves' poem is a skillful example of a dramatic speech dealing with every detail of the desired imprecation.

The last poem of these four short pieces suggests that the poems were written for children, but certainly not for children who are very young. They employ a sophisticated technique of juxtaposing statements in order to suggest a meaning for the reader to resolve. They are tantalizing, rather like riddles.

PROBLEMS

1. In the first poem, what is the implied contrast between deer and men?

2. In the second poem, is the herring merely a fish or is it a metaphor or symbol for something else? (Don't overlook the last two lines.)

3. Paraphrase the statement of the third poem. What is the relevance of lions to crowns?

FOR FURTHER CONSIDERATION

A bestiary was a catalog or dictionary of beasts, a very popular kind of work for several centuries. The compilers of bestiaries had very little actual anatomical information to include, since the books were written by scholars who got their information out of other books. The accounts of animals—actual and mythical—included a great deal of fantasy, much distortion, and a great deal of moral instruction, for the compilers used the behavior of beasts to contrast with the spiritual nature of man. One of the typical bestiaries, a twelfth-century Latin text, was translated and published by the late T. H. White under the plain title, *A Bestiary*. The range of fantasy is demonstrated by the fantastic beasts, shown with illustrations drawn from the original manuscript. A few minutes' perusal of this book will clearly show Mr. Rexroth's purposes in these poems.

THE UNKNOWN CITIZEN · W. H. AUDEN
page 320

PROBLEMS

1. What does the epitaph under the title contribute to the meaning of the poem?

2. Why is the citizen "unknown"?

3. What words or phrases are most effective in setting the citizen in the framework of his time?

4. What aspects of "the Greater Community" is Auden satirizing?

5. Is the poet speaking for himself, or does he adopt the "voice" of someone else? Explain.

6. What is the difference between the poet's attitude toward the "unknown citizen" and that expressed by the speaker? Explain.

Since the customary meaning of *dirge* does not apply to this poem, the title may seem misleading at first. The discrepancy between the assumed and the actual, however, is intentional, underlining Fearing's cynicism. Much of the meaning of the poem is expressed in the jarring rhythm, best conveyed when you read it aloud.

PROBLEMS

1. As a preliminary to appreciating the irony, define a *dirge*.

2. Why is there a change of tenses in the third and fourth lines?

3. What is the meaning of *denouement* as it is used here?

4. How are the men characterized who are carrying the casket in the sixth stanza?

5. Do you see any reason for combining *Roosevelt, Sears Roebuck, big dipper*, and *summer rain* in the last stanza? Explain.

FOR FURTHER CONSIDERATION

Compare this poem to W. H. Auden's "The Unknown Citizen" (page 320). What aspects of society does each poet satirize? If either poem were directly applicable to the present year and the present place, which words or allusions should be changed to make the satire more immediate?

MY SWEET OLD ETCETERA · E. E. CUMMINGS
page 324

Cummings was famous for his technique of deliberately misusing English syntax and punctuation and his erratic capitalization. Indeed, if you read this poem aloud several times, it is apparent that the lines and stanzas are not arranged to help us discover the sentence units. After a little experimentation, you will discover that the explicit statement in each sentence unit can be made clear. Cummings used this technique to insure that he would force his readers to read his poems carefully, since a superficial reading would leave them quite incomprehensible. Although the reader must work a little for even the most literal level of communication, the work is also a part of the fun.

PROBLEMS

Begin by rewriting the poem in prose style, supplying the necessary punctuation and capitalization. The answers to the questions will be much easier to find from your prose version.

1. To whom does the narrator refer by "Your" at the end of the poem, and what may we infer about their relationship?

2. Where was the narrator or what was he doing during the time spoken of in the poem?

3. What does the narrator reveal about his attitude toward the other members of his family?

4. Is this a literal statement: "mother hoped that / i would die . . ." Explain the statement in the context of the poem.

5. Is this a love poem, a war poem, or does it have elements of both?

FOR FURTHER CONSIDERATION

1. Locate each "etcetera" and try to deduce what it means in the context.
2. The narrator capitalizes only two words. Why these two?
3. Explore the connotations of the adjectives ("sweet") and the things they modify, such as "fleaproof earwarmers" to see how they affect the tone of the poem.

FOR WRITING

Write a brief analysis of what the narrator has to say about the reactions of people in wartime. Consider the view the narrator gives us about each character and the implications of his own attitude in the situation.

WHEN MY LOVE COMES TO SEE ME IT'S · E. E. CUMMINGS
page 325

This is one of Cummings' lyrically sensual poems which celebrate love, sex, youth, and innocence. His unique combinations of slang and clichés with shockingly fresh word combinations contribute to his lasting popularity.

PROBLEMS

1. Like "my sweet old etcetera" (page 324), this poem presents us with a slight problem in punctuation and syntax. With what word would you begin the second sentence?

2. Find the words the narrator uses to describe how his love makes him feel. What do they all have in common?

3. The line, "a wonderful smell in my mind" makes no literal sense. What non-sense meaning does it express?

4. Why does the narrator speak of his body as a "corpse"?

5. The narrator compares his love to several things. Which two are explicit?

   a.

   b.

6. Why is orange an appropriate color in the fourth line?

7. "I" and "She" are conspicuously capitalized in the fifteenth line. What might be the reason?

FOR DISCUSSION

1. Does the last line have any relevance to anything mentioned earlier in the poem?

2. What is the effect of the line, "whose stilling lips murder suddenly me."

LOVE IS NOT ALL · EDNA ST. VINCENT MILLAY
page 326

PROBLEMS

1. From the statement in the first seven lines, what would you say is the "subject" of the poem?

2. What different *powers* does the speaker deny to love? (Paraphrase.)

3. Where does the speaker shift from a general comment (more or less in the "third person") to a personal comment (in the "first person").

4. What concrete images does the speaker employ? (Remember that *love, death, resolution,* and *peace* are abstractions. Look for the objects or words that provide a visual image.)

5. Are there any words or phrases in the poem that evoke *other kinds* of images? (Such as sounds, sensations of touch, and so forth.)

6. What situation might the speaker be in that would evoke the ideas of the last three lines? (Explain.)

7. The speaker is evidently addressing someone—a specific person. What value does she put on this person, or what quality in that person is evaluated in the poem?

Pieter Breughel (1520?–1569) was a Flemish painter who often painted lovely scenes of peasants at work and at play. "The Kermess" represents a celebration of a local saint's day with many people and much feasting and dancing. The poet here tries to create with words what the painting creates with colors and movement.

PROBLEMS

1. List four words in the poem which express a strong sense of *sound:*

    a.   c.

    b.   d.

2. List six words which convey a strong sense of *action:*

    a.   d.

    b.   e.

    c.   f.

3. List three references to parts of the body which might (if taken out of context) be considered "impolite" by some readers. Beside the words, write the "polite" equivalent.

    a.

    b.

    c.

4. What does *rollicking* mean?

5. What effect does the poet achieve by ending some of the lines with such words as "and," "and the" or "about"?

6. Whose "bellies" are "tipping" in line five? Whose "bellies" are "off balance" in line seven?

FOR WRITING

Find a painting which you like and describe it so that the reader feels and sees the picture through your words.

THE BULL · WILLIAM CARLOS WILLIAMS
page 327

PROBLEMS

1. Briefly explain the following phrases and metaphors in terms of the whole meaning of the poem. If possible, show how some of the images are linked with others.

   a. chained to a drag

   b. the bull is godlike

   c. . . . nozzles / the sweet grass gingerly

   d. Olympian commentary on the bright passage of days

   e. his substance hard / as ivory or glass

   f. milkless

   g. the hair . . . matted with hyacinthine curls

2. What is the poet's attitude toward the bull?

3. Although the first lines show the bull "in captivity," is this fact important in the characterization? Why?

FOR FURTHER CONSIDERATION

The bull is the subject of many ancient myths and appears as a symbol in ancient art, especially in that remaining from Minoan culture. Why would the bull be an appropriate symbol for an ancient civilization whose wealth was in land and cattle? And is the bull—as symbol—in this poem significant in the same way?

The poet's attitude toward his subject—the tone—is a problem in this poem, for it has elements of satire. Some of the irony is implied by the choice of words but more comes to us from the "character"—the lady herself.

PROBLEMS

1. What is the scene?

2. To whom is the woman talking?

3. Is she a "sympathetic" character in the sense that she makes the reader feel sympathetic to her? Why?

4. Are there any indications in the poem that the narrator or poet is sympathetic?

5. What kind of imagery is evoked in each of these lines?

    a. "smeared with smoke and laughter"

    b. "love's abrasions have left me sore"

    c. "My teeth are on edge at the maggotty core"

6. Are these lines funny or pathetic?

    To hairy Harry and half-mast Hugh
      I gave the love I was starving for

7. Why is the lady concerned about a "judgement due"?

VOCABULARY

Consider these words carefully for their precise meaning in the context of the poem:

maudlin	garrulous	inclement
fulvous	rag-time	potentate
decamps	bray	stark
welt	chittering	incredulous
wraith	atone	maggotty

DREAM VARIATION · LANGSTON HUGHES

page 329

This short lyric is one of the best examples of the poem that *is* rather than a poem that *says* or *does* something for its effect. The contrasts are sharp, expressed in concrete words, yet the elusive quality of the poem is the expression of emotion.

PROBLEMS

Read the poem aloud, accentuating the stresses, to get the feeling of the rhythm in the irregular lines. Then consider these questions:

1. List all the adjectives in the poem and arrange them in contrasting pairs beginning with

white—black

2. What qualities are associated with day?

3. What qualities are associated with night?

FOR FURTHER CONSIDERATION

William Blake, a contemporary of the earliest "Romantic" poets writing at the end of the eighteenth century, used the short lines and stark contrasts we find in Mr. Hughes' poem. In your library, find an anthology that contains examples of Blake's work, especially from the volumes originally published as *Songs of Innocence* and *Songs of Experience*. Blake was the illustrator of his own work and occupies an important niche in early nineteenth century art as well.

Langston Hughes says that he is a Negro in the line "Black like me." This line has been used by a modern writer as the title of a book. Use whatever standard reference source is available to you to locate the book and discover its subject.

PROBLEMS

1. Except for the two lines of *eggs,* what is the most repeated word in the poem? Why?

2. What effect does the poet achieve by ending the two lines of *eggs* with three repetitions of *egg?*

3. Why does the poet make use of larger and smaller spaces between certain words?

4. If we define *theme* as the statement which the author is making about his subject, what is the theme of this poem?

5. What qualities does the poet emphasize in the turtle?

FOR WRITING

Observe some simple action of either an animal or a person and write a paragraph describing the action from beginning to end. Use as much detail and as many vivid descriptive terms as possible. Examples: a cat walking in grass or lying in wait for a bird; someone asleep on the porch in the sun; a bee in a bright flower.

HURT HAWKS · ROBINSON JEFFERS
page 331

Jeffers was noted for his pessimistic poems full of images of the stark natural beauty of the California coast near Big Sur. He wrote of the contrast between the noble beauty of nature and the pathos of man whose modern civilization contaminates this beauty.

PROBLEMS

1. In Part I of the poem, Jeffers uses several phrases and images which show his attitude toward the hawk. List three of them:

a.

b.

c.

2. What is meant by *arrogant* in the fourteenth line? Notice the later use and consider the connotations.

3. Is the word *freedom* used ironically in this poem? Why?

4. Jeffers uses several figures of speech to convey a more-than-literal meaning, as in the phrase *lead gift* for bullet. List three more examples and explain their meaning:

a.

b.

c.

5. For what qualities does Jeffers admire the hawk?

6. What is the relevance of the analogy to killing a man?

Sometimes a poem is written in order to allow reflection and better understanding of why a particular experience may affect someone very strongly. Here Mr. Barker describes feelings about a scene familiar to anyone who has ever come upon an old shack or deserted house. This poem is a good example of the kind of poetry which is, as Wordsworth said, "an emotion recollected in tranquility."

PROBLEMS

1. How are the four stanzas organized into units of thought, or paragraphs? State what you think is the main idea of each.

a.

b.

c.

d.

2. The speaker says that he normally loves the wind. Why does he feel different about this particular wind?

3. What do the *flowers, wild oats, fields,* and *birds* contrast with in the poem?

4. In the second stanza, does the word *scythe* suggest a second meaning?

5. Who was Niobe? What does the allusion add to the meaning here?

FOR DISCUSSION

Children often have a favorite "haunted house." In what different sense is this house "haunted" for the speaker?

FOR WRITING

Try to make a one-sentence paraphrase of the theme of this poem.

THE FISH · ELIZABETH BISHOP
page 333

The speaker in this poem has caught a fish that has vanquished the tackle of many earlier sportsmen. The fish emerges as a "character" through precise description, metaphor, and simile.

PROBLEMS

1. At the end of the poem, "victory filled up / the little rented boat." Who was the victor? Why?

2. Write down the most striking metaphors and similes used to describe the fish:

3. How many battles had the fish fought and won?

4. Would you characterize the ending of the poem as *ironic*? Why?

5. The fish's eyes are especially important in the characterization. What do these lines imply: "They shifted a little, but not / to return my stare"?

6. Although the speaker gives no direct self-description, we can learn something of the speaker's personality and something of the *tone* of the poem by examining the speaker's reactions to the "tremendous fish." Briefly describe the kind of person who wrote the poem insofar as this information reveals the tone.

PROBLEMS

1. Read the poem aloud (but softly) to yourself, listening for its structure. How does the poet *organize* each stanza?

2. What effect does the description of the snow have upon the images and the movement of the poem?

3. What does the poet mean in the image, "dogs have hangmen's legs"?

4. Why is the fox's death compared to the death of a soldier?

5. What is implied by "no proportions" in the last line?

6. Is this poem about hunting? Or does it have another theme?

ELEGY FOR JANE · THEODORE ROETHKE
page 336

Theodore Roethke's poetry is notable for its deep tenderness and an almost mystical identification with the things of nature.

PROBLEMS

1. What three images show how nature seemed to serve Jane?

a.

b.

c.

2. How does the speaker describe Jane? Write the lines or phrases that actually describe her?

3. Jane is compared to a series of creatures that are much alike. List them.

4. From the cumulative effect of these images, how do we know what kind of person Jane was?

5. Why is *elegy* a proper title for this poem?

6. In what way does the speaker *love* Jane? Examine the last three lines and think about your answer.

A NOTE ON STUDENT WRITING

Among the pieces in this book we have included, with no special comment, several examples of student writing which seemed to be of special interest to student readers. The controversial essay, "Conscience of an Objector," by Michael Craig Patterson was written from the same sense of conviction that marks the work of the other essayists represented in this book. David J. Riley's story, "The Guy Who Owned the Pitcher's Mound," belongs thematically with the kind of reading that teachers—and their students—like to turn to in a lighter mood. The three poems by Stephan Taugher, Michaele Sherry, and Mary Phillips show another range of mood and style.

All these pieces were contributed by students to the literary publication sponsored jointly by the English and Journalism Departments at Monterey Peninsula College, whose faculty advisor is one of the editors of this book. The title of the publication, *e.g.,* is a key to our purpose here: these are examples of what students can do—and they enjoy doing it.

DATE DUE

GAYLORD   PRINTED IN U.S.A.

1 2 3 4 5 6 7 8 9 0